Libya's Fragmentation

R2P - week 11 - Libya →
Chapter on this

Peacekeeping versus
peace enforcement

Libya's Fragmentation

Structure and Process in Violent Conflict

Wolfram Lacher

I.B.TAURIS
LONDON • NEW YORK • OXFORD • NEW DELHI • SYDNEY

I.B. TAURIS
Bloomsbury Publishing Plc
50 Bedford Square, London, WC1B 3DP, UK
1385 Broadway, New York, NY 10018, USA

BLOOMSBURY, I.B. TAURIS and the I.B. Tauris logo are trademarks of
Bloomsbury Publishing Plc

First published in Great Britain 2020
Reprinted 2020 (twice)

Cover design by Dani Leigh
Cover image: Fighters loyal to Government of National Accord (GNA) clash against forces
loyal to strongman Khalifa Haftar, on May 25, 2019. (© Mahmud TURKIA / AFP/Getty Images)

A catalogue record for this book is available from the British Library.

A catalog record for this book is available from the Library of Congress.

ISBN: HB: 978-0-7556-0080-9
PB: 978-0-7556-0081-6
ePDF: 978-0-7556-0082-3
eBook: 978-0-7556-0083-0

Typeset by Deanta Global Publishing Services, Chennai, India
Printed and bound in Great Britain

To find out more about our authors and books visit www.bloomsbury.com and
sign up for our newsletters.

Force is the midwife of every old society pregnant with a new one.

Karl Marx

Contents

Illustrations

Figure

Table

Map

Acknowledgements

This book would not have been possible without the generosity of Libyan interlocutors, acquaintances and friends. Their readiness to place their contacts at my service enabled me to speak to a wide range of actors in the course of the research. Among the many people who were never tired to offer their help – and often their hospitality – I would particularly like to thank Abdallah Hadeed, Aly Masednah, Musab El Gaed and Ousama Assed.

I am grateful to Stiftung Wissenschaft und Politik for being accommodative and flexible in the arrangements that allowed me to pursue the PhD on which this book is based. My first year of research was funded by the SWP project Elite Change and Social Mobilization in the Arab World. Early stages of the PhD project benefited from the comments of Catherine Boone, Isabelle Werenfels, Jannis Grimm, my brother Hannes, Klaus Schlichte, Mohammed Hachemaoui, Muriel Asseburg, Stephan Roll, Thomas Hüsken and Tobias von Lossow. As the work evolved, discussions with Jean-Baptiste Gallopin and Ivan Ermakoff helped focus the argument. I received useful feedback from the participants of the workshop on 'Illegalism, violence and state avoidance in Libya, Chad and the Central African Republic' at All Souls College Oxford – in particular from James McDougall, the commentator on our panel – and from those of the panel discussion on 'La décision à l'ombre de la violence dans le monde arabe' at the congress of the *GIS Moyen Orient et Mondes Musulmans*.

Claudia Gazzini, Denis Tull, Frederic Wehrey, Jean-Baptiste Gallopin, Isabelle Werenfels, Mary Fitzgerald, Virginie Collombier and Yvan Guichaoua all read chapters of the thesis and provided valuable criticism and comments. Nura Liepsner and Shamail Qureshi proofread some of these chapters, and Ricarda Ameling helped with the bibliography. I also received helpful comments from the two reviewers of the thesis, Volker Perthes and Klaus Schlichte, as well as from the other members of the doctoral committee: Herfried Münkler, Sebastian Lange and Ilyas Saliba. Marc Lynch and Caelyn Cobb offered useful feedback on the overall manuscript; critical comments by three anonymous reviewers for Columbia University Press were instrumental in the transformation of the PhD thesis into a book manuscript.

The bulk of the work on this book coincided with the first three years of Victor's and Joseph's lives. I am grateful to my mother, as well as to Michel and Philippe, for helping out while I was away for research or writing. Anne weathered my obsessive working pace – particularly during the writing phase – admirably. I promise betterment.

Abbreviations

BDB	Benghazi Defence Brigades (May 2016–)
BRSC	Benghazi Revolutionaries Shura Council (June 2014–)
CBL	Central Bank of Libya
DMSC	Darna Mujahidin Shura Council (December 2014–)
GNA	Government of National Accord (February 2016–)
GNC	General People's Congress (August 2012–January 2016)
HoR	House of Representatives (August 2014–)
IS	Islamic State
JCP	Justice and Construction Party
LIFG	Libyan Islamic Fighting Group (ca. 1995–2011)
LROR	Libyan Revolutionaries Operations Room (May 2013–ca. July 2014)
LSF	Libya Shield Force
NFA	National Forces Alliance
NOC	National Oil Corporation
NMF	National Mobile Force
NTC	National Transitional Council (February 2011–August 2012)
PFG	Petroleum Facilities Guard
PIL	Political Isolation Law
PSL	Popular Social Leadership (1994–2011)
SSC	Supreme Security Committee (September 2011–ca. January 2014)
UNSMIL	United Nations Support Mission in Libya

Introduction

The puzzle

In October 2014, at the height of Libya's second civil war, I travelled to Misrata to meet with the city's political leaders and the commanders of local armed groups. These groups had formed three years earlier to break the vicious siege Muammar al-Qadhafi's forces were then laying to the city. After Qadhafi's demise, they had come to think of themselves as guardians of the revolution. In July 2014, they had remobilized against what they saw as counter-revolutionary plots, driving their Zintani adversaries out of Tripoli during a month-long battle in which the capital's airport burned down. With Misratan armed groups now controlling Libya's capital, the politicians who had masterminded the operation were getting ready to negotiate from what they considered a position of strength. But just as Misratan power brokers were meeting with UN secretary general Ban Ki Moon and his Special Representative Bernardino Leon in Tripoli, their political support base at home was riven by serious disagreements, raising doubts over the extent of their sway. Several militia leaders assured me that scheming politicians had drawn them into the war against their will. They had established a council of seventeen field commanders to represent their interests independent of these politicians. Others backed the self-declared government in Tripoli, which rejected the negotiations. There were at least several dozen, probably over 100 armed groups in Misrata at the time, most of the larger brigades being assemblages of smaller factions. On the surface, and towards political adversaries, Misrata's political elite and armed groups still displayed a remarkable degree of cohesion. But the deepening rifts among Misratan players would haunt efforts to resolve Libya's crisis throughout the following years, complicating attempts to negotiate local ceasefire agreements, and repeatedly threatening to provoke a showdown in Tripoli, between forces supporting the UN-backed Government of National Accord and those opposing it.

Misrata's emergence as a key power centre in 2011 and its increasing internal fractiousness thereafter reflects wider dynamics at work in Libya. Political, military and territorial fragmentation defines the nature of conflict and non-state order in the country. Since 2011, Libya has lacked not only a central authority worthy of that name, but also strong national political or military forces, as well as stable local authorities. This splintering of the political and military landscape has prevented the re-establishment of state authority since Qadhafi's fall, and frustrated attempts at brokering a sustainable solution to Libya's conflicts.

Political and territorial fragmentation characterizes failing states, and is common in civil wars. Splits and divisions among armed groups often impede conflict resolution efforts. Rarely, however, does fragmentation occur as radically as in post-Qadhafi

Libya, where by 2015, no national institutions survived and almost no nationwide or even regional organizations emerged among the conflicting parties. Libya also stands out with regard to the marked localism of political and military forces. Armed groups mostly organize on the basis of individual cities, neighbourhoods or tribes, and often define themselves by their local affiliation. Such localism therefore has both a geographical and an identitarian dimension, and is anchored in concrete, tight-knit relations in communities.

But Libya's fragmentation is not the work of reawakening tribes or nascent city-states. In virtually no locality has uncontested leadership emerged; in most towns and cities, rival political camps exist, each of them entering into divergent alliances with outside forces. In the northeastern region of Cyrenaica, attempts to promote regional autonomy have been bogged down by intra-regional divisions. And in contrast to common patterns of fragmentation in other civil wars, Libya's conflict landscape is not populated by distinct armed groups that suffer ever new splits. In many regions, political and military structures are both too fluid and too deeply embedded in communities to settle into clearly identifiable organizations.

Comparable cases are hard to find among contemporary armed conflicts. The war in Syria, for example, has often been highlighted for the fragmentation of its parties. But contrary to Syria, Libya since October 2011 has lacked both a state leadership that can function as the principal power centre, and organizations whose scope of action and support base far transcend particular localities, and which have exercised exclusive control over sizeable chunks of territory, such as the Islamic State or the PYD. In civil wars such as in Lebanon and Afghanistan, armed groups associated with particular ethnic or sectarian groups carved out spheres of influence. But many of these armed groups were hierarchical, relatively centralized organizations led by warlords who gradually consolidated their fiefdoms. To date, Libya has not witnessed such a consolidation of local or regional authority by individual figures, with the exception of Khalifa Haftar – once an army officer close to Qadhafi, later his exiled opponent who after 2011 emerged as a blatantly power-hungry warlord – in the country's northeast. The Somalian case, with its close ties between sub-clans, business networks and militias, probably comes closest to Libyan conditions, despite important differences. But even in Somalia, a regional polity established itself in Somaliland two years after the collapse of central authority.

Among contemporary civil conflicts, Libya therefore presents an extreme case of fragmentation. This book seeks to explain Libya's political and military fragmentation since 2011 – that is, not merely why central authority collapsed and competing factions carved up the territory into a complex patchwork of spheres of influence. What is puzzling about Libya's fragmentation is the difficulty political and military actors have faced in centralizing control even over entire cities or regions, and the emergence of ever new rifts at the local level. Against this background, the consolidation of authority under Haftar in the country's northeast also begs explanation, as do Haftar's difficulties in expanding his authority despite the many divides afflicting his adversaries in western and southern Libya. To address this puzzle, this book presents a novel approach to fragmentation in civil war, through a comparative analysis of social transformation in four Libyan localities.

Fragmentation in civil wars and collapsed states

Libya represents an extreme case of a phenomenon that is attracting growing attention from scholars and policymakers. Over the past decade, fragmentation has become the subject of a burgeoning subfield in the study of civil wars and armed groups. The growing interest in multiparty civil wars and splintering rebel groups likely reflects a trend in the nature of contemporary armed conflict itself. Some even argue that complex conflicts with many disparate actors are the 'new normal' for civil wars.[1] There are, as yet, no studies to examine whether we really are witnessing a new development, or whether analysts of civil wars are merely becoming more attentive to a long-standing phenomenon.[2] Be that as it may, it is now common to question and transcend the – previously widespread – assumption that civil wars are binary conflicts between a government and a rebel group.[3]

Current approaches to fragmentation in civil wars fall into two main types. Arguments drawing on rational choice theory see fragmentation as driven by armed groups' response to external threats or incentives – state repression or co-optation; battlefield losses or victories; the individual weight of rebel factions within winning coalitions.[4] Approaches that analyse armed groups as organizations claim that the pre-existing social structures on which these groups were built determine how they react to pressure amid conflict.[5]

Common to both types of approaches is the general focus on situations of state-insurgent conflict – in other words, on the state as the central actor in suppressing, co-opting or dividing armed groups.[6] More importantly, they invariably centre on armed groups – 'rebels', 'insurgents', 'warlords', or 'militias' – as units of action and analysis. Game-theoretic models conceptualize insurgent groups or their leaders as rational, unitary actors. They assume that rebel leaders or warlords seek to maximize political power and accumulate wealth, and that the constraints on their actions arise from the interplay of warring actors pursuing their self-interest – rather than from these actors' obligations towards their constituencies. Organization-theoretic approaches stress the organizational logics of armed groups – resource mobilization, recruitment and efforts to establish control and cohesion – as determinants of their actions and trajectories. Both approaches start from the assumption that armed groups are discrete actors, defined by particular preferences in the case of the former, and their internal structure in the case of the latter.

The nature of fragmentation in Libya calls these assumptions into question. First, since October 2011, the Libyan state has existed only as a vestige, not as an actor in the conflicts. Most armed groups do not understand themselves as rebels – there is no central authority to rebel against – but claim to represent state legitimacy. Violent conflict has generally been localized and temporary, with the exception of twelve months of civil war in 2014–15, and the third civil war that erupted in April 2019. The strategic conditions and the pressures amid which armed groups operate in Libya therefore differ substantially from those of state-insurgent conflicts.

Second, Libyan armed groups often display a very low degree of formalization and organizational continuity. Their members mobilize and melt back into their communities according to conflict dynamics. Instead of sharpening their public profile and developing a clear corporate identity, armed groups commonly disguise themselves by constantly changing their names. Many see rapid fluctuation in their component elements and individual membership. The decision-making mechanisms into which they are integrated frequently extend outside the armed group itself to include informal elite networks or community structures. In such a context, conflict dynamics can be reduced neither to the internal logics of armed groups, nor to the interactions between them.

This book argues that developments in Libya, as well as in similarly complex and fragmented conflicts elsewhere, can only be understood through an analysis of the fragmentation and cohesion of *social* groups – of the social networks and communities in which political and military actors are embedded. Previous work on the role of social networks in armed groups and their fragmentation limits itself to the pre-existing social networks on which armed groups were built, or to social networks within or between armed groups.[7] By contrast, I understand social embeddedness as the constraints and capabilities of actors emanating from their ongoing social relations.[8] I contend that the relevant unit of analysis may not be armed groups as much as networks straddling political elites, community leaders, members of armed groups and their quotidian relations, such as their families, friends and neighbours – in other words, the social networks in which members of armed groups are embedded. To varying degrees, armed groups are embedded in, or isolated from, their social surroundings. Depending on their extent of social embeddedness, the ties linking their members to people outside their fighting group may be decisive in shaping their constraints and capabilities, as well as their interests and identities.

To understand fragmentation in Libya, we need to look beyond organizational splits. I define fragmentation as the processes through which a multiplicity of competing political and military actors emerge and continue to proliferate, preventing the maintenance or establishment of a credible claim to the monopoly on the concentrated means of violence.

Fragmentation and social structure

If we seek to account for the fragmentation of social groups, rather than merely of organizations, it is tempting to search for an explanation to Libya's complex landscape since 2011 in structural features of Libyan politics and society. From a structuralist perspective, these features would have made Libya's fragmentation inevitable once central authority weakened and the country descended into civil war. This argument appears all the more obvious in view of the apparent commonalities Libya shares with other cases of fragmentation amid state collapse, such as Afghanistan and Somalia. All three had historically been fragmented societies that were incorporated into nation-states only recently, and unevenly.[9]

Structuralist approaches would emphasize the weakness of institutionalization and state penetration of pre-revolutionary Libyan society, as well as the fact that Qadhafi systematically blocked the development of independent organizations aggregating political interests at the national level, such as political parties. They would interpret the pronounced localism of Libyan political forces since 2011 as a resurgence of parochial – in this case, tribal – identities.[10] Depending on their particular theoretical viewpoint, they would see such identities as having remained hidden underneath the surface during the Qadhafi era, or as having been perpetuated and transformed to serve as the basis for the patronage networks that structured Libya's rentier economy.[11] The revolution, from such a perspective, only served to bring these structural characteristics of Libyan society to the fore.

In view of the marked localism of Libyan political forces, a structuralist approach to Libya's fragmentation could not content itself with highlighting the weakness of national institutions. Social microstructure – the cohesion of communities – would be key to a structuralist argument. As theorists of social networks have argued, 'strong ties, breeding local cohesion, lead to overall fragmentation'.[12] Pre-existing social networks clearly play a role in mobilization in social movements and militant organizations.[13] A long-running tradition in the study of rebellion holds that group cohesion facilitates collective action.[14]

Structuralist approaches, however, tend to overstate the extent to which pre-existing structural patterns determine outcomes – in this case, the fragmented nature of political and military mobilization. As a detailed analysis of the rifts and alignments in 2011 shows, the integration or marginalization of a given community by the Qadhafi regime did in some cases correspond to that community's alignment in the revolutionary civil war – but in other cases, it did not. Moreover, a close look at local communities during the Qadhafi era demonstrates that they were politically divided and lacked strong leadership – in other words, they did not constitute political actors, raising the question of why they appeared as such during the revolution. Besides, tribal solidarities are not fixed; in Libya as elsewhere, social change, government policy and tribal political entrepreneurs themselves constantly refashion the nature and role of tribes.[15] As a result, there are no predetermined fault lines for fragmentation along tribal lines. Political and military mobilization since 2011 has occurred at least as much at the level of individual towns or cities as it has on a tribal basis, which corresponds neither to traditional loyalties nor to the political legacies of the Qadhafi era. Finally, explanations that rely on the strength of pre-existing local ties have difficulties accounting for the evolving divides after 2011, with rifts within – and realignments between – local communities.

A convincing approach to fragmentation in Libya should explain both the pronounced localism of political and military forces in the 2011 war – the first manifestation of Libya's fragmented landscape – and the breakdown of local unity, the deepening fragmentation at the local level, as Libyan society lived through its post-revolutionary turmoil.

This book locates the key to such an explanation in social transformation amid civil war. According to one of the oldest axioms of sociology, violent conflict can either strengthen group cohesion or cause group fragmentation.[16] Community social structure therefore is not a constant factor in the development of armed groups. We need to analyse not only how social structure conditions the formation of violent contenders, but also how communities change under the impact of violence – including violence wielded by their own members. Community refers to groups characterized by a high level of face-to-face, multiplex and reciprocal relations, as well as a common set of beliefs and values.[17] The denser the network of such ties, the more cohesive a community.[18] How community exposure to violent conflict alters cohesion, and how this affects armed groups that are embedded in communities, is central to the approach to fragmentation presented here.

Civil wars radically transform the social fabric. The dynamics of collective violence, through which such transformation occurs, include self-reinforcing processes and chain reactions – in other words, causal relationships that are endogenous to civil wars, rather than rooted in antecedent conditions.[19] But theoretically informed analysis of social transformation amid violent conflict is still in its early stages.[20] This book aims to advance such analysis.

The argument

Violent conflict produces new realities and logics that deeply transform societies. Violence draws rifts through the social fabric; it either strengthens cohesion or causes fragmentation among groups that rely on solidarity among their members to defend themselves against threats. It thereby redefines political communities and creates new ones.

These changes appear most dramatically during the escalation into civil war, when society first faces the threat of widespread violence, and when individuals and groups are forced to position themselves in highly uncertain situations. Amid mutual uncertainty – with each actor searching for cues in the behaviour of others – small acts of violence can trigger exponential consequences, provoking the alignment of actors on both sides of the act. Such mechanisms result in rifts and alignments that are partially shaped by contingent events, and therefore have the potential to transform structural divides antecedent to the conflict.

Where collective struggle produces social cohesion, armed groups are often deeply embedded in communities. Social embeddedness means that armed groups do not exclusively, or even primarily, follow their internal organizational logics, or the individual interests of their leaders. They also respond to obligations towards other members of the community they are embedded in. Their positions towards other actors in the conflict are therefore in part conditioned by the social boundaries that define local cohesion. As actors in violent conflict, armed groups are both agents and objects of social transformation: they reshape the social ties they are themselves enmeshed in, as well as the social fabric more broadly.

Fragmentation occurs because of conflicting pressures originating from local social ties on the one hand, and strategic considerations on the other hand. Changing strategic conditions – configurations of threat, opportunity and uncertainty – lead actors in the conflict to reposition themselves and enter into new alliances and enmities, thereby inflicting ever new rifts onto the social fabric. Where social cohesion remains strong, it constrains actors in their strategic behaviour. Political fragmentation is most pronounced where social cohesion limits actors in their opportunism and ruthlessness. Where the experience of communities in conflict has failed to strengthen local cohesion, or weakened it, armed groups stand a better chance of centralizing control.

This approach to fragmentation makes three theoretical contributions to the study of violent conflict more generally. First, it theorizes processes of social transformation amid violent conflict, building on nascent work in this domain, and demonstrating the relevance of these processes for our understanding of civil wars. Second, it advances a processual perspective on violent conflict, underlining the importance of mechanisms that develop a causality of their own, and combining rational choice arguments with a social and historical dimension that is generally missing in such arguments. Third, it proposes a novel concept for the social embeddedness of armed groups that furthers our understanding of how social ties matter for the behaviour of actors in violent conflict.

Structure, process and social transformation in civil war

The formative period of Libya's fragmented landscape was the 2011 revolution and civil war, when political and military forces were overwhelmingly organized on the basis of local communities, and rifts emerged between communities that found themselves on opposite sides of the divide. The pronounced localism of Libyan forces is unique among contemporary civil wars. To what extent can structural features of Libyan society and the country's singular history of state formation explain these patterns?

A detailed analysis of events at the local level during the first days and weeks of the 2011 revolution shows that communal alignments did not correspond to the activation of predetermined fault lines, or to mobilization on the basis of pre-existing scripts. In western Libya, rifts emerged between individual communities, producing localism, whereas eastern Libya wholly escaped regime control early on, producing regionalism. These patterns owed as much to historical precedents as to – partially contingent – dynamics of violence. Communal positions in the 2011 war were not defined through collective decision-making. Rather, an unprecedented situation forced local actors to take sides amid high uncertainty, thereby allowing individual acts to develop a disproportionate impact by triggering the behavioural alignment of others. Violence, or the threat thereof, then fuelled the mechanisms that turned such nascent rebellions by small groups of actors into collective positions of communities. Violence, and the threat thereof, activated ties of solidarity within communities; gambling that community solidarity would falter, the regime threatened collective retribution, thereby accelerating the process.

The Qadhafi regime's record of collective punishment and its divisive tribal policies made it likely that a revolutionary situation would trigger such mechanisms. But antecedent conditions did not determine the rifts of the civil war. The extent to which ties of solidarity could be activated was uncertain for all actors involved. Whether some communities were more cohesive than others prior to the conflict mattered less than the ways in which the eruption of the conflict transformed them. Communities did not enter the revolution as political actors; they became actors through the conflict. The war created new communities and community leaders.

Social cohesion and community are central to this book's overall argument. Neither is a fixed entity, as an analysis of social transformation through escalation and conflict shows. The experience of the 2011 war shaped political and military organization in

Libyan communities for years to come. In communities that had been welded together by collective struggle, armed groups emerged that were deeply embedded in the local social fabric.

Social embeddedness

Armed groups or their leaders are a key unit of analysis in current research on violent conflict. But a close look at the forces in Libya, as well as in similarly fragmented conflicts elsewhere, suggests that this may be inappropriate in situations where the boundaries of groups are fluid, and community structure plays an important role. Understanding armed groups as driven by their leaders' rational self-interest risks under-socializing these groups; focusing on their organizational logics overemphasizes social ties internal to the group.[21]

Instead of assuming that armed groups are discrete organizations that can serve as a unit of analysis, I analyse the members of a fighting group within the web of ties linking them to each other, as well as to political players, financial backers, external patrons, friends, families and neighbours. This web of ties, which goes far beyond what is commonly understood as an armed group, enables and constrains political and military actors, and influences how they conceive of their interests and identities. Such ties, built through repeated or everyday interactions, can carry relationships of trust, reciprocity, or loyalty, and can facilitate coordination by channelling information outside formal organizational structures.[22]

The more an armed group polices its boundaries, the better it can be analysed as a distinct organization. The more it is socially embedded, the more permeable its organizational boundaries are, and the less centralized its command structures. I will, at times, casually call such a network a 'socially embedded force' – a term that is intentionally vague – to avoid evoking a clearly defined group. Total social embeddedness would mean that the fighting group is identical with the community.

A comparative analysis of four Libyan localities shows that socially embedded forces emerge in communities that forge a high degree of social cohesion through collective struggle. Examples from conflicts elsewhere suggest that the wider contexts in which this tends to occur are complex political and military landscapes that fall short of, or transcend, binary state-insurgent conflict – contexts that some call 'hybrid political orders' or 'social orders', among other terms.[23] But in these contexts, socially embedded forces always coexist with – and can be overtaken by, or turn into – more tightly run armed groups. The latter have a greater chance of succeeding where conflict erodes social cohesion, or fails to enhance it. By far the most significant example in Libya is the warlord structure led by Khalifa Haftar in eastern Libya.[24] Warlord structures distinguish themselves from socially embedded forces by their centralization, military ethos and measure of autonomy.

The process of fragmentation

To the extent that actors in conflict are socially embedded, their social networks enable and constrain their actions. At the same time, these actors respond to particular strategic conditions: the configuration of threats, opportunities and uncertainty in a given situation, which corresponds to the factors that are considered decisive in rational choice theory. Strategic conditions shape and transform social ties by guiding the use of violence, which in turn draws new rifts and redefines communities. The immediacy of threats and the high stakes in situations of civil war encourage ruthlessly strategic behaviour.

Strategic conditions and social ties can therefore present violent contenders with conflicting pressures. Moreover, in civil wars and collapsed states, strategic conditions change constantly, forcing actors to reposition themselves and enter into ever new alliances and enmities. As strategic conditions change, they leave lasting traces in the form of rifts within the social fabric. Taken together, these hypotheses form a theory of fragmentation.

Violent contenders who are deeply embedded in socially cohesive communities face greater constraints in their strategic action than armed groups that insulate their members from their social surroundings. In cohesive communities, actors will find it more difficult to opportunistically enter into ever new alliances with former enemies, or move ruthlessly against local rivals. In some instances, they even refrain from positioning themselves openly at all, due to constraints originating from social ties. This means that, contrary to intuition, political fragmentation is most durable and debilitating in socially cohesive communities.

For a situation to persist in which the logics of strategic action and social embeddedness compete and conflict with each other, without one prevailing over the other, at least one of the following conditions needs to hold: First, the absence of meaningful central authority makes it difficult for political alliances to coalesce. Second, foreign support to local actors in the conflict prevents a consolidation of alliances around a central authority. Third, strategic conditions change rapidly, forcing actors to constantly reposition themselves, with periods of political competition within communities alternating with situations in which communities close ranks against external enemies – a sequence of repeated social fusion and fission.

To varying degrees at different times, all three conditions applied to the turmoil Libya has undergone since 2011. With the collapse of the regime, central authority broke down, locking in a fragmented landscape, since such a dispersed configuration of forces would severely hamper any attempts to form solid coalitions to uphold central authority. Fragmentation thereby became both a cause and a consequence of the collapse of central authority. Since mid-2014, foreign support to various parties in the conflicts has posed a major obstacle to a settlement.

Meanwhile, strategic conditions fluctuated heavily: during the 2011 war, individuals were forced to unequivocally choose sides, frequently aligning themselves with the side their community found itself on, and cutting off ties with communities on the other side of the divide. With the regime's demise, the threat posed by regime forces vanished, and with it the key factor subduing rivalries within and between revolutionary strongholds. The scramble for suddenly available state assets and budgets fuelled competition, including among rivals within the same communities who entered into diverging supralocal alliances. In 2014, the coalescence of such alliances into two broad opposing camps led to a second civil war that once again forced actors to take sides. Actors in the conflict sought to redraw clear lines between allies and enemies, and strove to refashion local unity. The split through government institutions threw patronage networks into disarray, prompting a search for new alliances and external sponsors. From early 2015 onwards, actors had to choose whether to bet on the UN-led negotiations for the formation of a unity government, or remain locked in polarization. The benefits from participating in negotiations and supporting a compromise were highly uncertain. Actors who chose compromise had great difficulties holding on to their local support base. Fresh political rifts emerged at the local level. Divisions multiplied further as the unity government's power base and ambitions narrowed over the following two years. In April 2019, Khalifa Haftar's offensive on Tripoli yet again prompted his adversaries in western Libya to close ranks.

In sum, the polarization of the 2011 civil war gave way to a differentiation of local positions in 2012–13; renewed polarization in 2014–15 was again followed by the fragmentation of the two rival camps in the context of negotiations; in 2019, polarization returned. At the local level, strategic conditions twice impelled actors to close their communities' ranks against external adversaries, only to subsequently switch to local competition over access to patronage. Successively, social processes that originated in different strategic conditions interfered with each other, gradually dividing the clearly defined groups of 2011 and tracing ever new fault lines. Actors not only responded to the exigencies of particular strategic conditions. Their room for manoeuvre was also constrained by social networks that had been shaped in radically different strategic environments.

Mechanisms and processes

The above argument represents a processual perspective on fragmentation in particular, and violent conflict in general. Social mechanisms, and processes of social transformation, serve as the missing link between structural conditions and the outcome of fragmentation. Mechanisms are not merely a combination of intervening variables or chains of events, but 'chains of interaction that filter structural conditions and produce effects'.[25] They are relational, and have a causality of their own. Feedback loops or path dependence are examples for endogenous, non-linear causality in mechanisms.[26] Mechanisms also differ from the sum of their composite events with regard to the importance of temporality: timing, sequence and acceleration.[27] Mechanisms should be portable to other contexts, in that they alter relations among actors in similar ways across different situations.[28] Processes are combinations and sequences of mechanisms.[29]

For example, two mechanisms in the escalation and early phases of a conflict cause a community to adopt a collective position, and draw rifts between communities (see Table 1). First, the community develops a reputation for being loyal to the party that exerts territorial control over it, which in turn provokes fear of collective retaliation against that community by the other side, thereby strengthening community loyalty to the controlling party. Second, individuals or groups on both sides of a dispute mobilize support by appealing to ties of solidarity, gambling that the solidarity of the adverse group will unravel. This redefines group solidarity just as it – potentially – provokes group conflict.

Table 1 Selected mechanisms in the process of Libya's fragmentation

Mechanism	Definition	References
Contingent sequential alignment	In situations of collective uncertainty, individual acts have a disproportionate impact by triggering the behavioural alignment of others.	Ermakoff (2015).
Security dilemma of solidary groups	Individual or group escalates by activating ties of solidarity to mobilize for collective action, gambling that solidarity within adverse groups will unravel, leading to group conflict.	Gould (1999); Schnell (2015).
Alignment lock-in	Territorial control generates reputation for community loyalty to controlling actor, provoking fear of collective retaliation by adversary, thus strengthening community loyalty to controlling actor.	Kalyvas (2006).
Cohesion through collective struggle	Collective struggle against outside actor strengthens mutual loyalties and increases density of ties within group, enhancing group cohesion.	Wood (2008); Whitehouse et al. (2014); Parkinson (2013).
Broker competition	Brokers compete for ability to represent a group, promoting group differentiation.	Tilly (2003).
Patron competition	Brokers/patrons compete in building clienteles within group, promoting group differentiation.	–
Fusion/fission	Repeated changes of strategic conditions alternately impel groups to close ranks against external adversaries, then cause brokers/patrons within group to compete, promoting fragmentation.	–

A mechanism that strengthens group cohesion amid conflict is the increased mutual dependence between members of a group that is in collective conflict with an outside actor. Group members strengthen their ties among each other, come to rely on and trust each other with their lives, and experience the loss of friends and relatives together.

Mechanisms that promote political differentiation within groups include the competition among leaders to represent that group towards the outside, and their competition in building up clienteles within the group. The process of fragmentation is driven by repeatedly alternating mechanisms promoting group cohesion and group differentiation.

Several of these mechanisms have been conceptualized in the literature; others have been described in other contexts but have not been explicitly formulated as portable mechanisms. This book identifies the mechanisms at work in the process of fragmentation through a comparative analysis of conflict and social transformation in four Libyan localities during 2011–19.

Research design and methodology

The approach adopted here relies on a subnational comparison of structures, mechanisms and processes in four locations: the Nafusa Mountains, Misrata, Bani Walid and Tobruk. The focus on communities as the primary level of analysis was prompted by the localism that has defined much of Libya's political landscape since 2011. But in-case comparison also makes it easier to control for historical, socioeconomic and cultural factors that may differ widely in cross-national comparative analyses.[30] The case – political fragmentation in Libya – serves as a basis for theory building. But the theoretical framework presented in each chapter also draws extensively on examples from other country cases.

Drilling down to the local level does not mean discounting national-level dynamics or the role of external actors. Both figure in the analytical framework as part of the strategic conditions in which local actors operate, and both feature in the empirical analysis. The next chapter examines Libya's overall trajectory since 2011, and thereby provides the context in which to situate the micro-level events that form the heart of the analysis.

The four localities were chosen in an effort to maximize differences among the cases, particularly with regard to the ways in which communities were exposed to, and participated in collective violence in 2011. Communities in these four regions also differed in their exposure to changing strategic conditions over the following years, and underwent diverging social transformations. In Misrata and the Nafusa Mountains, communities emerged from the 2011 war as cohesive local power centres. While both areas were revolutionary strongholds, they differ in that Nafusa towns are tight-knit rural communities, whereas Misrata is a diverse city. Their comparison reveals striking similarities in local cohesion and the social embeddedness of armed groups. Both areas subsequently became arenas for competing local camps that only united under acute external threat.

Bani Walid, a tribal stronghold that remained loyal to the regime in 2011, was initially riven by deep internal rifts, but constant victimization at the hands of stronger outside forces promoted internal cohesion. The town's weak leadership settled on isolationism to ward off the threat of open internal conflict. Tobruk remained at the margins of the transformations wrought by the 2011 war, and the weakness of socially embedded forces offered fertile terrain for the consolidation of control by Haftar.

Three of the four localities are located in the west, while Tobruk is in the east; the two regions differ substantially with regard to historical legacies and the experience of the 2011 war. The cases are relevant for Libya's overall trajectory and patterns across the country: with Misrata and Zintan, the analysis includes two key power centres in post-Qadhafi Libya; with Tobruk, the heartland of Haftar's power structure is accounted for – though this was not yet evident when I first visited the city in April 2014.

Pragmatic considerations such as security and accessibility also mattered for case selection. I chose localities that were comparatively stable, and avoided cities where security was already deteriorating in early 2014, such as Benghazi, Sirte or Sabha. I was unable to include a case study from southern Libya for that reason. I recurrently refer to communities that were riven by violent internal conflict to identify key differences in patterns.

Data collection

To establish precise chains of events in the localities under examination, as well as the protagonists and drivers behind these events, I gathered information through interviews with actors and observers on the ground. These interviews covered both historical and ongoing developments. Over time, through interviews that focused on actors and events, I collected detailed information on community structure, inter communal ties and the social networks in which members of armed groups and political actors were embedded.

I adopted an ethnographic approach to field research, drawing on participant observation and informal interactions as much as on formal interviews.[31] I conducted over 300 interviews specifically for this book, during nineteen weeks of field trips on eleven separate occasions between January 2014 and April 2018. These interviews were in Libyan Arabic without a translator. They were semi-structured or ad hoc, depending on the interlocutor and the situation. In most cases, I did not record the interviews, and often took few or no notes during the meeting, making notes afterwards instead, to put interlocutors at ease. Locations included Tripoli, Misrata, Bani Walid, Yefren, Zintan, Jadu, Nalut and Tobruk, as well as meetings during stopovers in Tunis and Istanbul. Interlocutors ranged from politicians and businessmen to army officers, leaders and members of armed groups, tribal notables, intellectuals and civil society activists. Many interlocutors were interviewed multiple times, which was important both to strengthen trust and to trace the changing representations of community, adversaries and social ties.

In addition, I drew on previous and subsequent research conducted during eighteen weeks of field visits on ten separate occasions between November 2011 and September 2013 – to the same locations, as well as to Benghazi, Sabha, Ubari and Murzuq – as well as between November 2018 and February 2019. In between research trips, I stayed in regular contact with interlocutors across the country to follow events, via web-based messaging and phone conversations. I engaged in such exchanges on an almost daily basis, and used them as an additional means of gathering and cross-checking information. Except for a small number of public figures, I have anonymized interviews to protect the interlocutors' identities amid a rapidly changing conflict landscape.

Conditions and constraints

Gathering evidence through field-based interviews is crucial for research on contemporary Libya, since there is a great dearth of reliable, written primary and secondary sources. Of all Arab states, Libya is probably the country that has attracted the least field research by social scientists. It was largely closed off to foreign journalists and social scientists for much of Qadhafi's rule, though a small number of anthropologists, historians and political scientists managed to navigate the maze of bureaucratic and political obstacles.[32] Authoritarianism also severely restricted the work of Libyan social scientists. As a means of information, rather than propaganda, Libyan journalism was virtually nonexistent.

After a brief opening in 2011–13, insecurity limited access yet again from early 2014 onwards. Several efforts at building reliable news outlets and TV channels withered away amid increasing polarization and the growing investment of political entrepreneurs in partisan media organizations. Rumours and deliberate disinformation thrived in social media, which became a leading source of information for most Libyans. Verifying or invalidating the flood of fake documents, leaked phone calls and invented articles attributed to foreign media could have been a full-time occupation in itself. Foreign journalists deserted the country. Those who continued to cover events in Libya often found it difficult to justify the relevance of even occasional reporting, as 'confusion is difficult to report'.[33] As a source of authoritative data, the state bureaucracy had collapsed. Given these circumstances, research on political developments that did not rely on first-hand observation and interviews on the ground was doomed to failure. But during 2014–18, the number of foreign researchers regularly visiting the country could be counted on the fingers of one hand, myself included.

In this difficult context, I invested much effort into gaining access to relevant interlocutors, establishing the necessary trust, and evaluating divergent accounts. The primary means of gaining access was referral and facilitation by people personally connected to a prospective interlocutor. As security conditions deteriorated, ensuring personal security by gaining the backing of influential local figures and arranging for private transport and accommodation took up an increasing amount of time and energy. Like researchers operating in similarly fragmented social landscapes elsewhere, I gradually built my own local network so I could carry out my work, which undoubtedly also impaired my objectivity.[34]

Nevertheless, I did what I could to diversify entry points, and was able to offset much of the potential network bias that could have resulted from such local-level research. Having worked on Libya since 2007 and made several visits per year since 2011, I built up a network of contacts even as my contacts were also constantly adapting their social networks and political affiliations, thereby continually opening up new connections. As time went by, I met people whom I had faced difficulties accessing for years. In my capacity as a researcher at an institute that advises the German government and parliament, not only did I approach prospective interlocutors but Libyan interlocutors unknown to me also sought me out. In addition, fragmentation offered advantages in gathering evidence, since interlocutors from particular cities often omitted inconvenient facts that representatives of neighbouring or estranged communities then happily divulged. I then cross-checked with insiders what I had gathered from outsiders. The same logic applied to divided communities, including in cases where particular political actors or entire families had sought refuge outside their hometowns.

One form of bias I was unable to avoid was gender bias. In Libya, few women play a role in public life, and cultural conventions impose gender segregation in most social contexts. I was invited to dozens of homes, but never met any female household members. When invited to a home, I would be ushered into the *marbu'a*, designed to accommodate male visitors and offer space for socializing. The *marbu'a* frequently has an entrance separate from the main entrance to a house, and is often located in a separate structure from the house. As a topic of conversation, female household members or relatives were largely off bounds, making it very difficult to understand their role in the processes under investigation. By extension, family relations via marriage or maternal ties also came up less frequently in conversations. Anecdotal information leads me to assume that such relations are crucial in Libyan social networks, including for political purposes; historical evidence from Libya and analyses from other contexts also suggest as much.[35] Female researchers, able to access both worlds of segregated Libyan society, have a distinct advantage in this regard.

I followed the events discussed in this book as they unfolded, over a period of nine years. In a context of civil war and state collapse, reliable information is scarce, and incentives for misrepresentation are great. Closely engaging with events over a relatively long period allowed me to differentiate between the logics of action as declared by protagonists, and *ex post facto* rationalizations influenced by subsequent developments. At the same time, it often enabled me to discover the hidden background to certain events at a later stage, when information concerning them was no longer considered as sensitive, or when the actors who had conspired in these events had fallen out with each other. Close observation also affords a better grasp of contingent elements, as well as the role of trial and error in political action, and is particularly important for the analysis of social ties. As political divides shift, political actors often downplay or conceal their past relations with their adversaries of the moment. Moreover, violent conflict generates new political identities. For example, I witnessed the emergence of an ethnic discourse stigmatizing parts of local communities as foreigners on the basis of (real or imagined) ancestries reaching back a century or longer. Such shifts would be much more difficult to identify for a researcher starting work in 2018, and due to the dearth of written documents in Libya, will probably be largely invisible to a historian working in 2038.

Where available, I have backed up information gathered through interviews with articles from Libyan news websites, posts from Libyan social media, or coverage from Libyan TV channels.[36] Just like individual interlocutors, such sources invariably spin events according to their particular political alignment, and I have treated them similarly: in no instance do I use these sources as the only reference for my account of a given incident, and in most cases their role is limited to supporting the more detailed information provided by multiple interviewees.

Plan of the book

The next chapter outlines the setting in which the processes under investigation unfold. It provides an account of Libya's trajectory from the 2011 revolution to the 2019 civil war. It introduces key political players and forces, identifies turning points, and weighs the respective importance of international actors, politicians with nationwide influence, and local forces in shaping events. It familiarizes the reader with the broader context of events that are subsequently analysed in detail, and specifies the nature of the fragmentation the book seeks to explain.

Chapter 2, 'Structure and Process in the Eruption of Civil War', gauges the weight of structural factors and political legacies, as compared to mechanisms set in motion by the 2011 conflict itself, in shaping the patterns of localism that emerged during the war. More specifically, it examines the widespread assumption that tribal solidarities determined collective positions towards the uprising. Analysing the former regime's tribal policies, I offer an answer to the question of what a Libyan tribe was in February 2011. I then provide a micro-level account of how local political communities formed and positioned themselves during the first weeks of the uprising, comparing events in the Nafusa Mountains, Misrata, Bani Walid and Tobruk. These cases show that the formation of local power centres and the emergence of rifts between communities did not amount to an activation of predetermined fault lines. Instead, they point to the importance of contingent events in a situation of collective indecision, and self-reinforcing mechanisms involving violence or the threat thereof.

Chapter 3, 'Social Embeddedness and Transformation in Violent Conflict', takes issue with dominant conceptions of actors in civil wars and collapsed states. I conceptualize these actors as socially embedded, and propose a typology of armed groups according to the extent of their embeddedness. The case studies highlight the constraints that social embeddedness imposes on politicians and the leaders of fighting groups. Communities in Misrata and the Nafusa Mountains emerged from the 2011 war more cohesive, with collective leaderships and socially embedded forces. These coexisted with more hierarchical or socially insulated groups, but the latter proved less resilient. In Bani Walid, the war weakened local leadership, but cohesion recovered in the face of external threats, preventing the establishment of distinct armed groups. In Tobruk, leadership and cohesion were largely unaffected by the war, and no socially embedded forces emerged. The chapter focuses on events between 2012 and 2015.

Chapter 4, 'The Process of Fragmentation', examines the interplay between changing strategic conditions and the evolving social fabric in which local forces are embedded. The case studies show how the rapid change of strategic conditions during 2011–19 repeatedly forced political actors to change course in ways that clashed with their social ties. This impeded the consolidation of local leadership, and inflicted ever more fractures on communities. In Misrata and the Nafusa Mountains, social embeddedness and cohesion constrained political actors in their moves against local rivals and their alliances with outside forces, leading competing camps to coexist alongside each other within communities. In Bani Walid, cohesion facilitated the isolationist stance adopted by the town's leadership, and inhibited the establishment of divergent alliances with outside actors. Tobruk was largely shielded from the momentous changes taking place, and was easily taken over by a warlord structure that drew its power not from social embeddedness, but from external support. The focus of this chapter is on events between 2015 and 2019.

I conclude by drawing out the implications of my findings for wider theoretical debates in the literature on civil wars and collapsed states, as well as for Libya's predicament. Both Libyans and foreigners often venture either strongman rule or decentralization as solutions to Libya's fragmentation. But the warlord route to centralization hits a dead end when it encounters cohesive communities with powerful, deeply embedded forces. Conversely, as long as no meaningful central authority exists, local authorities will be paralysed by debilitating rivalries, besides lacking the resources needed to deliver services. Overcoming fragmentation will take time, but the approach most likely to succeed consists in the gradual consolidation of patronage networks around a central government in which local forces compete for influence.

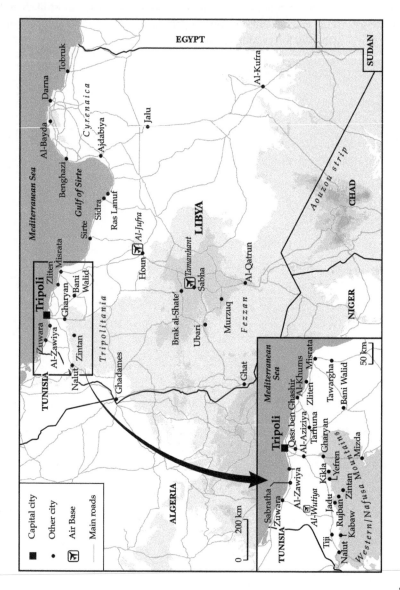

Map 1 Libya.

1

Libya's unravelling (2011–19)

Libya's fragmentation was not a linear process. Recent comment frequently draws a direct line between the 2011 NATO-led intervention and the chaos engulfing Libya since 2014. But the collapse of the post-Qadhafi transition was by no means inevitable. The dynamics and turning points that prevented the re-establishment of state institutions and the formation of cohesive national political forces deserve careful analysis.

This chapter draws the big picture of Libya's evolution during 2011–19, providing the context for subsequent chapters, which delve into the details of local struggles. It introduces the key political actors and traces changes in the political landscape. It identifies the events and dynamics that defined Libya's path towards fragmentation, and failed efforts that could have altered that path – such as attempts to form broader, more cohesive or more centralized institutions and political forces. It examines the nature of fragmentation, and underlines its central importance for Libya's overall trajectory during the period under investigation.

Revolution (February–October 2011)

The Libyan revolution erupted as a dramatic chain reaction that was sparked by spontaneous protests and regime violence. Within ten days of the first protest on 15 February, events had reached a revolutionary situation: a state of split sovereignty, with rebels taking over major cities and regions, contesting the Qadhafi regime's claim to legitimacy, and establishing their own leadership.[1] Local revolts had snowballed into a revolution and become militarized long before the NATO-led intervention began on 19 March.

The first protests were spontaneous and unorganized, erupting under the impact of the toppling of Ben Ali and Mubarak in neighbouring Tunisia and Egypt, which suddenly made the overthrow of Qadhafi seem equally possible. They preceded the 'day of rage' scheduled for 17 February, which exiled opposition groups had called for. The first instance of unrest erupted in Benghazi on the evening of 15 February, in reaction to the pre-emptive arrest of a lawyer representing families of victims of a 1996 massacre in a Tripoli prison. The families had staged periodic sit-ins in Benghazi over the preceding years. Though the lawyer was released after several hours, a small protest that included family members of the victims ballooned into a crowd of several hundred people at the courthouse in downtown Benghazi that was dispersed by tear gas and hot water cannons, with some protesters clashing with regime supporters in stone-throwing battles.[2]

The very next day, protests erupted in several cities, and were met with violence by security forces. In the eastern city of al-Bayda, security forces killed two protesters on 16 February. The following day, the funerals led to large protests in which fifteen people were killed.[3] Their funerals on 18 February, in turn, exploded into rioting. Protesters looted and torched the facilities of the internal security service and the Revolutionary Committees, seized weapons and lynched a member of the security forces.[4] The following day, people from al-Bayda and neighbouring Shahat attacked and seized the base of an army brigade that informally carried the name of al-Jareh Farkash, a relative of Qadhafi's wife who had long led the unit. They subsequently fought to gain control of nearby al-Abraq airport, through which reinforcements had been arriving, eventually seizing the airport on 21 February.[5]

In town after town, the pattern of regime violence provoking the rapid escalation of initially small protests repeated itself. In the eastern city of Darna, three protesters were killed on 17 February, triggering large protests and clashes after the funerals the following day, during which buildings of the security services were attacked and set on fire. During the night, Darna rebels had already taken over the nearby army base at Bombah, seizing weapons. On 23 February, fighters from Darna captured and later executed twenty-two soldiers.[6]

In Benghazi itself, security forces adopted a shoot-to-kill policy in their attempt to quell protests on 17 February, killing twenty-eight people and injuring scores.[7] The following day, regime forces opened fire on a funeral procession, causing protests to escalate further; thirty-five people were killed.[8] On 19 February, protesters attacked facilities of the security services and prisons, seizing weapons, and began attacking the base of the city's key praetorian unit, the Fadhil Bu Omar Brigade, initially armed mostly with stones. The decisive moment for the uprising in Benghazi – and in Cyrenaica as a whole – came on 20 February, when rebels seized the base. Interior minister Abdelfattah Younes, who also commanded the Benghazi-based Saeqa Special Forces, negotiated the evacuation of Qadhafi's son Saadi, his intelligence chief Abdallah Senoussi, and the bulk of the forces in the base, before it fell to the rebels. Younes officially defected to the rebels two days later; the same day, lawyers and academics at the courthouse formed a local council for Benghazi.

By 22 February, the eastern region from Benghazi to the Egyptian border therefore largely escaped government control. In the west, too, the uprising was in full swing. In the Nafusa Mountains, protesters on 16 February torched the seats of the Revolutionary Committees and Internal Security services in Zintan and neighbouring Rujban. In Rujban, a brigade sent to re-establish control that evening killed a young protester. Both towns were in open rebellion as early as 17 February. Zintani rebels formed a committee to organize the town's defences on 19 February, and seized a weapons depot several hundred kilometres away on 20 February. In Amazigh towns across the mountains, small protests erupted on 18 February; in Jadu, rebels seized their first weapons the next day. By 24 February, most towns in the mountains from the Tunisian border to Kikla had joined the rebellion.[9]

In the coastal city of Misrata, the first instance of unrest on 19 February led to the death of a young man at the hands of the security forces; his funeral the following day triggered larger protests and attacks on the security forces, which then temporarily withdrew from the city. Misratans formed their first local committee on 22 February. In Tripoli, the first major protests erupted on 20 February; as in Benghazi, regime forces followed a shoot-to-kill policy that claimed around 200 victims in the capital that night.[10] Large protests once again erupted on 25 February, whose repression caused dozens of casualties.[11] The western coastal cities of Zawiya and Zuwara escaped state control from 24 February onwards.

A spate of high-level defections accompanied the breathtaking dynamic of cities erupting in rebellion. Suleiman Mahmoud, commander of Tobruk military region and a longtime Qadhafi companion, publicly declared on 20 February that he had 'joined the people'.[12] Qadhafi's justice minister Mustafa Abdeljalil, from al-Bayda, resigned on 21 February in protest against the violent clampdown, and presided over the newly formed local council in his home city. The same day Libya's deputy ambassador to the UN and the ambassador to India both resigned. On 22 February, after Qadhafi's infamous speech, in which he called protesters 'rats' and 'cockroaches' that would be hunted down 'house by house', interior minister Abdelfattah Younes defected, as did Libya's ambassador to the United States. Many other senior diplomats and officials joined them over the next days, not least UN ambassador and long-standing senior regime figure Abdelrahman Shalgham, on 25 February. Rumours disseminated through the international media – most prominently by al-Jazeera – significantly contributed to this momentum. Allegations relayed on 21 February that the regime's air force was strafing protesters in Tripoli later turned out to have been false; so was the UK foreign minister's statement the same day that Qadhafi had fled the country.[13]

The defection of senior officials provided the spontaneous rebellion with a political leadership and channels to foreign governments. The lawyers and academics of Benghazi's local council reached out to these officials, as well as to the councils that were forming in other eastern cities. On 26 February, they established a national council headed by Abdeljalil. The National Transitional Council (NTC) was officially announced on 5 March, with the aim of representing all Libyan regions – though the only names they made public were those of eleven members from eastern cities. Rebels in several western and southern cities had designated representatives whose names were withheld to protect their security, and the council stated that some of its thirty-one seats were yet to be filled by representatives for Tripoli and other cities.[14] Even so, the council was clearly dominated by eastern figures.

The nascent revolutionary leadership was a diverse group. It included officials who had defected, like Mahmoud Jibril, who had been a prominent figure among the reformists promoted by Qadhafi's son Saif al-Islam, and who oversaw the NTC's foreign relations before becoming head of the council's Executive Office. They also included long-standing regime figures like Shalgham and Younes, the latter named chief of staff of the council's (largely imaginary) army. Members of the Benghazi intelligentsia and respected figures from other eastern cities formed a third constituency; a fourth were exiled opposition activists, many of them representatives of historically prominent families that had been sidelined under Qadhafi.[15] Who was really in charge remained unclear, and initial shortcomings in clarifying competencies led to recurrent quarrels between factions within the NTC.

The elite figures in and around the NTC quickly lost control over the revolutionary forces as they emerged on the ground. The groups of young revolutionary fighters that formed in Benghazi, al-Bayda and Darna to fight Qadhafi's forces on the eastern front had seized weapons in the initial chaos; they escaped central oversight, and many were deeply suspicious of Younes and other senior army defectors. Eastern dominance in the council and the isolation of the embattled western revolutionary strongholds from the NTC in Benghazi further compounded the problem. In Misrata and the Nafusa Mountains, highly localized armed groups developed as rebels defended individual towns or neighbourhoods. Gradually, civilian fighters and defected officers who had shown particular charisma or skills emerged as leaders of local factions and established local military councils. The NTC and its military leadership had few connections with these groups, and little to offer them.

The problems caused by the absence of strong central leadership would gradually come to the fore as the rapid momentum of the uprising's first two weeks gave way to a stalemated civil war. After regime forces re-established control in Tripoli in late February, the spate of defections shrank to a trickle. During the first two weeks of March, Qadhafi's forces violently suppressed rebels in Gharyan, Zawiya and Zuwara, established a foothold in Misrata, and laid siege to rebellious Nafusa Mountains towns. On the eastern front, regime forces drove the disorganized rebels from their positions at Ras Lanuf, and by 19 March appeared on the outskirts of Benghazi, when the onset of the French-led (later NATO-led) intervention annihilated the advancing column. Thereafter, the front lines would remain largely static until early June, when rebels in Misrata and the Nafusa Mountains began making steady progress.

In the six months between the eruption of the uprising and the fall of Tripoli in August 2011, the diverse factions that joined the revolution for the most part deferred internal conflicts that could be exploited by the regime – though there were many sources of tension, and several moments in which the coalition could have fallen apart. Within the NTC, Jibril was criticized for spending most of his time abroad and inaccurately presenting himself as the revolutionaries' prime minister.[16] Leading figures in the Muslim Brotherhood and other Islamist movements attacked the NTC for what they saw as its excessive reliance on secularist intellectuals; the absorption of several Muslim Brothers into the NTC from May onwards introduced a new political divide within the council.[17]

Frictions between the NTC leadership and the Islamist-leaning commanders of revolutionary armed groups in Benghazi also appeared early. In late March, Ismail Sallabi, one of the leading commanders in Benghazi, prepared a petition to alter the composition of the NTC. Sheikhs and armed men seeking to stop him confronted Sallabi at his house, and shots were fired before the situation de-escalated. Younes failed to assert his authority over the civilian fighters who were risking their lives on the front line, and harboured doubts over his competence, as well as suspicions that he retained ties with Qadhafi. He also faced a rival contender for the army leadership in Khalifa Haftar, a former army officer and Qadhafi protégé who had joined the exiled opposition after being captured by enemy forces during the 1980s Libya-Chad war, and arrived in Benghazi in early March. Crisis struck when Younes was assassinated in late July, in circumstances that remain murky. Under intense pressure from Younes' tribe, the Obeidat, the NTC dismissed its Executive Office, several members of which were alleged to have played a role in the events leading up to Younes' killing.[18]

Rivalries over weapons supplies to the revolutionary forces exacerbated such tensions. At first, Qatar channelled its weapons shipments to Younes, under NTC oversight. But from April onwards, competing networks emerged through which rival factions in the NTC and its Executive Office connected local revolutionary forces to regional governments. The prominent Doha-based religious scholar Ali Sallabi used his connections to route subsequent shipments to a coalition of Islamist-leaning revolutionary battalions in Benghazi in which his brother Ismail was a leading figure. Ali Sallabi was also instrumental in brokering Qatari and Sudanese weapons shipments to two groups that had established themselves in the Nafusa towns of Nalut and Rujban, and were led by former members of the Libyan Islamic Fighting Group (LIFG). In turn, Jibril and the Sufi scholar-cum-businessman Aref al-Nayed successfully lobbied the UAE for weapons shipments to their contacts in Zintan, and brokered their own Sudanese supplies to groups in Misrata and Benghazi. Misratan businessmen and military leaders gradually established their own links to Qatar and Sudan.[19]

The emergence of competing factions, each with its own local and international connections, thwarted all efforts by the NTC and its Executive Office to direct the capture of Tripoli, and ensure its stabilization under a central authority. The fall of Tripoli in August was chaotic, as forces from Nafusa Mountains towns, Misrata, and clandestine networks in Tripoli itself failed to coordinate, and almost instantly began to vie for control of the capital. Dozens of armed groups began competing for military and security facilities, government buildings and files of Qadhafi's intelligence services. They also began looting the assets of state-owned companies and the private property of senior regime figures. Zintani units seized the international airport. Predation and the seizure of strategic sites vastly increased the power of revolutionary commanders.

The security landscape in Tripoli evolved into an anarchic patchwork. Former LIFG commander Abdelhakim Belhaj, relying on the Qatar-backed units that had fought in Nalut and Rujban, declared himself the head of a 'Tripoli Military Council', though he had consulted only a fraction of the forces now scrambling for control in Tripoli, and had not received formal NTC approval. Zintani commanders, nascent armed groups from Tripoli, and many others immediately contested Belhaj's move.

In an attempt to establish a single command structure under the NTC and contain Belhaj, Jibril and another senior figure in the NTC's Executive Office, former exiled dissident Ali Tarhuni, created a Supreme Security Committee (SSC) to register and oversee all civilian fighters in the capital.[20] In reality, the SSC became a structure parallel to Belhaj's, who pressured Abdeljalil into handing control over the SSC to a politically diverse group of NTC members: the prominent businessman and Muslim Brother Abderrezak al-Aradi from Tripoli; the Misratan revolutionary leader Fawzi Abdelali, and the longtime exile Abdelmajid Saif al-Nasr, scion of a historically influential family from Fezzan. The SSC provided payments to the fighters who registered with it, initiating a cycle of competition that led to the formation of rival factions in new security sector institutions, and caused the membership of armed groups to skyrocket.[21] But neither

Belhaj's council nor the SSC succeeded in concentrating authority over the plethora of armed groups that formed in Tripoli. Many retained close ties to their towns of origin – Misrata, or towns in the Nafusa Mountains – while others adhered to particular strands of Islamism. Yet others were akin to criminal gangs. Outside of Tripoli, too, local armed groups and military councils mushroomed as the regime's arsenals were looted.

Even as revolutionary forces converged on the regime's last two strongholds in Sirte and Bani Walid, tensions in the revolutionary coalition increasingly spilled into the open. In Tripoli, competition over control led to frequent skirmishes. Both Ali Sallabi and the prominent Misratan politician Abderrahman al-Sweihli vociferously attacked Mahmoud Jibril in international media outlets, with Sallabi accusing him of being a 'secular extremist' and Sweihli accusing him of retaining ties to the former regime.[22] Sallabi and Sweihli were but the most high-profile of the many figures jockeying for influence in the formation of an interim government.[23]

The final months of the revolutionary civil war also revealed a much darker reality than the NTC's insistence that it represented all Libyans suggested. As the revolutionary forces advanced, they exacted revenge on neighbouring communities they collectively stigmatized as regime loyalists and accused them of having abetted crimes committed by Qadhafi's forces. In August, Misratan forces emptied the neighbouring town of Tawargha of its population, looting and destroying homes and infrastructure, and warning residents never to return. Zintani forces had done the same to neighbouring al-Aweiniya and western Riyayna; members of the Mashashiya tribe and residents of al-Qawalish fled from their towns as forces from Zintan and other revolutionary strongholds in the mountains advanced. Forces from Nalut targeted the population of nearby Tiji and Badr.[24]

The retreat of Qadhafi's inner circle and remaining loyalists to Sirte and Bani Walid reflected the widespread support the regime enjoyed among some constituencies. Many in these two cities experienced their capture in October 2011 not as a liberation but as a defeat. This sentiment was also widespread among some groups in southern Libya: many Qadhadhfa in Sabha, for example, suffered looting by forces affiliated with the Awlad Suleiman tribe as the city fell. Libya's social geography was transformed as entire towns were displaced and their residents dispersed across the country, members of particular tribal constituencies were forced from their homes, and many regime officials fled abroad with their families.

On 20 October, revolutionary fighters executed Qadhafi in Sirte. Three days later, Abdeljalil declared that Libya had been liberated, thereby activating the transitional roadmap laid out by the NTC. Though the euphoria of liberation and ebullient expectations of a bright future prevailed, the war had inflicted deep fractures on society, and created sizeable groups of losers. It remained far from clear who, exactly, would ultimately emerge as the winners.

Sharing the spoils (November 2011–July 2012)

The task set before the NTC with the collapse of the Qadhafi regime was daunting. A heterogeneous collective leadership without meaningful authority over the plethora of armed groups was to lead a transition towards no less than the establishment of a new state. Qadhafi's Libya had no constitution, and had functioned with unstable and highly idiosyncratic institutions that were inextricably tied to the leader himself. The army and security apparatus had largely collapsed with the regime. The NTC rejected any presence of foreign troops to help stabilize the country, and its foreign backers acquiesced, judging that foreign forces would be widely rejected in Libya and would severely undermine the NTC's legitimacy, thereby jeopardizing the transition.[25]

In its August 'Constitutional Declaration', the NTC had set out a highly ambitious roadmap. The document foresaw elections to a legislative body, the General National Congress (GNC), within eight months of liberation. The GNC would replace the NTC, appoint a new government and a constituent committee that would have two months to present a draft constitution. Within seven months of the constitution's adoption by popular referendum, new elections would complete the transition, less than two years after the regime's demise. The roadmap had been a victory for representatives of Islamist movements and western Libyan cities who had insisted on the need for an elected legislature and government to manage the process, calculating that elections would endow them with greater influence than they enjoyed in the NTC. Jibril and Tarhuni, who wanted the NTC itself to steer the transition and appoint a constituent committee, had lost out.[26]

Some observers have since argued that holding elections before the security situation stabilized was bound to provoke violence.[27] But in the months after the regime's demise, it became clear that the NTC lacked the legitimacy needed to manage the transition. The council was under attack for being unelected, self-appointed and opaque; even after it belatedly published a list of its (then 61) members in December 2011, it remained unclear how these members had been chosen. Representatives of the revolutionary fighters – the *thuwwar* – and their political allies criticized the prominent role of former regime officials in the council.[28]

With the appointment of an interim government under Abdelrahim al-Kib in November 2011, the NTC sought to signal a departure from the Executive Office of the Benghazi days. Contrary to Jibril's team, Kib's cabinet did not include any former regime officials. The repartition of the defence and interior portfolios unmistakably reflected the new balance of power in Tripoli: Defence Minister Usama al-Juwaili was the head of Zintan military council; interior minister Fawzi Abdelali, a former public prosecutor, had been among the revolutionaries of the first hour in Misrata. Former LIFG member al-Siddiq al-Mabruk al-Ghithi was named deputy defence minister with authority over the border guards; an influential Muslim Brother, Omar al-Khadrawi, became deputy interior minister. On the whole, however, government formation had withstood pressure to appease the new strongmen and factions to a surprising degree. Most ministers were technocrats, many of them – like Kib himself – former exiles without a local power base. Inevitably, several local constituencies reacted to the cabinet's announcement by protesting their exclusion – not least groups from Benghazi, where sentiments that the city was once again being marginalized were on the rise since the NTC's move to Tripoli.[29]

The Kib government soon faced the full brunt of pressure from the *thuwwar* and nascent political factions. The registration and payment of fighters through the SSC had set competitive cycles in motion. These were most intense in Tripoli. Military councils burgeoned across the capital as the SSC used them to distribute payments, based on lists the councils had themselves submitted, offering opportunities for massive corruption, and infuriating those who were excluded.[30] Before he had even presented his cabinet, Kib had to contend with angry armed men who burst into the finance ministry demanding payments and jobs.[31] Kib's calls for patience were swept aside when the UN Security Council lifted sanctions on the Central Bank in December 2011, suddenly making dozens of billions of dollars available to the NTC. With the arrival of Abdelali at the Interior Ministry, the SSC was re-established as a nationwide institution, and its opportunities for patronage and enrichment were rolled out to other cities. By August 2012, the SSC had reached a headcount of 149,000, but SSC officials estimated that less than half that number actually showed up for work.[32]

Other emerging factions in government institutions quickly emulated the SSC model. Both, Defence Minister Juwaili and the chief of staff appointed in January 2012, Youssef al-Mangush, signed off on dozens of new army units, which officers across the country were forming to build their own power base, often mixing regular soldiers with civilian fighters, and generously inflating personnel lists. Juwaili established several new army units to absorb Zintani fighters, and appointed dozens of military attachés to embassies abroad, the vast majority of whom were from Zintan. He also turned the Qaʿqaʾ Brigade founded by Zintani businessman Abdelmajid al-Mlegta into a unit of the border and petroleum facilities guards. Mlegta's men protected Jibril on his visits to Tripoli, and Mlegta would soon emerge as a leading figure and financier of Jibril's new party. Deputy Defence Minister al-Ghithi absorbed selected armed groups across the county into the border guard, several of them headed and dominated by former LIFG members.[33] Groups that had seized oilfields, refineries or export terminals were converted into units of the petroleum facilities guards, which went from 2,000 members before the revolution to a nominal headcount of over 25,000 in 2014.[34]

The politically most significant of these schemes was the Libya Shield Force (LSF). In early 2012, a series of local conflicts in western and southern Libya and the perceived threat emanating from regime loyalists led the leaders of revolutionary armed groups to deploy forces in several conflict areas, including in Kufra and Mizda. They obtained official mandates to act as peacekeeping forces. The regular army was in disarray, and many revolutionary leaders insisted that its ranks should be purged of regime loyalists before the institution was re-established; in the meantime, the *thuwwar* were to fill the vacuum.

In this context, the idea of a temporary paramilitary force called the Libya Shield Force surfaced. A prominent army officer and revolutionary leader from Misrata, Salem Jha, proposed that fighters from different groups within a particular region be dispersed across newly established units, thereby breaking up the structures of existing armed groups, and centralizing control over their heavy weapons under the command of army officers. Due to resistance from revolutionary commanders, however, the model eventually adopted was one in which existing armed groups simply joined an LSF unit and received salaries for their fighters, but otherwise retained their structures, loyalties and weapons.[35] After the chief of staff formally established the LSF in June 2012, its divisions multiplied as local commanders exerted pressure to obtain their separate units. The most active and militarily powerful were the Western Region Libya Shield, two Misrata-based units and a Benghazi-based unit that included many of the city's Islamist-leaning factions.[36]

In the struggles over new security sector institutions, factions that had a presence in Tripoli were at an advantage, and the embattled NTC was increasingly eager to appease them. In February 2012, the NTC decided that all revolutionary fighters should receive a one-off payment of LD2,200 ($1,700 at the time) as compensation for their role in the revolution, with married fighters being paid LD 4,000 ($3,000). Payments were to be made via the military councils, based on lists prepared by the councils themselves. Large-scale misappropriation followed, provoking protests by fighters who claimed to be eligible but excluded; in one such protest, *thuwwar* besieged the finance ministry, trapping the minister inside the building until he issued orders to pay out funds. By April, when the government suspended the payments due to massive abuse, it had disbursed LD1,8bn.[37] The suspension caused further violent protests; in May, fighters from the Nafusa Mountains towns of Yefren and Kikla tried to force their way into the prime minister's office, killing a security guard.[38] During this period, revolutionary leaders made numerous attempts to form councils or unions to represent the *thuwwar* politically, but most were narrowly based, and all failed.[39]

Beleaguered by armed groups and lacking electoral legitimacy, the Kib government and NTC deferred most urgent issues. The massive public works projects begun in the years preceding the revolution remained on hold, as the government shied away from settling disputes over foreign companies' losses since 2011. Capital expenditure plummeted, while spending on state salaries exploded, driven by the security sector payroll. The government took no strategic decisions to restore the army, police and judiciary, resorting, instead, to temporary stopgap measures such as the LSF and SSC.

The government also failed to invest in a demobilization programme: the Warriors' Affairs Commission established for this purpose by Mustafa al-Saqizli, who together with Fawzi Bukatef and Ismail Sallabi had been a leading figure in Benghazi's largest coalition of revolutionary groups, was largely reduced to operating expenditures. Its proposals for offering training, education or public sector jobs to the *thuwwar* went unheeded, not least because ignoring them raised no direct threat from armed groups.[40] If the policy of deferring decisions was meant to ensure that a future elected government would have the full range of options, it had the opposite effect: once initiated, the distributive policies and haphazard institutions of this period developed their own dynamics, and rapidly ruled out other choices. Establishing centralized control in the security sector soon became impossible.

As the struggles unfolded in Tripoli, frustration was mounting elsewhere. In the east, the sentiment spread that the region was once again ignored. Conflicts in southern Libya received scant attention from the government. In spring 2012, as negotiations over the geographical distribution of seats in the upcoming elections intensified, proponents of Cyrenaican regional autonomy staged two conferences at which they unilaterally announced the creation of a federal region in *Barqa* (Cyrenaica). The move had no concrete implications, as most former revolutionary armed groups in the region strongly opposed the autonomy movement. Nevertheless, it did pose a direct challenge to the NTC, and Abdeljalil reacted by denouncing the meetings as a conspiracy and a threat to national unity.[41]

Soon, however, the NTC changed track to placate the autonomy movement with two fateful amendments to the Constitutional Declaration. In March, the NTC decided that representatives of Libya's three historic regions should have equal weight in the Constituent Committee, just like the committee that had drafted the first constitution of independent Libya in 1951. As the 7 July elections drew closer, the Barqa Council called for a boycott, and armed proponents of regional autonomy turned to violence to sabotage the poll, setting up a roadblock to stop ballot boxes from reaching the east, shutting down oil terminals and ransacking electoral commission offices.[42] Two days before the vote, Abdeljalil unexpectedly announced another amendment: instead of being appointed by the GNC, the Constituent Committee would be elected through direct vote, giving voters in the less populated eastern and southern regions equal weight with those in the west. The decision meant a more drawn-out transitional process and an additional element of uncertainty, since the GNC was bound to challenge the decision. Equally important, it was the first concession to violence aimed at altering the transitional process, and thereby set an inauspicious precedent.

An experiment with democracy (July 2012–May 2013)

To the surprise of outside observers and many Libyans themselves, the elections were highly successful, given the difficult circumstances in which they were held.[43] Participation stood at over 60 per cent, and voters in the east squarely ignored boycott calls. The minor acts of violence and irregularities that occurred were limited to a few districts. Revolutionary armed groups played a decisive role in securing the vote. Electoral campaigning did not have a polarizing effect; the many newly founded parties were largely indistinguishable in their bland commitments to vague ideals such as the rule of law and transparent institutions. By and large, the Islamist-secularist divide was not salient in the run-up to the elections, although the mufti and revolutionary firebrand al-Sadeq al-Gharyani virulently attacked Jibril's National Forces Alliance (NFA) for its alleged secularism on the eve of the vote. Former LIFG commander Abdelhakim Belhaj even founded a party whose candidates ranged from former jihadis to unveiled women – though the party, Al-Watan, flopped in the elections.

The fact that not all were able to exercise their new rights was largely ignored in the euphoria surrounding the elections. In yet another attempt to appease the *thuwwar*, the NTC had passed a lustration law in April 2012 that barred certain categories of former regime officials from running for office or holding top positions, unless they had joined the revolution early on. The Integrity Commission[44] established to oversee the law's enforcement disqualified 300 candidates prior to the elections; in the following months, it suspended fifteen from among the GNC's 200 members. In addition, the NTC deliberately excluded groups associated with the former regime from voting. It opened voting centres in several Western states, the UAE and Jordan, but not in Egypt and Tunisia, where several hundred thousand Libyans had fled as the regime collapsed.[45] Nevertheless, on the whole, the elections united Libyans more than they divided them, and strengthened the sway of the February revolution as the founding myth of a new Libyan state.

The electoral system adopted by the NTC produced a legislature that mirrored the fragmentation of the political scene. Of the 200 seats, only eighty were allocated to party lists, the reasoning being that there were no established parties. The remaining 120 seats were reserved for individual candidates, with seats going to the candidate with the largest number of votes in a constituency. Confounding expectations of an Islamist landslide, Jibril's NFA won nearly half of the party list seats, while the Muslim Brotherhood's Justice and Construction Party (JCP) secured less than a quarter. The remainder went to lists that gained three seats or less, most of them local organizations. Both the NFA and the JCP also fielded independent candidates, who taken together won around a quarter of the seats reserved for independents. Salafis performed strongly in Tripoli and Zawiya. The first-past-the-post system meant that many independents were elected with only a few hundred votes.[46]

The GNC's fragmentation made for an equally fragmented government, and protracted decision-making. After the GNC had charged Mustafa Abushagur, a former exile and minister in the Kib government, with forming a government, Abushagur failed twice in obtaining approval for his proposed cabinets. Ali Zeidan, another long-standing member of the exiled opposition, eventually succeeded in late October. His government reflected a complex formula of NFA and JCP nominees, Salafis and representatives of particular local constituencies, all checked for regional balance – with the east strongly represented. Technocrats held the key portfolios of Foreign Affairs, Defence, Interior, Justice and Finance, though even in their case, geographical balance had a bearing. The deputy ministers for these ministries were political nominees. In other cases, ministries headed by an NFA representative had deputy ministers from the JCP, and vice versa. Revolutionary and Islamist factions were represented with such figures as former LIFG commander Khaled al-Sharif and the Misratan commander al-Tuhami Buzian as deputy defence ministers, as well as Ahmad Dromba from Zintan and former LIFG member Abdelbaset Buhliqa as deputy interior ministers. Zeidan qualified for the post of prime minister primarily because he lacked a power base of his own, and therefore did not pose a threat to any of the groups in his government.[47]

If Kib had sought to resist factional demands for representation in government, and had deferred decisions as a matter of policy, the Zeidan government was entirely carved up among factions large and small, in a way that ensured its internal paralysis. The practice of security sector officials sponsoring particular units and institutions, as initiated under Kib, expanded further, and rivalries over security institutions intensified. Factionalism in the security sector, in turn, spelled the government's impotence. Around 7,000 prisoners arbitrarily detained by revolutionary armed groups during and after the 2011 war, many of them from stigmatized communities such as the Qadhadhfa, Tawargha or Bani Walid, continued to languish in prisons outside state control. The government had no loyal force to deploy in the conflicts erupting in the southern periphery. It had no recipe for the stabilization of Benghazi, where a string of assassinations was targeting Qadhafi-era security officials. In September 2012, a terrorist attack on the US consulate in Benghazi had prompted civilians, backed by elements of the old army, to attack the bases of three powerful armed groups, among them Ansar al-Sharia.[48] The government also stood by as smuggling networks benefiting from Libya's multibillion dollar subsidy budget consolidated into vested interests, and criminal gangs thrived in large cities.

Zeidan's task of building consensus was all the more difficult as parts of the political spectrum were growing more radical in what they saw as the defence of the revolution. In October 2012, representatives of former revolutionary strongholds in the GNC pushed through a decision to launch a military operation against the former regime bastion of Bani Walid, ostensibly to arrest fugitives there. Bani Walid had openly defied the new order since early 2012, and armed men from Bani Walid had seized several hostages from Misrata, of whom one – a former revolutionary fighter who had been among Qadhafi's captors in Sirte – succumbed to his injuries shortly after being released. Several Misratan politicians, with Abderrahman al-Sweihli at their head, led in obtaining GNC approval for the operation, which was mainly carried out by Libya Shield units from Misrata and Zawiya. The campaign displaced thousands of families from Bani Walid, and starkly illustrated the impunity with which the armed groups could act under the banner of defending the revolution.

The proponents of a hard-line revolutionary stance gradually emerged as a camp within the GNC, which flexed its muscles by referring several of Zeidan's cabinet nominees to the Integrity Commission, preventing them from taking office for over a month.[49] In late 2012, demonstrations in former revolutionary strongholds began demanding the 'political isolation'[50] of former regime officials, meaning their exclusion in a more comprehensive manner than that assured by the Integrity Commission. In the GNC, the 'Honouring the Blood of the Martyrs'[51] bloc formed in January 2013 with precisely that goal. The Martyrs Bloc was a wildly heterogeneous group. It included a former senior LIFG member, Abdelwahab Gaid; several parliamentarians from Salafi currents; representatives of revolutionary strongholds, such as the Amazigh towns; members associated with the National Front party, the successor of the main exiled opposition movement; as well as various disgruntled members from southern Libyan districts. Political isolation was the only thing the group agreed on, though views differed over who exactly should be excluded.[52]

The struggle over the Political Isolation Law (PIL) entirely preoccupied the GNC between January and May 2013, distracting it from the most urgent task it had been set by the Constitutional Declaration: deciding whether the Constituent Committee should be appointed or elected, and providing the legislative framework for its election. But the tug-of-war over the PIL also had a wider significance. It would define the formation of camps within the GNC and the wider political scene beyond 2013. The push for political isolation not only sent a strong signal for the continued marginalization of former regime elements and the rejection of reconciliation; it also spelled a definitive rupture within the coalition that had led the 2011 revolution. Newly empowered forces now intended to rid the political scene of the regime defectors who had played such a critical role in the revolution's early stages. The most prominent target, and one that most proponents of political isolation agreed on, was Mahmoud Jibril.[53] Beyond Jibril, there was much disagreement over the scope of exclusion: Should the law punish involvement with the regime going back to 1969? This would mean that GNC president Mohamed al-Magariaf, who served as ambassador in the 1970s but defected in 1980 and then led the main exiled opposition movement, would fall under the law's criteria. Should the law target members of the Muslim Brotherhood and the LIFG who reconciled with the regime in the years preceding the revolution?

Equally important was the use of violence in the struggle over the PIL. Dozens of GNC members from all parts of the spectrum had close links with armed factions; several ran their own armed groups. In March 2013, the Misratan GNC members Abderrahman al-Sweihli and Salah Badi called in armed groups from Misrata to intimidate GNC members meeting to debate the PIL in a location that been held secret, to preclude the frequent disruption of sessions by armed men. The armed groups surrounded the meeting venue for twelve hours, demanding that GNC members pass the law then and there, and leaving only after other armed groups arrived to bail out the parliamentarians.[54] Over the following weeks, some GNC members received threatening text messages pressing them to pass the law, and the mufti called for demonstrations to exert pressure on the GNC. In late April, armed groups from Misrata, Tripoli and other cities began besieging the foreign and justice ministries to demand that the law be passed. The groups were led by the Coordination for Political Isolation headed by former LIFG ideologue Sami al-Saadi, and two hard-line *thuwwar* organizations with overlapping membership, the Libyan Revolutionaries Operations Room (LROR) and the Supreme Council of Libyan Revolutionaries.[55]

The sieges on ministries and the GNC were by far the most brazen acts yet by armed groups to influence the political process, and starkly illustrated the government's impotence. The widespread impression that the law was adopted at gunpoint – though inaccurate – severely damaged public confidence in the GNC and the political process as a whole. But rather than the threat of violence, miscalculation eventually broke the deadlock over the law. Apparently expecting that the prospect of an overly sweeping exclusion of former officials would lure their adversaries into concessions, senior NFA figure Abdelmajid al-Mlegta and several NFA parliamentarians proposed a draft that concerned officials who had been working with the regime from its start, and made no exceptions for the early defectors of 2011. The JCP and the Martyrs Bloc called the NFA's bluff, and the law passed on 5 May.[56] The GNC emerged from the struggle as a broken institution.

Escalating tensions (May 2013–June 2014)

The Political Isolation Law triggered far-reaching changes within the GNC and the political landscape at large. The balance of power within the GNC had already been shifting due to the suspension of fifteen members by the Integrity Commission, disproportionately affecting NFA members or representatives of constituencies that were stigmatized as former regime strongholds. Following the law's passage, GNC president Mohamed al-Magariaf and his deputy Jum'a Atiqa – both moderate, consensual figures – resigned to avoid being suspended. In Magariaf's place, the ascendant revolutionary camp installed Nuri Abusahmain, an Amazigh member of the Martyrs Bloc, who arrogated the title of 'supreme commander of the armed forces' on a contested basis, using it to accord official status and budgets to *thuwwar* armed factions. Among Abusahmain's first actions were the officialization of the LROR and the unlawful transfer of major funds to the Shield forces.[57] Abusahmain also instated an Integrity and Reform Commission for the armed forces that applied the principle of political isolation to the military, and would suspend or forcibly retire hundreds of officers before the end of the year – among them Khalifa Haftar.[58] Revolutionary hard-liners in the GNC began plotting Zeidan's dismissal, but continuously failed in assembling the necessary majority.

The NFA initially attempted to renegotiate and amend the PIL. Faced with intransigence from the revolutionary camp, the NFA announced in July 2013 that it was boycotting the GNC except for sessions concerning the law on the Constituent Committee elections.[59] After the law passed later that month, the NFA expanded its boycott by suspending its participation in both the GNC and the Zeidan government 'until the constitution is adopted'.[60] The strategy backfired, as it further weakened the NFA in a legislature that continued to meet as if nothing had happened, aided by the fact that many NFA members and associated independents continued attending GNC sessions. After all, the NFA was not a cohesive political party, but an assemblage of interest groups hastily cobbled together before the 2012 elections.

During autumn 2013, the NFA leadership switched tactics and started working towards the GNC's downfall and new elections. TV channels and social media outlets associated with the NFA began insisting that the GNC's mandate expired in February 2014, although this was a creative reading of the Constitutional Declaration.[61] In December 2013, a movement opposing the 'extension' of the GNC's mandate began mobilizing demonstrations in Tripoli and other cities. Sympathetic TV channels considerably exaggerated the magnitude of the demonstrations and suggested that they represented the popular will. Although the movement claimed to be politically independent, a senior NFA figure professed that the party leadership was driving the protests behind the scenes.[62]

In addition to the PIL, the sea change in regional politics following the July 2013 military coup in Egypt contributed to this shift towards increasingly confrontational tactics in Tripoli. The NFA's mobilization of demonstrations to bring down the GNC appeared to be taken straight from the Egyptian playbook. This, in any case, was the prevailing view within the revolutionary camp, where paranoia of counter-revolutionary plots spread following the coup in Egypt. On the other side of the divide, politicians increasingly labelled their adversaries as 'the Islamists' or advanced the idea that the Muslim Brotherhood had hijacked government institutions – thereby seizing on the discourse promoted by media outlets in Egypt, Saudi Arabia and the UAE, and positioning themselves as potential allies of these states.

While this struggle paralysed the institutions and the political climate grew increasingly poisoned, distributive conflicts escalated. The resort to violence in exerting pressure on state institutions had been a recurrent feature since the beginning of the transitional period. But as the countless local armed groups competed with each other for state resources, their readiness to use violence increased steadily. The brazen manner in which revolutionary hardliners had sought to push through the PIL incited others to let their inhibitions fall further.

In the months following the law's passing, Zintani armed groups increasingly recklessly attacked institutions in Tripoli. When in May 2013 oil minister Abdelbari al-Arusi attempted to curb the rapid growth of payrolls in the Petroleum Facilities Guards (PFG), Zintanis closed the pipeline of the giant Sharara oilfield. The following month, Zintani units attacked the PFG headquarters in Tripoli to demand jobs and salaries, clashing heavily with Tripoli-based forces.[63] In July, the Zintani-led Sawaeq Brigade seized the Interior Ministry building and held it for more than a week, ransacking it before withdrawing.[64] Such confrontations increasingly pitted Zintani-led units in Tripoli against groups associated with Misrata. These conflicts were closely intertwined with the political tug-of-war: the largest Zintani-led unit, the Qa'qa' Brigade, was led by a brother of senior NFA figure Abdelmajid al-Mlegta.

In the peripheries, some groups had begun to erode the competitive advantage of armed factions in Tripoli from late 2012 onwards, when the first closures of oilfields and export terminals occurred near Ajdabiya and Ubari. The demands in these early protests were modest, but the government's accommodating approach quickly emboldened other groups. In August 2013, such incidents acquired a wholly new significance when a commander in the PFG, Ibrahim al-Jadhran, harnessed initially separate protests at the al-Zuwaitina, Ras Lanuf and Sidra oil terminals to announce the creation of a 'Cyrenaica Political Bureau' with himself at its head. The government dismissed Jadhran and threatened military force, but Jadhran persevered, gathering support in the east by denouncing alleged corruption in the oil industry, and openly attempting to sell oil outside official channels. The blockade of the eastern oil ports would last until April 2014, when the government eventually agreed to negotiate directly with Jadhran, after losses that went into dozens of billions of dollars. Two of the ports Jadhran controlled only reopened when a deal was reached, in June 2014.[65] In the west, disgruntled PFG units from Zintan and Amazigh groups protesting against the election law for the Constituent Committee also repeatedly shut down major pipelines. During September 2013, oil production temporarily slumped from a post-revolution high of 1.6m barrels per day to below 200,000 b/d, choking government revenues.[66]

Meanwhile, escalating violence signalled the failure of the new security institutions. In Benghazi, a series of killings targeting officers of the old army and security services accelerated throughout 2013, expanding to journalists, judges and activists, and reaching the rate of several per day in early 2014. The Zeidan government failed to conclude any investigations of these cases, let alone prosecute suspects. Extremist Islamist groups were widely suspected; the jihadist group Ansar al-Sharia was by then openly recruiting and operating in Benghazi, and its militants had close relations with some members of Libya Shield units. The leaders of these units, while acknowledging that extremists were likely responsible for some assassinations, accused Qadhafi loyalists or criminal elements in the Benghazi-based Saeqa Special Forces.[67] Ansar al-Sharia affiliates and other extremist groups were also increasingly active in Darna and Sirte, both of which saw a string of assassinations.

The glorification of the *thuwwar* that had been so widespread in the months following the regime's collapse turned into a general disdain towards the armed groups. In June 2013, a protest in front of a Libya Shield base in Benghazi turned into clashes in which forty people were killed, the vast majority of them protesters.[68] Chief of staff Mangush resigned, and the GNC vainly decreed that the government should dissolve all armed groups operating under official authorizations into the army or the police by year's end. In November, a Misratan armed group opened fire on a peaceful protest in front of their base in Tripoli, triggering clashes in which forty-three died, most of them protesters.[69] Misratan units withdrew from the capital in response to what the city's leadership saw as a demonization campaign, and several large Tripoli-based militias – among them the three largest Zintani-led units – organized ceremonies during which they ostensibly handed over their bases to the authorities. In reality, however, they stayed put.[70]

A stunning illustration of the government's impotence came in October 2013 with the kidnapping of Prime Minister Zeidan from his hotel suite by an armed group affiliated with the Libyan Revolutionaries Operations Room (LROR). Following his release after several hours of detention, Zeidan accused a hardline faction in the GNC headed by the Zawiyan Salafi battalion commander Mohamed al-Kilani of being behind the incident.[71]

After the kidnapping, Zeidan moved his office to a compound held by the Zintani-led Sawaeq Brigade, thereby taking sides in the escalating struggles over control in Tripoli. Zintani units expanded aggressively in Tripoli after the Misratan withdrawal, drawing the ire of the revolutionary camp. Both the Qa'qa' and Sawaeq had some former members of Qadhafi's notorious security brigades within their ranks. Misratan leaders and LROR representatives saw this as evidence of Zintani collusion with counter-revolutionary elements. They repeatedly – but unsuccessfully – engaged with the Zintanis on the issue.[72]

At the same time, punitive expeditions by forces associated with the revolutionary camp provoked growing resentment. In January 2014, forces from Tripoli and the Nafusa Mountains fought with armed groups in the Warshafana area south of Tripoli, where they accused former regime figures of stoking lawlessness. The same month, major fighting erupted between armed groups drawn from different tribes in Sabha. Awlad Suleiman leaders in the city alleged that they were under attack from former regime loyalists. The Zeidan government tasked the Third Force, a Libya Shield unit from Misrata, with intervening.[73]

In public opinion, the view that the GNC was the root of Libya's problems became increasingly widespread. Politicians and media outlets associated with the NFA, Zintan, marginalized communities such as Warshafana, and the eastern autonomy movement all heaped blame on what they described as an Islamist-controlled GNC that was refusing to hand over power. Those insisting that the GNC's mandate ended on 7 February expected that Islamists and revolutionary hardliners would be defeated in new elections. The latter, in turn, feared losses, and sought, instead, to convert their position of strength in the GNC into a new government, to replace the fractious power-sharing cabinet of Ali Zeidan.

While the GNC remained deadlocked over these issues, events accelerated after 7 February, pushing the political process to the verge of collapse. On 14 February, retired General Khalifa Haftar announced on satellite television that he was suspending the GNC and the Constitutional Declaration, and handing power to a Presidential Council.

But nothing happened. Haftar was speaking in the name of a 'General Leadership of the Libyan Army', but he obviously did not have an army to move with. His announcement was met with widespread ridicule.[74] Over the next three months, however, he mobilized significant support from army officers in the east, where resentment over the continuing assassinations and the region's perceived political marginalization was reaching boiling point.

On 18 February, the Qa'qa' and Sawaeq Brigades issued a televised statement in which they gave the GNC five hours to hand over power – to whom, they did not say – or face its forced dissolution and the arrest of GNC members.[75] As Tripoli braced for major clashes, the head of the UN Mission in Libya, Tarek Mitri, intervened with the two brigades' leaders, who eventually relented. In March, Zintani-led forces looted an army base in southern Tripoli and attacked the chief of staff's office, forcing its relocation. The revolutionary camp in the GNC and associated armed groups in Tripoli now began pressing insistently for the dissolution of the Qa'qa' and Sawaeq, and the surrender of Tripoli's international airport by Zintani units.[76]

While tensions mounted in Tripoli, the oil ports crisis was coming to a head. In early March, a North Korean-flagged tanker entered the port of Sidra and started loading the crude oil Jadhran had been seeking to sell for months. In response, Abusahmain issued a decree authorizing the formation of a military force to take back the oil ports. When the tanker left Sidra, Zeidan ordered the Libyan army and air force to intervene, but neither acted. Instead, the US Navy seized the ship and brought it back to Libya. The incident finally brought about the necessary majority in the GNC for a deal to remove Zeidan, replace him temporarily with his defence minister Abdallah al-Thinni, and amend the Constitutional Declaration to pave the way for new elections. As with many GNC decisions by that time, however, it was taken on a questionable basis, and later found to have lacked the necessary quorum.[77]

The first crack through the formal institutions opened up on 4 May, when the Misratan businessman Ahmed Maitig was elected to replace Thinni in a controversial GNC session. Abusahmain maintained that Maitig's election had followed GNC regulations, but his deputy Ezzeddine al-Awami from the eastern town of al-Marj insisted, along with a large group of GNC members, that Awami had lifted the session before Maitig's election. Although the Thinni government remained in office, Maitig began acting as though he was the legitimate prime minister, and received a group of Western ambassadors.[78]

While the deadlock over Maitig's election persisted, Haftar's launch of a military campaign against revolutionary and Islamist factions in Benghazi dealt a blow to the transitional institutions that would prove fatal. On 16 May, Haftar attacked the bases of several armed groups using ground forces and warplanes, announcing 'Operation Dignity to cleanse Benghazi of extremists and outlaws'. TV channels owned by Haftar's political allies described the operation as led by the Libyan army. Haftar's targets included the jihadist group Ansar al-Sharia, but also a former revolutionary armed group turned army unit (Brigade 319), as well as the 17 February and Rafallah Sahati battalions – two Islamist-leaning revolutionary armed groups that had lost the cover of the Libya Shield after the latter was dissolved in Benghazi in June 2013. These forces had already clashed on several occasions with the Saeqa Special

Forces in Benghazi, in November 2013 and February 2014. But Haftar's operation was an entirely different matter, since it was openly defiant of the Tripoli-based army leadership. GNC president Abusahmain and prime minister Thinni immediately denounced the operation as a coup attempt – rightly so, since five days later, speaking in the name of a 'supreme council of the armed forces', Haftar declared his intention to hand over power to an emergency government.[79] Across the country, military officers, army units and tribes began expressing their support for Haftar, as did Jibril's NFA.[80] Meanwhile, the self-described revolutionaries saw themselves confirmed in their fear of counter-revolutionary plots.

Two days after Haftar launched his operation in Benghazi, the Qa'qa' and Sawaeq attacked the GNC in Tripoli while it was in session to vote on Maitig's proposed government, killing two staffers, abducting several members, looting the legislature's archives, and declaring it dissolved. By this time, Zintani-led armed groups in Tripoli had entered into a tactical alliance with Haftar, and their spokesmen equally announced the suspension of institutions in the name of the 'army'.[81] The attack triggered major clashes in Tripoli, and prompted the return of Misratan forces to the capital after their departure the previous November. Under heavy protection, the GNC met again on 25 May and approved the government proposed by Maitig. But on 9 June, the Supreme Court declared Maitig's election void, ending the dispute and leaving the Thinni government in office.

As the elections to the House of Representatives approached, UNSMIL head Tarek Mitri and Western diplomats attempted to gain the commitment of leading political and military players to a dialogue process. Jibril and his ally Mahmoud Shammam, who ran an influential Cairo-based news website, openly rejected such proposals as foreign attempts to secure a place in government for Islamists who were certain to lose the elections.[82]

Far from presenting a way out of the crisis, the 25 June elections revealed that the political process was moribund. Voter participation was only a third of that seen during the 2012 elections; less than a fifth of the overall electorate participated, reflecting widespread disillusionment with the formal institutions. Violence and boycotts prevented voting in several areas, leaving fifteen among the 200 seats vacant. In Benghazi, unknown perpetrators assassinated prominent rights activist and former revolutionary figure Salwa Bugaighis after she casted her vote.[83] The elections to the Constituent Committee in February had hardly gone better: participation had been even lower; the Amazigh, Tuareg and Tubu had largely boycotted the vote; and jihadi groups had prevented voting in the eastern city of Darna.[84]

By the time of the elections, formerly separate conflicts and forces had coalesced into a nationwide confrontation, and violence had superseded the formal political process. The tug-of-war in the GNC, rivalries between armed groups over territorial control in Tripoli and their competition over access to state budgets, the extortion of the government by armed groups blockading energy facilities, and the revolt by eastern army officers against those whom they held responsible for assassinations had all become intertwined as their protagonists searched for allies in intensifying struggles. For one side, their adversaries were all 'Islamists'; for the other, they were the forces of the counter-revolution. The Political Isolation Law and other attempts to purge or punish former regime elements had done much to produce this convergence: Jibril fell under the law, as did Haftar; several of Haftar's closest associates had been ousted from the army by the Integrity Commission or its equivalent in the army. For different reasons, the militant autonomy movement in the east shared these groups' interest in toppling the Tripoli institutions. As civil war beckoned, it dawned on former proponents of Political Isolation that they had gone too far.[85] But by then, it was too late.

The second civil war (2014–15)

Following the attack on the GNC in May and the return of Misratan forces to the capital, both Misratan leaders and hard-liners associated with the Libyan Revolutionaries Operations Room (LROR) increased their pressure on Zintan, holding a flurry of meetings with Zintani leaders to demand the dissolution of the Qa'qa' and Sawaeq and the surrender of Tripoli International Airport.[86] No agreement was reached, and tensions continued to mount. As election results were announced on 7 July, heavy clashes raged in western Tripoli between the Sawaeq and Fursan Janzur, a local militia. For many observers, the question was not if, but when, a major confrontation between Zintani and Misratan units would erupt.

On 13 July, forces from Misrata, Tripoli and Zawiya attacked the bases of the Qa'qa' and Sawaeq, as well as the airport. The operation, initially called *Qaswara* (Lion), was led by a small group of hardliners associated with the LROR, including Salah Badi and Salem al-Zufri from Misrata, Abdelghani al-Kikli and Salah al-Burki from southern Tripoli, Naji Gneidi of Fursan Janzur, Said Gujil from the Tripoli-based, Amazigh-dominated National Mobile Force, and the Zawiyan Salafi preacher Abu Obeida al-Zawi.[87] Influential figures from Misrata, Zintan and other cities mediated between the conflicting parties over the following days, and on 19 July reached an agreement under which a neutral force from Jadu would take over the airport. But Misratan negotiators failed to convince Badi, who continued to attack regardless of the agreement.[88]

Over the following week, most large Misratan units joined the operation, now billed Libya Dawn. The airport war raged for 43 days, ending in late August with Zintan's withdrawal after heavy losses, and the airport's destruction. By that time, state institutions had split in two, and the country had descended into full-blown civil war.

The newly elected House of Representatives (HoR) adopted a partisan stance to the crisis, in line with the forces prevailing in the new parliament. There had been no party lists, but independent candidates backed by the NFA had a strong showing. In the east, many proponents of regional autonomy had been elected. By contrast, candidates associated with the Muslim Brotherhood and other Islamists had performed poorly. The Amazigh had boycotted the elections, further weakening the revolutionary camp in the HoR.

The dominant forces in the HoR set its direction even before the parliament's first session. The HoR was to convene in Benghazi, but the city witnessed ongoing fighting, and in late July, the coalition of Ansar al-Sharia and former revolutionary forces calling itself the Benghazi Revolutionaries Shura Council (BRSC) dislodged many units aligned with Haftar from their bases.[89] Eastern HoR members had been strong advocates of Benghazi as the seat of the new parliament – among them Abubaker Baera, a proponent of regional autonomy from Benghazi, who as the oldest elected HoR member enjoyed the privilege of presiding over the opening session. But as the date of the inaugural session, 4 August, approached, Baera organized a meeting in Tobruk on 2 August. To other HoR members, he described it as informal, adding that a formal meeting could be held if enough members attended. Parliamentarians from across the country were ferried to Tobruk on planes chartered by the Benghazi businessman Hassan Tatanaki, whose TV station strongly backed both Haftar's operation and the autonomy movement.[90] Meanwhile, GNC president Abusahmain invited HoR members to a handover ceremony in Tripoli on 4 August. For some parliamentarians, it was unclear whether Baera's initiative was legitimate. Moreover, travelling to Tobruk meant entering territory controlled by Haftar, which for some raised risks to their personal security.[91]

When the HoR convened its inaugural session on 4 August, 158 out of 188 members attended; among those who boycotted the meeting were all of Misrata's representatives, as well as influential figures from Tripoli and other cities. Despite the boycott, the HoR moved ahead with electing its president, Agila Saleh, a tribal politician from the eastern town of al-Qubba who had publicly reassured Qadhafi of his tribe's loyalty just days before the 2011 uprising broke out, and had been elected with a mere 913 votes in his constituency. Saleh's election showed how radically the mood in the HoR differed from that of the GNC. The HoR's decisions throughout August had a distinct partisan slant, such as its decree to dissolve all 'irregular armed entities' – without clarifying how irregular and legitimate units would be distinguished from each other – and its call for international intervention to protect civilians.[92]

The divide hardened after Libya Dawn pushed Zintani forces out of the airport and the capital as a whole, on 23 August. The HoR reacted by calling both Libya Dawn and Ansar al-Sharia terrorist entities.[93] Several members from western Libyan cities now left Tobruk to join the boycotters, and HoR attendance plummeted.[94] On 25 August, the HoR appointed a close associate of Haftar, Abderrazeq al-Nadhuri, as chief of staff. The same day, representatives of the revolutionary camp reconvened the GNC in Tripoli, arguing that the HoR was illegitimate, due to the absence of a handover ceremony and the 'illegality' of the inaugural meeting in Tobruk. The rump GNC tasked Omar al-Hassi, a Benghazi university professor who was close to the armed groups fighting Haftar, with forming a government. The HoR, in turn, charged prime minister Thinni, who had fled east alongside several of his ministers, with presenting a new government.[95] The UN and Western states rapidly clarified that the HoR and the Thinni government were the only internationally recognized authorities. But the emergence of two parallel governments and parliaments in August 2014 ushered in a struggle over legitimacy and an institutional divide that had yet to be overcome at the time of writing.

Its detractors alleged that Libya Dawn was a deliberate attempt to overturn the results of the elections and force a negotiated settlement with the groups that had established control over Tripoli. But the tensions between Tripoli-based militias had been on the rise throughout the preceding months, and after the attack by Zintani-led forces on the GNC in May, a major confrontation loomed irrespective of the electoral outcome. Most figures directly involved in launching Libya Dawn were local militia leaders rather than national-level political strategists – with the notable exception of Fathi Bashagha. A former air force pilot turned businessman who had been Misrata's liaison with NATO in 2011 and controlled one of the city's largest battalions, Bashagha had been elected as HoR member with the second-highest number of votes in Misrata. During July 2014, Bashagha helped prepare the offensive behind the scenes, and a group from Bashagha's Hatin Battalion – including one of his sons – participated in the operation from its very start.[96] Once Libya Dawn had defeated the Zintanis, Bashagha shifted towards a more conciliatory stance, and subsequently became Misrata's leading representative in the UN-led negotiations. Bashagha certainly had the political acumen needed to engineer an operation designed to trade territorial control over Tripoli for political influence. Whether this had been his intention from the beginning remains unclear.

Rather than a tightly run operation with a clear objective, Libya Dawn was a tactical alliance between diverse actors. International media outlets simply described the operation as led by 'Islamist militias'. This was misleading. Undeniably, a network of mostly Islamist militia leaders that largely overlapped with the LROR was at the core of Libya Dawn, but the leadership of the Misratan forces that formed the military heavyweight of the operation was separate from this network. The mufti lent his support to the operation, as did the JCP leadership and former leaders of the Libyan Islamic Fighting Group such as Khaled al-Sharif.[97] But the majority of the forces from Misrata, Zawiya, Sabratha, Zuwara and Gharyan that joined the operation had no Islamist orientation; rather, they defined themselves by their local origin in cities that were considered revolutionary strongholds. In fact, their leaders were often deeply suspicious of – or even hostile to – the Islamist networks. They followed the rallying cry of defending the revolution and the transitional institutions. Libya Dawn leaders portrayed the Zintani-led forces in Tripoli as the vanguard of the counter-revolution, pointing to the Qa'qa' and Sawaeq Brigades' alliance with Haftar, their attacks on the GNC, and allegations that both units included members of Qadhafi's security brigades.

The Tripoli operation stood in a de facto alliance with the coalition of jihadist and revolutionary armed groups that fought Haftar's forces in Benghazi. The BRSC relied on support networks in Misrata, Tripoli and other cities in the west to channel funds, weapons and recruits to Benghazi, and treat or evacuate its wounded fighters. Such support aimed not only at blocking Haftar's advance in the east and thereby preventing him from expanding to the west. Ideological affinities played a role for Islamist networks surrounding the mufti and the former LIFG leadership. Social ties were also important: many BRSC leaders came from families whose origins went back to Misrata. (Militia leaders from the Benghazi-based Awaqir tribe, who formed the bulk of Haftar's forces, openly threatened to expulse all 'Misratans' from the city.)[98] The self-declared Tripoli government and Misratan leaders insisted that the Benghazi coalition were *thuwwar*. They downplayed the role of Ansar al-Sharia, and denied that IS cells were emerging among the forces fighting Haftar.[99]

The first rifts began appearing in Libya Dawn the moment the alliance achieved its original objective of driving the Zintanis out of Tripoli, in late August. Hard-line revolutionary leaders and the Muslim Brothers supported the resurrection of the GNC and the formation of the Hassi government. Representatives of the armed groups obtained posts as ministers or deputy ministers.[100] In contrast, political heavyweights in Misrata's business elite, such as Bashagha, kept their distance from the Hassi government, and began positioning themselves for the negotiations over the formation of a unity government. The components of Libya Dawn also began diverging over military strategy, with Tripoli-based hardliners pushing to take the war to Zintan, and the majority of Misratan commanders rejecting this.[101]

The enemies of Libya Dawn were similarly diverse, and their alliance was equally loose. In the east, the early core of Haftar's operation was formed by army officers disgruntled by the government's immobility towards the assassinations in Benghazi, or by their forced retirement by the Integrity Commission. Some proponents of regional autonomy, such as Colonel Hamed al-Hassi's Cyrenaica Defence Force, also joined Haftar early on. They were awkward allies for Haftar, who emphasized the need for a strong central state backed by the army, and as a member of the Firjan tribe of central Libya was considered a 'westerner' by many advocates of eastern autonomy. The bulk of Haftar's forces was made up of civilians, many of them organized in militias from Benghazi and its outskirts.[102] Most were led by members of the Awaqir tribe, who demanded revenge for the victims of assassinations – and in some cases the expulsion of 'western' families and the restitution of Benghazi to Cyrenaican tribes. In contrast, several of Benghazi's army units were slow in joining Haftar. Al-Mahdi al-Barghathi's Brigade 204, for instance, rallied to Operation Dignity only in October 2014.[103] Throughout its first year, Haftar's operation was marked by serious tensions between his inner circle and the commanders of army units and militias in Benghazi, who at times openly contested his authority and accused him of withholding ammunition from them.

In the west, Zintani armed groups formed the bulk of Libya Dawn's adversaries, but they were divided over their attitude towards Haftar. The commanders of the Qa'qa' and Sawaeq Brigades associated themselves closely with Haftar, who also appointed an officer from Zintan as his commander for Western Libya. But the bulk of Zintani forces were led by the military council under Usama al-Juwaili, who remained hostile to Haftar.[104] At risk of being overpowered by Dawn militias, Zintani leaders recruited Tubu fighters from Niger and Chad.[105] More significantly, they struck up alliances with armed groups from communities that were considered former regime strongholds. In May, Zintanis had still reacted with dismay when representatives of such constituencies had held a conference in the Warshafana area. But soon after the airport war began, Zintanis freed hundreds of members of Qadhafi's forces from their prisons, to fill the ranks of a self-styled 'Army of Tribes' that was heavily dominated by forces from Warshafana.[106] Dawn militias drove the 'Army of Tribes' back to the Nafusa Mountains during September 2014, but these groups would return in early 2015 and act increasingly independently of their former Zintani sponsors.

External support was critical for the loose alliance led by Haftar and Zintani figures. In August, foreign fighter jets struck Libya Dawn positions in the Tripoli area several times. They were almost certainly UAE warplanes flying from bases in Egypt, though neither state ever admitted its involvement.[107] Both HoR president Saleh and chief of staff Nadhuri undertook frequent visits to Egypt, whose support to Haftar became ever more obvious. Power brokers with good contacts in Egypt and the UAE now acted as gatekeepers and helped shape these states' policies: the Libyan ambassador to the UAE Aref al-Nayed; Mahmoud Jibril; and the Benghazi businessman Hassan Tatanaki.[108] Like Haftar himself, these figures played to the virulently anti-Islamist discourse prevailing in al-Sissi's Egypt and the UAE. Overt Egyptian and Emirati interference provoked fury in Misrata and among other constituencies supporting Libya Dawn, not least because Emirati airstrikes killed over a dozen Misratan fighters, and ten businessmen from Misrata and Tripoli were arbitrarily detained in the Emirates.[109] For Egypt and the UAE, Libya was an arena for their rivalries with Qatar and Turkey, which were supporting Islamist movements, including the Muslim Brotherhood. Allegations of Qatari and Turkish support to Libya Dawn were widespread. But such support was much more discreet, and most likely much more limited than that provided by Egypt and the UAE. Qatari backing mainly came in the form of funds, which were used to buy weapons from Sudan or other foreign suppliers, as well as the local black market.[110]

Despite such foreign backing, the conflict rapidly settled into a stalemate. In mid-September, a local conflict in the southern town of Ubari escalated when Tuareg armed groups associated themselves with Libya Dawn and their Tubu adversaries adopted the Dignity discourse of 'the army' fighting against 'terrorists'. But the war in Ubari would rage on over the coming year without either side being able to dislodge the other. In the north, Zintani forces warded off the threat to their town by shelling the Nafusa Mountains town of Kikla in early October, to pre-empt a move by Dawn forces from Tripoli and Zawiya to take the war to the mountains. Dawn forces failed to make significant progress in their attempts to capture the Zintani-held Wutiya air base south of Zuwara. The last major attempt to fundamentally shift the balance of forces came in December, when Misratan forces launched a large-scale offensive to seize the export terminals in the 'oil crescent' between Sirte and Ajdabiya. The offensive became stuck in the Sidra area, where the Misratans faced off with Ibrahim al-Jadhran's forces, and were targeted by Haftar's air force.[111]

As a military stalemate took root, both sides also lost hope of winning international political backing. Western governments made it clear that they would not deal with the reconstituted GNC and its Hassi government, thereby thwarting the latter's move to convert facts on the ground into international recognition. At the same time, Western states refused to recognize the new executives appointed by the HoR and Thinni for the Central Bank (CBL) and the National Oil Corporation (NOC), instead sticking with CBL governor al-Saddiq al-Kabir and NOC chairman Mustafa Sanallah, who had both been appointed prior to the institutional split and continued to work in Tripoli. Both jealously guarded their independence from the two rival governments, and al-Kabir's Central Bank continued disbursing salaries on the basis of 2014 payrolls, which included parliamentarians in both bodies and armed factions on all sides of the conflict. Both governments therefore faced difficulties accessing funding, and had to resort to practices such as using budgets left over from the previous fiscal year, or taking up loans from state-owned banks.[112] This limited their capacity to fund armed groups.

In November 2014, Libya's Supreme Court overturned the GNC's March 2014 amendment to the Constitutional Declaration, which had paved the way for the HoR elections. Western governments and the UN adopted an ambiguous position.[113] They refused to accept the GNC's position that the ruling invalidated the HoR, but insisted less on the HoR as the only legitimate legislative body, and more on the HoR's need to unite with its boycotting members to become fully representative. Western refusal to extend full political backing to either side reflected the assessment that a military victory of either side was impossible.

As the conflict dragged on without any prospects for a decisive advantage for either camp, the two alliances fragmented. In western Libya, leading figures in the war effort positioned themselves as proponents of détente and negotiation, while others adopted a hard-line position. In Misrata, Bashagha declared Libya Dawn 'over' as early as December 2014.[114] Together with several other Misratan figures, he emerged as a key proponent of the UN-led negotiations over a unity government. His leading local rival, Abderrahman al-Sweihli, rejected the talks. Following two unsuccessful attempts in autumn 2014, UN Special Representative Bernardino Leon succeeded in late January 2015 in bringing together active and boycotting HoR members as well as representatives of several municipalities and independent figures in Geneva.[115] Though the GNC initially boycotted the talks and provocations from both camps repeatedly caused hiccups, the process developed momentum during spring 2015.

Simultaneously to, but largely independently of, the UN-led process, local notables and commanders in western Libya began reaching out to adversaries. Misratan and Zintani delegations began meeting in mid-February; representatives from Nafusa Mountains towns started holding talks in early March. This occurred amid ongoing fighting and tense relations between communities, as armed groups from Zintan as well as those from Gharyan and Zawiya were cutting off supplies to their respective enemies, making life difficult in and around the Nafusa Mountains. Airstrikes by both sides repeatedly caused talks to break down; fighter jets flying from Misrata's air base bombed Zintan's airstrip, while Haftar's air force conducted strikes on Misrata's port and airport, as well as Mitiga airport in Tripoli.[116]

Ceasefire efforts succeeded where a balance of power had emerged and the warring parties grew tired: at the end of March, Misratan forces withdrew from Sidra after reassurances from their adversaries that they would not capture the vacated terrain. In April, Misrata's Halbus Brigade negotiated a ceasefire with armed groups from Warshafana that had just seized back their home turf after descending from Zintan.[117] Though former Libya Dawn allies from Zawiya repeatedly violated the ceasefire, Halbus elements interposed themselves between groups from Warshafana and their enemies, and remained steadfast in their support for the truce. The Halbus and Mahjub Brigades, two of Misrata's largest forces, publicly advocated a general ceasefire, earning much disdain from more hardline elements in the former Libya Dawn alliance. The breakthrough came in May, after Zintani forces had heavily shelled positions of armed groups from Gharyan, displaying unexpected strength. During late May and June, Zintani leaders negotiated a series of accords with their neighbours in the Nafusa Mountains, as well as Gharyan, Zuwara and Zawiya. Each agreement included a ceasefire, an exchange of prisoners and the restoration of free movement.[118]

The détente between former warring factions meant that the polarized landscape gave way to a more fragmented and chaotic scene. Hardliners on both sides opposed the ceasefires – among them the mufti; the Tripoli-based prime minister Khalifa al-Ghwell from Misrata, who had taken over from Hassi in March 2015; the former core of Libya Dawn around Salah Badi and Abu Obeida al-Zawi; and factions in Zintan and Warshafana that were associated with Haftar's LNA. Those who negotiated the ceasefires did so in the name of their local communities. The civil war abated, although confrontations continued in several hotspots. But in the meantime, the political and military landscape had changed. Former regime elements who had previously been imprisoned or exiled emerged as prominent actors in Haftar's coalition – among them Haftar's man in Warshafana, Colonel Omar al-Tantush, who had been imprisoned in Zintan and was released to lead the offensive to recapture the Warshafana region; and Mohamed ben Naiel, a former intelligence operative who now led a small armed group in his native Wadi al-Shati' area in southern Libya.

Another important change was the emergence of local affiliates of the Islamic State (IS), which benefited from the chaos. In Benghazi, where the loose alliances of forces led by Haftar began to slowly take back territory from October 2014 onwards, members of Ansar al-Sharia joined a local IS affiliate that became an increasingly potent force among Haftar's adversaries. In Darna, which was controlled by armed groups that opposed Haftar, a local IS group established the headquarters of a *Barqa* (Cyrenaica) emirate and began clashing with local rivals.[119] In Sirte, Ansar al-Sharia expanded after Misratan forces had dislodged its rivals in their March 2014 offensive against Jadhran. In early 2015, as Misratans yet again confronted Jadhran's forces in Sidra and sought to avoid opening another front in their rear, the bulk of Ansar al-Sharia in Sirte morphed into IS and seized control of the city.[120] The local IS affiliate turned Sirte into its Libyan headquarters and accommodated leading figures from Iraq and Arab Gulf states, as well as hundreds of foreign fighters.

In Misrata, proponents of an offensive against IS in Sirte had difficulties convincing local politicians and militia leaders, who were reluctant to withdraw forces from Tripoli and the front lines in the west and south. In the former Dawn camp, the attitude towards the rise of IS oscillated between outright denial and allegations that former regime elements were masquerading as IS in Sirte to justify Haftar's counter-terrorist campaign.[121]

In July 2015, the parties to the UN-led negotiations reached an initial agreement, without settling on names to lead a unity government. By that time, the key actors who had driven the descent into civil war – Haftar; the leaders of the Qa'qa' and Sawaeq Brigades; Jibril; Bashagha; a handful of militia leaders from Tripoli – had lost all control over the dynamics their actions had spawned. The allies they had mobilized had become increasingly independent or even turned against them; the governments in Tripoli and al-Bayda and their respective parliaments lacked influence over the forces nominally aligned with them; and the fragmentation of the two camps meant that any settlement would be prone to fail.

The elusive agreement (July 2015–September 2016)

The progress of talks to establish a unity government ushered in a period of deep uncertainty for political players across Libya's chaotic landscape. Would a deal be reached? Could a foreign-backed unity government succeed against the range of forces opposing it? Was there more to be gained by supporting the talks, by holding out and wearing down the parties until they made larger concessions, or by leading the opposition?

Calculations were made even more difficult by the complex nature of the negotiations. The UN faced great difficulties in identifying the key political and military forces. The first talks in September 2014 had brought together Tobruk-based and boycotting members of the HoR. After the Supreme Court ruling deepened the controversy over the legitimacy of the HoR in Tobruk, Leon broadened the political negotiations to include active and boycotting members of the GNC, as well as several moderates without direct affiliation with any of the conflicting parties. But both the HoR and GNC were hamstrung by their internal divisions, and had no control over the parties to the conflict. These parties were loose, constantly changing alliances; there were few clearly identifiable organizations and cohesive forces.

The UN dealt with this diffuse landscape by launching several parallel dialogue tracks from February 2015 onwards. In addition to the core political negotiations, it brought together mayors from important cities in a municipalities track. Algeria hosted several meetings between representatives of political parties and civil society activists. UNSMIL also organized several meetings of women's representatives. The key talks between representatives of armed factions never got off the ground; UNSMIL never succeeded in bringing the different parties together in a security track. Leon's plans for a track gathering tribal leaders in Egypt equally failed. At first, the Egyptian government convened its own meeting of Libyan tribal leaders to promote its partisan stance. When UNSMIL cooperated with the Egyptians to organize another meeting, most invitees failed to show up.[122]

The divisions within each of the two negotiating parties – the GNC and HoR – and the difficulties in bringing together the actual parties to the conflict would continue to dog the UN's efforts to reach a deal and implement it. Both parliaments resorted to delaying tactics and avoided clear negotiating positions. In July 2015, the parties initialled a draft agreement on the formation of a Government of National Accord (GNA) in the Moroccan resort town of Skhirat. But the GNC delegation did not attend due to pressure from hardliners, although a bloc within the GNC was represented by the head of the JCP, Mohamed Sawan. Both bodies then delayed their response to the initialled draft, and were slow in proposing names for the GNA's five-member Presidency Council. The GNC, where a substantial bloc was forming in favour of a deal, was unable to agree on its candidates. Eventually, during talks in Skhirat in October, two members of the GNC's negotiation team went along with Leon's proposals despite formal instructions from GNC president Abusahmain to desist.[123] They did so not least because their own names had been shortlisted by Leon: Abderrahman al-Sweihli, who had suddenly gone from hawk to dove, and Mohamed al-Ammari from Benghazi.

On 8 October, Leon announced the names for a six-member Presidency Council, along with another twenty names as suggestions for ministerial and other posts.[124] The two bodies were then expected to endorse the agreement, but opponents blocked votes in both legislatures. They accused Leon of having overstepped his remit by proposing names for positions that were to be appointed or elected by the Presidency Council or the High Council of State, the GNC's reincarnation under the agreement. Leon's proposal of Sweihli as head of the latter body also provoked angry reactions because Sweihli had become one of the most widely hated politicians in the country. In addition, some questioned Leon's nomination for prime minister, Faiez al-Serraj, whose name had not come from the negotiating parties, but was presented by Leon minutes before the announcement.[125] Most notably, hardliners in both bodies argued that the members of their negotiation teams were not authorized to agree on the names. The HoR dissolved its negotiation committee, while the GNC's team had broken apart. To win some opponents over, Leon later expanded the Presidency Council from six to nine members, to establish parity between representatives of Libya's three historic regions.[126]

Meanwhile, tensions between proponents and opponents of the agreement within each body were mounting. In the HoR, support mostly came from western Libyan representatives eager to return to their homes, as well as some southern members; the bulk of eastern parliamentarians – including HoR president Saleh – were staunchly opposed to the agreement. The sticking point for many eastern representatives was the negotiators' convergence on a formula to dismiss Haftar by declaring top military positions vacant unless the Presidency Council agreed on their incumbents. This left Haftar and his supporters fiercely opposed to the agreement, but it was essential to mobilize support for the deal in the GNC. There, most members associated with the JCP backed the agreement, as did most Misratan representatives; figures associated with the former LIFG and other Islamists were against the deal, and could count on GNC president Abusahmain to block any votes on the issue. Many Misratan armed groups also came out in favour of a deal – a necessary, but not sufficient, condition for a prospective government to establish itself in Tripoli. The Misratan forces backing the agreement had a substantial presence in the capital, but so did forces associated with the Ghwell government and the GNC hardliners. Misratan units were on both sides of this divide, and as some positioned themselves in favour of an agreement, they suffered internal splits.

The negotiations were almost thrown off their track when it emerged that Leon had accepted an offer to become director of the UAE's diplomatic academy, and had negotiated the terms with Emirati officials even while he was mediating in Libya, where the UAE was strongly backing one side.[127] Shortly after the scandal erupted in November, Leon gave up his position to Martin Kobler, who pushed for a rapid conclusion of the negotiations despite shaky support in both parliaments. Western governments, worried about the expansion of IS in the Sirte area, saw the establishment of a unity government with whom they could cooperate in fighting IS as increasingly urgent, and were losing patience with the talks. Proponents of a deal among the negotiating parties equally urged swiftness, fearing that the Leon scandal would erode existing support within the HoR and GNC or among their constituencies.[128] The sense that the UN-led talks were faltering increased in late November, when opponents of the agreement from the GNC and HoR launched parallel talks.[129] The so-called Libyan-Libyan initiative sought to peel away support from the Skhirat process. On 15 December, two days before the agreement was to be signed in Skhirat, Abusahmain and Saleh even met personally in Malta to mobilize support for an all-Libyan initiative.[130]

Unable to obtain formal backing from either body, and under increasing pressure from Western governments and Libyan stakeholders, Kobler opted to have the agreement signed by individual HoR and GNC members without an official mandate from their respective bodies. To demonstrate broad-based Libyan support, the UN ferried dozens of parliamentarians and mayors, as well as figures who had participated in the civil society and political parties track to the signing ceremony on 17 December. But it was obvious that the deal stood on a weak foundation. Of twenty-one Libyan signatories, eleven were elected members of the GNC or HoR, while ten were independent participants in the negotiations who had been hand-picked by the UN in an arbitrary fashion, and in most cases lacked any significant power base.

Among the Presidency Council's five deputy prime ministers, Ahmed Maitig represented Misrata; Fathi al-Majbari was a representative for eastern Libya who enjoyed the backing of militia leader Ibrahim al-Jadhran, while the other eastern representative, Ali al-Qatrani, had been designated by Haftar loyalists in the HoR; and Musa al-Koni was a representative of southern Libya and the Tuareg. Omar al-Aswad from Zintan and the GNC member from Benghazi, Mohamed al-Ammari, were named as ministers, who contrary to the deputy prime ministers had no veto over decisions. The remaining two seats on the Presidency Council were filled in a last-ditch negotiating drama. The JCP leadership designated the fifth deputy, Abdelsalam Kajman, for southern Libya. A third minister, Ahmed Hamza, also came from southern Libya, and was close to Qadhafi's former chief of staff, Bashir Saleh. Kajman and Hamza were both relative unknowns.[131]

The combination of a nine-member executive body with the requirement that decisions be taken unanimously reflected the fragmentation of the negotiating parties – but it virtually guaranteed paralysis. None of the members had a strong power base, with the partial exception of Maitig and Aswad. Moreover, both Qatrani and Aswad began boycotting the Presidency Council in mid-January during negotiations over the government. In Qatrani's case, this was predictable, given that he represented a major opponent of the agreement; the very day before the ceremony, Kobler had tried to win Haftar's support for the deal – in vain. In the case of Aswad, it reflected Zintani anger at their junior role in the Council, compared to Misrata. The seven acting council members failed to obtain HoR approval for the two cabinets they presented in January and February 2016.

In the HoR, an initially small group of rejectionists led by Agila Saleh blocked the formal endorsement of the deal. In late January 2016, a narrow majority in the HoR backed the agreement in principle, but voiced its objection to Article 8 of the agreement's 'Additional Provisions' – the article effectively spelling Haftar's dismissal by requiring the Presidency Council to agree on all senior military positions.[132] By failing to formally vote on the deal in its entirety, the HoR left both the agreement and the government in a state of limbo. The main source of opposition clearly came from

Haftar's allies in the HoR, who were determined to block Haftar's dismissal according to the mechanism foreseen in the agreement.

The array of opponents widened after the Presidency Council took office in Tripoli, in late March, and called on its designated ministers to start working despite lack of formal support from the HoR. Contrary to the terms of the agreement, the Presidency Council did not attempt to mobilize neutral security forces to enable its members to work in Tripoli. Instead, it obtained the support of a handful of militias from Tripoli that, when the Presidency Council arrived in the capital, narrowly avoided an open confrontation with forces backing the Ghwell government. To the surprise of many observers, the Ghwell government then retreated without putting up a fight. But the success of taking up office in Tripoli without provoking conflict came at a high cost. The Presidency Council's accommodation with local militias alienated many who had supported the agreement on condition that it would lead to a re-establishment of state authority in Tripoli. It particularly angered the Zintanis, who refused to accept that the capital would remain controlled by forces that had expelled them in 2014.[133] Zintan had been a key stakeholder of the agreement, but now sided with its adversaries.

Libyan politicians and Western governments backing the Government of National Accord (GNA) had gambled that it would gradually win over fence-sitters and holdouts as it took the purse strings in Tripoli and created facts on the ground, despite its weak legitimacy basis. Central to that premise was that Majbari, several eastern ministers designated by him, and his backer Jadhran would wear away at Haftar's support base in the east. Defence Minister al-Mahdi al-Barghathi had a particularly important role to play in this scheme. He hailed from the Awaqir tribe that dominated the forces aligned with Haftar in Benghazi, and led a unit against the anti-Haftar coalition there. Now, he was to encourage defections from Haftar's forces towards the GNA. Government spending would do the rest: Central Bank governor al-Kabir and NOC chief Sanallah had signalled to Western diplomats even before the agreement was signed that they would work with the GNA.

The gamble backfired badly. Sanallah and Kabir did, indeed, recognize the Presidency Council's authority, but Kabir was reticent to provide access to funding as long as the designated finance minister – one of Majbari's eastern nominees – had not taken up office and the HoR failed to approve the government, let alone its budget. Meanwhile, Sanallah was disgruntled with the Presidency Council's concessions towards Jadhran, who kept the export terminals shut to demand ever-greater payoffs. Sanallah protested fiercely when Kobler met Jadhran in July 2016 to broker a deal – followed, a few days later, by Presidency Council members Koni and Hamza.[134] Far from re-uniting the Central Bank and NOC under its authority, the Presidency Council alienated both institutions' top executives, and proved incapable of restoring oil production. The economic crisis, manifest in liquidity shortages, a plummeting exchange rate and rising inflation, continued to deepen under the GNA's watch.

Expectations that eastern ministers would rally support for the GNA in their region were similarly frustrated. Defence Minister Barghathi was the only one of Majbari's nominees to make it to Tripoli, belatedly, in May. Barghathi gained the backing of several Awaqir militia leaders from Benghazi who had been on bad terms with Haftar, sparking an open power struggle over loyalties within the tribe. Haftar and Barghathi each mobilized Awaqir elders to voice their support. A similar tug-of-war was ongoing among the Magharba between Jadhran and the tribe's leading notable, Saleh Latiwish, who had opposed Jadhran's rise for some time and now allied with Haftar against the upstart. In July, the Presidency Council was forced to dismiss four designated ministers from the east, after they had refused to take up their posts as long as the HoR did not endorse the government.[135]

Steady external support from Egypt, the UAE and France – in contradiction with the official French policy of supporting the GNA – allowed Haftar to gradually tilt the balance in the east.[136] Since December 2015, local forces loyal to Haftar had clashed with Islamist-leaning militias in Ajdabiya, forcing them out in February 2016. Around the same time, Haftar's alliance made substantial progress in Benghazi.[137] To prevent defections to the GNA, Haftar loyalists intimidated HoR members, tribal notables, and designated GNA officials. In Ajdabiya and the oil crescent, Haftar allegedly bought loyalties with payoffs and presents. In June, the struggle in Ajdabiya escalated after the Benghazi Defence Brigades, a new group of Benghazi militants who had assembled in the Jufra area, bypassed Ajdabiya and were stopped only a few dozen kilometres outside Benghazi by (probably Emirati) airstrikes. Credible allegations that Jadhran had provided safe passage to the group provided the pretext for Haftar's air force to bomb Jadhran's positions in Ajdabiya.[138] Eventually, in September, Haftar's forces took over Jadhran's oil export terminals without major military confrontation; most of Jadhran's forces melted away, while he and his core followers escaped to the Jufra area to link up with the Benghazi Defence Brigades.

Impasse (September 2016–January 2019)

Haftar's takeover of the oil ports ushered in a new balance of power, in the east as well as nationally. With Jadhran, a significant military counterweight to Haftar in the east had fallen away. Barghathi's efforts to turn political and military figures in Benghazi against Haftar faltered. Barghathi himself, who was in Benghazi at the time of the ports takeover, escaped with some difficulty to Tripoli, where he began plotting a counteroffensive with Jadhran and the Benghazi Defence Brigades, his erstwhile enemies. Haftar's forces took over Barghathi's former unit in Benghazi, killing and arresting several of its members.[139] The path was clear for Haftar to consolidate power in the east. Only Darna, under the control of a local coalition that included Islamist and jihadist elements, for now held out against the siege Haftar's forces were imposing on it. Across the country, the fact that Haftar opened up the ports despite revenues accruing to the Central Bank in Tripoli gained him widespread popularity.

The consolidation of authority in the east by the GNA's leading opponent failed to provoke alarm among the Western governments that had so resolutely pushed for the establishment of the GNA a year earlier. The reason was that in the meantime, IS had been annihilated as a territorial force. This was the result of disparate local developments, among them Haftar's progress in Benghazi. In Darna and Sabratha, IS affiliates had become embroiled in conflicts with local armed groups that ejected IS from both cities during the spring of 2016. In Sirte, IS attacks on Misratan checkpoints and a looming offensive by Haftar's forces triggered a mobilization of Misratan armed groups in May 2016. Misratan action then ballooned into a major operation that ended in December 2016 with the defeat of the last remaining IS fighters in Sirte. Although the international media described the Misratan forces as loyal to the GNA, their support for the GNA – which had neither launched the operation nor overseen it – was lukewarm at best. The mere existence of the GNA did, however, facilitate the provision of foreign support for the operation in the form of US airstrikes, UK special forces and an Italian field hospital.[140]

Its status as the internationally recognized authority was what kept the GNA alive even though the Skhirat agreement had, for all intents and purposes, failed. The GNA never broadened its support base; indeed, the opposite happened. Two of the Presidency Council's nine members had suspended their participation since January 2016; with Musa al-Koni, a third resigned in January 2017; the remaining members did not work together, and Serraj made most decisions without consulting the others. Constituencies that had been crucial in supporting the Skhirat agreement, such as Misrata, grew disillusioned with the GNA's ineffectiveness. The Tripoli militias that protected the GNA acquired unprecedented influence over state institutions in the capital, intimidating officials, filling posts with their protégés and infiltrating the administration. This made a mockery out of the GNA's ambition to function as a national unity government. The largest four of these militias – Haytham al-Tajuri's Tripoli Revolutionaries Brigade; the Suq al-Jum'a-based Nawasi Brigade; Abdelghani al-Kikli's forces in the Abu Slim area; and Abderrauf Kara's Special Deterrence Force in Mitiga airport – gradually consolidated control over central Tripoli, in several brief rounds of major clashes with forces opposed to the GNA, between December 2016 and May 2017.[141]

The self-described revolutionaries who opposed the GNA suffered setbacks not only in Tripoli, but also elsewhere. Lacking an alternative political project with which to rally broader support, they resorted to ill-fated military operations. Jadhran and the Benghazi Defence Brigades (BDB) failed to wrest control over the oil crescent back from Haftar. During autumn 2016, BDB leaders assembled a diverse coalition of forces with the backing of GNA defence minister Barghathi, mobilizing funds from Qatar, and bribing Sudanese and Chadian mercenaries deployed by Haftar in the oilfields to switch sides.[142] Despite these preparations, the BDB's first offensive against the oil export terminals in December 2016 collapsed after a mere twenty-four hours. In early March 2017, the BDB temporarily took control of the oil crescent, but ten days later, Haftar's forces drove them out again.[143]

In May, Misrata's Third Force, backed by Chadian mercenaries, attacked the Brak al-Shate' air base in southern Libya held by forces loyal to Haftar, killing dozens in apparent executions.[144] Following an outcry across the south, the Third Force first withdrew to the Jufra area; then, after Egyptian airstrikes, to Misrata. Haftar's forces took over the Tamanhant and Jufra air bases from the Misratans, further bolstering their strategic position, and preventing the BDB from using Jufra as a launching pad for attacks against the oil crescent.[145]

Haftar's consolidation in the oil crescent, as well as his expansion in central and southern Libya, stoked expectations that he would continue to extend his sphere of authority – and possibly even seize control of Libya as a whole, ending the country's fragmentation. Such calculations caused both foreign and domestic actors to reevaluate their positions. In Misrata and other cities in which anti-Haftar sentiment had been almost unanimous, some politicians and army officers reached out to Haftar, seeking a new settlement in which he would play a leading role, or even declaring their outright support for him. Recognizing his growing importance, Western governments intensely courted Haftar during the first half of 2017, trying to broker a deal that would include him. Previously, Haftar had rejected all overtures at negotiations. But in the summer, Haftar made his first visits to Paris and Rome, which gave him a wholly new international stature. He also regularly met with the new UN Special Representative, Ghassan Salamé, after having consistently rebuffed his predecessor Kobler.

Western diplomats now believed they could win Haftar's support for a transitional arrangement leading up to new elections, in which he would be able to present himself. Salamé, however, made no progress in negotiating such an arrangement. The two legislatures that had functioned as the negotiating parties in Skhirat, the HoR and the former GNC, were hopelessly divided, but those interested in maintaining the status quo – and thus holding on to their privileges – prevailed within them. Whether Haftar genuinely supported free elections could be considered doubtful at best. International meddling also posed obstacles to progress. Russia, France, Egypt, and other states all undertook their own mediation efforts, undermining the UN role.[146] Through military support, France associated itself increasingly closely with Haftar. While Italy tried to improve its relations with Haftar, it nevertheless remained focused on western Libya. Italian officials apparently engineered a shift by key militias in western Libya from migrant smuggling to blocking departures from the Libyan coast.[147] Not least due to such divergent alignments, the Italians remained at odds with the French over their approach to the Libyan crisis.

While the political process remained stuck, so did the military balance of power. Haftar's anticipated further advance failed to materialize. In central Libya, Haftar's forces refrained even from attempting to wrest Sirte from the Misratans. Visibly short of forces, Haftar deployed Sudanese mercenaries in the Jufra area. In the south, Haftar exerted no territorial authority beyond the air bases his forces controlled. The region was a patchwork of armed groups that were each drawn from particular tribes. Haftar did not command sufficient forces to act as a neutral arbiter between these groups. When he allied with a given tribe's militias, he attracted the enmity of their adversaries. In Sabha, for example, some Awlad Suleiman militia leaders sought Haftar's support after the departure of their former allies, Misrata's Third Force. This caused the Awlad Suleiman's opponents – the Tubu, whose armed groups had previously acted as Haftar's allies in the Ubari conflict – to turn against Haftar.[148] After months of fighting, Tubu militias captured the principal base held by Awlad Suleiman forces in May 2018, dealing a blow to Haftar's designs.

In the west, Haftar not only failed to expand, but saw his influence recede. In June 2017, Serraj appointed Usama al-Juwaili of Zintan as commander of the western military region, thereby weakening the position of Haftar loyalists in the town.[149] Juwaili made no secret of his fierce opposition to Haftar. His actions followed the interests of Zintan military council, rather than orders from Serraj – but their impact was to block Haftar from making any further inroads into greater Tripoli. Most notably, in November 2017, Juwaili deployed Zintani forces to the Warshafana area, dislodging several units loyal to Haftar from their bases.

That period also saw the last challenges to Haftar's authority in the east. In August 2017, Serraj appointed the Benghazi militia leader Faraj Qa'im – an ally of Defence Minister Barghathi – as deputy interior minister. Qa'im took up his functions in Benghazi, openly defying Haftar's authority.[150] In November, after Qa'im escaped an assassination attempt, he called for Haftar's removal from the military command. In response, Haftar loyalists captured Qa'im and took over his bases.[151] A handful of other eastern politicians defied Haftar in more subtle ways. The mayor of Tobruk, for example, met with GNA officials in Tripoli to mobilize budgets and investments, ignoring Haftar's ban on all interaction with the GNA.

Speculation over Haftar's health came to compound the doubts over his capacity for expansion. In April 2018, Haftar was hospitalized in Paris, and for several weeks, wild rumours of his incapacitation, or even death, spread. He returned later that month in apparently robust health, and immediately sought to underscore his vigour by launching a long-delayed offensive to capture Darna, the only eastern city to remain outside Haftar's control.[152] Haftar's forces initially made swift progress in Darna, but were able to dislodge the last forces holding out in Darna's old city only in February 2019.

The deployment of forces towards the Darna front, in turn, made the oil crescent vulnerable to attack. In June 2018, Ibrahim al-Jadhran yet again captured the export terminals that he had once controlled.[153] Even though Jadhran's operation triggered an outcry across the political spectrum and the lack of GNA support meant that he could not hold on to the ports, the incident once more tainted the image of invincibility Haftar sought to cultivate. After he had re-established control in July, Haftar blocked oil exports by the National Oil Corporation (NOC) in Tripoli and attempted to export oil on the account of the parallel NOC in the east, effectively causing exports from terminals in the oil crescent to shut down. Haftar sought to use the closed ports as a bargaining chip to gain greater access to funds from the Central Bank, going as far as demanding the replacement of its governor. But his brinkmanship pushed oil prices on global markets higher just as the Trump administration was preparing to reimpose sanctions on Iranian oil exports. Haftar's move therefore sparked rare high-level interest in the United States. Intense international pressure forced him to back down without concrete gains, allowing the NOC to resume its operations.[154]

In western Libya, too, efforts to alter the distribution of benefits from state wealth sparked military action, but produced only limited change. From late 2017 onward, resentment grew among many political and military factions over the stranglehold of a handful of Tripoli militias over state institutions. Some Misratan politicians and militia leaders repeatedly sought to mobilize for an offensive against the Tripoli groups. They reached out to similarly disgruntled elements in Tarhuna and Zintan – groups that had, in the case of Zintan, been their sworn enemies only three years ago. In Tarhuna, a powerful armed group had emerged under the name of the 7th Brigade – also known as the 'Kaniyat', for the three brothers of the Kani family who ran it – and monopolized control over the city, while remaining ambivalent over its political loyalties.[155] Eventually, in August 2018, the Kaniyat launched an offensive on Tripoli with the support of some Misratan factions, triggering a month of fighting on the capital's southern outskirts. The bulk of Misratan forces stopped short of entering the war, while Zintan's Juwaili used the opportunity to return Zintani forces to western Tripoli without confronting the Tripoli militias. UN Special Representative Ghassan Salamé then helped broker an end to the war. In exchange for their nonintervention, Misratan power brokers negotiated the key post of interior minister for Fathi Bashagha, and the imposition of a fee on foreign exchange that destroyed the business model used by Tripoli militias, who had exploited their privileged access to hard currency at the official exchange rate. The Kaniyat had to retreat empty-handed. But the Tripoli militias retained much of their control over the capital and its institutions.[156]

In sum, a set of circumstances combined to preserve the political impasse after the failure of the Skhirat agreement. Renegotiating executive authority was not possible, as Western governments clung to the GNA and insisted that only the institutions recognized by the Skhirat agreement – now along with Haftar – were legitimate negotiating parties. But these parties benefited from the status quo, and had little interest in changing it. While the formal divide between the GNA and the eastern government persisted, the polarization had long receded, and many ties crossed the divide. Some ministers and other senior officials in Tripoli had close relations with the circles around Haftar and found ways of sharing budgets with them. Moreover, the Tripoli government continued to pay the salaries of most civil servants in the east, and many soldiers in Haftar's forces – who received a hefty bonus on top from Haftar's command structure.[157] In Misrata and other former revolutionary strongholds in the west, Haftar gradually lost his bogeyman image, and there was increasing openness to negotiate with him.[158] Most fundamentally, the political and military landscape in western and southern Libya had become even more fragmented. Shifting alliances in the struggles over Tripoli reflected increasing opportunism, and proliferating political divides in cities such as Misrata made it difficult for any side to mobilize support for significant military action. The enmities of the past had lost much of their sway.

Haftar's expansion and the third civil war (January 2019–)

In mid-January 2019, Haftar deployed a modest contingent of forces from eastern and central Libya to the southwestern region of Fezzan. Haftar's swift – albeit superficial – takeover of that region finally destabilized the fragile equilibrium that had been kept in place for the preceding two years. The operation's stunning success raised expectations that a push towards Tripoli would be the logical next step. Instead of condemning Haftar's military expansion, western governments rushed to court Haftar even more, leading him to conclude – correctly – that a move on Tripoli would not provoke significant international opposition. That move, which occurred in April and provoked Libya's third civil war, therefore stood in close relation with Haftar's Fezzan operation.

Before Haftar's forces deployed to Fezzan, anger over rampant insecurity and the breakdown of public services had reached breaking point in the region. The GNA, under the clutches of Tripolitanian interest groups and their associated militias, had almost entirely ignored the south, and had notably refrained from even attempting to expand its military command structures to the region. The increasingly widespread presence of Chadian and Sudanese fighters – some of them on the payroll of Haftar's forces, others associated with local Tubu armed groups – was a source of growing resentment, particularly where such elements engaged in criminal activities including kidnappings.

As Haftar's forces deployed to the south, under the banner of 'cleansing the south of Chadian gangs and terrorists', they therefore encountered much approval. Haftar allied closely with armed groups recruited from the Awlad Suleiman, one of which – Brigade 128 – played a central role in the southern operation. Many Awlad Suleiman groups in Sabha and Tuareg units in Ubari that had formerly been officially aligned with the GNA switched sides. Through such realignments, triggered by promises of material benefits, Haftar's forces also succeeded in taking over one of Libya's largest oilfields, al-Sharara. They only ran into resistance when they attempted to advance towards Murzuq, a town with a sizeable Tubu population. Tubu armed groups had handed over their positions in Sabha and withdrawn to demonstrate their cooperation with Haftar's forces' declared objective of restoring security. But the advance of an Awlad Suleiman-dominated force towards Murzuq triggered violent resistance by Tubu factions. The eventual takeover of the town by Haftar's forces saw killings as well as the burning and looting of the properties of prominent Tubu figures. In other Tubu towns, such as al-Qatroun and Umm al-Araneb, local factions nominally switched sides and declared their loyalty to Haftar's forces, to avoid a similar fate.[159]

By late February, Haftar could claim that he had taken over southern Libya – and that he had done so largely peacefully. To be sure, his claim to control over Fezzan was mostly nominal: the configuration of forces on the ground had changed little, and Haftar soon withdrew the contingents he had sent from eastern and central Libya. But the impact of the successful southern operation on Haftar's fortunes was dramatic. Public figures overwhelmingly portrayed it as a patriotic effort to rid Libya of fighters and criminals from Chad and Sudan. Even political adversaries of Haftar, such as the interior minister and Misratan power broker Fathi Bashagha, expressed their appreciation. Few in western and southern Libya dared speak out against Haftar's exploitation of inter-communal conflicts and his brutal repression of Tubu resistance.

At the international level, Haftar's southern operation produced even more significant changes. Western diplomats were impressed by the fact that Haftar now controlled the quasi-totality of Libya's oil production and the fact that the population of the south had overwhelmingly welcomed his forces. Although the operation dramatically changed the balance of power in ways that presaged further conflict, western reactions were exceptionally subdued. UN Special Representative Salamé and western diplomats interpreted the new situation as an opportunity to finally negotiate a political deal that would accord Haftar the political influence to match his territorial sway.

In late February, Salamé as well as US, French and Emirati officials brokered a meeting between Haftar and Serraj in Abu Dhabi. At that meeting, Haftar and Serraj verbally agreed to the broad outlines of a deal that would establish a single, unified interim government and military command, combined with a roadmap towards elections.[160]

Although the deal foresaw a collective body to act as the supreme commander of the army, it clearly would have made Haftar the dominant actor not only on the ground, but also in state institutions. In western Libya, leading figures began negotiating with Haftar's representatives over the composition of the government. This exacerbated divisions among western Libyan forces in a way that would have further strengthened Haftar's position, had the deal gone through. Salamé now scheduled a long-delayed National Conference that would have given broader legitimacy to the roadmap. Western diplomats argued that Haftar felt a genuine urge to make concessions and reach a deal.[161] Privately, however, some western officials said that Haftar would capture Tripoli – and power – one way or another; the agreement was preferable to a war in western Libya.[162] But soon after the Abu Dhabi meeting, Haftar reneged on key aspects of the deal, notably on the collective nature of the supreme military command.[163]

While Salamé prepared for the National Conference and sought to broker another meeting between Serraj and Haftar to revive the talks, Haftar on 4 April launched a surprise offensive on Tripoli, shattering all designs for a negotiated solution. The offensive was massive, with Haftar mobilizing the bulk of his eastern forces and allied militias from southern Libya. With the help of a key militia leader in Gharyan – Adel Daab, who in 2014 had led Dawn forces from Gharyan against Haftar's Zintani allies – Haftar's forces reached Tripoli's southern outskirts within twenty-four hours of setting out from their bases in the Jufra region. The following day, the Kaniyat militia of Tarhuna joined Haftar's forces, pushing into the southeastern Ain Zara suburb of Tripoli.

The offensive took western Libyan forces by surprise. There had been some concertation between leading military actors in the west in the month preceding the attack – notably including Zintan's Usama Juwaili and Misratan leaders, as well as some Tripoli militia commanders – to prepare for anticipated attempts by Haftar to make inroads into western Libya. But suspicion between western Libyan forces that had not so long ago fought against each other, or were at loggerheads over the distribution of resources in Tripoli, impeded the formation of a cohesive alliance.[164] In any case, few had expected such a brazen, all-out offensive. Only with Haftar's forces appearing at Tripoli's southern outskirts, the threat became acute enough for western Libyan forces to overcome their divisions, and for massive mobilization to begin in Misrata, Zawiya and the Amazigh towns, as well as Tripoli itself.[165] That mobilization and the closing of ranks behind the GNA – even by forces from Misrata and Zawiya that had hitherto rejected the GNA – fundamentally transformed the balance of power in western Libya overnight. After the operation's initial four days, Haftar's forces made no more advances, and began slowly losing territory to their adversaries.

Even more stunning than Haftar's offensive itself was the international reaction to it. Western governments, whose intelligence services had tracked the military buildup to the operation, feigned surprise. Several Western states then moved rapidly to condemn Haftar's move, although French and Russian opposition prevented strong statements – let alone measures – by the European Union and the UN Security Council. Quickly, however, western governments settled into an ambivalent position, refusing to come to the rescue of the government they had helped install and kept in place for so long, and not taking any steps beyond tepid calls for all sides to commit to a ceasefire and

return to the political process. French diplomats began a cc
playing field by accusing Serraj of having blocked a deal witl
the forces fighting Haftar as being dominated by criminal n
jihadists.[166] The impression of Western complicity with Hafta
emerged that the US National Security Advisor John Bolton had
light in a phone call a day before the offensive began.[167] Repo.
Saudi Crown Prince Mohamed bin Salman had promised Haftai
a meeting in Riyad, a week before the start of the operation.[168] A   ⌐undant
evidence for new weapons shipments as the war dragged on, particularly noteworthy
were drone strikes that pointed towards the UAE – and that would later prompt Turkey
to provide combat drones to Haftar's opponents.[169] Western governments remained
silent, apparently judging that Haftar was backed by such a powerful constellation
of foreign interests that opposing him was futile. And yet, robust western Libyan
resistance to Haftar's offensive confounded all expectations that Haftar would prevail.

Haftar's attack on Tripoli and the civil war it caused – Libya's third since 2011 –
led Libya's fragmented political landscape to crystallize yet again into a new state
of polarization. Given that Haftar had long eliminated all opposition to his rule in
the east, the fault line this time was more neatly between east and west. In the west
itself, some cities were yet again united in their resistance to Haftar, while a few –
most notably Tarhuna – were collectively stigmatized as supporting Haftar's offensive,
due to the alignment of the armed groups that controlled them. But the many divides
afflicting these apparently united blocs were discernible underneath the surface, and
they were certain to return to the fore soon.

Patterns, turning points and paths not taken

As this account has made clear, fragmentation has been a defining feature of Libyan
politics since the revolution. The local cohesion of revolutionary forces prevented the
emergence of an effective national leadership during the revolution, and in its immediate
aftermath. Some Western observers – and possibly Western leaders who supported
the rebels – expected the 2011 intervention to establish a friendly government in
Tripoli.[170] They were mistaken. The suave figures that acted as the political leadership
of a spontaneous movement rapidly lost control over the forces it unleashed, and most
were pushed aside after Qadhafi had fallen. Few continued to play influential roles
after 2011, when the stakes in struggles over the state and its assets surpassed by far
the resources that those with connections to foreign governments could muster. Local
forces carved up the landscape in the absence of a national leadership. Lavish state
funding for armed groups, which originated in an ill-advised attempt by the NTC to
establish control, then spawned rivalries both between local factions, and within them.

Foreign support regained importance from 2014 onward. There were perhaps a
dozen notable figures with international networks and clienteles that transcended a
particular locality – people like Mahmoud Jibril, Aref al-Nayed, Ali Sallabi, Khalifa
Haftar, Hassan Tatanaki and Abdelhakim Belhaj. Most were based abroad and used
their foreign connections to mobilize support for their political, military or media

...ations and media outlets. But none – with the exception of Haftar, from mid-...o onwards – marshalled centralized forces that could shape national politics in any meaningful way.

Attempts to form cohesive national forces failed over and over again. The first examples for such failures were the numerous attempts in late 2011 and 2012 to form councils or unions representing *thuwwar* leaders from across the country. The experiment with party politics then revealed how poorly organized national political forces were. Jibril's NFA, while electorally successful due to the popularity of its founder, quickly became internally riven as the political landscape in which it had been formed had changed beyond recognition. The Muslim Brotherhood's JCP was more cohesive, but eventually also suffered splits and defections over the party leadership's support for the GNA. After the collapse of the political process, the Dignity and Dawn alliances proved short-lived, with each camp quickly breaking up into new configurations of its component elements.

Moreover, localism and fragmentation did not imply the emergence of monolithic local or regional forces. Cohesive groups formed in revolutionary strongholds during the 2011 war, but did not evolve into tribal fiefdoms or city-states thereafter. Crucially, the nature of fragmentation changed as the conflicts raged on. Even cities that had become renowned for their unity of purpose, such as Misrata or Zintan, suffered divides during the conflicts of 2015–19. Competing factions within the eastern autonomy movement ruled out the possibility of its leaders making any meaningful progress towards their stated goal. Haftar alone was successful in building a centralized structure and a solid regional support base, but faced great difficulties in expanding his reach across the country.

A corollary of these local divides was the dearth of strong local leadership figures. Unchallenged, pre-eminent local leaders were extremely rare. So were warlords. With the exception of Haftar, no militia leaders succeeded in consolidating and holding on to power over more than tiny bits of territory. This was partly due to the rapid changes in the security landscape – such as the slow annihilation of Benghazi's powerful Islamist-leaning militias, the turf wars in Tripoli and, from 2014 onward, the emergence of local military forces in communities that had been subjugated in 2011. But these changes in military capabilities are insufficient to explain the absence of centralized local authority. Accounting for this degree of fragmentation at the national and local level is the object of the present analysis.

Libya's fragmentation was not simply due to the breakdown of the state monopoly on violence. Localism preceded the dispersal of the state's arsenals and the inflows of weapons from foreign states backing the rebels. The emergence of cohesive local factions in the early weeks of the revolution was the reason why local groups subsequently seized state arsenals, and why foreign states directly supported what they saw as the effective actors on the ground.

Nothing was inevitable about the patterns of fragmentation that developed thereafter, as several plausible counterfactual scenarios suggest. The events in Libya were shaped by singular international circumstances: the UN Security Council decision and the NATO-led intervention that followed were exceptional enough, but even more extraordinarily, the states that supported Qadhafi's overthrow withdrew after the war and did not establish a stabilization mission. Without UN Security Council backing for an intervention, a longer civil war might have ensued that could have forced rebels to integrate more, or led to a takeover of the rebellion by jihadists or secessionists. Alternatively, a prolonged stalemate enforced by an international no-fly-zone – as opposed to the authorization to use 'all necessary means' to protect civilians of UN Security Council resolution 1973 – could have led to a consolidation of an eastern structure, and de facto partition.

The element of time also mattered greatly. The formation of armed factions; the gradual intensification of rivalries; the recourse to ever more brazen steps to exert influence, such as blocking oil export terminals or attacking the GNC: all of this took time to unfold. Had the NTC's Abdeljalil not caved in to pressure from armed proponents of regional autonomy in July 2012, much faster progress towards the drafting of a constitution and new elections might have been possible. State institutions might have had a chance at taking root before armed factions grew too powerful and power struggles escalated.

These observations are not intended to reduce Libya's trajectory to mere randomness. Rather, they illustrate why we should not dismiss Libya's fragmentation as an inevitable outcome of structural sociopolitical conditions. Instead, we need to analyse fragmentation as a process in which time, sequence, and the impact of sudden changes to strategic conditions all have their place. Most of all, we need to delve into the depths of local politics to understand the mechanisms that engendered fragmentation at the micro-level.

Structure and process in the eruption of civil war (2011)

Localism and fragmentation have been the most striking features of Libya's political and military landscape since 2011. It is a landscape that mostly lacks national political or military forces, and is, instead, populated by innumerable actors whose reach is in most cases confined to a particular locality or region. These actors are localist in that they draw their support from a particular local constituency without attempting to appeal to groups beyond their home turf; and in that they claim the right to speak for that constituency. Their claims generally concern their position in matters of national political importance and their demands versus the central government; only in few cases have local or regional forces formulated agendas of self-rule.

Today's localism can be traced back to the beginning of the 2011 revolution, when community leaders and armed groups across Libya began speaking in the name of their towns or tribes, declaring their rebellion against the regime. They did so at an astonishing speed: whereas protests in Tunisia, Egypt and Syria took weeks or even months to build up and remained largely non-violent during that time, Libyan protesters seized weapons and entered into open revolt from the very first days of the uprising.[1]

This was a startling phenomenon. For the four decades of Qadhafi's rule, no social forces had been able to publicly articulate their interests and demands. Suddenly, the society that had been shrouded by the regime's security apparatus for so long appeared to be stepping into the light. Libyan political players and foreign media outlets quickly seized on this perception. As early as 20 February, people calling themselves 'Faraj al-Zwayy' or 'Akram al-Warfalli' – names merely composed of a common forename and the tribal epithet, which made it impossible to identify them – phoned into the Qatari satellite channel al-Jazeera claiming that their entire tribe had joined the revolution.[2] The international media and foreign experts took them at face value, referred to them as tribal leaders, and began describing Libya as a tribal society, asserting that tribal support would be crucial for the fate of the regime and the rebels.[3]

Was Libya really witnessing the resurgence of hidden structural features of its society? Were communities dividing into revolutionary strongholds and loyalist towns according to whether they had been marginalized or integrated into the regime over the past decades? Did the apparent revival of tribal loyalties show that the Libyan state and national identity had been nothing more than a veneer, as foreign observers were quick to conclude?[4]

This chapter examines to what extent collective positions in 2011 formed on the basis of pre-existing factors – a group's social structure and its ties with central authority – and to what extent they emerged through processes endogenous to the conflict. It offers a reappraisal of Libya's legacies of statelessness, societal divisions and idiosyncratic institutions. A detailed analysis of events in four Libyan cities and regions during 2011 – the Nafusa Mountains, Misrata, Bani Walid and Tobruk – then shows how processes propelled by violence, or the threat thereof, fundamentally altered Libya's political landscape. A situation of collective indecision allowed contingent events to trigger chain reactions that deviated from the pathways set by pre-revolutionary structures. Positions for or against the regime were not the outcome of collective decision-making within a predefined community. Rather, community leadership, the capacity for collective decision-making, and the strong solidarities in revolutionary strongholds formed during the uprising and ensuing struggle. As much as they were the product of a particular history, the forces in Libya's revolutionary politics were shaped by the self-reinforcing dynamics violence sets free.

Structure, process and violence

The post-Cold War era has seen a boom in research on the causes of civil war. Much of this research relies on cross-national comparisons – generally large-sample statistical analyses – of variables attached to the pre-conflict properties of actors or states.[5] Although the methodological pitfalls of such studies are well established, their popularity is unbroken.[6] More recently, they have been joined by rational choice approaches that explain the outbreak of civil war as bargaining failures.[7]

Both types of approaches – the search for correlations between variables and the eruption of civil war, as well as the analysis of strategic interaction between antagonists – miss a crucial point. All politics is made of interaction and process, but violent interaction is particularly transformative. The eruption of civil war may resemble a sudden escalation or a gradual descent, but it invariably involves violent acts that alter the realities in which they occurred. The sudden irruption of violence often confronts actors with unprecedented choices in highly uncertain situations. In such contexts, otherwise fixed political parameters are suspended, and processes spawned by violence create new structural divides. The forces interacting in the escalation into civil war do not remain constant; in many cases, the antagonists emerge only during the escalation.

Libya descended into civil war within three weeks of the first protests. By early March, eastern Libya, the Nafusa Mountains, Misrata and several other coastal cities escaped regime control; rebels there had seized arms to defend themselves against regime forces; and in the east, a rebel leadership had emerged that claimed to be the legitimate representation of the Libyan people. Asking why local protests in Libya spiralled into revolution means asking why local communities entered into rebellion, closing ranks in defiance against the regime. In short, asking *why* the Libyan revolution erupted is synonymous with asking *how* it erupted.

Collective indecision, contingency and violence

A revolution is a critical juncture: a situation in which well-established institutions break down, dramatic changes become possible and individual agency can have an extraordinary impact.[8] But immediately before a revolution or a civil war breaks out, there is often a situation of pervasive uncertainty: a state of collective indecision that arises when exceptional developments suspend established expectations about the behaviour of political actors. Faced with an unprecedented choice and high risks, each actor searches for cues in the behaviour of others, who are similarly disoriented. Adopting a position or taking action can have irreversible consequences, forcing actors to stick with their decisions and encourage others to support them.[9] In such a situation, individual actions can trigger rapid behavioural alignment, and small causes can therefore end up having big effects.[10]

The first days of the Libyan revolution were just such a situation of collective indecision. In February 2011, the regional context led Libyan actors to interpret the first protests not as isolated outbursts, but as the potential onset of a revolutionary situation. The fall of Ben Ali and Mubarak in neighbouring Tunisia and Egypt directly inspired Libyan protesters of the first days, as their adoption of the slogan 'the people want the fall of the regime' showed. The events of the first days therefore confronted people across Libya with the choice of whether or not to rise up. Even as some actors were unequivocally taking sides (and risks), the great majority was undecided and hesitant, but increasingly forced to choose amid high uncertainty.

Situations of collective indecision amplify the impact of individual agency. Unexpected decisions by prominent actors can suddenly open up the possibility of open rebellion, and trigger the behavioural alignment of others: a local notable who joins young protesters, for example, or the first commander of a major army base to declare his defection. Once such acts breach the wall of fear, protests or desertions can cascade rapidly as others join.[11] Such contingent events, deriving their power from the unprecedented situation in which they occur, therefore provoke ruptures in patterns of social causality.[12]

Contingency and non-linear causality are even more important where violence is involved. More than most kinds of social interaction, collective violence generates a momentum of its own.[13] The dynamics triggered by violence are often self-reinforcing or entail chain reactions.[14] Random micro-level incidents – say, police killing an infractor in the context of an unintended altercation – can set off riots. In a situation where two groups face each other – for example, friends or relatives of the infractor, and police reinforcements – escalation can take the form of reflexive anger spirals.[15] Even where violence is used strategically, it frequently spirals out of control; at other times, violence is unintended and arises spontaneously from a tense confrontation or a loss of command and control.[16] The violent repression of protests can trigger moral outrage, leading to yet greater unrest.[17]

Violence, group structure and social transformation

The role of contingent events in situations of collective indecision, and the self-reinforcing dynamics unleashed by violence, are important because they transform social boundaries and solidarities in ways that cannot be predicted on the basis of extant structures.

Pre-existing social structures and relations between central authority and local society, as well as between local communities, clearly matter for collective action during the eruption of rebellions and revolutions. Analyses of peasant rebellions have long emphasized the importance of strong communal traditions and horizontal ties of solidarity and reciprocity.[18] Likewise, social movement theorists have highlighted the role of pre-existing social networks as bases for mobilization.[19] Tight-knit social networks offer access to information on others' preferences and allow for the coordination of decision-making through relationships of trust. Cohesive, close-knit communities will also more readily confer status rewards upon individuals taking risks for causes that the community deems laudable, and will furnish greater assurances over the risk of denunciation and the ability to prevent collaboration.[20]

However, arguments that focus on the role of pre-existing social networks neglect the fact that the onset of violence transforms social ties in ways that are decisive for the eruption of all-out civil war. This applies both to group identities and to solidarities. In Somalia, political divides cut across clan lines in the months preceding the outbreak of fighting in Mogadishu, in 1990. But as violence erupted, it set in motion processes that led to the emergence of warring camps associated with particular clans.[21] In 1941 Bosnia, ethnic divides only became salient with the onset of mass killing, which was itself driven partly by the motivation of material gain, and escalated due to mutually reinforcing fears.[22] In the Vendée, in 1793, French authorities stigmatized the population of an entire region as counterrevolutionaries, and through their repression created the regional identity they had imagined.[23] In El Salvador, pre-war social networks in communities were too weak to solve the collective action problem of insurgent mobilization. The networks that fulfilled this purpose formed during mobilization itself.[24]

From the very beginning of an uprising, new social groups form and existing ones are transformed. Whether or not protesters or rebels are linked to each other through pre-existing social ties, collective risk-taking transforms their bonds, or creates new ones.[25] Anonymous participants in protests can experience an intense joy of collectivity as they overcome their fear of state violence, thereby strengthening their solidarity and contributing to the formation of a common identity.[26] New political communities form in the very midst of the action.

Escalatory dynamics involve mechanisms that draw or activate social boundaries, thereby redefining groups and group solidarities. Individual acts of violence can usher in a Hobbesian security dilemma for entire groups, if an adversary identifies a perpetrator as a member of that group, or if the perpetrator can push close contacts to intensify their commitment to solidarity.[27] The sociologist Roger Gould theorized this mechanism, which we could call the *security dilemma of solidary groups*. In contexts of weak state authority, individuals or small groups engaged in contention threaten larger group action to deter an adversary, but the deterrent effect of this threat will depend on the credibility of group solidarity. Because of the fundamental tension between individual and group interests, group solidarity is invariably imperfect. People gamble that the adversary's solidarity will crumble if the conflict intensifies, provoking escalation between groups rather than individuals.

> Expressions of group solidarity are therefore double-edged: They may succeed in forestalling escalation, but if they fail to do so they intensify the violence that occurs ... it is the fragility of group solidarity, not its strength, that leads to the intensification of conflict.[28]

This mechanism applies to all situations in which ties of solidarity matter, or the actors perceive them to matter – including in confrontations between protesters and government forces. The case of a village community in the Russian civil war illustrates the mechanism well. An unplanned act of violence by villagers against state representatives raised the threat of retaliation. Perpetrators and their close associates invoked community solidarity to prepare for collective defence, which increased the stakes of the conflict and the level of violence. Escalating in ways that made collective retaliation more likely further facilitated the mobilization of allies. A single act of violence thereby triggered a chain of events that led to the formation of a local militia and a new power structure in the village.[29]

The transformative impact of this mechanism will be particularly pronounced where confrontations are not routine, and where, therefore, uncertainty prevails on both sides to what extent the adversaries benefit from group solidarity, or are able to activate solidary ties. This applies to a situation of sudden, open revolt in communities, as in Libya in February 2011. In such a context, escalation that seeks to break perceived or actual community solidarity is a high-risk gamble that can either re-establish government control, or cause communities to close ranks against the government. Inter-group conflict, then, does not inevitably lead to greater group cohesion or cause a group's fragmentation. But by forcing group members to take sides, it redefines group solidarity as well as group boundaries. Escalation and group transformation are closely linked. Groups change even as they enter violent conflict.

Crucially, new political communities can also emerge where there had been none, because an adversary perceives them to exist. During the escalation into civil war, patterns of territorial control can spawn path dependencies that turn accidents of location into enduring political identities, in a mechanism we could call *alignment lock-in*: areas that are controlled by a belligerent may develop a reputation of loyalty towards this belligerent. Whether or not that reputation reflects actual loyalties in the area at the outset, it may lead to indiscriminate reprisals – or the fear thereof – thereby strengthening loyalties to the controlling belligerent.[30]

Once violent conflict activates social boundaries, and once adversaries start using social categories to designate their enemies – cities or tribes, in Libya's case – self-reinforcing dynamics of polarization unfold.[31] Such categories can suddenly determine whether one lives or dies.[32] Channels of communication between groups become fewer, heightening uncertainty over the intentions of the adverse group, which in turn encourages an aggressive stance.[33] Groups segregate through displacement and resettlement along political lines; people who happen to find themselves on opposite sides sever ties. Pre-war social networks, including marriages and friendships across political or ethnic divides, break apart.[34]

Within the groups whose boundaries are redefined through violence, collective struggle creates new and lasting loyalties between individuals who depend on each other for their common survival. Where such individuals are linked through pre-existing ties – such as kinship or friendship – these ties may acquire wholly new qualities, but equally strong loyalties can form between brothers-in-arms who did not know each other before the conflict.[35]

Taken together, these mechanisms imply that violence draws new divides and thereby produces new collective actors. The categories violent contenders use to define their adversaries – such as clans, tribes or cities – may, indeed, refer to groups with dense social networks and a degree of solidarity, but the threat of violence facing these groups nevertheless transforms them. Where violence escalates in a situation of collective indecision, contingent acts acquire a disproportionate impact; in such cases, how violence transforms social networks is not predictable on the basis of pre-war structures. To understand to what extent localism is a product of structural societal characteristics, we need to examine not only historical legacies, but also how violence transformed social ties during the 2011 revolution.

Structural aspects of Libyan localism

Writing in 1990, Lisa Anderson pinpointed the unique nature of the relationship between tribes and the state in Libya. Tribal challenges to state-building enterprises are a common phenomenon. But in Libya, from the monarchy (1951–69) to Qadhafi, state elites themselves displayed an 'aversion to the reliance on state institutions and ideologies for political legitimacy and loyalty'.[36] Qadhafi's overt hostility to the state, Anderson concluded, while rooted in Libyans' negative experiences with attempts at state-building, was a luxury afforded by oil. She closed with an extraordinarily perceptive warning: 'No doubt Libya will eventually be forced to come to terms with its statehood, and only at that point will the true costs of today's refusal be apparent'.[37] Had the writing been on the wall for decades?

A century of turmoil (1911–2011)

Few territories worldwide underwent state penetration as recently, discontinuously and violently as the region known today as Libya. During the late nineteenth century, the beginnings of economic commercialization along the Tripolitanian coast, combined with Ottoman attempts to modernize the administration of its Libyan provinces and expand into the interior, produced a nascent class of notables.[38] But Ottoman state-building came to an abrupt end with the start of the Italian colonial conquest in 1911. The Italians subdued the Ottoman-backed resistance in Tripolitania in 1913 and conquered Fezzan in early 1914. With the outbreak of the First World War, the rebellion renewed in Fezzan in late 1914, and by mid-1915, rebelling Tripolitanian forces pushed the Italian presence back to a few cities on the coast. In Cyrenaica, the Italians failed to vanquish the Bedouin resistance coordinated by the Sanusi religious order, and supported by the Ottomans. During the First World War, Italian forces in Cyrenaica were largely confined to the cities of Benghazi and Darna.[39] In 1922, the fascist authorities launched fresh offensives and eventually subjugated Tripolitania by 1924, Fezzan by 1930, and Cyrenaica by 1931, through, among other actions, the brutal confinement of the Cyrenaican population in concentration camps. But already in 1943, Italian and German forces in Libya were defeated by Allied advances. Libya's colonial experience was therefore exceptionally brief, violent and disruptive. The Italian colonial administration and economy had provided no avenues for the formation of a local bourgeoisie. Many Ottoman-era notables had been exiled, imprisoned or marginalized; egalitarianism was revived in tribal communities.[40]

Libya emerged in 1951 as an 'accidental state', the outcome of US and Soviet opposition to French, British and Italian designs for trusteeships over each of the territory's three regions.[41] In Cyrenaica, ambitions for an independent state had been prevalent, and were eventually assuaged with the establishment of a federal system headed by the head of the Sanusi order, now turned king, Idris. The nascent Libyan state's central authority was weak; its territory was then one of the poorest countries in the world, offering few opportunities to extract resources; and the three provincial administrations enjoyed extensive competences.

This changed after the discovery of oil in 1959, which allowed the king to abolish the federal system and centralize authority in 1963. The ensuing influx of revenues not only massively accelerated urbanization in what had largely been a subsistence economy dominated by pastoralism and agriculture. It also led to rampant corruption, and provoked intensifying rivalries among the urban notables, tribal leaders and businessmen whose interests the king sought to juggle. The life span of successive governments shortened, inequalities surged dramatically, and a budding bourgeoisie once again built clientelist networks that wore away at the ideology of tribal egalitarianism.[42]

After a group of young military officers led by Qadhafi toppled the monarchy and suspended the constitution in 1969, these processes were yet again interrupted. From the very beginning, Qadhafi deliberately targeted the elites of the monarchy. In the two years following the 1969 coup, administrative borders were redrawn to cut across tribal territories; tribal notables lost their function as state officials; large businesses were nationalized; and many tribal leaders, members of prominent bourgeois families, and top-ranking military officers were imprisoned or executed.[43] Initially, these measures met with much resistance, particularly in rural areas, where tribal notables retained much of their sway.[44]

To overcome such opposition, Qadhafi, from 1973 onwards progressively introduced his vision of direct democracy, a stateless society in which popular committees would disrupt the rule of elites. While in practice this meant that power was increasingly concentrated in Qadhafi's hands, Libya's cultural revolution also mobilized young men and women from modest social backgrounds against established families. In 1978, Qadhafi felt secure enough to attack such elites head-on: a new property law paved the way for a wide-ranging expropriation of wealthy families. Homes could be claimed by those inhabiting them, land by those cultivating it, companies by their employees. Property rights dissolved into chaos.[45]

The beneficiaries of these capricious measures were many. More broadly, Qadhafi gained substantial support from distributive policies that ensured free healthcare and education, as well as public sector employment. Social hierarchies were flattened further, and class formation forestalled, by a massive increase in labour migration to Libya from neighbouring countries, which meant that few Libyan citizens did manual labour.

The following decades were defined by frequent upheaval in state institutions, at constant threat of being reshuffled or overruled by the 'revolutionary sector' – the Revolutionary Committees and other entities that were considered outside formal state authority, at their top Qadhafi himself.[46] Qadhafi recurrently threatened to dissolve most or all government ministries, temporarily following through with this threat in 2000. Oil revenues, he repeatedly proposed, should be distributed directly to the people.[47]

Qadhafi's notion of statelessness undeniably drew on deeply rooted local, particularly tribal, traditions: an aversion to central authority, and esteem for direct participation in decision-making by consensus or mediation.[48] In this sense, Qadhafi's revolution was a 'reassertion of hinterland culture in national life'.[49] But localism was also a default consequence of the inability of political and social forces to organize themselves across the country. Qadhafi's Libya knew neither political parties nor independent associations. Formal politics was a struggle over the allocation of budgets between ever-changing local administrative units. The informal politics of spreading patronage through state funds, jobs or influence over decision-making produced clientelist networks that were heavily tilted towards their patrons' regions and communities of origin.

Statelessness, of course, was a fiction. In reality, the state came to spawn vested economic interests in the form of informal or illegal arrangements. With the reintroduction of private sector activity in 1987 after a decade of socialism, entrepreneurs with close links to regime officials emerged. The UN economic embargo in place for much of the 1990s produced a group of black market profiteers among regime cronies.[50] In the late 1990s, the regime began reaching out to exiled opponents and offered commercial opportunities to those returning. Linked to this was the growing role of Qadhafi's sons, most prominently Saif al-Islam, who built up a clientele of businessmen. When rising oil prices and the end of Libya's international isolation led to increasing state expenditures during the 2000s, the opportunities for embezzlement of public funds and manipulation of payrolls expanded massively. The Libyan state was once again spawning powerful patron–client networks that stood in stark contrast to Qadhafi's ideology of egalitarianism.

The contradiction between the rhetoric of statelessness and political realities was most obvious at the regime's core: its security apparatus. From the mid-1970s onward, Qadhafi began attacking the army as an instrument of repression, calling for it to be disbanded and replaced by a 'people in arms'.[51] A growing array of paramilitary and civilian militias were established to check the army and persecute regime opponents, including the Revolutionary Committees, the Revolutionary Guards and the People's

Guards.[52] Until the mid-1980s, the army was a national institution: a melting pot for recruits from across the country. After Libya's defeat in Chad in 1987, and under the impact of economic sanctions, the army fell into neglect. The regime allowed officers to join units in their towns of origin to compensate for stagnating salaries, closing an eye on their pursuit of side jobs. During the 1990s, the regular army therefore devolved into local units closely linked to their garrison towns.[53]

In the army's place, Qadhafi established praetorian units – the security brigades – defined by their recruitment from among tribal constituencies that were considered particularly loyal. They were part of a complex system of security institutions designed to protect Qadhafi's rule. In these institutions, close relatives of the leader and other members of the Qadhadhfa tribe held key positions, and members of the Warfalla and Magarha also came to be over-represented.[54] This was not simply a matter of trust: since the mid-1970s, Qadhafi had gradually shifted away from his rejection of tribes, and begun drawing on them as a political resource.

What is a Libyan tribe?

At this stage, it is necessary to clarify the notion of tribe, and the changing empirical realities it denotes, over the century preceding the 2011 revolution. Social scientists encountering tribes in their field research have increasingly felt obliged to defend their use of the term against the dominant academic fashion of dismissing tribes wholesale as colonial inventions reified by political entrepreneurs, administrators and anthropologists.[55] Those defending a considered use of the term recognize its ambiguities and connotations, as well as the fact that it covers societies diverging in their hierarchization and the centralization of power. Their definitions of the term vary, but most agree that tribes are characterized by their reliance on an ideology of common belonging – and very often of common descent – as the basis for shared solidarity. They concur that tribes never evolved in isolation from states; instead, tribes were influenced by their relationship with the state, just as states were shaped through their interaction with tribes. They further stress that tribes thus understood have proven adaptable and innovative, confounding the predictions of modernization theorists that they would disappear with the inexorable rise of the state.[56] Some have seen in this adaptability the transformation of tribes into something wholly new or even artificial: 'neo-tribal associations' or 'tribalism without tribes'.[57] Others have attributed the resurgence of tribal politicians and militia leaders in Iraq or Afghanistan exclusively to the support they receive from the US military.[58] But the resourcefulness of tribal political entrepreneurs in manipulating kinship and genealogies is as old as their interaction with foreign military forces. The continuity of the tribal phenomenon in Libya, as in many other societies, justifies the use of the term, but the changes it underwent require analysis.

During the Ottoman and Italian colonial eras, tribes in Cyrenaica, Fezzan, and the Tripolitanian hinterland were tribes in the sense of a 'society that lives by appropriating and transforming the resources of a territory', a society that 'exerts its sovereignty over a determined territory'.[59] Land rights were at the core of this society, and defined relations between groups, including between 'free' and 'tied' tribes. They were also the driver behind the formation of alliances and the persistence of conflicts between groups competing for territory. It was not, however, a society that existed in an equilibrium, immune to historical change. Nor were tribes necessarily units of action. Edward Evans-Pritchard's efforts to apply his model of a segmentary, acephalous society to Cyrenaican tribes were meticulously rebutted by his student Emrys Peters.[60] According to Peters, who conducted his field research in the late 1940s, entire tribes were never at war; indeed, as tribes, they lacked the leadership to wage war.[61] The actual lines of conflict between groups did not correspond to the divisions of tribes according to lineage – that is, to the ideology of common descent. Instead, leaders emerged by constituting a following through marriage strategies and the adoption of clients, forming patchworks of power groups that competed and feuded with each other.

In the Tripolitanian hinterland, Ottoman and, later, Italian efforts to rule by co-opting tribal notables produced tribal leadership structures that were more centralized, hierarchical and dependent on state support. They also exacerbated factionalism within tribes and lent greater weight to political rivalries between tribal leaders in conflicts.[62] In relation to the Nafusa Mountains during the colonial era, Mouldi Lahmar has emphasized the opportunism and weak social base of tribal leaders, claiming that they lacked authority over their tribes and commanded a ragtag following that combined close relatives and mercenaries from other tribes. According to Lahmar, the tribe was politically meaningless, the relevant socioeconomic and political unit being the extended family. But Lahmar does not back up this argument, which, while plausible for the sedentary Amazigh communities, lacks credence with regard to semi-nomadic groups in and around the mountains.[63]

Lahmar's thesis is also contradicted by the well documented role of tribal alliances (*suff*, pl. *sufuf*) in Tripolitania and Fezzan during the nineteenth and early twentieth centuries. Tribes allied with more distant groups against their immediate neighbours, in coalitions that remained remarkably stable over the course of a century because they were rooted in common interests in land use regimes.[64] Nevertheless, as in Cyrenaica, Tripolitanian tribes were not fixed units of action. Lahmar may exaggerate the extent to which they suffered internal splits in the period of pervasive conflict between 1911 and 1924, but such splits were certainly common.[65]

During the Ottoman – Italian war of 1911–13 and the First World War, the units fighting the Italians with Ottoman support were formed of volunteers who came together on a tribal basis, and were headed by tribal leaders. In Tripolitania, Italian divide-and-rule tactics caused much internecine warfare between such tribal forces. Virtually all leading Tripolitanian figures repeatedly switched back and forth between fighting the Italians and collaborating with them. These struggles escalated into a local civil war in and around the Nafusa Mountains during 1920–21. In Cyrenaica, the unifying structure of the Sanusi religious order prevented such infighting, but there too, forces from distinct tribes remained separate.[66]

In both regions, the leaders of the anti-colonial struggle emerged as prominent notables during the monarchy, and as the founders of notable families.[67] The tribal fighters who withdrew to Egypt after the 1931 defeat of the Cyrenaican resistance returned as an auxiliary force of the British army in 1943, and subsequently became the Cyrenaica Defence Force, a paramilitary unit designed to be loyal to King Idris by virtue of its tribal makeup. British military administrators tried unsuccessfully to govern through the appointment of tribal notables according to the segmentary tribal structure, failing to grasp that power groups did not correspond to lineages.[68] But during the monarchy, tribal leaders – along with representatives of prominent urban families – gained influence as ministers, parliamentarians, members of the king's entourage, or provincial governors.[69] Administrative divisions were drawn on the basis of tribal territory; tribal notables were tasked with tax collection in their groups, and competed with other notables of their tribes for access to state patronage.

The rapid process of sedentarization and urbanization with the shift towards a rentier economy from the mid-1960s onwards could have been expected to gradually dissolve tribal ties. Instead, tribes changed shape. Outside coastal Tripolitania, private land ownership was often weakly developed, and urbanization occurred at such a breathtaking pace that relatives settled in close vicinity to each other. In towns where several tribes settled, such as Ajdabiya or Sabha, they did so in tribally homogeneous neighbourhoods. Where towns were inhabited by a single tribal confederation, such as in Bani Walid, each area came to be inhabited by a particular component tribe or subtribe. Even in large cities such as Tripoli or Misrata, recent settlers from rural areas clustered with fellow tribesmen in particular districts. When John Davis conducted research in Ajdabiya in the late 1970s, tribal relations remained central, despite the fact that people from different tribes were now working alongside each other:

> The relaxed, friendly informal sociable occasions at which people gossiped and discussed affairs and policy were generally restricted to members of the same tribe, section or lineage. By 1979, cadres from different sections had not married into each other's families.[70]

Settlement patterns helped preserve tribal ties and allowed political entrepreneurs to play the tribal card in elections. Tribal politicians typically whipped up support in their own group by pointing to the threat that other tribes or sections could seize control of the Popular Committees or Basic People's Congresses of Qadhafi's 'direct democracy'.

By the late 1970s, tribes had lost their economic autonomy, as rent distribution had replaced pastoralism as the foundation of the economy. Claiming sovereignty over territory was no longer possible, nor was it economically vital. The transition from collective to individual ownership of land was already well under way before Qadhafi turned much tribal territory into state property. Gaining influence over the distribution of budgets and public sector jobs had become crucial, and tribal relations were converted into networks that connected local communities with state institutions and public sector companies. Though such clientelist networks benefited communities unevenly, they generally did not exacerbate inequality during the first two decades of the Qadhafi era. The tribal notables of the monarchy were frequently marginalized during this period, and the turnover of officials in local institutions was high, preventing the consolidation of tribal elites. Moreover, tribes retained some of their institutions, such as welfare systems whereby sheikhs collected funds to cover the costs of members in need. In Cyrenaica, Fezzan and pockets of Tripolitania, the tribal framework continued to supply recognized mechanisms for the settlement of disputes.[71]

Regime policies also breathed new life into tribes, even as they were transforming them. Though Qadhafi initially displayed hostility towards tribes and abolished the office of sheikh, he rapidly began invoking tribal values and myths of common origin, and exploiting legacies of inter-communal rifts. The first illustration came in 1975, after an alleged coup attempt led by Omar al-Muhaishi, an army officer from Misrata, long-standing confidant of Qadhafi and member of the Revolutionary Command Council. Two months after the purported coup plot was discovered and Muhaishi fled the country, Qadhafi met with tribal leaders in Bani Walid for a public show of allegiance, playing on the history of conflict between Misratan leaders and Bani Walid's Warfalla tribe during the early twentieth century.[72] The outreach to Bani Walid was helped by Qadhafi's invocation of the historically close ties between the two tribes. The Qadhadhfa had been a client tribe of the Warfalla; the two tribes had been allied in the struggles over pasture of the nineteenth and early twentieth centuries, had fought together against the Italians, and had intermarried extensively.[73] But Qadhafi's efforts to mobilize tribal loyalty also extended to the manipulation of genealogies: in 1980, for example, a delegation of Qadhadhfa elders met with notables of the Nuwail tribe in al-Jumail, near the Tunisian border, to sign a document stating that the two tribes had a common ancestry – contrary to the hitherto accepted genealogies of both groups.[74] At the time, Qadhafi often phrased his idea of a 'people in arms' in terms of tribes taking up arms to defend their homeland.[75]

Through the expansion of clientelist networks and the diffusion of notions of tribal loyalty, tribalism progressively pervaded the entire security apparatus. After the alleged coup plot of 1975, Qadhafi increasingly relied on relatives to staff the top echelons of the security apparatus, who, in turn, recruited a growing number of Qadhadhfa. His associates from other tribes, in turn, boosted recruitment from among their own groups. Such was the role of Ali al-Fituri, a *Warfalli* army officer close to Qadhafi, who from 1975 onward oversaw heavy recruitment from Bani Walid into the army, the Revolutionary Committees and other security institutions, which would continue for almost two decades. Two prominent figures played the same role among the Magarha: Qadhafi's right-hand man during the 1970s and 1980s, Abdesselam Jallud, and the leader's brother-in-law and top intelligence official, Abdallah Senoussi. Over time, such tribes came to be perceived as pillars of the regime, whether by local communities, the exiled opposition or regime officials themselves.

Eventually, Qadhafi turned tribal membership and loyalty into formal principles of his rule. In 1994, he established the Popular Social Leadership (PSL), an institution designed to represent and control communities on a tribal basis.[76] Three years later, he passed a 'pact of honour' under which families, tribes and cities were to be held collectively responsible for their members' subversive activities, and could face indiscriminate punishment, such as deprivation of water, electricity or access to public jobs. The PSL were placed in charge of enforcing this law.[77]

The immediate trigger for these measures had been the discovery, in October 1993, of a coup plot in which a number of Warfalla military officers from Bani Walid were implicated. Even though Warfalla did not represent the majority among the officers involved, the regime quickly began portraying the plot as a tribal conspiracy – perhaps because all three leaders who succeeded in escaping abroad were from Bani Walid.[78] A wave of arrests among Warfalla ensued, provoking repeated protests in Bani Walid in 1994 during which facilities of the security services were attacked and torched.[79] Tribal elders from Bani Walid, among them notables who had wielded influence during the monarchy and preserved their social standing, reached out to close associates of Qadhafi in an attempt to ease regime repression. But they opposed Qadhafi's plan to have the suspected coup plotters executed in Bani Walid itself, displaying a degree of unity that Qadhafi likely perceived as a threat.

With the PSL, Qadhafi groomed figures from a modest social background, or upstarts who owed their recent rise to the regime. Some prominent monarchy-era notables also joined the PSL, such as al-Tayyeb al-Sharif, an Obeidat sheikh who had been governor of Darna under the monarchy, was repeatedly imprisoned under Qadhafi, and then became head of the Tobruk PSL in 1995.[80] But within the PSL, notables drawing on historical legitimacy had to compete with figures whose sole source of influence was the regime. Representation was modelled on the tribal structure of each community, though the PSL were also established in cities such as Misrata, where only part of the population saw themselves as belonging to tribes. The PSL therefore reproduced tribal divisions and fuelled rivalries over the claim to community leadership. At the same time, those joining the PSL often saw their credibility as community representatives decline, due to their association with the regime.

Qadhafi's will to reduce the tribes to mere instruments of his rule, and break their capacity to represent community interests independently of the regime, emerged most starkly in subsequent events in Bani Walid. Eight alleged coup plotters were executed in 1997, but in a concession to the demands of tribal elders, the execution took place neither publicly nor in Bani Walid. In 1999, however, an alleged co-conspirator was taken from the prison in Tripoli to Bani Walid and hanged in public, and local regime henchmen razed the houses of the coup plotters' families – the ruins of some are still visible in Bani Walid today. Those overseeing the demolition were the heads of the PSL for each tribal section of the Warfalla, joined by cheering cohorts from the same tribe. The coup plotters' families were barred from jobs, their children banned from schools, and several were banished to other towns.

Another upshot of the failed coup plot was the expansion of the security brigades, whose composition was clearly based on tribal affiliation. Even before the coup plot, Qadhafi had established the Imhemmed al-Magariaf Brigade, which was led by Qadhadhfa, with a large proportion of Warfalla and Tarhuna soldiers, and charged with protecting his Bab al-Aziziya headquarters in Tripoli.[81] During the late 1990s and early 2000s, similar units were established in Misrata, Sirte, Benghazi, Bayda, Tobruk, Gharyan, Sabha and Ubari – each of them, at its core, recruited from a well-thought-out combination of tribes, generally from the area where the units were based. For example, the Gharyan-based brigade, informally named after its commander, a *Magrahi* officer called al-Mabruk Sahban, was staffed primarily by Zintani soldiers and recruits from historically underprivileged tribes from the Nafusa Mountains such as the Mashashiya and Asabea.

Recent returnees or immigrants from Sahelian states formed another important recruitment pool for the security brigades. Since the 1970s, Qadhafi had accelerated the repatriation of descendants of tribesmen who had fled to Chad and Niger following their defeat against the Italians in the 1920s, or the Ottomans in the nineteenth century – among them Awlad Suleiman, Warfalla, Qadhadhfa and Magharba. They gained Libyan citizenship, but were stigmatized by the administration and local communities as *a'idoun* – returnees.[82] In the early 1980s, Qadhafi also reached out to other Arab tribes in the Sahel, offering them second-class citizenship as 'Arab nationals' on condition of their recruitment into the army. The Torshan from Niger even gained full citizenship and were incorporated into the Qadhadhfa, where a section of the same name existed.[83] Tuareg from Mali and Niger had fought for Qadhafi in several conflicts since the early 1980s, and were later gathered in a force of their own, the Ubari-based Maghawir Brigade; many never obtained the citizenship they had been promised in exchange.[84] The invocation of tribal values and identities to ensure the loyalty of such fighters often served to conceal their dependency and exploitation.

These observations suggest that by the early 2000s, instrumentalization and manipulation by the regime had turned tribes into shadows of their former selves, and had irreversibly compromised those claiming tribal leadership. And yet, the evidence is somewhat more ambiguous. It is well documented, and was confirmed to me by interlocutors from Tobruk to Bani Walid and Zintan, that many legal disputes and even murder cases continued to be solved by tribal elders dispensing customary law (*'urf*), rather than by recourse to the state. According to a leading tribal figure in Zintan, the havoc Qadhafi's policies wreaked on property rights prompted local elders to resurrect practices of mediation that had been almost forgotten.[85]

Just as the role of tribes in the Qadhafi era remains somewhat ambiguous, so does the nature of the state. Thomas Hüsken has argued that tribal networks in eastern Libya infiltrated the security services and organized the bypassing of state law within the state apparatus itself. According to Hüsken, tribal politicians in the borderland of Egypt and Libya lamented that competition between these networks had 'turned state institutions into a rag rug of factions', and that the state was no longer *primus inter pares* vis-à-vis competing tribal groups.[86] This is a matter of perspective: certainly, tribal factions and other clientelist networks did operate within state institutions. Allowing these networks to embezzle and smuggle was at the core of the regime's political economy. It did not, however, signify a loss of control; Qadhafi and his close associates chose to ignore or penalise transgressions as a means of managing competing factions, the better to rule them. No operator in such networks could be in any doubt over his vulnerability to Qadhafi's whims. Qadhafi's power to savagely punish any given figure, regardless of how well-respected he was, was absolute. Finally, Qadhafi never allowed collective decision-making within tribes, independently of the regime's divisive structures. Tribal politicians could not mobilize their communities to press collective demands. To speak of 'intermediary rule'[87] therefore overstates the role of tribal politicians under Qadhafi.

Tribes can be an identity, an institution, an arena and an actor.[88] In Qadhafi's Libya, their role in furnishing an identity remained unbroken, due to the regime's efforts at mobilizing tribal support and exploiting communal divisions. They also functioned as an arena for political players competing for community leadership and representation, the arbiter in this competition being the regime, rather than local communities. As an institution, some retained a modest capacity for local dispute resolution, but most had otherwise lost their autonomy in decision-making. Historical accounts show that we should not assume Libyan tribes to have been unified, collective actors in the past, but they were clearly even much less so following four decades of Qadhafi's divide-and-rule policy. Against this background, the sudden appearance of cohesive local communities as leading forces in the revolution is all the more puzzling.

The myth of the marginalized cities and regions

A common explanation for the localism of Libya's revolutionary forces rests on the claim that certain cities, tribes, ethnic groups, or regions were deliberately marginalized by Qadhafi, and rose up because of their grievances. But this argument does not hold up to a close look at the patterns of rebellion and loyalism in 2011.

From the first days of the uprising, foreign media and experts described Benghazi and eastern Libya in general as 'a traditional hotbed of anti-Gaddafi sentiment among tribes hostile to his rule'.[89] Cyrenaica, it was widely claimed, had been deliberately marginalized by Qadhafi because it had been the power base of the monarchy, as well as the main locus of a low-level Islamist insurgency during the 1990s. Likewise, with regard to the rebellion in the Nafusa Mountains, the media pointed to the marginalization of Libya's Amazigh minority.[90] Similar claims would later be made about the Tubu minority in southern Libya, despite the relatively late formation of revolutionary armed groups among the Tubu.[91]

Yet, most such claims fail to convince. Certainly, Cyrenaican influence in government declined after Qadhafi took over, moved the capital from the eastern city of al-Bayda to Tripoli, and arrested or sidelined most leading figures of the monarchy – a disproportionate number of whom were from the east. On the eve of the 2011 uprising, the region's infrastructure was indeed run-down, though not more so than that of many other provincial areas, including purported regime strongholds such as Bani Walid. It is also true that clandestine Islamist opposition movements such as the Libyan Islamic Fighting Group (LIFG) were most active in the eastern cities of Benghazi and Darna, and that the clampdown on these groups was particularly heavy-handed in these two cities. But it is incorrect to claim that most victims of the 1996 massacre in Tripoli's Abu Slim prison were from the east.[92]

The east was not less integrated into the regime than other regions. Indeed, proportionally to its population, its share of holders of ministerial portfolios was higher than that of the west and south during 1969–99.[93] Many close and long-standing associates of Qadhafi, as well as senior figures of the security establishment, were from Cyrenaica.[94] The region's most influential businessman, Hassan Tatanaki, had close ties with Saif al-Islam. The three security brigades based in the east were recruited primarily from among eastern tribes: the Fadhil Bu Omar Brigade in Benghazi; the Tobruk-based Omar al-Mukhtar Brigade, and the Bayda-based Hussain al-Juwaifi Brigade, informally named after its commander al-Jareh Farkash, an uncle of Qadhafi's wife Safiya, who was herself from Bayda's Barassa tribe.

Misrata, which emerged as a key revolutionary stronghold in 2011 and was the city that suffered most from Qadhafi's counterinsurgency campaign, had been well represented in the regime. More of Qadhafi's ministers had come from Misrata than from any other Libyan city.[95] Many of the city's leading merchants were in partnership with regime cronies. By contrast, few sons of Bani Walid held ministerial office or other top governmental positions. The town benefited little from public investment despite widespread recruitment into the poorly paid public sector or security services. The vicious repression of the 1990s had left hundreds of people among Bani Walid residents deeply resentful of the regime. In the words of one politician from Bani Walid: 'strange things happened in February 2011. You should have expected Misrata to back the regime, given how much they had benefited from it. Bani Walid should have risen up, given how much it had suffered.'[96] And yet, the opposite occurred.

In the Nafusa Mountains, the Amazigh did, indeed, harbour profound grievances over Qadhafi's denial of their culture and language, right down to his banning of Amazigh forenames. They also chafed at what they perceived as Qadhafi's promotion of neighbouring Arab communities through their recruitment into the army and the security brigades. But the first town in which major unrest erupted in February 2011 was Zintan, which was perceived as a pillar of the regime by its Amazigh neighbours. One revolutionary from Yefren recalled how stupefied he and others were over events in Zintan: 'We didn't understand why they were rising up, and at first, we didn't believe it was real.'[97] Without Zintan joining the uprising, it is doubtful whether protests in Amazigh towns would ever have developed momentum.

The Tubu had a turbulent relationship with Qadhafi, who recruited heavily from among that group during his war with Chad, in the 1980s, and granted Libyan citizenship to thousands of Tubu in Chad to bolster his claim to the disputed Aouzou strip. After the International Court of Justice ruled against Libya's claim to Aouzou, Qadhafi stripped these people of their citizenship, and stopped recruitment from among the Tubu. Several small Tubu armed groups joined the rebels in 2011, but it was only in the final months of the war that these groups seized control over vast areas in the name of the revolution. Conversely, the several thousand Tuareg soldiers in Qadhafi's forces remained overwhelmingly loyal during the war despite having a similarly checkered experience with broken promises of citizenship.[98] They would struggle to shake off the stigma of regime loyalism for a long time to come.

Who joined the revolution and who remained loyal in 2011, then, was hardly predictable on the basis of perceived or actual marginalization and promotion by the regime. The reason lies in the endogenous conflict dynamics that unfolded in the first weeks of the uprising, and the role of contingency in shaping them.

The irruption of localism in 2011

A local civil war in the Western/Nafusa Mountains[99]

In early February 2011, under the impact of the momentous events in neighbouring Tunisia and Egypt, the Libyan regime began staging displays of popular support to

Qadhafi, who toured the country to receive declarations of loyalty from tribal politicians. On 15 February, the head of the People's Guard in Zintan – a reserve force recruited from among civilians – held a meeting with the town's Popular Social Leadership to discuss the regime's plan to mobilize Zintani volunteers and deploy them in eastern Libya in anticipation of unrest. The matter was deferred to a committee of twenty tribal figures that was to meet the next day. That very night, the first protests erupted in Benghazi. When the meeting was taking place on 16 February, in the late morning, a handful of enraged Zintanis forced their way in, breaking up the meeting. A few men – among them one of the elders, Milad al-Amin – went from the meeting to the town's main square and started shouting slogans against the regime. One participant recalled the scene around noon:

> There were around twenty people there, shouting 'the people want the fall of the regime'. I joined them. I was surprised by their courage, and by my own. The police did nothing. All the while, more people were joining.[100]

The astonishment of participants and bystanders grew further when a well-known Zintani religious sheikh, a man in his sixties called al-Taher al-Jdi', joined the small group of protesters, and began calling on Zintanis to come out of their houses and support their brethren. Slowly, the crowd grew. In the early afternoon, the protesters looted and burned the police station, the seat of the Revolutionary Committees, and the office of Internal Security, seizing a few weapons. Milad al-Amin spoke to the crowd shortly afterwards, declaring that the 'wall of fear has been broken'.[101] Later, a contingent of Central Security Forces entered the town and arrested several people in the square, but then withdrew again.[102]

The same evening, as the news of events in Zintan spread, a group of young men torched the facilities of the Revolutionary Committees and Internal Security in neighboring Rujban, a town with close social and historical ties to Zintan. They were dispersed with live ammunition by Central Security Forces, who killed one of them, provoking larger protests in Rujban the following day, and spurring the protesters' efforts to arm themselves. Across the mountains, in Nalut, Hawamid, Jadu, Yefren, Kikla and Gharyan, small, spontaneous protests erupted in the following days, escalating in response to arrests made by security forces. As in Zintan, protesters looted and burned the facilities of the Revolutionary Committees and Internal Security – in Jadu on 18 February, in Nalut the following day, in Yefren on 20 February – and began seizing small stocks of weapons.[103]

At first, communities in the mountains were divided over the unrest. The two Zintani notables who had shown such courage on the day of the first protests were hardly representative; across the mountains, most protesters in the first days were young men who acted spontaneously. Parents sought to dissuade their sons from protesting; elders tried to convince protesters to calm down to avoid provoking regime repression. But for those involved in attacking the symbols of the security apparatus, there could be no turning back. Fearing arrests, their families began throwing their support behind them. In each town, these small groups began organizing and arming themselves. They were tight-knit communities, and protesters drew on their close social ties with former and active officers in the army and the security services.

In Zintan, a core circle of rebels formed around Mohamed al-Madani, a retired army officer and preacher. Madani began reaching out to army officers and civilians who had joined the rebellion in Nalut, Jadu, Rujban and Yefren. On 20 February, Zintani rebels seized major stocks of ammunition at the Qariyat base, 300 km southeast of Zintan.[104] At that point, protest leaders in Yefren were still undecided over whether they should arm themselves and risk being attacked as armed rebels. The decision was forced upon them the next day, when a group from Zintan arrived to negotiate with Zintani officers at an army base in Yefren to hand over several hundred assault rifles that had just been delivered in preparation for a clampdown.[105] These initial seizures of weapons raised expectations of a violent response, and efforts to seize weapons by negotiating or forcing the handover of army bases now accelerated across the mountains. In Zintan, rebels formed a local council on 21 February, led by Madani, which included civil and military committees. In Nalut, Jadu and Yefren, defence and crisis committees were formed over the following three days. Several of Nalut's and Jadu's army officers joined the uprising in its first days – as one rebel from Nalut explained, 'they were more Nalutis than army officers'.[106]

Throughout this first week, most people in towns across the mountains were undecided over whether to join the rebellion. The situation was one of deep uncertainty. Developments in eastern Libya loomed large in the calculations of actors: by 24 February, the entire east had been liberated, and the regime appeared to be on the verge of collapse. But obtaining reliable information was extremely difficult, and foreign media reports had a major impact. From the very first days of the uprising, allegations that Qadhafi had sent African 'mercenaries' to suppress protests in Benghazi, al-Bayda and Darna circulated, stoking xenophobia and fear of transgressions against the civilian population. These claims were partly true, but also contained much confusion and deliberate disinformation.[107] On 21 February, foreign media relayed reports that Qadhafi's air force was bombing protesters in Tripoli – a claim that later turned out to be false, but was impossible to verify or dismiss at the time.[108]

In the mountains, many towns were rife with rumours that a regime offensive was imminent. The regime's shoot-to-kill response to protests in Tripoli and Benghazi meant that its approach in the mountains would likely be similarly violent. Qadhafi's infamous 22 February speech, in which he called protesters 'rats' and 'cockroaches' that would be hunted down 'house by house', suggested that his response would be brutal. Army officers in active service had to decide whether to side with their community in the event of regime repression, and be court-martialled if the rebellion failed. The security apparatus turned to tribal profiling, fearing that anyone who hailed from a rebellious town was compromised. Already during the first week, Zintani soldiers in the Gharyan-based Sahban Brigade were withdrawn from ammunition depots in the region and disarmed, thereby pushing them towards defection.[109] Initially, the core group in rebels in Zintan was made up of retired officers and civilians; active officers began defecting after a delay of several days. In Jadu and Nalut, a handful of active army officers joined the rebels in the first three days, but others were more hesitant.[110]

Meanwhile, regime emissaries were reaching out to notables and protest leaders with offers of concessions. A Zintani figure sent by Qadhafi's son Saif al-Islam arrived on 19 February offering large sums of money to each Zintani family if the rebels stood down. The offer remained open until military operations started in mid-March.[111] The regime's efforts to co-opt leading figures in rebellious towns raised doubts over who could be trusted, but they were undermined by the evident distrust within the security apparatus towards members of these communities, and its drive to mobilize against the rebellion in neighbouring towns.

In each town, those gauging how to position themselves were warily watching moves in neighbouring communities. Before the first protests erupted, Amazigh community leaders had sought to dissuade restless youth from making any move, out of fear that the regime would mobilize Zintan and other Arab communities against their Amazigh neighbours.[112] Some watched the unfolding upheaval in Zintan in disbelief, but rebel leaders in Amazigh towns linked up with Madani's group in Zintan from the first days of the uprising. Delegations of elders began visiting neighbouring towns to probe their position. A group from al-Qal'a went to see Mashashiya elders in al-Aweiniya as early as 18 February, advocating a common stand against the regime. They encountered scepticism over the rebellion in Zintan – a community which the Mashashiya, just as their Amazigh neighbours, perceived as a regime bulwark – and more deep-seated distrust related to the Mashashiya's land disputes with Amazigh communities. Two further meetings over the following week failed to bring results.[113]

Similar meetings took place in late February and early March between Zintani rebel leaders and the Mashashiya, as well as elders from Nalut and the Si'aan towns of Tiji and Badr. Mashashiya and Si'aan representatives, facing internal disagreements, tried to adopt a balanced position, making clear that they would not join the rebellion, while assuring their neighbours that they meant no harm. But for Nalut and Zintan, this was insufficient. Zintani rebels needed guarantees of safe passage for their wounded through the Mashashiya town of al-Aweiniya to the hospital in Yefren. And Nalut community leaders already knew that the People's Guard had begun registering volunteers and distributing weapons in Tiji and Badr.[114]

By the second week of the rebellion, then, the initial acts of individuals and small groups had triggered a concatenation of moves by the regime and within communities. The determination of the rebels spread fears that the entire community would be attacked, which in turn led to the emergence of dominant positions and new local leadership structures in each town. From 24 February onwards, leading figures in the rebellion began appearing openly on videos to issue statements in the name of their towns. The regime's security apparatus, meanwhile, was hard at work mobilizing support, focusing on mountain communities where the rebellion had failed to take root: the Si'aan, the small town of Haraba, the Arab population of Ruheibat, the Mashashiya towns of Zawiyat al-Bagul and al-Aweiniya, the village of al-Qawalish near Kikla, and the town of al-Asabea. Most of these communities had historically been socioeconomically disadvantaged vis-à-vis their neighbours.

Rumours that the regime was trying to exploit long-standing disputes over land to mobilize such groups against their neighbours promoted the closing of ranks in the emerging revolutionary centres. The fact that the Si'aan and Mashashiya were now collectively perceived as hostile by their rebellious neighbours, in turn, strengthened the case for taking up weapons in support of the regime. In mid-March, the regime began forming auxiliary units for each of the tribal communities in the coastal plain north of Nalut – the Si'aan, Nuwail and Orban – to support the Sahban Brigade within a command structure carrying the ominous name of 'Operations Group for the Cleansing of Nalut'.[115] By this point, communication between communities on opposite sides of the divide had broken down.

*

It is tempting to draw parallels between the conflicts that divided communities in and around the mountains in 2011, and those that erupted a century earlier. To advance its conquest, the Italian colonial power exploited rifts that partly derived from rivalries between local leaders, and partly from long-standing alliances and conflicts between tribes over land rights.[116] In 1916, Zintan and Rujban fighters forcibly displaced the Amazigh population of neighbouring towns, whose leaders had collaborated with the Italians. In 1921, the Zintan, Rujban and Asabea forced the quasi-totality of the mountains' Amazigh population to seek refuge in the Italian-held coastal strip. The Italians mobilized *bandas* (irregular auxiliary forces) from Amazigh communities and the Arab Mashashiya tribe to lead a counteroffensive that drove Zintan and Rujban fighters to the desert valleys south of the mountains, thence to Fezzan, and for some, eventually into exile.[117]

These conflicts remained acutely present in the minds of communities in the mountains well into the twenty-first century. The Qadhafi regime worked to accentuate inter-communal rifts, rather than smooth them over. Qadhafi's policies of nationalizing and redistributing the property of wealthy elites hurt notable Amazigh families rather than neighbouring, more egalitarian Arab communities. Amazigh landowners saw parts of their property awarded to former client tribes such as the Mashashiya, Asabea and Si'aan. Many members of established Amazigh families joined clandestine or exiled opposition groups, and some were executed or saw their houses destroyed in several waves of repression. The regime's denial of Amazigh culture and language exacerbated discontent in Amazigh towns.

Qadhafi's divide-and-rule strategy did not mean that entire communities either supported or opposed the regime. Amazigh towns all had their regime henchmen, and Zintan, while strongly represented in Qadhafi's army and considered by many a pillar of the regime, lost several sons in the 1996 prison massacre in Abu Slim. But the apprehension with which Amazigh activists eyed Zintan and smaller neighbours in February 2011 suggests that particular communities were perceived to have proclivities towards rebellion or loyalism.

The events of February 2011 confounded such expectations. The front lines opening up in the mountains were not simply historical fault lines rising to the surface. The most obvious digression from historical precedents was the fact that Zintan and Amazigh towns found themselves on the same side of the conflict. The uprising in Zintan remains as puzzling today as it was to the town's neighbours at the time. No other tribal constituency in western Libya comparable to Zintan in its integration into the regime's army and praetorian units joined the uprising. And without Zintan entering into the rebellion, Amazigh towns likely would not have risen up in the first place, or the protests would rapidly have petered out.

What had happened? In a situation of collective indecision, small acts prompted the alignment of others – in this case, the key act being the spontaneous decision of a handful of individuals in Zintan to disrupt the 16 February meeting and start a protest. The small minority of rebels in Zintan then rapidly took steps that made it difficult to turn back, and sparked fears that the regime response would target the community as a whole. The regime accelerated the closing of ranks in Zintan by disarming Zintani soldiers in the Gharyan-based brigade. Similar processes then played out in Amazigh towns, where the accelerator was the regime's arming of volunteers among neighbouring communities.

Whether or not the first acts of revolt led to all-out rebellion therefore depended on processes of coordination in which the history of relations among communities did figure, as did actors' expectations of how the regime would react. But at least as important were factors that arose from the moment itself: the mutual uncertainty of actors in the mountains over each other's position, and the viability of open rebellion.

A crucial element in making that assessment was geography – a factor that was unrelated to the degree of social cohesion within a community and to its relations with the regime, but that figured in calculations concerning the threat of violence. Mountain towns west of al-Asabea were natural fortresses, each of them accessible only through its dedicated, meandering access road from the foot of the mountains, as well as the main road connecting the towns on the mountain ridge. During the first week of the uprising, small, spontaneous protests erupted in many towns and cities across western Libya, including communities that later gained the reputation of being regime strongholds. In many cases, the location of these towns meant that rebellion simply was not a viable option, and the regime quickly re-established control. For example, Gharyan, the biggest city in the mountains, boasted large troop contingents and was strategically important due to the fact that the main road connecting Tripoli to southern Libya ran through it. After a week of protests, regime forces conducted a violent clampdown, and then remained solidly in control of the city until August. Only one community among the numerous towns at the foot of the mountains joined the revolution: Hawamid, a small town with close ties to Nalut. When regime forces occupied the town in April, its civilian population fled to the mountains, and subsequently to Tunisia.[118]

Geography also had a bearing on relations between communities and their rebel leaderships. Mutinous towns were dependent on each other to prevent regime forces from ascending the mountains, or advancing westwards from Gharyan. This was not only the logic behind attempts to sway the Mashashiya in their position. It was also the imperative that encouraged close relations between army officers who had defected and civilian rebels from Jadu, Zintan and Rujban from the very beginning. It led to early contacts between rebel leaders from Zintan and Nalut to ensure that Naluti control over the border crossing with Tunisia kept supply and evacuation lines open. Tellingly, the very first operation against advancing regime forces was conducted jointly by rebels from Zintan, Yefren and al-Qal'a to prevent a convoy of the Sahban Brigade from climbing the road to al-Qal'a on 7 March. Rebels from across the mountains came to the help of Zintanis in the first major battle in the mountains on 17 March, repelling the regime's attempt to capture Zintan. After regime forces occupied Kikla and fought their way into Yefren in early April, rebels from Kikla moved to the besieged heights of al-Qal'a and Yefren, forging close ties with fighters from both towns. Once an army convoy in mid-April ascended the mountains to deploy at the small town of al-Haraba, which remained under regime control, fighters from several towns forced the convoy to retreat, and then closed the road leading to Haraba from the foot of the hills, as well as that of the neighbouring Amazigh community of Tamzin, which had also remained immobile throughout the uprising. Finally, when regime forces captured the border crossing in mid-April, a joint effort by rebels from across the mountains wrested back control.[119]

In sum, the threat of violence brought upon entire towns by the initial acts of a small minority, and shaped by the regime's knee-jerk reactions as well as the accidents of geography, prompted communities to close ranks and reach out to some of their neighbours, while growing hostile towards others. What happened during the first month of the uprising was less the surfacing of old structures than a rupture provoked by violence through which new social boundaries were drawn and new political communities were created.

*

Events during the uprising's first month were foundational for political dynamics during and after the revolution, and decisive for the irruption of localism. But they did not yet determine the future shape of relations between revolutionary strongholds in the mountains, nor relations between communities and armed groups. In the five months between the onset of fighting in mid-March and the fall of Tripoli in mid-August, leadership structures, coordinating mechanisms and the makeup of armed groups in the mountains continued to evolve under the impact of conflict dynamics and the growing influence of external actors.

In Yefren and al-Qal'a, whose heights were besieged by regime forces from all sides, small, tight-knit armed groups formed among relatives and friends. They had no centralized leadership, and were cut off from the coordinating structures in the western part of the mountains.[120] In Zintan, which was closest to the front line across the mountains, armed groups emerged on a similar basis. They initially remained informal and deferred to the unrivalled leadership of Mohamed al-Madani, who managed supplies and directed the retired officers and civilians leading these groups.[121] A charismatic leader, al-Madani also commanded wide respect among revolutionaries from Amazigh towns, and had established close ties with some of them. Led by Mukhtar Fernana, another group of Zintani officers, most of whom had been in active service when the uprising erupted and had not been among the revolutionaries of the first hour around al-Madani, formed a 'Western Mountains Military Council' to coordinate between the leadership of each town. But in practice, the body was Zintani-dominated with some participation from Rujban and Jadu, and its role was largely confined to liaising with NATO, which began conducting airstrikes in the mountains in late April. In Jadu, which was removed from the front line and only occasionally exposed to shelling from the foot of the mountains, military officers formed a council that trained the town's civilian fighters, centralized control over weapons and ammunition, and directed operations in close coordination with Zintan.[122] Nalut, which was more exposed, also had a military council that managed supplies and ammunition, but only loosely coordinated the close-knit civilian armed groups that were forming in the town.[123]

From these starting points, in April 2011, various trajectories were conceivable with regard to the formation of armed groups and their integration across the mountains. The evolution of armed groups could have ranged from a consolidation of town-based units under the tight control of local military councils to the formation of rebel groups escaping local control and integrated into national or transnational networks, such as jihadist movements. Relations between forces across the mountains could have evolved towards closer coordination or towards increasing rivalry between local power centres. The fragmented landscape that eventually emerged after the 2011 war was defined by Zintan's increasing alienation from Amazigh towns, and a pre-eminence of local decision-making structures over regional coordination. Relations between armed groups and communities differed from one town to another. The two most important factors shaping this landscape were the short duration of the conflict and the networks of external support to rebel forces.

The patterns of military organization outlined above evolved after revolutionary forces secured control over the border crossing with Tunisia in late April. Weapons shipments via Tunisia increased, provided by Qatar and other regional states, and initially distributed across the mountains by Nalut military council. Greater numbers of fighters from Tripoli, Zawiya and other coastal cities began establishing themselves in Nalut, Jadu, Rujban and Zintan, forming their own armed groups, some of them led by members of the former Libyan Islamic Fighting Group (LIFG), and bringing their own support networks with them. Mohamed al-Madani's death in battle on 1 May removed a crucial link between Zintan and Amazigh towns, and triggered a scramble for leadership in Zintan. Al-Madani's commanders blocked a takeover bid by the Fernana's Western Mountains Military Council. From centralized leadership under al-Madani, Zintan went to collective leadership within a military council headed by another retired officer, Usama Juwaili, formerly a close ally of al-Madani. Distinct armed groups – *saraya*, or battalions – now emerged, whose leaders sat on the council.[124]

In retrospect, revolutionary leaders across Amazigh towns dated the beginning of the decline in their relations with Zintan to al-Madani's disappearance.[125] But important though the role of al-Madani had been, larger dynamics were at work behind the growing rivalries within and between revolutionary strongholds. Instead of centralizing the provision of external assistance, foreign powers supporting the rebels established direct relations with individual actors on the ground. Qatari advisers were present in several towns, including Zintan, but Qatari weapons shipments were channelled primarily to two battalions of Tripolitanian fighters in Nalut, one of which was linked to the networks of the former LIFG. Emirati officers established an operations room in Zintan that worked with Juwaili's and Fernana's councils, and Emirati arms supplies went first and foremost to Zintan. Moreover, as the crucial role of forces in the mountains in any attempt to capture Tripoli became clearer, political players external to the mountains built privileged relations with forces in particular communities and facilitated foreign support for them, drawing them into their struggles with rivals. Qatari supplies to forces in Nalut and Rujban associated with the former LIFG were channelled through a network led by Ali Sallabi and Abdelhakim Belhaj. Weapons flows from the UAE to Zintan were facilitated by Mahmoud Jibril and Aref al-Nayed – a close ally of Jibril's at the time, before the two fell out – via the Zintani businessman Abdelmajid al-Mlegta. Jibril and al-Nayed were hostile towards Sallabi and Belhaj, who, in turn, were critical of what they saw as Jibril's and al-Nayed's secularist tendencies and their ties to the former regime. Mlegta arrived in Zintan in July and established a well-armed battalion from scratch, just weeks before the offensive on Tripoli began.[126]

As revolutionary forces in the mountains went on the offensive, they exacted vengeance on neighbouring communities they held collectively responsible for having supported regime forces. In most cases, the civilian population of these towns had fled before rebel forces captured them and looted or burned many homes. The frenzied descent towards Tripoli then showed that the unity that had characterized relations between revolutionary strongholds in February and March was fading, as the imperative of communal defence began to give way to the lure of spoils and power. Rivalries between the political players from outside the mountains who were sponsoring armed groups there frustrated all attempts to coordinate a joint offensive on Tripoli. On the day the capital fell, Zintani fighters were furious about Belhaj's appearance on al-Jazeera from inside Qadhafi's headquarters, which portrayed him as the leading commander among the forces entering the capital.[127] Forces from across the mountains scrambled for control over strategic locations and key government buildings with groups from Misrata, which were entering the capital from the east. Armed groups mushroomed as commanders from Zintan and other towns formed new militias by recruiting from among the young men in the capital, removing themselves from the decision-making structures of their communities of origin. The chaotic capture of Tripoli prefigured the struggles over influence in the capital over the following years.

Since February, a common threat had forged close relations between communities in the mountains and had led to varying degrees of oversight over armed groups by military councils. With the fall of Tripoli, this threat vanished. A longer conflict in the mountains and closer coordination of external support by the NTC might have led to closer integration between town-based forces; without such coordination, it could have brought their gradual takeover by external actors that controlled access to foreign assistance, such as Islamist networks. But the swiftness of rebel victory in Tripoli – followed two months later by the defeat of remaining regime forces in Sirte and Bani Walid – had the effect of locking in the localism that marked armed groups from the mountains at the time.

The war transformed the communities in the mountains. In revolutionary strongholds, new leaders had emerged through their courage in the first days of the uprising and their military skills in the battles that followed. These leaders, as well as families and friends of those killed in battle, formed a powerful group that defined these towns' new identities as guardians of the revolution. Deep divides ran between them and the neighbouring communities that had failed to rise up.[128] Many of the latter had fled and were prevented from returning, developing a sense of collective victimhood. In the mountains, violence not so much brought the return of old patterns as the formation of a new social order.

Misrata: Rise of a revolutionary bulwark

In contrast to the small towns of the Nafusa Mountains, with their communal history of historical struggles, Misrata was a large and diverse city that had been a melting pot of sedentarizing groups throughout the twentieth century. And yet, the collective struggle in the revolution would transform Misrata into a highly cohesive power centre.

The events in eastern Libya made a deep impact in this port city and trading hub, which had dozens of wealthy merchant families whose commercial interests spanned the country. Many Misratan families had close relatives in Benghazi, to where large numbers of Misratans had moved from the 1920s onwards. On 19 February, Abderrahman al-Sweihli, member of a historically prominent Misratan family, called into al-Jazeera to denounce the violence against protesters in eastern Libya, and declared that the blood of Libyans was a 'red line' that could not be crossed.[129] That evening, the first protests erupted in Misrata, which were relatively small, including perhaps a few hundred demonstrators. Security forces shot and killed one protester, causing over a thousand people to turn out to his funeral the following day, braving the threat of further killings, and eventually torching facilities of the security services.[130]

Arrests prompted the protests to swell further, and on 21 February, a crowd of several hundred people seized a small number of light weapons at an army base without resistance from the two dozen under-armed officers at the base.[131] The next day, hundreds of protesters assembled at the courthouse in central Misrata, where a group of judges, prosecutors and lawyers formed a judicial committee to oversee the city's administration.[132] Regime forces led by the Misrata-based Hamza Brigade killed dozens of protesters over the following three days, and arrested scores. Representatives of the rebels negotiated the withdrawal of the Hamza Brigade from the city centre and its base to the air force base south of the city.

From 25 February to 6 March, central Misrata was left to rebel control. Retired army officers and others who had defected, led by Salem Jha and Salah Badi, formed a military committee and began preparing the defence against the expected return of regime forces. Across the city, unarmed young men in each neighbourhood began forming small groups and controlling movements through their areas. Small bands of poorly armed rebels waged attacks on the air force base to seize weapons and ammunition. Meanwhile, senior regime figures reached out to prominent Misratans, among them Sweihli, trying to woo them into persuading the rebels to stand down.

On 6 March, a large contingent of the Hamza Brigade moved into the city centre and was beaten back by rebels guided by the military committee, who were vastly outgunned, but able to exploit the element of surprise.[133] This improbable military success boosted morale among the rebels, and shored up support for their emerging leadership. It also meant that military defence was the only way forward. Locals expected Qadhafi's response to be violent and indiscriminate, even more so given that regime forces were using Grad rockets, tanks and vehicle-mounted anti-aircraft guns in their recapture of Zawiya, between 1 and 9 March.[134] In early March, Misratans began hearing of the recruitment of volunteers for Qadhafi's forces in Tawargha, a neighbouring community of dark-skinned descendants of slaves who were socio-economically disadvantaged vis-à-vis Misratans.[135] Rumours were spreading that mercenaries recruited by Qadhafi were raping women in rebellious towns.[136] Fear of collective retaliation galvanized Misratan rebels.

As in the case of the mountains, geography played an important role in making rebellion a viable option in Misrata. The port, in the city's east, offered a lifeline for the rebels. As they were preparing for another regime onslaught, according to Salem Jha, an army officer who had defected and had emerged as a leading figure in the military committee and later Misrata's Military Council, 'we knew well that the port was our only hope. If the port fell, then Misrata would fall with it.'[137] Defending the port was a strategic priority for the military council.

The battle for Misrata began in earnest on 16 March, with regime forces pushing into the city from three directions, and occupying Tripoli Street in the city centre. The forces were led by the 32nd Reinforced Brigade, the largest and best-equipped security brigade, headed by Qadhafi's son Khamis. Snipers took positions along Tripoli Street, several of them mercenaries from South American and Eastern European countries. The offensive was accompanied by a wave of arrests in areas of the city that were under regime control. Navy ships began blockading the port, though their blockade was broken on 23 March with the onset of NATO airstrikes in Misrata. Over the following weeks, NATO struck at the supply lines of regime forces, but was otherwise reluctant to target positions in the densely populated city centre. Until early May, Misrata would remain besieged, partially occupied, and the site of the heaviest street fighting of the war.

This was the formative period for Misrata's armed groups, which emerged spontaneously, without coordination from the military council. In most cases, these groups were forming on the basis of individual neighbourhoods amid networks of friends and relatives. Businessmen from their families or neighbourhoods supplied funds, vehicles and other assets, and began organizing shipments of weapons, food and medicine by boat from Benghazi, since Misrata was wholly surrounded and cut off from supplies. As a result, close relations formed from the outset between members of Misrata's merchant elite and the developing armed groups.[138] On the battlefield, leaders emerged through displays of bravery and fighting skills. According to Brian McQuinn, who conducted detailed research among Misratan combatants during and after the war, a typical fighting unit during this phase of the war would comprise around thirty to fifty combatants, developing out of an initial nucleus of three to five people. Decision-making was generally by consensus, and group membership stabilized as the conflict raged on, with group members forging close bonds.[139]

Misratan revolutionaries dislodged Qadhafi's forces from Tripoli Street by late April, and seized the air force base on 11 May. The priority now lay in pushing regime troops away from the city, out of artillery range. Static front lines were established, and the small fighting groups merged into larger ones: the revolutionary battalions. Along each front line – east, west and south – the leaders of these groups coordinated closely with each other. The size of the battalions also grew due to an exponential increase in recruits, now that revolutionary forces were moving on the offensive. By the end of the war, Misrata's armed groups comprised around 40,000 members, the most formidable military force in post-Qadhafi Libya.[140]

Misratan groups established a major presence in Tripoli as the capital fell, and began arresting former regime officials and suspected members of Qadhafi's forces. They devastated Tawargha and warned its residents never to return, alleging that Tawarghans had enrolled in Qadhafi's forces in large numbers, and had raped Misratan women. Eventually, they vanquished the remnants of Qadhafi's forces in his hometown of Sirte. Qadhafi himself was captured and killed by Misratan fighters, and his body put on public display for three days in a Misratan meat locker. In a city of 500,000, the war had claimed more than 1,300 victims.[141] Misrata's armed groups would become notorious for their brutal persecution of those they alleged had participated in the regime's onslaught on their city.

*

Whether during or after the war, Misrata's revolutionary leaders invariably described their city as united in the fight against Qadhafi. With the appearance of Misrata's armed groups and political figures as key players in post-revolutionary politics, Libyan and foreign observers frequently saw Misrata as a unitary actor. But the emergence of Misrata as a revolutionary bulwark occurred through the violent exclusion of groups that were perceived as contradicting the city's new identity.

Relations between Misrata's elite and the regime had been complex and often difficult – it could hardly have been otherwise with as fickle and ruthless a dictator as Qadhafi – but they had been extensive. Prominent members of the city's notable families had been persecuted after 1969, and the regime's nationalization and expropriation measures severely hurt Misrata's capitalists. But in several cases, representatives of these families reconciled with the regime: Abderrahman al-Sweihli, for example, had been active in the exiled opposition until his return in 1988; but his brother Hamdi subsequently rose to become chief of staff of the Navy, a position he would retain throughout the 2011 war. Several members of the Muntasser family – historical rivals of the Sweihlis for political pre-eminence in Misrata – were imprisoned or exiled under Qadhafi, and one member was even assassinated by Qadhafi's agents in Beirut, in 1980; but Omar al-Muntasser held leading positions in the oil sector and in government throughout the 1970s and 1980s. Indeed, Qadhafi's cabinets always included several Misratan figures.[142] However, with the exception of a number of fighter pilots – Misrata's air force base also boasted an associated academy – Misratans were weakly represented in the military and security services. In a city that prided itself on its thriving businesses, low-paid jobs in the army were generally considered unattractive.

With the timid economic liberalization measures that were adopted from the late 1980s onwards, Misratan businessmen associated themselves informally with regime figures for political protection. A Misratan school friend of Qadhafi's, Ali Dabeiba, was central in connecting the city's business elite with the regime. In the final years of Qadhafi's rule, Dabeiba oversaw a multibillion dollar infrastructure investment programme that offered vast opportunities for corruption. As a senior regime figure from Misrata and long-standing acquaintance of Dabeiba remarked, 'He was always generous with his stolen money, he shared it widely in Misrata.'[143]

Many Misratan businessmen were quick to support the revolution, whether out of conviction, obligation towards their relatives and neighbours, or opportunism. While there were little weapons and ammunition the rebels could seize in the first weeks of the uprising, the collective support of the business elite allowed Misratan fighters to arm themselves by buying weapons in Benghazi. Dabeiba was abroad when the revolution erupted and – after a period of hesitation – began disbursing substantial funds to back the struggle together with his nephew Abdelhamid, among other things sponsoring their own battalion. The Dabeibas thereby protected their interests, and would re-emerge as influential players behind the scenes in post-revolutionary Misrata. Only a handful of prominent Misratans who had been at the core of the regime and failed to jump ship fled the country.[144] Hamdi al-Sweihli remained Navy chief of staff until the regime fell, and unlike many other officials of comparable rank was not imprisoned, due to his brother's revolutionary credentials. After the revolution, Misratan politicians would take the lead in demanding the exclusion of former regime officials from political life, conveniently sweeping their own past association with the regime under the carpet. The post-revolutionary leadership of the city was largely formed of established businessmen, professionals and notables who had acquired revolutionary legitimacy through their actions and material support.

The city's social fabric, however, was deeply affected by the conflict. An estimated 200,000 of the city's population of 500,000 fled during the war, to Tripoli, Sirte, Bani Walid or elsewhere, many of them from neighbourhoods that were under regime control.[145] The accidents of territorial control – with the city centre held by the rebels, and several suburban areas controlled by the regime – sparked rifts along community lines in the city.

Misratans had long categorized themselves into different ethnic and tribal components, the main distinction being between families of Turkish or Circassian origin, and members of Arab tribes.[146] Intermarriage and business relations had been extensive across these categories, forming a dense, integrated social fabric.[147] But given that specific areas of the city were dominated by particular tribal constituencies, patterns of territorial control in 2011 impacted Misrata's social components differently. Those most numerous to flee the city were from formerly semi-nomadic tribes such as the Maadan, who had largely settled in the suburbs, most of which were now controlled by the regime. Because the Maadan had also settled in Sirte, where some had been recruited into a Maadan unit to fight for Qadhafi, they came to be collectively suspected of being regime loyalists. Unlike the Maadan, Warfalla were spread across the city, but they faced similar suspicions due to their ties with the supposed loyalist stronghold of Bani Walid. While there were some prominent Warfalla in Misrata's revolutionary battalions, many members of the community had fled.[148]

After the war, those who left were eyed with suspicion, and often hostility, by neighbours who had supported the revolution, and in several neighbourhoods, local notables formed committees to mediate between returnees and their neighbours.[149] However, many families who had fled the city did not return, fearful that they would be imprisoned or face retribution for their alleged support for the regime.[150] Many of their houses had been looted and burned when revolutionary forces seized the area, or were subsequently reoccupied by others.[151] The Maadan were forcibly displaced from two entire neighbourhoods in which they had previously predominated, and revolutionary leaders encouraged their clients to occupy their land, claiming Qadhafi had illegally allocated it to them.[152]

Most of my Misratan interlocutors glossed over these divides, and many emphasized that the city was united in its support for the revolution. When the displaced came up, they were often described as being 'not originally from Misrata' or 'not real Misratans'. The overall effect of these developments was to politicize communal identities, and render them salient. A Maadan notable later recalled:

> Mohamed [he points to his son] was born in 1991. Before the war, he had barely heard about the Maadan, about bedouins and Karaghla and Awlad Sheikh. But because of all the discrimination against the Maadan, we became more aware of our shared interests.[153]

Misratan unity and cohesion, therefore, was not a condition for the city's emergence as a revolutionary bulwark. Rather, unity in support for the revolution was forged through the conflict, in tight-knit networks straddling armed groups, families and influential businessmen, and in part by excluding a significant proportion of the city's population. The lines along which the new Misratan revolutionary identity included or excluded particular families were partly drawn by the accidents of territorial control.

The rebellion itself had erupted not because of Misrata's political marginalization, but in spite of the close ties between its business elite and the regime. It had been provoked by events in eastern Libya and the Nafusa Mountains, as relayed by the international media, and by the death of a protester during the first small demonstration. The emergence of a rebel leadership in the first few days, in a situation in which regime collapse appeared to be imminent, set the direction: for those involved in the rebellion, military defence was the only way forward – and given the city's access to a port, rebellion was also a viable option in the calculations of others. The example of the regime's recapture of Zawiya and rumours concerning the indiscriminate threat of transgressions by regime forces then had a galvanizing effect. Misrata's rise as a political and military power centre defined by a revolutionary identity was a contingent outcome of conflict dynamics.

Bani Walid: Loyalism and victimization

From the beginning of the uprising, a struggle over the allegiance of members of the Warfalla began. Though no official figures exist, the Warfalla are considered Libya's largest tribe, and most estimates, all of them of doubtful reliability, range around 1 million members. In the media coverage of the revolution's first weeks, it was assumed that tribes such as the Warfalla would adopt a common position as a community – despite the fact that most Warfalla had been living for several generations in the cities of Tripoli, Benghazi, Misrata and Sabha, and had no political ties to elders in Bani Walid, the tribe's home and a town of 80,000. On 20 February, an anonymous person calling himself Akram al-Warfalli phoned into al-Jazeera, presenting himself as a 'leading tribal representative' of the Warfalla, and telling Qadhafi to leave the country, in a quote that was widely spread by the media and experts as suggesting that the tribe had defected.[154] Two days later, Aref al-Nayed – a prominent businessman and scholar who had spent many years abroad and lacked strong ties to Bani Walid – went on Sky News posing as a 'Warfalla tribal spokesman', and claiming that 'Warfalla completely renounces Qadhafi ... and asks all sons and daughters to enter into full rebellion'.[155]

On the ground, the reality was entirely different. On 20 February, around three dozen people came out to demonstrate in Bani Walid, many of them former prisoners or family members of those arrested in the wave of repression following the 1993 coup plot. Members of Bani Walid's Popular Social Leadership (PSL) engaged with the protesters, discussing their demands for political reforms and an end to the use of force against demonstrators in eastern Libya.[156] The following day, after security forces had set up several checkpoints across the town, a handful of activists torched the seat of the Revolutionary Committees in the dead of night. But the momentum stopped there. As a sympathizer of the protesters recalled, 'if Jibran [the head of a local paramilitary force] had given orders to shoot or arrest, the protests would have escalated. That way, they simply petered out.'[157] On 3 March, around fifty people came out into the open again, recording a video statement in which they declared their allegiance to the NTC in Benghazi. Under pressure from the PSL and the security services, they then stopped mobilizing in public, and moved underground.[158] Many saw their attempts as dangerous and naïve: 'Bani Walid is exposed in the desert and cannot be easily defended. There were no weapons here, and we have no port. We had no way of moving against the regime,' one tribal politician remarked.[159] Even if this may partly be an *ex post facto* rationalization of the events in February 2011, the geography certainly did play a role.[160]

In the meantime, regime officials had started working to ensure Bani Walid's loyalty. The recruitment of volunteers for Qadhafi's forces had begun in Bani Walid as early as 21 February. Volunteers were given cars and weapons, promised money and integrated into Warfalla units of the People's Guard or attached to Jibran Hussein's *jahfal*, a paramilitary regime protection unit based in Bani Walid that had enforced much of the repression of the 1990s.[161] After the war, tribal elders in Bani Walid often claimed that they had adopted a position of neutrality, telling those who supported the revolution to leave for the Nafusa Mountains, and others to go and join Qadhafi's forces, but refrain from sowing internal conflict among Warfalla in Bani Walid.

In fact, Bani Walid as a community was rapidly drawn into the loyalist camp. Part of the *jahfal* was deployed to Zawiya in early March, where a senior officer from Bani Walid was killed. Another part led the column of regime forces that moved towards Benghazi in mid-March, and four of its members, including Jibran Hussein himself, were killed in the French airstrikes that stopped the convoy on Benghazi's outskirts, on 19 March. These deaths buttressed support for the regime line that Libya was facing a foreign conspiracy, and created a constituency of people who saw regime forces as fighting against foreign domination, akin to the anti-colonial resistance of their forefathers. A big crowd attended Jibran Hussein's funeral in Bani Walid, and swore revenge. Those killed were henceforth referred to as 'martyrs', implying that their struggle was legitimate, even sacred. Mobilizing support for the revolution became much more difficult, since it risked offending their families.[162]

The initial military losses therefore rapidly narrowed down available choices in Bani Walid. The regime's continuing efforts did the rest. According to several former revolutionaries, Warfalla regime figures gave cash and vehicles to a number of tribal notables to buy their loyalty.[163] As an indication of how much importance the regime accorded to courting the tribe's loyalties, two dignitaries from Bani Walid, Ali al-Ahwal and Mohamed al-Barghuthi, acted as the chairman and his deputy at the Conference of Libyan Tribes in Tripoli, which the regime staged in May 2011 to rally tribal support.

By 28 May, when Bani Walid's revolutionaries made their final attempt to mobilize, the regime was firmly in control of the town, and few continued to harbour sympathies for the rebels. Around 150 people staged a demonstration that day, and were scattered by gunfire from elements of the *jahfal* and local volunteers. One protester was killed, as was Khalifa Hussein Jibran, who had succeeded his brother as head of the *jahfal*. Twelve protesters, who likely carried some weapons, sought refuge in a nearby house, where regime forces killed them. Shocked, other revolutionaries – many of them close friends and relatives of the victims – hurriedly escaped from Bani Walid and fled to Zintan. Those who did not were arrested. The incident cut a deep rift through Bani Walid. As the brother of one of the victims recalled, 'I would never have imagined that members of our own tribe could turn on us.'[164]

Among those who fled was Mbarek al-Futmani, a merchant and religious sheikh who had played a prominent role in Bani Walid's PSL, but whose brother and son were killed on 28 May. Futmani became Bani Walid's NTC representative, and together with other escapees formed the Martyrs of 28 May Battalion, as well as a local and military council, while preparing for the military capture of the town. Mohamed Bashir Tuti, one of three leaders of the 1993 coup plot to have escaped abroad, linked up with the group and became another leading figure. When Tripoli fell, dozens of men from Bani Walid who had been imprisoned in the capital were freed, and many joined the 28 May Battalion.[165]

In late August, remnants of Qadhafi's forces retreated to Bani Walid, turning it into the regime's last stronghold along with Sirte. The town's revolutionaries claimed that regime forces had taken Bani Walid hostage. In fact, the revolutionaries lacked support in the town, and Warfalla were a minor component of the revolutionary forces massing around Bani Walid. Inside the beleaguered town, many viewed the prospect of outside forces entering with apprehension. Fighters from Bani Walid returning from Qadhafi's defeated army with their weapons and cars, and people implicated in the regime's crimes in Bani Walid, had an obvious interest in preventing the entry of revolutionary forces.[166] But opposition went far beyond these groups; by this time, revolutionary discourse often collectively stigmatized the Warfalla as loyalists, provoking defiance in Bani Walid. In negotiations with tribal elders over the town's surrender, Futmani and Tuti demanded that the Local and Military Councils take control. But the takeover of a body formed outside the town by a small minority that harboured a deep-seated desire for revenge was not a proposition that could find acceptance in Bani Walid. Dozens of young men who had not previously joined Qadhafi's forces took up weapons to resist the revolutionary armed groups, which eventually captured the town after several weeks of fighting in September and October 2011.[167]

In Bani Walid, the violent takeover was widely perceived as a humiliation, and shaped majority opinion towards the revolution as synonymous with Bani Walid's defeat and marginalization. Revolutionary battalions from Tripoli, Zawiya and elsewhere had engaged in rampant looting during their capture of Bani Walid, and the 28 May Battalion began arresting suspects in regime crimes. In Tripoli, revolutionary battalions from Misrata and the capital itself were searching for alleged accomplices in the regime's counter-insurgency and repression, and were seizing dozens of Warfalla. Bani Walid had lost much of its political elite, as its top regime figures had been killed, or imprisoned, or had fled abroad.

Given their numerical weakness and lack of acceptance in Bani Walid, the revolutionaries soon felt compelled to call in external support. When they did, in late November, former fighters in Qadhafi's forces and other armed locals attacked the armed group that had come in support of the 28 May Battalion from Tripoli's Suq al-Jum'a area, killing thirteen of them and taking several prisoners. Armed groups from Suq al-Jum'a retaliated by randomly kidnapping Warfalla in Tripoli, and Futmani accused a rival armed group from Bani Walid led by Salem al-Waer, another one of the 1993 coup plotters who had recently returned from exile, of being behind the fighting. Waer was forming his group in Tripoli, calling it the Warfalla 1993 Battalion in reference to the coup plot. He accepted the revolutionary order, but also reached out to Bani Walid elders who were opposed to the revolutionaries then trying to dominate the town.[168] As a result, the 28 May Battalion became even more isolated. In January 2012, after yet another arrest, armed locals attacked the 28 May Battalion's base and forcibly ejected the battalion as well as the local and military council from the town.[169] The Libyan media – and many international outlets – uncritically espoused the revolutionaries' version that regime loyalists had ousted government forces and raised Qadhafi's green flag, further adding to the stigma attached to the community.[170]

In place of the NTC-accredited Local Council, Bani Walid tribal figures formed the Social Council of Warfalla Tribes, which neither in its name nor in its insignia made any nod to the new order. Rather than using the monarchy-era tricolour that was Libya's new official standard and was adopted by all newly formed councils and armed groups, the Social Council's logo was a pale green. As the PSL, the Social Council's membership structure was based on the Warfalla's five sections.[171] In fact, many Social Council members had previously been in the PSL. Its chairman, Mohamed al-Barghuthi, a prominent religious sheikh, had been key in mobilizing support for the regime during the war, and had acted as the deputy chairman of Qadhafi's Conference of Libyan Tribes in May 2011.

But the council could not be reduced to supporters of the former regime. Barghuthi's deputy Salem al-Ahmar had been imprisoned for five years in the post-1993 wave of repression, and had initially sympathized with the revolutionaries.[172] Waer, who gained the Council's backing to establish his Warfalla 1993 Battalion in Bani Walid, had been among the coup plotters of 1993, and had only just returned from exile. By contrast, the head of the Local Council and the 28 May Battalion, Mbarek al-Futmani, had been head of a section in the Bani Walid PSL – 'and then he suddenly turns into a revolutionary and calls us *azlam* [regime stooges]. Well, what is he?' as one local expressed a widely shared sentiment.[173]

What united supporters of the Social Council was their rejection of the new order, in which Bani Walid was collectively stigmatized, politically marginalized and had been militarily humiliated by armed groups from other cities, while dozens of its sons languished in the prisons of these same groups. The council reached out to other ostracized constituencies, holding two Conferences of Libyan Tribes in May and June 2012 to denounce their political exclusion, the arbitrary reign of armed groups, and the forced displacement of several communities. In these meetings, Libya's new tricolour flag was nowhere to be seen.

At this point, support for the Social Council's position was considerable in Bani Walid, but by no means unanimous. To foment discontent over the council's confrontational approach to the new authorities, the Local Council withheld the resources it received from the Tripoli government, such as medical supplies, after council members were thrown out of Bani Walid and unable to return. And, indeed, a considerable fraction of Bani Walid's professional and social elite advocated a middle course between the revolutionary hard-liners of the 28 May Battalion, and the isolationists of the Social Council. It was not least lobbying from this current that pushed the Social Council to allow preparations for the July 2012 GNC elections to proceed in Bani Walid. The electoral result then offered proof of the Social Council's influence: the two winning candidates had been agreed upon within the Council, and voting recommendations handed down to families within each tribe.[174] One of Bani Walid's two elected GNC members was Salem al-Ahmar, the council's deputy chairman.

Then, the crisis between the Social Council and the revolutionary camp came to a head. In Bani Walid, former fighters in Qadhafi's forces had linked up with other armed locals in a number of small, informal armed groups to police and defend the town's territory. Waer's 1993 battalion was only one among several armed formations. In July, such groups seized five Misratans on roads near Bani Walid. While the Social Council sought to swap the hostages against Bani Walid prisoners held in Misrata, it was not in control of the armed groups that held them.[175] One of the five hostages, Omran Shaaban, had been among Qadhafi's captors in Sirte. He was injured during his capture by Bani Walid fighters and died of his wounds shortly after being released in late September.

In the GNC, the revolutionary camp mobilized to authorize military action against Bani Walid, ostensibly to arrest the suspects in his abduction and injury, as well as other suspects allegedly hiding in Bani Walid. Armed groups from Misrata, Zawiya, Gharyan and other towns massed around Bani Walid, joined by parts of the 28 May Battalion, and began attacking before the deadline set in the GNC decision expired. After major shelling, they captured Bani Walid yet again, driving out the bulk of the civilian population, then engaging in looting and hoisting the picture of Ramadhan al-Sweihli, a Misratan chieftain who had been killed in Bani Walid during a conflict with Warfalla leader Abdelnabi Belkheir in 1920. The historical symbolism was all the more offensive as a scion of the Sweihli family, Abderrahman, had led political mobilization for the Bani Walid operation in Misrata and the GNC. Dozens of men from Bani Walid were arrested, among them Barghuthi. Many Social Council members fled.

Resistance and renewed humiliation united Bani Walid. To defend their town, former revolutionaries joined with former fighters in Qadhafi's forces; teenagers who had not fought before took up weapons, as did old men. Having suffered such deep divides for the past two decades, Bani Walid became very nearly united in enmity towards its oppressors. But this unity required the exclusion of a minority. For several hundred families associated with those who supported the second military capture of Bani Walid, this would mean exile in Tripoli.

*

Clearly, there was no 'Warfalla position' during the 2011 war, despite the propaganda from revolutionaries and the regime alike. To the extent that Bani Walid had a position, it was produced by the conflict, not constitutive of it. There was no collective decision-making at the beginning of the conflict; rather, the regime's recruitment of volunteers and the death of several at the hands of Western airstrikes during the first weeks set the path that eventually led to Bani Walid's emergence as a loyalist stronghold. Who knows what direction events in the town might have taken, had the *jahfal* responded to the first protests with deadly force?

Of course, there were also structural reasons why Bani Walid was likely to tilt towards the regime in the conflict. The town's population depended on public sector employment to a much greater extent than a commercial centre such as Misrata. The clientelist networks spreading out from Tripoli had penetrated the community deeply. At the apex of these networks were two ministers who hailed from Bani Walid. Ma'tuq Mohamed Ma'tuq, who since the late 1980s had held various positions as minister for labour, education and infrastructure, had promoted students from Bani Walid in the award of scholarships to study abroad, which explained not least the preponderance of Warfalla in the diplomatic service by the time of the revolution. Omran Bukra'a had headed the electricity utility as well as its line ministry, and had placed graduates from Bani Walid's Electrotechnical Academy in these bodies and their foreign contractors.[176] Then, there were the army and the security services, which had extensively recruited in Bani Walid until 1993. The networks that linked regime figures to Bani Walid families had much to lose from the political upheaval. Equally significant was the fact that Bani Walid had no businessmen of note who could finance the revolutionary effort with their private means. Bani Walid's dependence on the state, however, did not endow it with a corporate interest that made the town choose sides in 2011. Following the repression of the 1990s, the clientelist networks covered a deeply divided community.

In the end, what really united Bani Walid, or at least a majority there, was its collective stigmatization and victimization by the victors. Defiance in the face of defeat and humiliation explains the paradoxical attachment of many in the town to a regime that had inflicted deep wounds on the community through its sadistic methods of repression. (This defiance, and the denial of local responsibility in the course of events, also made it extremely difficult for me to uncover the facts of 2011, particularly as they pertained to the engagement of the town's notables and young men in the regime's war effort.)

It was not because but in spite of the Social Council's leadership that the community closed ranks. In the words of one local observer, in addition to being internally divided, the Council was 'permeated by the feeling of defeat'.[177] Many members of the Council had emerged as tribal politicians during the sordid clampdown of the 1990s, when the coup plotters' families were collectively punished and humiliated by their own neighbours and tribesmen. As a local notable recalled, the regime had set to work slowly following the 1993 plot, watching parts of the community rise up, then empowering others to crush them:

> People couldn't believe that this was possible, especially in such strong a tribal society as Bani Walid. But the regime triumphed. It picked those who excelled in carrying out its orders against their own people, and promoted them.[178]

Those Social Council members who were in the PSL at the time had been petty accomplices or bystanders in these acts; their ringleaders fled abroad or were captured during the revolution, leaving behind a decapitated community riven by past injuries. Significantly, however, the divides of 2012 were not those of 1999. As the examples of Salem al-Ahmar, Salem al-Waer and Mbarek al-Futmani show, some victims found themselves siding with those who had been silent over their persecution, while on the other side of the rift, some perpetrators joined their former victims.

Like those of 1993–99, the rifts of 2011–12 could not be explained in terms of Bani Walid's tribal structure. Historically, political competition in Bani Walid had frequently played out between the five sections of the Warfalla, with politicians mobilizing support by promising benefits to tribes in their respective section, or to allies who vowed to deliver their own section. A typical pattern had been that of three sections uniting to outbid two others, but at times, sections had also split during the bargaining process. Competition on the basis of sections had defined the parliamentary elections of the monarchy – in 1952, armed members of three sections had attacked local government buildings after their candidate lost against that of the two other sections. During the Qadhafi era, representatives of the sections vied for influence within the five-member popular committees, each of which, under an unwritten rule, included one member for each section.[179] These rivalries underlined the role of the tribe as a political arena. Some even argued that the tribes did not really exist, except as a sentiment political entrepreneurs instrumentalized when competing for office and contracts.[180]

The coup plotters of 1993, however, came from all sections, and in all but one section were officers executed and their houses razed. The victims of 28 May were also spread across the five sections. The rifts of 2011 went through tribes and extended families. As one sympathizer of the revolutionaries said, 'I still don't know how my cousin and close friend, who I used to sit and joke with, suddenly became my enemy.'[181] Several local politicians ended up longing for the return of tribal politics along sectional lines to overcome the divide that had forced the exile of the minority of revolutionary hard-liners.[182]

Bani Walid's position in the conflict, just as the rifts that cut through the town, was less the reflection of political structures than the outcome of processes driven by violence, through which old divisions were overcome, and new ones produced. Some of the events that shaped these processes were heavily influenced by chance: who killed or chose not to; who was killed or escaped. Once the path had been set, Bani Walid eventually became the counter-revolutionary stronghold others made it to be, despite all the divisions that ran through it.

Tobruk: Revolution at the margins

On 17 February, under the impact of the previous day's events in Benghazi and al-Bayda, a few dozen young men came out to protest in Tobruk. Representatives of the city's PSL, including its head at the time, Omar Rashwan, met with the protesters at the house of a local notable, and asked them to go home – in vain. Later that night, armed regime supporters confronted the protesters and staged a large, televised demonstration in the town's main square. Clashes ensued, and internal security arrested several protesters. The next day, Tobruk's PSL met to declare its loyalty to the regime and denounce foreign attempts to destabilize Libya.[183] But the tribal figures were rapidly overtaken by events. A few hours later, larger numbers of demonstrators assembled on the main square, some of them armed with hunting rifles. Two protesters and a policeman were killed in altercations as the protesters torched the seat of the Revolutionary Committees and occupied the police station and criminal investigations department, seizing small amounts of weapons.[184] Contrary to events in Benghazi, al-Bayda and Darna, regime forces in Tobruk undertook no serious efforts to suppress the unrest. Further attempts by PSL representatives to reason with the protesters also failed. Over the following days, the protesters swelled to several hundred people who kept Tobruk's main square permanently occupied.

Meanwhile, military officers in Tobruk assessed the difficult choices before them. The commander of Tobruk military region was Gen. Suleiman Mahmoud, a long-standing companion of Qadhafi who had recently fallen out with him. Mahmoud, a member of the local Obeidat tribe, ordered the Tobruk-based Omar al-Mukhtar Brigade not to shoot at the protesters, arguing that the brigade was largely composed of locals and many of its members might sympathize with the protesters, whereas killings would provoke feuds that could draw in the brigade. An officer in the brigade later argued that a shooting order would have provoked defections: 'Qadhafi thought that he had formed this brigade from local tribes that were loyal to him, but it turned out they were more loyal to their tribesmen.'[185] Nevertheless, the brigade's commander and several of its senior officers remained staunchly loyal to the regime throughout the first week.

On 18 February, Tripoli notified Tobruk commanders that troops would be airlifted to the city to restore order. Mahmoud agreed with the commander of the local air base, Saqr al-Jarushi, on feigning a fault in the runway lighting. Both officers thereby treaded a thin line between executing orders and defecting. According to Mahmoud, the same day, Qadhafi's secretary instructed him and two other Obeidat officers – among them Abdelfattah Younes, the interior minister who was in Benghazi at the time – to lead an offensive of Obeidat forces against neighbouring Darna. By this time, Darna had already escaped regime control. It had not only long been a stronghold of jihadi underground networks, but also differed in its social makeup from surrounding areas, in that the majority of its population traced its origins to families that had come from western Libya several hundred years ago. Mahmoud recalls that he discussed the matter with several Obeidat elders from Tobruk and al-Qubba, all of whom rejected the regime's plans, pointing to the Obeidat's extensive social relations and intermarriage with Darna families. He then informed Younes of their collective refusal.[186]

In sabotaging the regime's efforts to put down the uprising, Mahmoud had the backing of several local officers. On the evening of 20 February, as the battle over the base of the Fadhil Bu Omar Brigade was raging in Benghazi, Mahmoud announced his defection to the rebels in Tobruk's principal mosque, amid a crowd that included several tribal leaders and army officers.[187] At this point, the commander of Tobruk's security brigade as well as several of its officers remained loyal; the commander of the air base continued to cooperate with Tripoli's orders; and a number of tribal figures were continuing to rally support for the regime. Jarushi thwarted an attempt by protesters to seize the air base, and only under heavy pressure from rebelling officers prevented reinforcements from landing in Tobruk. But given the inexorable drift towards revolution in Cyrenaica with the fall of the Fadhil Bu Omar base in Benghazi and Abdelfattah Younes' defection on 22 February, Tobruk's remaining loyalists soon lost hope. Faced with the choice of defecting or handing over the air base to an officer who had defected, Jarushi chose the latter. The commander of the Omar al-Mukhtar Brigade fled to Tripoli on 23 February along with the brigade's Qadhadhfa officers, taking with them whatever weapons they could load on their vehicles, after blowing up the brigade's ammunition storage.[188]

Thereafter, the situation in Tobruk stabilized, and the social order remained largely untouched. Over the next two weeks, local revolutionaries formed committees to run the city's affairs and control the border crossing with Egypt – with officers such as Mahmoud playing a leading role. 'The first thing we did was to secure the civil registry office, to make sure it wouldn't be attacked and citizenship documents destroyed,' one local professional who participated in these efforts recalled.[189] This was seen as critical because around a third of Tobruk's population of 180,000 were Egyptian citizens – most of them members of the Awlad Ali tribe – who during the 1970s and 1980s had obtained the second-rate 'Arab citizenship' granted by Qadhafi to supposed 'returnees from exile'.[190] Locals derogatively called them 'Sad Shin', an abbreviation for 'eastern Sahara', the category employed by the Qadhafi regime to extend 'Arab citizenship' to them. Having originally been summoned by Qadhafi in the 1970s to fill the ranks of a 'Desert Brigade' with poor recruits who could be easily exploited, these groups had a comparatively low social status. They also formed the bulk of the Omar al-Mukhtar Brigade's rank and file.[191] Tobruk's revolutionaries, then, made sure that social hierarchies were not challenged by political turmoil.

More generally, Tobruk was shielded from revolutionary upheaval. From 23 February onwards, the city's geographical isolation at the Egyptian border, surrounded by the sea and vast expanses of desert, and the fact that its air base was under rebel control, meant that the city faced no serious threat from loyalist forces anymore, short of a major ground offensive by the regime from western Libya. While Qadhafi's counteroffensive eastwards in mid-March sent jitters through Cyrenaica, the threat vanished after the onset of foreign airstrikes on 19 March. In Benghazi, al-Bayda and Darna, hundreds had been killed in clashes with regime forces, and the rebels had seized control over substantial arsenals. In Tobruk, however, the revolution had only claimed two victims, and senior officers had shaped events and retained control of military infrastructure. Moreover, contrary to Benghazi and Darna, Tobruk had no dark history of regime repression that would have created a hard core of fervent and vengeful revolutionaries.

Tobruk rapidly fell back into its backwater status. Its involvement in – and transformation through – the revolution was limited. Out of 270 military officers from Tobruk, only four went to fight Qadhafi's forces at the front.[192] Several dozen young men from Tobruk entered the revolutionary struggle, but most of them joined groups from Darna, al-Bayda and Benghazi to do so. As a result, no powerful local armed groups emerged after these fighters returned. Many joined a border guard unit that was created as part of the Omar al-Mukhtar Brigade.[193] State security institutions in the city lost much of their power, since they were no longer backed up by central authority. Drawing on their clientelist networks, tribal politicians regained control over the management of local affairs, reaffirming the principle of seniority, and shutting out women and youth from decision-making.[194]

*

Tobruk did not emerge from the revolution as a power centre. The revolution did not unite its population, nor create new divides, or overturn the established local order. Contrary to towns in the Nafusa Mountains, Misrata or Bani Walid, the events of the war shaped no new local identity in Tobruk. The characteristic localism of Libya's post-revolutionary forces was conspicuously absent in Tobruk.

The reason for the divergent pathways between western Libyan towns and Tobruk is obvious. In western Libya, communities divided into loyalist towns and revolutionary centres within the first two weeks of the uprising, and the regime re-established control over key cities within the first week of March. Eastern Libya wholly escaped regime control by the end of the uprising's first week, and regime forces failed to regain control. As a result, rebels in the east were under no pressure to defend their cities, and did not form tight-knit armed groups for this purpose. The armed groups that emerged often included members from various eastern cities, and tensions would soon arise between different armed groups within cities. Developments in Tobruk broadly followed the trend across Cyrenaica, with the differences that little bloodshed had happened in Tobruk, and that the city was geographically isolated from the rest of the region, and, particularly, far from the front line.

Why did the entire east fall to the rebels so quickly? Why were Qadhafi's attempts to exploit inter-communal rifts unsuccessful there? The explanation most commonly put forward points to the region's alleged marginalization. Yet, as discussed earlier, marginalization does not provide an adequate guide to the divides on 2011; the east was no more marginalized than most provincial towns in western Libya, and there were numerous senior regime officials from the east who had little interest in a popular revolution.

Another explanation centres on the role of the region's tribes, and their relations among each other. Both Libyan and foreign analysts have portrayed the defections of senior officers and politicians in the east as reflecting their tribes' decision to turn against Qadhafi.[195] From this perspective, the division into loyalist and revolutionary strongholds was avoided in the east because the region boasted a strong regional identity, rooted in the myth of common ancestry shared by Cyrenaica's 'free' tribes, as well as in the unifying function of the Sanussiya Brotherhood during the late Ottoman era and the anti-colonial struggle.[196]

Yet, a closer analysis reveals problems with this interpretation. As in other eastern cities, the uprising in Tobruk was not led by tribal figures. Rather, these figures were blindsided by the spontaneous protests of young men, which forced them to position themselves after considerable hesitation. Suleiman Mahmoud's account shows that his defection did not follow a decision by 'the tribe'; instead, Mahmoud consulted with five tribal notables in three separate conversations, and avoided informing one of them – al-Tayyeb al-Sharif – of his discussion with three of the others, due to the bad relations between them.[197]

This was hardly collective decision-making. Indeed, personal quarrels forestalled any collective action by Tobruk's Obeidat during the revolution. Faraj Yasin al-Mabri, the Obeidat notable who was chosen to sit on the NTC by its chairman Mustafa Abdeljalil, was on notoriously bad terms with two of his tribesmen whom Mahmoud had consulted: al-Tayyeb al-Sharif, and Faraj's cousin Mansur al-Salihin al-Mabri. Asked to designate a second NTC member for Tobruk, Faraj Yasin then chose Othman al-Mgairhi, ostensibly because his family had roots in western Libya, and therefore his choice would not fuel rivalries between the city's other two main tribes, the Mniffa and Qutaan.[198] Tobruk's tribes did not appear as actors during the revolution, but individual notables with their respective networks did.

Historically, it is certainly true that Cyrenaica had developed a regional identity of a kind that existed neither in Tripolitania nor in Fezzan. Though by no means devoid of internal conflicts, Cyrenaica experienced nothing comparable to the struggle of tribal alliances and the colonial strategy of divide-and-rule in the other two provinces during the early twentieth century. While coordinated by Ottoman officers and the Sanussiya, anti-colonial fighters during the Ottoman – Italian War and the First World War were organized along tribal lines – but contrary to developments in Tripolitania, the eastern tribes did not turn on each other, despite the Italians' best efforts.[199] However, the lasting impact of the Sanussiya and the sway of the myth of common origin should not be exaggerated. As Italian settlers withdrew from Cyrenaica's Green Mountains, protracted conflicts raged between tribes over ownership of land.[200]

Moreover, the myth of common origin did not extend to the families of western Libyan provenance who formed the bulk of the population of Benghazi and Darna.[201] This genealogical distinction had long been politically relevant: in 1949–51, tribal leaders had supported Cyrenaican independence or a loose federal system under King Idris, while in Darna and Benghazi, a nascent nationalist movement had advocated a strong central government, or even a republic.[202] During the Qadhafi era, political figures in the east played on the subjacent divide between 'indigenous' eastern tribes and the groups of western Libyan origin. As Qadhafi's attempt to mobilize Obeidat officers for an offensive against Darna shows, the regime intended to exploit such rifts for its counter-insurgency. In Benghazi and Darna, many leading figures in the uprising's first weeks were urban intellectuals and professionals to whom tribal affiliation meant little, or who hailed from families whose origins lay in western Libya.

In sum, the hypothesis that events in Cyrenaica were driven by the collective defection of eastern tribes does not stand closer examination. The question, rather, appears to be why the regime's attempts at mobilizing certain tribal constituencies against other groups failed in the east, while they succeeded in the west. The most plausible answer to this question is not differences in structural conditions such as marginalization or inter-communal rifts, but the dynamics of protests, repression and defection themselves.

In the east, the regime's botched attempts to suppress the protests caused dozens of casualties in Benghazi, al-Bayda and Darna as early as 17 February, provoking a much earlier and steeper escalation than in the west. The key military assets in the east had fallen to the rebels before the regime could recover from its surprise: the Jareh Brigade in al-Bayda on 19 February, the Benghazi-based Fadhil Bu Omar Brigade the following day, and al-Bayda's airport on 21 February. Insubordination by a few officers blocked the arrival of reinforcements via Tobruk's air base. With the seizure of these four locations before the regime could react, the balance of power in the east rapidly tilted towards the rebels, which, in turn, provoked further defections (most importantly that of Abdelfattah Younes on 22 February) or the hurried departure of loyalists (such as that of several officers in Tobruk's Omar al-Mukhtar Brigade on 23 February). In the west, the military infrastructure was much denser, and the delay of several days in the escalation of protests enabled a more coordinated response that was either more measured – such as in Misrata and Bani Walid – or more decisively crushing, such as in Tripoli.

Suleiman Mahmoud's actions in the uprising's first four days appear crucial in this respect. Had Mahmoud not fallen out with Qadhafi a few years earlier, it is far from certain that he would have sabotaged the arrival of reinforcements, and refused to participate in an offensive against Darna. Though this counterfactual argument cannot be substantiated further, it suggests that in the first days of the uprising, collective indecision allowed individual whims to play a significant or even decisive role in spreading the rebellion across Cyrenaica.

Conclusion: Violence and the formation of new political communities

Contrary to what rebels and the regime claimed in February 2011, Libyan communities were united neither in support for the revolution, nor in loyalty to Qadhafi. Local unity only came about through collective defence, and through its enforcement by the political and military leadership in each community, for whom the suppression of dissenting voices was essential for survival. For communities to achieve a semblance of unity, some groups had to be physically excluded: such as members of the Maadan tribe in Misrata, or Bani Walid's revolutionaries. But perceptions of united communities turned out to be a self-fulfilling prophecy: regime forces regarded anyone hailing from rebellious towns with suspicion, meaning that their residents were safer in revolutionary strongholds, supporting the rebellion. Members of alleged loyalist communities feared collective retaliation, which strengthened their support for the regime. With the advance of revolutionary forces, they were exposed to the threat of looting, displacement or imprisonment merely due to their tribal identity, which further entrenched counter-revolutionary sentiment in these communities. The experience and the threat of violence transformed communities. A city such as Tobruk was largely shielded from the conflict, and its social structure consequently remained largely unchanged from the Qadhafi era.

The rapidity with which the uprising spread, and the fact that it took the form of open revolt by rebels claiming to represent their community, owed much to antecedent factors. The track record of the Qadhafi regime in exploiting communal divides, and holding communities collectively responsible for subversive acts by individual members, made it highly likely that repression would take the form of collective punishment. A revolutionary situation was therefore likely to initiate mechanisms of solidarity. The regime's establishment of security brigades on a tribal basis and its neglect of the army, which pushed officers to retire or demand their transfer to their hometowns, facilitated coordination among civilian and military members of the same communities during the first days of the uprising.

Underlying such coordination were the dense social ties that characterized these communities: relations of trust and solidarity in tight-knit, overlapping networks of friendship, kinship and neighbourhood. These ties certainly aided the rapid defection of officers in communities whose young men were rising up, and the formation of small groups to defend particular neighbourhoods. By the same token, they helped deter defections and protests in towns where the regime recruited volunteers for its counter-insurgency.

But such structural and antecedent factors determined neither the side a community ended up on in the civil war, nor whether the divides of the war would emerge between neighbouring communities – as in Tripolitania – or between an entire region and central authority, as in the east. Localism in western Libya, and its weakness in Tobruk, was a contingent outcome of conflict dynamics that underlines the transformative power of violence in the first weeks of the uprising. Nor did communities engage in bargaining over their position towards the conflict. The alignment of communities with either side was not the outcome of collective decision-making; the capacity for such decision-making only emerged with the new leadership and solidarities that formed in the very act of rebellion. Communities did not enter the revolution as actors; they became actors through the conflict.

Whether some communities were more cohesive than others prior to the conflict mattered less than the ways in which the eruption of the conflict transformed them. The towns of the Nafusa Mountains, for example, had a history and identity as communities, whereas a large, diverse city such as Misrata did not. But through its collective struggle against a regime that treated any Misratan as a rebel – and through the exclusion of groups that revolutionary leaders regarded with suspicion – Misrata became a cohesive community. The Libyan civil war, then, created new political communities, and community leaders, even where such communities had initially been an illusion exploited by the opposing sides.

Contingent events in the first few days of the uprising disrupted predetermined patterns. In the unprecedented situation of 17 to 22 February, with high uncertainty over whether Qadhafi would last much longer, collective indecision accorded a disproportionate weight to individual whims and small, spontaneous acts. Among the most significant of these were the decision of a handful of individuals in Zintan to start a protest and the decision of a respected Zintani religious sheikh to join them, as well as the insubordination of Suleiman Mahmoud in Tobruk. Without the former, the regime might have retained control over western Libya; without the latter, eastern Libya could have witnessed a conflict along inter-communal lines.

The spontaneous protests and individual acts of the first days then set in motion mechanisms of diffusion. For rebels and defectors of the first hour, as well as the perpetrators of regime crimes, there could be no turning back, pushing them to mobilize support on the basis of solidary ties. Repression by regime forces triggered anger spirals, as the recurrent catalysing effect of funerals of victims shows. Communities quickly began to expect collective reprisals for the actions of a minority, accelerating the drive to seize weapons. Parallel processes in various locales mutually reinforced each other: the uprisings in the Nafusa Mountains and Misrata likely would not have gone as far, had they not been accompanied by the simultaneous rebellion in the east – and vice versa. The spate of defections of Libyan diplomats, the rumours and disinformation spread via satellite television – all of these events played a role in the chain reactions unfolding at the local level.

The processes that set a community on the path towards rebellion or loyalism played out over a very short period of time. In many cases, the point of no return was reached within three or four days of the first protests. But in that short time span, local actors who were under pressure to position themselves engaged in an intense search for cues. Calculations about the viability of open rebellion were visibly influenced by a factor that was endogenous to the developing situation: the geography of territorial control, as it stood around 21 to 25 February. The loss of regime control over key military facilities across the east; Misrata's access to a port; and the defensibility of Nafusa Mountains towns all featured heavily in the considerations of local actors. The geographic factor was contingent both in that individual agency played an important role in the distribution of local revolts in the first week, and in that defensibility was causally unrelated to group social structure and the history of group relations. But the geography of territorial control at a critical point in time clearly contributed to the lock-in of patterns of rebellion and loyalism as they had emerged by late February.

Because the moment of collective indecision was crucial in shaping subsequent developments, timing also influenced whether the processes that led to communities rising up and closing ranks could develop a momentum of their own. Rebellion was generally successful where it erupted early, taking the regime by surprise and provoking uncoordinated or counterproductive responses – such as in the east and the Nafusa Mountains. In towns that rose up early, protests and defections could gather a critical mass before the regime's machinery spun fully into action, and while it appeared as if Qadhafi could fall within days. Qadhafi's blood-curdling speech of 22 February strengthened convictions in rebellious towns that there could be no turning back, while sowing terror in towns that remained under regime control. In Bani Walid, protests were too hesitant and came too late to cascade further, with the tragic attempt of 28 May ending in a bloodbath. Foreign military intervention became likely only in mid-March, and therefore had no impact on the calculations of actors in the crucial first three weeks of the uprising.

The collapse of central authority with the fall of the regime locked in the localism that had developed during the brief civil war. Re-establishing central authority would prove difficult in such a fragmented landscape. But localism was also the outcome of deep and lasting transformations of the local social fabric. Hundreds of families had to flee Bani Walid because one or two of their members had supported the revolutionaries, and the rift through the town spread distrust among many of those who stayed. In Misrata, the arbitrary lines of territorial control dictated whether an entire tribal constituency would be expelled for being considered loyalist. Pre-existing ties among those defending their city together were significantly reinforced. The next chapter shows just how lasting the impact of the social transformations wrought by the 2011 war would be.

3

Social embeddedness and violent conflict (2012–15)

The actors in Libya's post-revolutionary conflicts are often collectively labelled as 'the militias'. For some, this category includes the forces under the control of Khalifa Haftar, while those who see Haftar's forces as Libya's army apply the term to all other armed groups. In its contemporary usage in Libya, as well as in many other contexts – such as that of the Lebanese civil war – 'militia' has overwhelmingly negative connotations, evoking unruly, ruthless, predatory armed groups. Reflecting a widespread view among Libyans and foreign observers, well-respected international media outlets have described militias as the forces 'who are really calling the shots'[1] and are 'holding Libya hostage'.[2] Pessimistic or even cynical views of Libyan armed groups as opportunistic and greedy have also shaped foreign policies towards the Libyan crisis since 2014. In countless discussions I had with Western diplomats and security policymakers, my interlocutors left no doubt that they saw 'the militias' as chiefly concerned with their revenue sources, be they state salaries or various kinds of criminal activity, as well as their own protection against future prosecution.

To be sure, many actors in Libya's military landscape do, indeed, come close to the stereotype of unscrupulous, self-interested armed groups conveyed by the term 'militias', as it is commonly used in Libya. But a blanket usage of the term for all actors in Libya's conflicts obscures important differences between them. Forces that are deeply socially embedded in communities, and in some cases almost indistinguishable from them, have been a central feature of Libya's conflicts. While they have at times deployed brutal violence against other communities, such forces have been subject to social control, rather than purely driven by the opportunistic gambles of politicians. Amid state collapse, such forces have also maintained stability within communities without forming predatory or repressive power structures.

Analysing such socially embedded forces and the conditions under which they emerge is not only crucial for understanding processes of fragmentation in post-revolutionary Libya. It also requires tackling a key weakness in much of the literature on civil wars, namely, an almost exclusive focus on armed groups as the central unit of analysis. The comparative analysis presented in this chapter shows how social transformation driven by conflict shaped the organization of violence at the local level.

Resocializing armed groups

Over the past two decades, armed groups or their leaders have been the dominant units of analysis in research on civil wars. This was not always the case. Not so long ago, analysts focused on social forces and collective interests as the drivers behind rebellions, revolutions, 'peasant wars' and 'ethnic conflicts'.[3] The shift towards armed groups during the 1990s went along with a tendency to view actors in contemporary civil wars as motivated by individual self-interest. Rebels, or warlords, were seen as driven by greed and a hunger for power.[4] The methodological individualism and normative bias implicit in such assumptions linger on in part of the literature. The most influential recent effort to transcend unitary actor models of rebel behaviour has been the literature on the organizational logics and constraints of armed groups.[5] But as the bulk of current research on civil wars, the 'organizational turn'[6] retains the focus on armed groups as the units of analysis.

There is reason to question the widespread assumption that armed groups or their leaders are the relevant analytical categories in all situations of violent conflict. From Afghanistan to Central Africa, civil wars frequently exhibit two seemingly contradictory phenomena, both of which should raise doubts over the utility of taking armed groups for granted as discrete actors. First, the membership of armed groups is often highly fluid, with fighters moving effortlessly between seemingly distinct organizations, or leaving to form offshoots. Second, it is frequently difficult to distinguish armed groups from their social environments; in many conflicts, analysts see direct links between particular armed factions and specific clans, tribes or other communities. The opportunism of actors in the first case appears to contradict their rigid ties to particular tribal or ethnic groups in the second. In both cases, however, the appearance of an armed group as a distinct organization carrying a particular name disguises the actual structures, which are far more diffuse.

To give but a few examples, during the Afghan struggle against the Soviets, many local commanders 'tried of their own free will to avoid any professionalization or militarization that might threaten traditional society's structure'.[7] In many parts of the country, the fighting group was 'the civil society, with the same leadership and no professionalization of fighters'.[8] South Sudan's Nuer self-defence militias have maintained substantial autonomy from external political actors and military forces; they are self-mobilizing, deeply rooted in their communities, and lack a military hierarchy.[9] In northern Niger, the short-lived insurgency of 2007 was a 'hop on-hop off rebellion' launched by opportunistic professionals of violence, but driven by a rank and file of self-motivated youth seeking to assert their rights.[10] In northern Mali, ephemeral alliances and fluid boundaries between armed groups are an 'inherent feature of Tuareg rebellions', but so are the tribal divisions underlying these groups.[11] In Chad, ex-fighters made use of kin-based and war-based networks while moving from one insurgency to another, crossing borders while doing so.[12] Somalia and Darfur offer further examples for armed groups of rapidly changing form, but with deep roots in local social networks.[13] In eastern Congo, certain Mayi-Mayi militias are deeply embedded in local communities, and social control puts a cap on abusive behaviour, while others have become predatory enterprises co-opted by local politicians.[14] In Colombia, local self-defence groups fought as liberal guerrillas in the civil war of the 1950s, then demobilized, only to re-emerge as communist guerrillas in the late 1960s.[15]

On one end of the spectrum, then, are violent self-help systems in which clans or tribes institutionalize collective responsibility, and 'all adult males take part in organized violence and share the risks involved'.[16] On the other end are armed groups that form haphazardly from disparate elements, only to dissolve again or mutate into something different before they can settle into a neatly identifiable organization.

But while the examples just cited may be extreme, they underline a broader problem with dominant approaches to violent actors. The social surroundings into which armed groups are embedded, sometimes to the point of being indistinguishable from it, barely feature in these approaches. Just as the sociologist Mark Granovetter assessed classical and neoclassical economists' conceptions of economic action as under-socialized, and those of new institutional economists as over-socialized, the same can be said for much of the recent literature on armed groups. Game-theoretic approaches abstract away from the social relationships and structures in which members of armed groups are enmeshed, while organization-theoretic approaches overemphasize relations and structures among the groups' members. What are largely missing are analyses of 'attempts at purposive action [that] are … embedded in concrete, ongoing systems of social relations'.[17] Granovetter's point is all the more relevant because trust is central in both economic behaviour and violent conflict.

Recent, groundbreaking work has enhanced our understanding of the role of pre-war social networks from which armed groups emerge for the command structure and cohesion of these groups.[18] In addition to determining a group's initial structure, strong pre-existing social ties – such as marriage or kinship – may also transform it, as group members activate such ties to deal with growing pressure on the organization from an adversary.[19] Such work shows that what is commonly understood as an armed group can be viewed as a network of ties linking the members of a fighting group to political players, financial backers, friends, families and neighbours.

Previous contributions to the literature recognize the importance of social ties, but focus on the impact of pre-existing ties on organizations. They say little about how social bases and armed groups interact with, and transform, each other.[20] Moreover, they invariably assume the existence of armed groups as organizations that are distinct from their social environments. They conceptualize ties with communities as relations between them and armed groups, implicitly supposing that the two are analytically separate. This may be in part because much of the work on armed groups has focused on insurgencies, in which armed groups have greater incentives to distinguish themselves by their demands, ideology and leadership, for purposes of mobilization, bargaining and foreign relations.[21] But in fragmented landscapes, in which many violent actors classify neither as insurgents nor as state-sponsored militias, only some groups come to be moved by such incentives, while others remain locally embedded to an extent that makes it difficult to even speak of distinct groups. Such socially embedded forces never come out on top in prolonged civil wars; any successful, large armed group needs to centralize command and establish rules and hierarchies.[22] But they are key to understanding fragmented civil wars and collapsed states.

Rather than assuming armed groups to be analytically separate, I suggest that such groups are socially embedded or insulated from their surroundings to varying degrees. All action is socially embedded, but the extent to which formal organization trumps other social ties varies. In other words, whether internal organizational logics dominate the workings of an armed group, and therefore merit analytical focus, depends on that group's ability or willingness to police its boundaries.

Social embeddedness versus formalization

Modern armies decouple civil and military society and reshape individual identities through boot camp and initiation rituals to build primary group cohesion.[23] Robust internal controls enforce the boundaries between civil and military life. Strongly institutionalized armed groups mimic such mechanisms by indoctrinating members, ensuring compliance with internal rules through disciplinary force, and discouraging or regulating marriage, such as by demanding that group members' families settle in military camps.[24] As they expand, such groups can embark on a trajectory of formalization and bureaucratization that brings them even closer to the traits of formal armies.[25] Less institutionalized groups rely more heavily on rites of passage, such as swearing on sacred texts or oath-taking.[26] Some authors have associated gang rape and other atrocities with groups that forcibly recruit their members or face challenges in ensuring their loyalty, and make them commit crimes to deal with such challenges.[27] In clandestine organizations, militants progressively reduce affective ties to the intense relations they have with comrades, closing channels of communication with outsiders. Such closed groups eventually become the sole point of reference for their members; ideological discourse becomes primarily for internal consumption.[28]

The less armed groups try to isolate their members and decision-making structures from their social environment, the more broadly and deeply embedded they are in a society, and the less they can be usefully understood as discrete groups. The more they seek to segregate their members from their former social surroundings and centralize decision-making, the more formalized they are as an organization, and the more insulated from the influence of social networks external to that organization. In other words, the behaviour of deeply embedded forces is shaped less by internal organizational logics than by the social ties of their members.

I conceptualize the social embeddedness of armed groups as a function of two parameters: first, permeability; that is, the openness or closeness of the group within a given community with regard to recruitment patterns and information outflows; second, the degree to which its command structures are centralized or decentralized.[29]

Total social embeddedness would mean that a fighting group is identical with a local community. This is the case for tribal societies in which all males are potentially part of the fighting group and the entire community is threatened by conflict, splitting and aligning under the impact of conflict dynamics.[30] Formalization means that the networks linking combatants to their social surroundings are curtailed and policed; centralized command further limits the impact of social ties outside the organization.

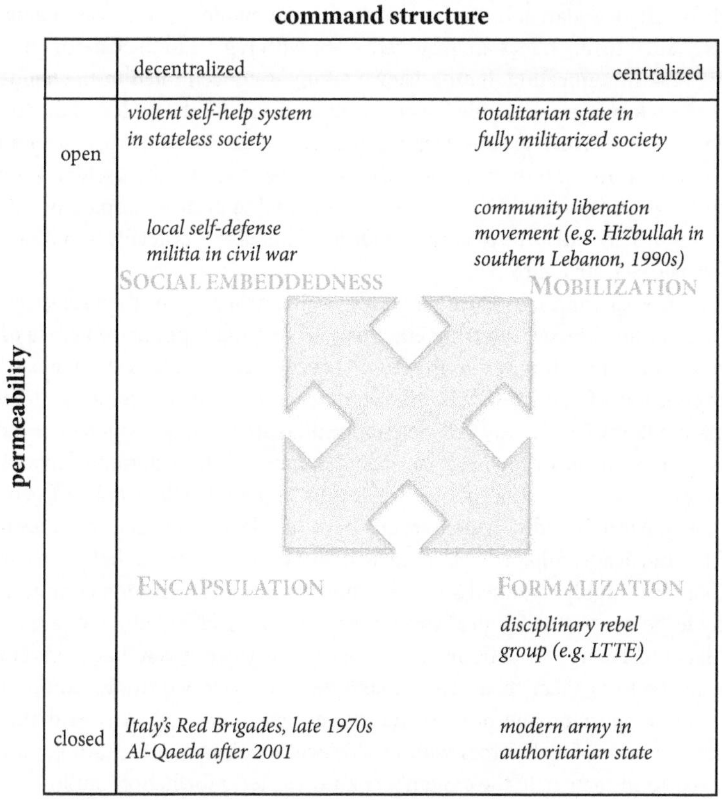

command structure

	decentralized	centralized
open	*violent self-help system in stateless society*	*totalitarian state in fully militarized society*
	local self-defense militia in civil war	*community liberation movement (e.g. Hizbullah in southern Lebanon, 1990s)*
	SOCIAL EMBEDDEDNESS	MOBILIZATION
	ENCAPSULATION	FORMALIZATION
		disciplinary rebel group (e.g. LTTE)
closed	*Italy's Red Brigades, late 1970s Al-Qaeda after 2001*	*modern army in authoritarian state*

permeability

Figure 1 Social embeddedness versus formalization.

This applies to modern armies in authoritarian states, as well as to tightly run, disciplinary rebel groups such as Sri Lanka's LTTE.[31]

Between the two ends of the spectrum, there are various possible combinations. An organization such as Hizbullah in southern Lebanon during the 1990s was highly centralized, but mobilized local communities so effectively that it came to be identified with them, ensuring steady recruitment and the reproduction of control by members of the communities themselves. The organization's military and intelligence compartments were hierarchical and closed, protected by the outer layers of more permeable networks that were deeply embedded in the local social fabric through its charitable activities.[32] Under the impact of repression, a tight-knit clique of war veterans such as al-Qaeda may evolve into a highly decentralized network that is hermetically closed to the outside due to its clandestine nature.[33] A local jihadist group such as the offshoots of Ansar al-Sharia in several Libyan cities has a decentralized structure that is closer to local communities, is more open towards locals about its activities, but makes recruits undergo intensive indoctrination.[34] Finally, there are loose and open alliances of more cohesive subgroups. For example, close-knit groups of opportunistic fighters have moved from one fleeting insurgency or counter-insurgency to another in the triangle of Chad, Sudan and the Central African Republic, a recent case being Seleka in CAR.[35] Such insurgencies are relatively open with regard to the ease of joining and the flow of communication, but decision-making is concentrated in the hands of the leaders of each sub-group – unless it concerns decisions of the rank and file to desert.

Why are some armed groups deeply embedded in the social fabric of a community, while others form tightly run organizations that isolate themselves from their surroundings? Consistent with the process-oriented approach adopted in this book, the answer lies not only in two scope conditions, but also – crucially – in how conflict transforms social structures.

First, the social infrastructure on which armed groups graft themselves evidently matters. A group whose leadership emerged out of a tight, politicized circle of fellow students welded together by the threat of surveillance – such as the Libyan Islamic Fighting Group of the 1990s[36] – will exercise great control over recruitment and information flows. Conversely, self-defence militias are frequently open to all members of a kin group, village or town; recruitment happens on the criterion of mere kinship or location, and information about the group's activities will circulate freely in the community. More broadly, armed groups have to adapt to societal attitudes towards authority and leadership, as well as to whether or not societies have a tradition of statehood.[37] In highly stratified societies, military mobilization on a communal basis is likely to be controlled by local strongmen. Socially embedded forces are therefore most likely to emerge in cohesive local societies with relatively flat hierarchies and a propensity for collective decision-making – in other words, in communities.[38] Mobilizing support on the basis of defensive communal solidarity and traditional loyalties can endow such forces with broad local legitimacy, which, in turn, reduces their need to indoctrinate their members and restrict information outflows. Instead, communal solidarity activates 'mechanisms of control located within the social fabric of the population itself'.[39]

Second, socially embedded forces are most likely to emerge where communities exert territorial control. In areas of split control, or occupation by an adversary, the clandestine nature of an insurgency requires the tight policing of group boundaries and a heavy reliance on strong ties of trust such as those among close friends and relatives. Amid state repression and the risk of denunciation, distrust will spread among community members who share weak social ties.[40] More generally, a binary conflict between a state and an insurgent group allows comparatively little space for the formation of socially embedded forces. Broad popular support for an insurgency has to be harnessed by a centralized organization, lest it lead to organizational fragmentation and, eventually, multiparty conflict. A conflict in which the state is absent or only one actor among many – that is, a fragmented situation – provides more opportunities for local forces to organize on a communal basis.

However, as the preceding chapter has underlined, localism and communal cohesion are at least as much the product of social transformation amid conflict, as they are structural factors that shape military organization. At the core of the processes through which socially embedded forces emerge are mechanisms that redefine community boundaries and solidarities. To the extent that armed groups are socially embedded, they are both agents of, and subject to, such changes. They are, indeed, built on a pre-existing infrastructure of social ties that include bonds of trust, solidarity and loyalty. But more important is how the formation of socially embedded forces transforms such ties, strengthens loyalties among parts of the community while excluding other parts, and creates strong bonds of trust and common identities among individuals who collectively face unprecedented and existential external threats. What differentiates distinct armed groups from socially embedded forces is the extent to which ties of trust, solidarity and loyalty are forged primarily among combatants, thereby detaching them from their community.

Bonds of trust, solidarity and loyalty forged through collective struggle may be intertwined with pre-existing or newly established relationships of political alliance, economic exchange or patron – client ties. But the former differ qualitatively from the latter in that, once broken, it is much more difficult to restore them. The cohesive, socially embedded forces that can emerge from a community's defence against an external adversary therefore rely on a precious type of ties: ones that can be particularly enduring, but are hard to replace once they are lost. This means that, like other armed groups, socially embedded forces are subject to change. External support can be channelled in ways that promote divides and hierarchization, or fusion between separate groups. Local self-defence militias or vigilante groups that are decentralized and close to communities can be co-opted by political players who promote particular militia leaders.[41] Finally, the presence or absence of a charismatic figure may explain why socially embedded forces centralize into a distinct armed group.

Social embeddedness and transformation in Libya's conflicts

Before we delve into a comparative, micro-level analysis of social embeddedness and social transformation in Libya's conflicts, a few general observations about social microstructures in contemporary Libya are in order. A field researcher has ample opportunity to experience first-hand how dense and effective the social networks of Libyan interlocutors are. Even after diversifying entry points to access different political constituencies within a single city, one gets the impression that everyone seems to know everyone. During meetings or home calls, I often ran into a contact I knew through a separate set of relations. Socializing takes up much time in Libya, and can run late into the night. Calling an acquaintance at midnight is perfectly normal, and Libyans are heavy users of mobile phones, as well as of web-based services to communicate with interlocutors abroad. Formal social occasions such as funerals were a frequent reason for why meetings had to be rescheduled, showing that people are expected to attend the burial of members of their extended family, or of acquainted families. Libyan contacts at times spontaneously invited me to accompany them to wedding celebrations or condolence receptions, which typically involve over a hundred people at any given time.

The strongest indicator of network density was the ability of my interlocutors to facilitate contact with others who would then meet me at least in part as an obligation to those who asked them to. On countless occasions, trusted contacts got relatives or friends to host me, give me rides or arrange meetings with others. These experiences underlined the multiplicity of ties of obligation and trust that connected people I met to others. Sometimes, I had the impression that an interlocutor would arrange assistance for me from someone in part because it presented a good occasion to ask for a favour from someone he knew could not refuse it.

While private networks of friendship and kinship only partly overlap with business or political networks, there is no discernible boundary between the two. Informal socializing in the evenings and on Fridays can include both, often at the same time. Friends and relatives are routinely mobilized to intercede with a given individual or organization they have access to, powering circuits of favours and obligation that straddle the private and political worlds. There really is no strictly private social life. This is not merely a post-revolutionary phenomenon, nor is it a relic of 'traditional' society. Rather, the density and pervasive role of social networks in Libya is not least the product of an authoritarian regime that deliberately weakened state institutions and threatened arbitrary intervention in every sector of society, thereby according crucial importance to informal social ties for everything from a public sector job to the resolution of land disputes.

At the core of individual social networks is typically the extended family. It remains important, although somewhat diminished by a long-term trend towards nuclear families. Cousins, uncles and in-laws frequently featured among people I ran into while meeting with someone, as well as among allies or associates of political and military actors. When my contacts arranged for someone to facilitate my visits or meetings, it would often be a member of the extended family – unless, of course, it were a brother or son.

The extended family owes its resilience not only to patterns of urbanization that saw relatives settle next to each other, but also to the dominance of endogamy in marriage strategies. Leaving aside the Tuareg and Tubu communities, consanguineous marriage remains widespread in Libya. Marriages among first cousins were estimated at a staggering 43 per cent of all marriages in 1995, the last year for which figures are available.[42] The nuclear family itself remains large: an average household included seven members in 2009.[43] This is a remnant of the 1970s and 1980s, when Libya had some of the highest population growth rates worldwide; over the following two decades, the fertility rate dropped dramatically. The patterns I just outlined are therefore subject to change. But in the period under investigation, extended families continued to embody complex, dense webs of kinship, affinity, influence, economic dependency and association. These networks were of crucial importance in everyday life.

Historically, consanguineous marriage served to maintain the socioeconomic and political unity of extended families, while exogamous marriage was a way of diversifying economic risk and building political alliances.[44] Both strategies coexisted with each other. Today, as a result of urbanization, exogamous marriage is much more widespread. But the patterns of marital ties are far from random. Marriages concluded before the mid-1960s, when economic diversification and group alliance was still the defining aspect of such bonds, have created path dependencies by establishing ties between families or communities that are continually reinforced through new marriages. Among certain groups, intermarriage remains taboo, such as between Amazigh in the Nafusa Mountains and their Arab neighbours in Zintan, Rujban and other towns. Parents exert much influence over the choice of wedding partners, and considerations of a family's social status and respectability are decisive; tribal identity and the existence of prior ties between extended families can also be important. Moreover, between influential families, marital alliances remain a strategic instrument, and are yet another illustration of the absence of a boundary between private and political ties. For example, Misrata's big merchant families are extensively intermarried with each other. Qadhafi and his intelligence chief, Abdallah Senoussi, married two sisters to seal the bond between themselves. Qadhafi's prime minister al-Baghdadi al-Mahmoudi is linked to leading businessman and Muslim Brother Abderrezak al-Aradi through the marriage of al-Aradi's brother to the sister of al-Mahmoudi's wife. During their three decades of exile, members of the National Front for the Salvation of Libya intermarried extensively, forming a dense social network that proved cohesive after many of the group's members returned to Libya in 2011.[45]

Of course, we cannot assume that extended, related or even nuclear families operate as groups with a common political interest. This may apply in some cases, but more often such networks comprise divergent interests. In 2011, al-Aradi was a leading figure in the NTC and subsequently became the *eminence grise* behind the Muslim Brotherhood and its newly founded party, while al-Mahmoudi remained loyal until the very end, and was imprisoned in Tripoli after his extradition from Tunisia. In Tobruk, the three leading notables of the local Obeidat section, the Ait Mariam, have a common great-grandfather, but have long been bitterly divided over land ownership disputes and the fact that one of them, al-Tayyeb al-Sharif, reconciled with the regime. In Misrata, Abderrahman al-Sweihli supported the uprising, while his brother Hamdi remained the regime's Navy chief of staff until the fall of Tripoli. Sweihli twice opposed the ambitions of his nephew Ahmed Maitig – when the latter ran for prime minister in 2014, and when he sought membership of the Presidency Council in the UN-led negotiations in 2015 – and only supported the political agreement Maitig was pushing once he was sure to obtain an influential position of his own. In Benghazi, the family ties across the divide that has torn apart the city since 2014 are extensive, and even members of a single nuclear family have positioned themselves in opposing camps. I was often stunned by offhand remarks revealing social ties that linked Libyan political players across deep divides – jihadis and self-styled liberals, for example.

Dense, highly interdependent social settings such as cohesive neighbourhoods, villages and small towns or family businesses – and we could add the Libyan extended family to these – 'tend to be simultaneously close-knit and intensely competitive, outwardly unified and internally divided, "familistic" but also conflictual'.[46] In such environments, political conflicts can be privatized and exploited for personal enmities among relatives or neighbours. Amid civil war, such conflict can have a highly destructive impact on the pre-war social fabric. Such conflict among close relatives is *fitna* – chaos and disorder within a community.

Misrata: Power politics and social embeddedness

In October 2011, Misrata emerged deeply transformed from eight months of civil war. The armed groups that had cropped up to defend the city, mostly on the basis of neighbourhood or pre-existing family or friendship ties, had reshaped the social networks and loyalties of thousands of people. In the vast majority of cases, these groups counted fewer than 100 members.[47] Most armed groups were not only associated with particular neighbourhoods and families, but also with particular backers among the city's businessmen and notables. But although the war had welded fierce loyalties within these tight-knit networks, they remained deeply embedded in the city's wider social fabric.

Strong pre-existing social ties often cut across individual armed groups. For example, the Halbus Brigade, which was among Misrata's largest units, had attracted fighters from across the city. Contrary to other large forces, it was not an alliance of smaller groups but had developed out of a single core. The brigade's members were often closely linked to those of other groups. As one of the brigade's commanders recalled:

> In the early days of the war, Mohamed al-Halbus led a group that fought in Misrata's eastern district, and gained a reputation for being very effective and courageous. Friends of those who fought there, or simply people who heard about the group, joined them. I had a friend in there, and even though I'm from a different neighbourhood, I went and joined. At the time, there were no battalions yet in my neighbourhood, they only formed later. My brother later formed a battalion in our neighbourhood, which he still leads today. But I've stayed with the Halbus Brigade.[48]

Such networks shared a revolutionary spirit that shaped the city's new identity. Misrata's new leaders laid claim to a degree of political influence commensurate with the city's central role in the war, and tangible benefits for revolutionary fighters. They also intended to settle scores with the former regime: two prisons in the city confined almost two thousand soldiers and civilians seized in the final months of the war; individual armed groups held yet others.[49] A man's reputation and influence directly depended on the contribution he had made to the revolutionary war effort, the relations he had built during it, or the courage he had shown in battle. Almost two fifths of the city's pre-war population of 500,000 was excluded from this new identity, and unable to claim revolutionary legitimacy, having fled during the war. Many of these people were members of tribes that were alleged to have predominantly supported the regime, including the Maadan, the Burkat, the Warfalla and others.

The war had produced a new Misratan leadership, because it had created a political and military force where there had been none. Previously, the Misratan elite had occupied an intermediary position between central authority and the population, without being able to mobilize popular support to exert influence on the government. Now, the city was mobilized, and there was no central authority in any meaningful sense any more. But while many of the new leaders had risen to the fore through their courage, skills or commitment, their rise had not overturned the city's social order. Few of the new leading figures were social upstarts. Many had already been well-respected members of the community, and were often representatives of wealthy, established families.[50] Field commanders from more modest backgrounds, who had distinguished themselves by their valour, kept close ties with the establishment. Only a handful of the city's prominent regime figures were imprisoned or forced into exile.[51] Others kept a low profile, remained in Tripoli, or redeemed themselves by backing revolutionary armed groups and cultivating allies among the new leaders.[52] The general pattern, then, was one of continuity in elite composition, combined with a sharp increase in elite influence and vastly strengthened ties between elites and their clienteles.

With regime collapse and the scramble for influence over state assets and institutions, relations within the Misratan elite became intensely competitive – or rather, they reverted to internal competition, a condition many locals described as integral to the mercantile culture prevailing in the city.[53] Various Misratan networks successfully lobbied the NTC or the Kib government to place Misratans in ministerial positions or in control of financial institutions and state-owned companies.[54] Amid such rivalries, successive attempts to form a united, Libya-wide body to represent the interests of the *thuwwar* (revolutionaries) foundered, among them several initiatives led by Misratan figures. In Misrata itself, *thuwwar* established the Union of Misratan Revolutionaries, led by Col. Salem Jha. But in the context of intra-Misratan competition, that body failed to unify *thuwwar* interests. In November 2011, three members of Misrata's Military Council oversaw the disbursement of LD14 million to a list of fighters prepared by the council amid contestation.[55] Competition also marked the elections for a local council held in February 2012 – a purely local initiative – and the GNC elections in July. Most successful candidates mobilized on the basis of revolutionary legitimacy.

As Misrata's socially embedded forces were drawn into such rivalries, the tight-knit webs embedding fighting units in the social fabric began to change. Since the fall of Tripoli, the establishment of the Supreme Security Committee (SSC) and the pressure for payouts to the *thuwwar* had set in motion competitive cycles. Misratan fighters who had established themselves in Tripoli were most directly exposed to them. They competed with Zintanis and others over the control of state institutions, and developed notoriety for increasingly brazen acts of looting, as well as drug consumption and drunkenness. Socializing mostly with their brothers-in-arms, returning to Misrata for a day every now and then, members of such groups progressively escaped the social control of their families and neighbourhood networks.[56]

Another case in point was the formation of a jihadist group that was partly recruited from among Misratan fighters. The Faruq Battalion, led by the Imam al-Tuhami Buzian – who became deputy defence minister in late 2012 – was a group that had emerged in Misrata's Ramla district, home to the eponymous tribe. Within the battalion, regular revolutionary youth and hardened jihadists from the same area mingled. In June 2012, the jihadists within the battalion went to Benghazi to join a public display by Ansar al-Sharia, which thereby made its first appearance in the city.[57] This provoked a rift within Faruq, and part of the group, including most of its jihadists, subsequently moved to Sirte. There, they formed the nucleus of what later became the local branch of Ansar al-Sharia. As the group in Sirte radicalized, several of those who had moved to Sirte due to close personal ties with the jihadists left and returned to Misrata.[58] Having initially been deeply embedded in the social fabric, a faction within Faruq had spun off and isolated itself both ideologically and geographically.

The bulk of the city's forces, however, remained in Misrata. Many fighters went back to their former jobs, or simply stayed home. Their heavy weapons remained under the collective control of the leadership of individual units, or were held directly by field commanders in each group. During early 2012, Misratan leaders lobbied the chief of staff for the establishment of a temporary paramilitary force drawn from among revolutionary fighters. They were driven by the political rivalries in Tripoli, but also by the threat of escalating local conflicts in western and southern Libya. Jha proposed a reserve force into which existing armed groups from a region would dissolve, diluting their attachment to individual commanders, neighbourhoods or cities, and allowing army officers to centralize control over heavy weapons. Several Misratan politicians mobilized against that idea, likening it to a conspiracy aimed at disarming the *thuwwar*.[59]

Eventually, the Libya Shield Force (LSF) was set up as a set of regional units, but within these units, the leadership and structures of existing armed groups remained intact, as did their control over their weaponry. Misratan fighters formed the bulk of the Central Shield, which also included groups from nearby towns, and was headed by Misratan army officer Colonel Mohamed Musa. The access to budgets and influence over *thuwwar* forces the Central Shield offered immediately whetted the appetite of others. Several politicians and commanders successfully pressured the chief of staff to establish a second unit, the Third Force, which was exclusively composed of Misratan fighters and led by Colonel Jamal al-Triki. In addition to the two Shield units, four army units were established in Misrata, the biggest among them Brigade 166; they, too, were conglomerates of revolutionary armed groups.[60]

As they entered the Shield units, Misratan forces became actors in the rivalries over budgets and their distribution that were playing out in Tripoli, and within Misrata itself. The absence of oversight over the accounts of the Shield units accorded commanders substantial leeway in embezzling budgets and using them to strengthen their clientele.[61] But the impact of the new bodies and their money on the structure of socially embedded forces was surprisingly limited. The Shield leaders were unable to centralize command over the battalions in their units. 'Mohamed Musa was at the head of Libya's biggest military force,' one commander recalled later, referring to the Central Shield. 'He could have ruled the country, had he made hard choices and taken control of that force.'[62] Despite the Shield's nominal power and its vital role as a safeguard for Misratan interests in Tripoli, commanders were often dismissive of the Shield's capacities. According to another prominent field commander:

> Central Shield, Third Force, Brigade 166 – these are all just names. When the salaries end, you won't find anyone in these units. At one point, the Central Shield controlled Misrata's three entrances – east, west and south. But then the salaries stopped, and Mohamed Musa called me, asking me to send guys to man the deserted checkpoints. The Third Force was first and foremost a business venture formed by political interests. There was big money in it: the salaries, the vehicles, the funding for logistics, and later the opportunities for profiting from smuggling

in the south. But after the budget ran out, most of them came back from the south. Now, there are only about sixty of them left down there.[63]

In other words, the revolutionary armed groups and their networks continued to be the decisive units of action. In the western district of Zawiyat al-Mahjub, for example, around twenty local armed groups had joined together in August 2011, ahead of the offensive towards Tripoli, to form the Martyrs of al-Mahjub Brigade, which was among Misrata's largest. The brigade was a relatively loose coalition of more cohesive sub-groups. In 2012, several of these component elements – the small, neighbourhood-based armed groups that were often linked to particular families – joined the Central Shield, while others entered the Third Force. Individual fighters signed contracts for a duration of one or two years, but the Shield unit they enrolled in depended on which battalion they belonged to.[64] In January 2014, the chief of staff tasked the Third Force with overseeing a ceasefire in the southern city of Sabha. The task came with major budgets and supplies of vehicles, which in itself created fortunes among battalion leaders.[65] The decision to join the operation was taken at a battalion or individual level. Those who did were deployed for twenty days at a time, then spent ten days at home, receiving a substantial monthly payment of LD 3,000 – about four times an army officer's salary. But when money ran out in mid-2015, few maintained their commitment. Similarly, in August 2014, Central Shield contracts expired; the Shield simply vanished, and the battalions that had made up its components reappeared.[66]

Control over salary budgets, then, was insufficient to centralize command structures. None of the existing bodies – the Local and Military Councils, Union of Revolutionaries and the command of the Shield units – were on their own able to take decisions committing Misratan forces to a major operation. The multitude of intertwined networks commanding military forces meant that decision-making was complex, involving formal political representatives, informal power brokers, businessmen and dozens of leaders of armed groups.

To bring these different constituencies together, the Local and Military Councils as well as the Union of Revolutionaries, in mid-2012, called a big meeting to establish a 120-member Shura Council. The Shura Council became an important locus for consultation, though any single meeting would typically attract only around a third of its members.[67] The key players in the council had been leading figures in the revolution, and were now pushing a hardline agenda hostile to anything they saw as counter-revolutionary.[68] But they were not a united group, nor were they able to simply impose their will on others. Misrata no longer spoke with one voice. As the city's GNC representative Hassan al-Amin put it in March 2013:

> The situation in Misrata does not differ from that of any other Libyan city … there is a weak Local Council, a Security Committee, a Military Council, and a Union of Revolutionaries. Each one is working on its own, and none of them has the power to make decisions, or the legitimacy to speak for Misrata.[69]

The uncompromising stance of the city's new leaders set it on a collision course with other communities. It also produced new losers within the city itself. The trigger for the formation of the Shura Council was the seizure of six Misratans by armed men on the outskirts of Bani Walid in July 2012. Pressure mounted in Misrata to launch an operation against the town. Mobilization began in earnest when one of the hostages – Omran Shaaban, who had been among Qadhafi's captors in Sirte – died of his wounds shortly after his release. Prominent revolutionary hardliners led the drive for a punitive expedition, sidelining Salem Jha, who had tried to reach out to Bani Walid and firmly opposed the war.[70] Denounced as a traitor, Jha left the country, and later became the military attaché at the Libyan embassy in Abu Dhabi – the first of several prominent Misratan revolutionary figures to go into exile.

The violent recapture of Bani Walid in October 2012 upended the efforts Jha and others in Misrata had made at fostering reconciliation with the town. Two volunteer units from Bani Walid had fought in Misrata in 2011. Dozens of men from Bani Walid languished in Misratan prisons, and hundreds of families from Misrata had sought refuge in Bani Walid – many originating from Bani Walid, or members of tribes that were stigmatized as regime loyalists.[71] The October operation against Bani Walid cemented the divide between the two communities.

The gulf widened further in March 2013, after it emerged that twenty-one men from Bani Walid who had been taken prisoner in the operation had died in Misratan prisons, apparently under torture.[72] Though there was extensive intermarriage between families from both cities, mutual visits became exceedingly rare.[73] The direct road between the two cities was hardly used anymore. Misratan trucks began circumventing Bani Walid on their way to southern Libya, using longer roads instead; those risking the passage through Bani Walid stopped after a Misratan truck driver disappeared in the town in early 2014. Merchandise from Misrata, such as the dairy products of the Naseem factory owned by the prominent businessman Mohamed al-Raedh, could neither enter nor transit Bani Walid due to the threat of confiscation by locals manning checkpoints at the town's entrances.[74]

The aggressive posture of the city's leaders also damaged Misratan commercial interests more broadly. Several drive-by shootings targeted Misratan-owned shops in Sirte and Sabha during and after the Bani Walid operation, and Misratan trucks took to forming convoys in their journeys to the south. Misrata's two largest wholesale markets, for vegetables and meat, moved to neighbouring Zliten because buyers from other towns were reluctant to pass through Misrata's checkpoints.[75]

The hardliners further strengthened their hold over Misrata with their push for the Political Isolation Law, which in principle enjoyed widespread support in the city. In March 2013, armed men from Misrata trapped GNC members in their meeting venue to force the law's passage. Misratan GNC member Salah Badi, a former member of the military council and prominent revolutionary commander, had close ties with the group.[76] After the siege was lifted without having reached its objective, another Misratan GNC member, the longtime exile Hassan al-Amin, accused his colleague Abderrahman al-Sweihli of having incited the men to pressure the GNC.[77] A few days later, al-Amin publicly asserted that armed gangs had taken Misrata hostage.[78] Having received death threats, he then resigned and left the country. Another moderate Misratan politician, GNC deputy president Jum'a Atiqa, resigned after the isolation law was adopted in May. Somewhat later, yet another prominent dissident emerged in Fawzi

Abdelali, ambassador to Bahrain and former interior minister, who publicly claimed that Islamists had taken control of Misrata. Revolutionary hardliners stigmatized Abdelali, Jha and al-Amin as 'traitors', and accused them of conspiring with former regime elements, political opponents such as Mahmoud Jibril, or foreign powers such as the UAE.[79] Several of my Misratan interlocutors at the time said they were afraid to speak out against the direction the city had taken, and to discuss issues such as political isolation or the forcibly displaced population of neighbouring Tawargha. Some spoke of a climate of fear.[80]

*

In the period following the passage of the isolation law and before the escalation into civil war in mid-2014, Libyan public opinion began seeing Misrata as an Islamist stronghold, and the city's Shield units as the armed wing of the Muslim Brotherhood. This image was promoted in the media outlets owned by the political adversaries of the Misratan-led camp in the GNC, and was adopted uncritically in much foreign media coverage and analysis.[81] It was far from accurate, but contributed greatly to the collective demonization of the city.

To be sure, there was a tactical alliance between Misratan politicians and Islamist parliamentarians in the GNC, which had been forged over issues such as the Bani Walid operation and the Political Isolation Law. The ascendant camp in Misrata also converged with many Islamist figures in their hardline revolutionary discourse. But the Shield units had no discernible link to the Brotherhood or other Islamist organizations. Adverse media outlets so often targeted Misratan politicians such as Sweihli as 'Muslim Brothers' that many began to believe them, even though such claims were baseless. Few influential figures in Misrata were self-declared Islamists, and few leading Muslim Brothers were from Misrata.[82]

The collective vilification of the city, and the bunker mentality it produced there, received a significant boost in November 2013, when a Misratan armed group opened fire on a peaceful protest in front of their base in Tripoli, triggering clashes that killed forty-three people, most of them protesters.[83] The incident occurred against the backdrop of intensifying rivalries in Tripoli between Misratan, Zintani and Tripolitan armed groups. Faced with a public outcry, the Local, Military and Shura Councils at first denounced a conspiracy against Misrata. Then, two days later, they announced the withdrawal of all Misratan forces from the capital.[84] Misratan fighters in Tripoli complied, but many were furious that they had not been consulted on so far-reaching a decision. Battalion commanders called a big meeting in which some urged the formation of a Council of Revolutionaries to dissolve and replace the Local and Shura Councils. Leading politicians reined in the rebellion, channelling it into the formation of a committee of twenty-one commanders that quickly faded into irrelevance.[85]

The city's hardline leaders had manoeuvred Misrata into isolation. Commercial exchanges with other cities were diminished. Ties with some communities were almost completely cut off, and communication with former allies in the revolution was increasingly burdened by mutual distrust. Even contacts with Misratan revolutionary heroes who were now defamed as traitors were considered suspicious.

For the new leaders, this situation opened up opportunities for brokerage – that is, controlling connections across political boundaries. From late 2013 onwards, a group including the Shura Council members Fathi Bashagha and Khalifa al-Zawawi held several meetings with Qadhafi's former foreign minister Abderrahman Shalgham – the first of which took place in Bahrain, together with Fawzi Abdelali – to discuss the political tug-of-war that formed the backdrop to the struggles over control in Tripoli. In the first half of 2014, Bashagha, the Shield commanders, and leaders of armed groups repeatedly negotiated with Zintani strongmen, including Usama Juwaili and Qa'qa' commander Othman Mlegta, seeking to curb Zintani expansionism in Tripoli in the wake of Misratan fighters' departure.[86] The descent into full-scale civil war in mid-2014 further increased these opportunities for brokerage. A battalion commander later recalled:

> We eventually understood that all the talk about *azlam* [regime stooges] and the counter-revolution was fake. They were telling us 'Ali al-Triki [a Qadhafi-era foreign minister from Misrata, exiled in Cairo] is a traitor' to keep us from speaking to him, even as they were themselves doing so.[87]

Mobilizing support for the war in Tripoli in July proved a difficult task for the hardliners, despite their apparent dominance and their control over channels of communication across political divides. The Zintani-led attack on the GNC in May 2014 strengthened the hand of those rallying with Misratan forces to resist what they portrayed as a counter-revolutionary plot to topple the legitimate order. Nevertheless, the Central Shield leadership was divided over the return to Tripoli following the attack on the GNC. Some of its battalions deployed in the capital, but several left again shortly after they had arrived, uncertain about what role they were being made to play in the political game.[88] Only two prominent Misratan commanders – Salem al-Zufri and Salah Badi – participated with their battalions in the forces that attacked Zintani positions in Tripoli on 13 July, though Bashagha coordinated in the background.[89] Seeking to stop the fighting, Shield commander Mohamed Musa, along with two commanders from the Halbus and Mahjub Brigades, negotiated an agreement with the Zintanis to hand over control of Tripoli International Airport to a neutral force.[90] According to one of the commanders, 'we told Badi we needed 72 hours to implement the deal. He responded, "I'm going to attack". We weren't able to stop him. We couldn't control our people.'[91]

The city's business elites and the bulk of Misratan forces initially opposed the war.[92] Several commanders who later joined the operation emphasized the social pressure that drew the city's forces into the war. From the first day of clashes, Misratan fighters were killed in battle, and supporters of the war became active on TV and radio to invoke the need to avenge the blood of the 'martyrs'. Families of those killed came out to public rallies to honour the dead, a well-established practice since 2011. Speaking out against the war meant offending these families. In public discussions and in the local media, those supporting the war incessantly labelled the forces that had not yet joined the operation as traitors. A group of Misratan religious scholars led by Ibrahim ben Ghashir put out a statement in support of the war.[93] Finally, even those who opposed the war feared the consequences of a defeat: 'if Misrata was forced to retreat from Tripoli, everyone would turn against us – all the towns that supported the regime. We'd not even be able to go to Zliten or Khums anymore.'[94] About ten days into the fighting, the big Misratan battalions joined the fray, mobilizing their fighters from 2011, as well as younger men who had not fought before. Most fighters had not carried weapons since 2011 or 2012. Around 180 Misratan men were killed in the airport war.

The deep embeddedness of Misratan fighters in dense local social networks is key to understanding their mobilization for the July 2014 Tripoli war. The war leaders drew their influence from their role in these same networks. As Fawzi Abdelali later said:

> There is no top-down command in Misrata. Nobody was ever forcibly drafted into a brigade. They either join for money or for the cause. And nobody does anything alone in Misrata. You cannot solely blame Fathi Bashagha for Libya Dawn. Nobody can accuse Fathi of leading our youth into a war serving his political aims, because they know he also has close relatives who were killed in battle, and others who are fighting.[95]

Bashagha was far from an exception. Among many other examples, the head of Misrata's Military Council Ibrahim ben Rajab lost two sons in the airport war. Ibrahim Bait al-Mal, a member of the military council, lost one son in the 2011 war, and another in the offensive against the Islamic State (IS) in Sirte, in 2016. Zeidan's minister of labour Mohamed Sawalem, who ran a battalion that was part of the Third Force, led ceasefire negotiations in Sabha in early 2014, and hosted a Libya Dawn operations room at his office during the Tripoli war, was himself killed in clashes with IS south of Sirte, in 2016.[96] Many of the wealthy families that sponsored Misratan battalions had members who were themselves fighting. Sacrifice, or the willingness to sacrifice, was central to the credibility of leaders, as were their personal relations with their fighters, and their fighters' families. In October 2014, I found leading political and military players in the war sitting in the same hotel lobbies and cafés frequented by ordinary citizens. They were accessible by anyone. Neither social class – inequalities are not very pronounced in Misrata – nor security measures separated them from other members of their community.

At the same time, many field commanders and the rank and file were wary of the designs of political power brokers. While the airport war was raging, doubts spread among commanders over the claims of Bashagha and others that they had obtained Western backing for the operation – particularly after unidentified foreign aircraft struck Libya Dawn positions in Tripoli on 18 August.[97] Misratan commanders fighting in Tripoli set up the Committee of 17 as a political representation of *thuwwar* interests. Its members emphasized their intention to distance themselves from the Islamist politicians whose backing for the war prompted Western media to describe Libya Dawn as an Islamist militia alliance.[98] As one of them said, referring to the head of the Muslim Brotherhood's Justice and Construction Party:

> When Mohamed Sawan and other Islamists expressed their support for the operation, we began wondering: are they instrumentalizing us as their armed

wing? So we established a separate political organization, the Committee of 17. The *thuwwar* are not associated with Islamist movements, nor with any political party.[99]

The Committee of 17 exerted significant influence over the formation of the so-called National Salvation Government of Omar al-Hassi, in late August.[100] Subsequently, it was decisive in supporting Bashagha's shift from war to negotiations, and stopping the bulk of Misratan forces from moving to the Nafusa Mountains to lay siege to Zintan. Thereafter, the committee fell into irrelevance as new political rifts pulled its members in opposite directions – rifts between supporters and opponents of the UN-led negotiations, and disagreements over the new offensives of Misratan forces against the Zintani-held Wutiya air base at the Tunisian border, as well as the oil export terminals to the east of Sirte, in December 2014. The committee thereby experienced the same fate as all previous attempts at institutionalizing collective decision-making, be it by the Military or Shura Councils, the Union of Revolutionaries or the Committee of 21. The stakeholders in collective decisions were not strongmen controlling stable command structures. Rather, they were members of constantly evolving political and social networks, with some individual figures remaining constant, while others exerted influence only temporarily.

*

Following the victory over the Zintanis in Tripoli, Misratan forces fragmented. Money had played no role in the mobilization for the Tripoli war, but now it became increasingly important. To raise fighters for the Wutiya fronts and the oil ports offensive, political figures baited field commanders with major sums of cash – at least some of it coming from foreign backers – but only managed to mobilize a fraction of the forces that had fought in Tripoli.[101] Political rivalries and the growing attraction of money in a rapidly deteriorating economy led different battalions within larger brigades to affiliate themselves with competing camps, and even individual fighters from the same battalion to join new units. These processes of fragmentation are analysed in detail in the next chapter.

Despite fast-changing political affiliations, the ties and loyalties that Misratans had forged during the 2011 war remained strong, as did the city's new identity as a revolutionary stronghold that cemented these ties. From late 2015 onwards, some Misratan forces based in Tripoli supported the UN-backed Government of National Accord (GNA), while others fiercely opposed it. Misratan opponents of the GNA repeatedly clashed with Tripolitan armed groups backing that government. But in 2017, none of my Misratan interlocutors could contemplate that the city's forces would ever confront each other in Tripoli, let alone at home. Even if fighters hired themselves out to one group or another, their true loyalties often remained unchanged. A Tripoli-based commander in the Halbus Brigade explained that the brigade did not receive any salaries, hence he could hardly stop his fighters from joining other Misratan units in Tripoli, such as the 'Presidential Security' guarding the seat of the rump GNC, or a force controlling the headquarters of the National Oil Corporation (NOC). 'They tell us, look, I need the money, so I'll go and work there, but I'll come back every night to sleep at the base, and if you ever need me, in case of fighting, just call me.'[102]

The large-scale Misratan offensive against the Islamic State in Sirte between May and December 2016 showed how cohesive the city's social fabric remained, and how competing networks continued to cooperate in the common interest of defending Misrata. Although widely portrayed in the Western media as an offensive by forces loyal to the GNA, the operation was not launched by the GNA but by Misratan commanders, in reaction to the expansion of IS towards Misrata and Haftar's announcement of an offensive to take Sirte. It remained without significant GNA support for several months. Its force derived from the participation of Misratans irrespective of political affiliation, which was far in excess of the membership of the battalions that had fought in the operations of the previous two years. Around 9,000–10,000 Misratan fighters participated in the Sirte war, not counting men who only joined the operation for a few days. Of the more than 700 fighters killed among the forces fighting IS, around 550 were from Misrata.[103]

The example of two closely related extended families from the Zawiyat al-Mahjub neighbourhood of Misrata illustrates the social embeddedness of the fighters who participated in the Sirte war. Families A. and B. each comprise around seventy to ninety members all living closely together in adjacent plots. The two families are extensively intermarried and have a common ancestor in the great-grandfather of the current family patriarchs. Several family members own medium-sized businesses. In 2011, around twenty of both families' men – most of them aged between fifteen and thirty-five – took up weapons to fight Qadhafi's forces. They did so in four different battalions that later united with around sixteen others to form the Martyrs of al-Mahjub Brigade. Additionally, one member supported the revolutionary war effort with media and communications work. The families' women joined with those of other households in the neighbourhood to cook food for the fighters.

After the fall of the regime, none of the two families' members remained active within their battalions or joined the Shield units. Several men had been wounded and were treated in hospitals abroad. None participated in the October 2012 operation in Bani Walid. When the July 2014 Tripoli war erupted, most of the families' members initially opposed it. Three of them joined in the final weeks of the war, after the number of Misratans killed in the fighting surged and social pressure to bring the war to an end increased. Following the war, one member of family A. stayed with a unit of the Mahjub Brigade that secured the prime minister's office in Tripoli. None joined the subsequent operations at al-Wutiya or the oil ports.[104] One member of family B. emerged as a prominent Misratan opponent of continuing war, and mobilized local political support for his efforts at reaching out to the adversaries of Misratan forces.

In April and May 2016, IS carried out devastating attacks on checkpoints manned by Misratan fighters, creeping steadily closer to the city. On 5 May, the second attack on the al-Sdada checkpoint a hundred kilometres south of Misrata killed three, causing the military council to declare a state of emergency and call for a general mobilization.

Abubaker* A., a young religious sheikh and father of two, joined the ad hoc counter-offensive that day with members of his old battalion. Less than a week later, four fighters were killed in renewed fighting near al-Sdada, among them a field commander from a family with which both A. and B. were intermarried; several members of A. and B. were cousins of the victim. The event caused more men from both families to join the war effort, among them Abubaker's brother Omar* A., who had been too young to fight in 2011:

> I joined the fight against IS the day after the third attack on the Sdada checkpoint. I joined because IS was moving closer to Misrata, even surfacing in Misrata itself, and because they were distorting the image of Islam. At first I worked as a nurse, but after a while I felt I could no longer stay behind the frontline. I had to fight. I joined a battalion from Zawiyat al-Mahjub. Most of its members are from al-Mahjub, they all know each other, but there are also others, *Sharaksa* and other tribes, many of them friends from university. If you have a friend in a battalion, you tell him you want to join, that's how it works. The battalions are very cohesive.[105]

Abubaker's brother Othman*, who had already fought in 2011, equally mobilized. Each of the three joined a different unit, all of them under the umbrella of the Mahjub Brigade. Their sister's husband Ali* B. was a field commander in one of the units, and Abubaker subsequently became field commander of another unit following the death in battle of his leader. Several other field commanders came from families that were intermarried with A. and B.

The Mahjub Brigade had formally declared its support for the GNA, but in reality its component battalions and individual members diverged politically. Attitudes towards the GNA also differed among individual members of both families. None of this mattered in Sirte, according to Abubaker:

> In our unit, there are people who support the GNA, and others who oppose it. In the evenings, there are fierce political disagreements between them. But during the day, they are fighting side by side.[106]

After the defeat of IS in December 2016, Abubaker was the only member of both families to remain active within the military operation, by assisting in the return of displaced families over the following months. All other family members again went back to civilian life. Lured by cash, a brother of Ali B. briefly joined an offensive led by the Benghazi Defence Brigades to seize the oil export terminals in March 2017, and was reprimanded by his relatives upon his return. Within and between the two extended families, information on the deals of Misratan political players and leaders of armed groups flowed freely, since individual members of the two families enjoyed privileged access to competing political networks.

Misratan forces, then, were constantly evolving networks that straddled political elites and their foreign backers, local professionals in violence, and ordinary men linked

---

* Names have been changed.

to each other through multiplex ties of kinship, affinity, friendship, neighbourhood and patronage. The members of these networks fluctuated between mobilization and civilian life. Most of the time, these networks were not discernible as active armed groups, and the social ties that linked members across battalion boundaries meant that the internal logics of these groups were not decisive in shaping their action. Despite this fluidity, these networks were far from inconsequential: taken together, they constituted Libya's most formidable military force. But centralizing command over these forces proved impossible, and the continuously changing alliances between Misratan politicians were unable to exploit these forces for their political ends except for limited periods at a time.

The cohesion and social embeddedness of the city's forces was not due to innate properties of Misratan society. These armed groups were not simply organic extensions of local society, let alone mere family-based self-defence groups. Their emergence deeply transformed this society. Moreover, what allowed them to operate in the way they did after 2011 were the substantial funds Misratan politicians channelled to them from state coffers. As the political struggles intensified after 2014 and payouts to fighters gained in importance for their mobilization, the networks of 2011 began to display a growing number of fractures. But while money did play a role, its impact also had limits. Money could not achieve a major mobilization, such as that for the 2016 Sirte war. Nor could it bring Misratan armed groups associated with competing political camps to turn on themselves. Misratan cohesion drew on the lasting impact of the social transformations of 2011: the strong ties and loyalties forged during the war and the city's new identity that cemented them, in combination with considerable continuity in its social order, and the composition of its elite.

Western/Nafusa Mountains: Militia conglomerates and community security

The principal counterweight to Misratan influence in Tripoli, Zintan, underwent very different changes following the regime's collapse. Zintani armed groups had emerged under slightly less external pressure than the battalions in besieged Misrata. But they, too, were tight-knit, and built on pre-existing family, neighbourhood and friendship ties.

Contrary to Misrata, however, Zintan had no established elite or prominent families, instead priding itself on its tribal egalitarianism. The rise of revolutionary leaders overturned the town's social order. Moreover, in contrast to Misrata, Zintan had no private sector economy fighters could return to. The attraction of sudden wealth and power proved far stronger in Zintan. The town's revolutionary armed groups were much more expansionary, aggressively taking control of key locations in Tripoli, as well as oilfields deep down in southern Libya. The ranks of Zintani armed groups in the capital swelled rapidly in the weeks following the fall of Tripoli, as Tripolitans of Zintani origin joined along with other neighbourhood youth.[107] As one battalion commander recalled:

When we held our first meeting of Zintani forces in Tripoli, at the airport in September, we were stunned at the number of people who showed up. Lots of young guys who had never fought, but somehow got hold of weapons and now all had their own armed groups. Where did they all come from so suddenly?[108]

This also reflected a demographic difference. Whereas the number of Tripolitans of Misratan origin was small compared to Misrata's population, Tripolitans of Zintani origin outnumbered the residents of Zintan. Compared with Zintan's revolutionary battalions, loyalties within the mushrooming Zintani-led armed groups in the capital were much weaker, and they were much less solidly rooted in pre-existing social networks. These groups rapidly escaped the social control of their community of origin, and became key actors in the almost daily succession of minor clashes in Tripoli during late 2011 and 2012.

Zintani forces underwent profound changes in the aftermath of the 2011 war. They were rapidly drawn deep into the political struggles over the security sector. As defence minister in the Kib government from November 2011 onwards, the former head of the military council Colonel Usama al-Juwaili used his authority to channel resources to newly formed units led by Zintanis. The largest among them, the Qa'qa' Brigade led by Othman al-Mlegta and the Sawaeq Brigade led by Emad al-Trabelsi, mostly recruited from among non-Zintanis whose principal motives for enrollment were the salaries. A senior Zintani commander in Tripoli closely familiar with both brigades estimated that only around a tenth of their membership comprised Zintanis, most of them Tripoli residents whose families were from Zintan.[109]

Juwaili also dissolved Qadhafi's security brigades and cut off the salaries of their members. Later, he oversaw the recruitment of members of Qadhafi's notorious 32nd Reinforced Brigade as well as the Ubari-based Maghawir Brigade, a Tuareg unit, into the Qa'qa' and Sawaeq Brigades, which offered them access to salaries.[110] As head of the Prisons Department in the Military Police, the former head of the Western Mountains Military Council Colonel Mokhtar Fernana equally built a Zintani-led militia conglomerate, as did Ahmed Dromba, the deputy interior minister. A Zintani unit controlling Tripoli International Airport recruited Tubu fighters to augment its ranks.[111]

The revolutionary battalions that had fought under the Military Council's direction in 2011 had created lasting relationships and loyalties, but they were eclipsed as the new militias expanded. The military council itself became largely irrelevant, even more so after Juwaili stepped down as defence minister in November 2012. The close relations established in 2011 between revolutionary leaders from Zintan and other towns deteriorated. In January 2012, Zintani battalion leaders formed the Western Libya Shield together with their former brothers-in-arms from Amazigh towns, as well as Zawiya and Sabratha. They deployed to separate the belligerents in several local conflicts. But in October 2012, the Zawiyan Shield forces joined the operation against Bani Walid, while the Zintanis and most Amazigh forces refused to do so. In the aftermath of the operation, the Western Shield's Zintani commander resigned, and the Zintani contingent left the unit.[112]

The aggressive expansion of Zintani-led militias, their enrollment of former regime elements, and the Mlegta brothers' political alliance with Mahmoud Jibril, all isolated the Zintanis from their former revolutionary allies. Among all militias in the capital, the Zintani-led forces became most notorious for looting and other criminal activity, as well as reckless attacks on state institutions.[113] But the town's representatives failed to distance themselves from the militia leaders. During 2013, Zintani tribal elders and revolutionary leaders negotiated with the Islamist militia leaders of the Libyan

Revolutionaries' Operations Room over control of several ministerial buildings in Tripoli – an issue that first and foremost concerned the Zintani-led militias in Tripoli.[114] The political discourse in Zintan became increasingly uniform in its denunciation of the rivals of the Qa'qa' and Sawaeq in Tripoli as Muslim Brothers or extremists. Though Juwaili and others retained ties with former revolutionaries on the other side of the divide, relations became fraught with distrust.[115]

Their adversaries in Tripoli saw the Zintani-led militias as representing Zintani collective interests: a way for the town to punch far above its weight and compete with forces from a city more than ten times its size – Misrata. A minority in Zintan, however, began seeing the new militias as instruments for individual interests increasingly at odds with those of the collectivity. The Qa'qa' and Sawaeq openly acted as the armed wing of Jibril's NFA, most blatantly in February 2014, when their leaders issued an ultimatum to the GNC to relinquish power within five hours or face its forced dissolution and the arrest of its parliamentarians.[116]

In Zintan, this act provoked discord; one of the town's leading notables even considered it a threat to Zintan's unity. Juwaili and several former revolutionary leaders were indignant. The Committee of Twenty, a council of tribal elders, resigned in protest, complaining that the militia leaders were risking escalation without consulting the community.[117] But tribal elders and revolutionary figures wielded little influence over the leadership of the Qa'qa' and Sawaeq. When Haftar launched his operation in Benghazi, in May 2014, the leaders of both militias allied themselves with him, as did Fernana. Their attack on the GNC that month deepened the divisions in Zintan. Before the 2014 war, then, collective leadership in Zintan was upended by the reckless politicking of a small number of militia leaders whose meteoric rise upset the town's revolutionary social order.

*

The mountains' Amazigh communities had proven far more resistant than Zintan to the pull of the post-revolutionary power struggles. As in Zintan, armed groups in Amazigh towns had formed among close friends, neighbours and relatives, and the revolutionary struggle had promoted local cohesion. But contrary to Zintan, Amazigh towns had established local elites – families whose political influence had been curtailed under Qadhafi and who had made a comeback with the revolution. In Zintan, military leaders were the town's face after 2011; in Amazigh towns, the standing, revolutionary credentials and social ties of established families anchored the leaders of armed groups more thoroughly in collective decision-making. On average, the population of Amazigh communities was also better educated, and many fighters were eager to return to their white collar jobs or business activities.

Some fighters from Amazigh towns took up positions in Tripoli, particularly in the city's western districts, where most families of Amazigh origin lived. Like groups from other towns, they remained mobilized to defend the revolution – a claim that all too often served to conceal the promotion of parochial interests in the distributive struggles that followed the regime's demise. Gradually, however, the Tripoli-based armed groups differentiated themselves from communities in the mountains.

Following an incident in May 2012, when armed men from Yefren and Kikla had tried to force their way into the prime minister's office to demand compensation, killing a guard in the event, sizeable contingents of fighters from Amazigh towns left the capital to distance themselves from such acts.[118] By this point, the bulk of these towns' fighters had demobilized and returned to civilian life. The substantial arsenals accumulated by their forces during and after the war were stored in the towns under the authority of their military councils – bodies that now only met in cases of emergency.[119]

Amazigh fighters who stayed in Tripoli were often closely integrated into networks that did not centre on Amazigh towns. In Nalut, three revolutionary battalions had formed during the 2011 war that included some Naluti *thuwwar*, but mostly fighters from elsewhere, many of them Islamists: the 17 February Battalion, Tripoli Revolutionaries Battalion and Martyrs of the Capital Battalion. The networks created by members of these groups were key forces in Tripoli's security landscape, and formed the core of the capital's Supreme Security Committee.[120] These networks linked revolutionaries from Nalut and other Amazigh towns much more closely to former brothers-in-arms than to their communities of origin.

The National Mobile Force (NMF), formed in July 2012, was initially less clearly distinguishable from the collective interests of Amazigh towns. The force, established by the NTC to provide security in Tripoli, included contingents from Amazigh towns, as well as Zawiya, Sabratha, Rujban and several other cities. Zintanis, who did not join the force, saw it as an 'Amazigh conspiracy against Zintan'.[121] The force operated in the greater Tripoli area, and many members of the contingents of Amazigh towns were, in fact, Tripoli residents. Its commander, Said Gujil from Jadu, increasingly drew the force into the political struggles in Tripoli. Gujil became a founding member of the Libyan Revolutionaries Operations Room (LROR), a temporary association of hard-line former revolutionary commanders that formed in mid-2013 as a counterweight to the Zintani-led militias in Tripoli.[122] In early 2014, Gujil led the NMF into an operation in the Warshafana area south of Tripoli targeting alleged criminals and former regime elements. In July, Gujil helped launch Libya Dawn, and sought to push Amazigh towns into the war, but achieved the opposite: the towns' collective leaderships made their neutrality increasingly clear as the conflict raged on.[123]

Over the preceding two years, the relations between Zintan and Amazigh communities had steadily deteriorated. By 2014, there was nothing left of the close alliance and cooperation during the 2011 war. Social ties between Zintanis and Amazigh communities had remained limited, and there still was no intermarriage. Fervent Amazigh activists ruffled feathers in Zintan, while the Arabist discourse of many Zintanis – who, for example, insisted on 'Western Mountains' as the name for the Nafusa Mountains – irked their Amazigh neighbours. When Zintan organized a Conference of Libyan Cities and Tribes, in July 2013, no representatives of Amazigh towns attended. Meanwhile, the only attempt to bring Zintani revolutionaries together with their former Amazigh brothers-in-arms, the Western Libya Shield, had foundered within less than a year's time.

The most important source of tensions was competition over control of the border with Tunisia. Forces from Nalut and Zuwara controlled both official border crossings and the immensely lucrative smuggling of subsidized fuel to Tunisia. In late 2011, units from Zintan had sought to establish themselves at the border, only to be pressured into retreating.[124] Later, Zeidan's minister of transportation, a Zintani called Abdelqader al-Ayed, tried to open a third border crossing in Si'aan territory – a community based in the coastal plain north of Nalut that had sided with the regime in 2011 – but was blocked by opposition from Nalut.[125] Such rivalries compounded the distrust between Zintanis and neighbouring Amazigh communities. When I visited Zintan and several Amazigh towns in January 2014, the mutual disdain and antagonism was palpable in many conversations.

*

The 2014–15 civil war profoundly transformed the political landscape in Zintan, as well as its relations with its Amazigh neighbours. The Zintani-led militia conglomerates disintegrated. The bulk of the Qa'qa' and Sawaeq's forces were unwilling to risk their lives for a mere salary and simply vanished, selling or abandoning their vehicles and weapons.[126] Zintani militia leaders' patronage networks crumbled after the Thinni government sought refuge in the eastern city of al-Bayda and lost access to budgets. Those who defended Zintani positions at the airport were the revolutionary battalions of 2011, who mobilized their former members as well as young Zintanis who had not fought before, and reorganized under Juwaili's Military Council. As a field commander and close associate of Juwaili's said: 'if they had attacked only the Qa'qa' and Sawaeq, we might not have intervened. But they attacked the airport, which had nothing to do with the Qa'qa' and Sawaeq. The attack targeted Zintan.'[127] In late August, having lost 400 of their men and running short on ammunition, Zintani forces withdrew from Tripoli to the mountains.[128]

At the time, external observers ranging from the international media to the protagonists of Libya Dawn saw Zintan as an integral part of an anti-Islamist alliance led by Haftar, and supported by the majority in the Tobruk-based House of Representatives. But contrary to the image promoted in the media, Zintani forces were hardly secularist: indeed, in early August, Zintani leaders felt compelled to issue a statement 'denying categorically that we adhere to secularist, liberal, democratic, or other ideas deviating from the Quran and the Sunna'.[129]

Moreover, Haftar's influence on Zintani forces was limited. Haftar appointed Colonel Idris Madi, a Zintani officer who had been loyal to Qadhafi in 2011, as his commander for western Libya. As such, Madi claimed command over forces from Zintan and fighters who had banded together as a self-styled 'Army of Tribes' that included combatants from Warshafana and several other tribes that carried the stigma of regime loyalism.[130] But after the Tripoli-based militias disintegrated in the airport war, the bulk of Zintani forces were led by Juwaili's Military Council, which mobilized to defend their community, not to fight for a political camp. Juwaili refused to accept Madi's authority and fiercely opposed Haftar.[131] He and his commanders still saw themselves as *thuwwar*, and snorted at the Dawn camp's portrayal of Zintan as the spearhead of counter-revolutionary forces. They were also irritated by Madi's reliance on former regime elements in his effort to assemble forces under his command.[132] In the fight against a common adversary, the Zintanis temporarily shelved such disagreements. But the town's defence against the existential threat it faced was assured principally by the socially embedded forces of the military council.

After the Zintani withdrawal from Tripoli and the defeat of the 'Army of Tribes' in the Warshafana area in September, hardliners within Libya Dawn began plotting the siege and capture of Zintan. They had already mobilized fighters from the Mashashiya, who had been forcibly displaced by forces from Zintan during the 2011 war, and joined the airport battle against the Zintanis on the promise of receiving Dawn support for returning to their homes.[133] But the hardliners encountered opposition from most Misratan battalion leaders.[134] What happened next is disputed. According to the Zintani version of events, Dawn commanders including Abdelghani 'Ghaniwa' al-Kikli, a Tripoli militia leader who was originally from Kikla, prepared to move forces up the mountains and camp in Kikla before laying siege to Zintan.[135] Kikla representatives acknowledge that such plans existed, but maintain that the community opposed them.[136] On 9 October, unidentified perpetrators sabotaged a bridge on the main road at the foot of the mountains, effectively cutting the road off to any Zintani forces moving eastwards.[137] Zintani leaders claim that this was the sign for the start of an operation to encircle their town. In response, Zintani forces occupied al-Qawalish, the highest point in that part of the mountains, and began shelling Kikla, eventually killing 170 people and displacing the town's entire population.[138]

The Zintani attack on Kikla very nearly provoked a conflict that could have engulfed the mountains as a whole. Up to this point, the Local and Military Councils in Amazigh communities had adopted a position of ambiguous neutrality – ambiguous, because several hundred men hailing from these towns had fought the Zintanis in Tripoli, in the ranks of the National Mobile Force. Amazigh leaders argued during this period that they could not prevent the men from fighting in Tripoli, but would shield the mountains from the struggles over the capital. The Zintani move on Kikla threatened to bring the war to the mountains. Now, more fighters from Nalut, Jadu and Yefren mobilized to help defend the town.[139] In Jadu, community leaders and members of the military council closed the road to Zintan, trying to avert a direct confrontation.[140] Local Councils across the mountains denounced the Zintani offensive, but failed to take a clear position in favour of Libya Dawn.

In late November, the onset of fighting over the Zintani-held Wutiya air base, halfway between the coast and the mountains, further raised the risk of a war in the mountains. Fighters from Nalut and the Dawn alliance plotted the takeover of the base with the support of commanders from Kabaw, Jadu and Ruheibat, who were to cordon off Zintani supply lines. Such an operation would have unequivocally made these Amazigh towns parties to the conflict. Forces from Nalut prepared to attack, waiting for their allies from Jadu and Ruheibat to deploy. 'But when we arrived at the front, they weren't there. We waited for a day, two days. Then we understood that they had betrayed us, and withdrew most of our forces,' an officer from Nalut recalled.[141] Zintani threats and pressure from community leaders opposed to the war had dissuaded forces from Jadu from deploying. The battle over al-Wutiya had risked drawing in Amazigh towns as a whole, but in the end, the fighters from Nalut and Jadu who participated were those who had already fought in Tripoli, most of them as part of the National

Mobile Force.[142] And according to the official position of their towns, they did so as individuals, not on behalf of their communities.

While local leaders were busy averting an inter-communal war in the mountains, relations between Zintan and its neighbours reached their lowest point. Zintani positions in the plain and the mountains cut off all supplies to Amazigh towns, while Dawn positions closed off all roads to the mountains from Gharyan and the coast – both to prevent supplies from reaching Zintan and, as Amazigh leaders suspected, to strongarm Amazigh towns into joining the war against Zintan.[143] Some individuals from Nalut, Jadu and Zintan with relations dating back to 2011 maintained contacts that allowed the Zintanis to evacuate their wounded via Nalut to Tunisia.[144] Otherwise, between October 2014 and February 2015, practically all communication between Zintan and its neighbours broke down.

An emerging ethnic discourse threatened to harden the divide. Zintani figures and their allies from tribes that were considered former regime loyalists began emphasizing their common Arab identity and called Misratans 'Turks', 'Janissaries' and 'Jews' who were allying with 'Berbers' against the 'indigenous Arab tribes'. One of the two names Haftar used for his organization, the 'Libyan Arab Armed Forces', clearly played to this discourse.[145] This ethnic reading of the conflict gained sudden popularity. I first encountered it in October 2014, in a discussion with a politician from Bani Walid who had been involved in forming the 'Army of Tribes', and again in meetings with tribal politicians in Tobruk in April 2015. I had met the same interlocutors before, but none had previously used such rhetoric.[146]

However, this emerging rift receded as the two opposing alliances in western Libya crumbled amid a series of local ceasefire agreements. The first – unsuccessful – attempt at negotiating a bilateral ceasefire was made between Misratan and Zintani representatives, who met in the town of al-Asabea, in the mountains, on 20 February 2015.[147] Misratan commanders and negotiators subsequently began meeting with representatives from Warshafana, while continuing to engage the Zintanis. In mid-March, community representatives from the Nafusa Mountains began a series of meetings.[148] All the while, fighting continued. In early April, groups from Warshafana descended from Zintan, forcing their way back to their home region. This increased pressure on Misratan forces in the area and led to the first ceasefire agreement, on 21 April, between Misrata's Halbus Brigade and representatives of Warshafana – which was violated the very next day by forces from Zawiya, but gradually came to hold.[149]

Dawn leaders from various cities initially demanded that Zintan negotiate with them as a bloc. But in mid-May, Juwaili's Military Council shelled Gharyan with heavy artillery, forcing the city's Dawn commanders into negotiations. This triggered a domino effect. In late May, representatives of all communities in the mountains, including Zintan, formally agreed that the conflict had to end and roads should be reopened immediately. On 9 June, Zintan and Gharyan reached an agreement on a ceasefire, the release of prisoners, and an end to the capture of persons simply on the basis of their adherence to either community, coupled with provisions on the location of the two parties' forces. The deal with Gharyan served as a blueprint for similar Zintani agreements with Zuwara, Sabratha and Zawiya over the following weeks. These agreements effectively ended the second civil war in western Libya – despite the fact that a final deal between Zintan and Kikla was only reached in January 2016, and that the Zintanis never reached a formal understanding with Misratan representatives.[150]

Two points are important to understand these local agreements. First, while the UN-led negotiations provided some impetus, the talks were driven by local actors, largely unrelated to the political negotiations hosted by the UN. In Misrata, a link did exist between the UN-led talks over the formation of a unity government and local negotiations: the Local Council played an important role in the initiative for talks with Zintan, and simultaneously backed Fathi Bashagha and Suleiman al-Faqih in their push for a political deal. But the agreement eventually reached with Warshafana representatives was concluded by the Halbus Brigade, whose commanders emphasized that they were acting on their own accord and independently of their city's politicians.[151]

Second, contrary to what might be assumed from the pictures of bearded old men in white robes signing such agreements, commanders were key in initiating, conducting and concluding the talks. Local divisions greatly impeded the efforts at negotiating local ceasefires, and were the cause of frequent setbacks. These divisions are discussed in more detail in the following chapter. What matters here is that they did not run between the representatives of armed groups and elders. In other words, it was not pressure from communities on armed groups that led to the conclusion of ceasefires. Rather, in each town, hardline commanders were linked to local notables and politicians who supported their stance, and the same went for those commanders who were driving the negotiations. In January 2015, for example, a delegation of elders from Jadu went to see their town's fighters on the Wutiya front, asking them to withdraw. But another delegation of notables met with these fighters shortly afterwards and expressed support for the war.[152]

A leading Zintani elder and negotiator explained to me that it was not reconciliation through tribal elders that caused stabilization, but the emergence of a balance of power that made victory unrealistic for either side. (He liked to quote Nietzsche on justice originating in the interaction of parties of approximately equal power). Extolling the accuracy of Zintan's heavy artillery bombardment on Gharyan in glowing terms, he emphasized that Zintan only entered negotiations once it had re-established a position of strength. This elder acted as a loyal adviser and negotiator for the military leaders of his community, rather than as a representative of interests distinct from these leaders.[153] Another, equally prominent Zintani notable recounted that elders routinely consulted with the military council to present a united position in negotiations.[154] By early 2015, Zintan had certainly grown tired of war – around 400 Zintani men had been killed in the airport war, double the number of those killed in 2011 – but civil society representatives did not have to remind commanders of this war weariness; they were fully aware of it.[155]

The very first talks between Misrata and Zintan included representatives of the Local and Military Councils as well as notables. They took place in the neutral town of al-Asabea, whose elders and religious sheikhs acted as mediators. But subsequent negotiations between representatives of the two cities were direct, without mediators and principally between commanders, who brought with them notables they trusted.[156] The negotiations between Zintan, Zuwara and Gharyan were essentially led by members of the Military Councils and battalion commanders, and they were direct.

A key negotiator for Zintan described the role of elders in the talks with Gharyan and Sabratha as honorary and symbolic: when negotiations between commanders had produced a mutually acceptable draft agreement, both sides would form committees of elders for the signing ceremony. He went on to reflect on the most difficult talks, those with representatives from Kikla:

> The first meetings were with elders from Kikla. But they don't have forces on the ground. When you meet with the commanders, you can judge whether an agreement will succeed or fail. There is no point in talking to the elders in a situation of war. You have to sit down with the guys who have the force, who can either reject an agreement or accept it. The elders may accept a given stipulation, as in the case of the first agreement with Kikla, and then the fighters reject it, and the agreement collapses. Anyway, we met with this commander, it went well, and five days later we met again and started drafting. Back then, there was also a committee from two other tribes that was trying to mediate between Kikla and Zintan. But we chose to talk directly to the guy who, because he had lost two of his brothers in the war and led part of Kikla's forces, had the weight to allow the negotiations to succeed or to fail. After around six months, we finally arrived at an agreement.[157]

Commanders negotiated on behalf of their constituencies, not as all-powerful leaders of centralized forces. The prospects for military victory and the risk of an enduring stalemate clearly played a role in their willingness to negotiate, as pointed out earlier. But they were neither free to act as they pleased, nor did they simply follow the designs of political figures. A commander in Misrata's Halbus Brigade and leading figure in its push for local ceasefire agreements explained the rationale behind opening talks with counterparts from Warshafana:

> I have experience in war. I fought in 2011, and I fought in 2014. I can tell when someone is fighting for principles. The Warshafana were fighting for their land, for their homes. We realized that the talk about the Army of Tribes and the counter-revolution was just manipulation. Along with a few others, I met with the Mufti to ask for his support for the ceasefire. But he clearly wanted the war to continue. I asked him, do you approve of the displacement of innocent families? He replied that it was necessary.[158]

Social embeddedness meant that the struggles over continuing the war or normalizing relations with neighbouring towns raged within the social fabric of communities themselves. It was neither a matter of civilian pressure on the leaders of armed groups, nor did it boil down to the calculations of warlords in their pursuit of wealth and power. There was no clear dividing line between civilians and combatants, and the bulk of the forces in the mountains did not correspond to clearly identifiable armed groups.

Of course, some forces – such as those led by Colonel Idris Madi – were controlled by a more or less hierarchical command structure, rather than diffuse social networks. Some held together largely due to salary payments or the inability of their members to return to areas controlled by their adversaries, such as the remnants of the Sawaeq.

When the latter's leaders, the Trabelsi brothers, called me in for questioning on my way to Zintan in April 2016, they continued to be torn between claiming to defend Zintani interests, and maintaining that theirs was a professional force with members from all across Libya, and answerable only to the Interior Ministry in al-Bayda.[159] Madi and the Trabelsi brothers advanced such arguments to escape Zintani collective decision-making. Some commanders of armed groups were moved by money or revolutionary fervour, and appeared to be immune to appeals from their social surroundings. Such groups mattered as actors in the conflict. But their weight was far inferior to that of forces that were deeply embedded in their communities.

The strength of socially embedded forces in the mountains was rooted in the lasting relationships and loyalties forged during the 2011 war. These ties survived the post-revolutionary transformations, and were reactivated as the relapse into civil war posed acute threats to communities. Socially embedded forces defended Zintan, and prevented Amazigh communities from entering the war.

Like the 2011 war, that of 2014–15 left a deep imprint on society in the Nafusa Mountains. The sense of siege induced by the war in communities far outlasted the state of acute conflict. Around 20,000 Tripolitans of Zintani origin had fled to Zintan during the war, and a majority were reluctant to return to Tripoli even long after the ceasefire agreements had been concluded. The displaced had made considerable investments in Zintan in housing and commercial real estate, suggesting that they were planning to stay, or at the least providing for the eventuality of renewed displacement in the future. Between mid-2015 and mid-2016, concerns over security in Tripoli limited the movements of most Zintanis to the town of al-Asabea as a hub for trade and supplies, the flight connection between Zintan and the eastern city of al-Bayda, as well as the land route to Tunisia via Nalut.

The overall effect of these new patterns of movement, communication and exchange was to promote even denser social ties within the community, as well as an increasingly homogenous political discourse that differed sharply from that prevalent in neighbouring towns. Only upon my return to Zintan in March 2017 had some of its residents begun to undertake occasional visits to Tripoli, and many of the displaced were moving back to the capital.

Related to these changes was the rise of community-driven law enforcement in Zintan. Prior to the second civil war, Zintan had acquired notoriety in Tripoli, in the mountains and in southern Libya for criminal activities and abuses by some of its young men. To rein in such abuses and the damage they caused to the community's reputation, a self-mobilized police force called the Committee of 200 sprang up. It owed its name to its founding act, the spontaneous mobilization of around 200 men who had called a Zintani armed group to order after it had forced hundreds of people from the town of Dirj to seek refuge in Algeria, in September 2013. The committee clamped down on crime by engaging with suspects' families prior to arrests, urging them to surrender suspects, and if necessary shaming them into doing so. With the collapse of the Zintani-led militia conglomerates in 2014 and the afflux of the displaced from Tripoli, the work of the committee enjoyed greater leeway, while also taking on greater urgency for community security. Over time, and after road movements across the mountains were restored, the committee gained a reputation for impartial law enforcement even beyond Zintan, and thereby helped to improve inter-communal relations somewhat.

Overall, however, relations between Zintanis and their neighbours remained marked by deep distrust. The rifts of 2011 separated some communities in the mountains from others. The 2014 war divided the allies of 2011.

Bani Walid: The difficult path to local cohesion

Bani Walid entered the post-Qadhafi era in profound disarray. The town's inhabitants had been humiliated by looting revolutionary forces, who also stripped the town's fighters of the weapons and vehicles they had brought with them from Qadhafi's defeated forces. What remained was woefully inadequate to protect the town against the exactions of revolutionary armed groups. The community had been decapitated of its political elite, whose members had been killed, were imprisoned or had fled abroad. Moreover, it was deeply divided, reeling from the killings of 28 May and the forced entry of its revolutionary fighters into the town. Many residents were frustrated with Bani Walid's new status as a renegade town, and the hardship and marginalization that came with it, after local armed men forced out the 28 May Brigade in January 2012. The Social Council that emerged in the wake of this event was mostly recruited from second-tier figures, some of whom remained under the influence of former regime officials who were now based abroad. Although the fifty-member Social Council had been established to represent each of the Warfalla's five sections equally, ostensibly through consultations led by a constituent committee, in reality it was largely self-appointed.[160]

The organization of violence in the town after the expulsion of the 28 May Brigade reflected that disarray. Bands of armed men emerged, many of whom had fought in Qadhafi's forces but, more importantly, had fought together in the town's defence against revolutionary forces in 2011. Salem al-Waer's Warfalla 1993 Brigade was the only group with a formal name, an authorization from the NTC, and a core membership that had supported the revolution, but not participated in the town's forceful capture. But it was a small, newly formed group that lacked both internal cohesion and weaponry. As the Social Council sought to negotiate the exchange of five Misratan hostages against prisoners from Bani Walid in Misrata, doubts emerged over whether the Council could negotiate the release of the hostages, or was powerless in the face of local armed men.[161] This reflected weak leadership in general, and weak links between the Social Council and those carrying weapons, in particular.

The 2012 siege and forceful takeover of the town had the unintended consequence of promoting unity in this deeply divided community. Even many who had supported the revolution saw the operation as an egregious injustice. Many ordinary citizens who had not fought in 2011, ranging from teenagers to retirees, helped defend the town in October 2012. Former exiled opponents such as al-Waer, and Bani Walid revolutionaries who had fought in Zintan, such as Mohamed Salama al-Wadani, played a leading role in the defence. Those members of the 28 May Brigade who participated in the capture and re-established themselves in Bani Walid in its wake lost all remaining sympathies.

In the aftermath of the October 2012 operation, the community's isolation deepened. Many residents were reluctant to go to Tripoli out of fear they would be pulled out at checkpoints and, in the worst case, captured by militias, merely because they were from Bani Walid – there had been recurrent cases. For former members of the army or security institutions, this concern loomed even greater. A young man with whom I fetched a ride back to Tripoli in April 2014 told me that most members of his extended family no longer travelled to the capital, because one of his uncles was a member of the Social Council, and another had been an officer in the security services.[162]

The community became increasingly inward-looking. This applied not only to personal interactions, but also to media consumption. In the homes I visited, people would watch either the al-Dardanil TV channel launched by the Social Council or al-Jamahiriya, the channel run by former regime officials based in Cairo – among them prominent Warfalla – who unabashedly indulged in the reverie of a return to the old days. Few sought to engage with the narratives and debates promoted in the leading Libyan media outlets. The political discourse in Bani Walid came to resemble that of an islet cut off from most of the rest of the country.

Social Council members had fled the town during the October 2012 capture, but they quickly returned and reorganized in clandestinity. In February 2013, they reemerged into the open and compelled the 28 May Brigade to leave the town. Armed local youth had already forced out a unit of the Tripoli Supreme Security Committee (SSC) in December 2012. Two army units dispatched by the government to Bani Walid later withdrew to a checkpoint about 70 kilometres north of the town, and eventually left after they were attacked by unknown assailants in June 2013.[163] Following this incident, no organized armed entities existed in Bani Walid until October 2014, when the Social Council formed a security battalion.

Having learnt a painful lesson in October 2012, the Social Council shed its former confrontational stance, particularly as several of its members – including its chairman, Mohamed al-Barghuthi – remained imprisoned in al-Zawiya until December 2013. In early 2013, the Social Council negotiated with the Zeidan government that a new local council be established, chosen from figures who accepted the new order in Tripoli but excluding the revolutionaries who had supported the town's second capture. The new Local Council gained some local acceptance by paying out compensation payments to those who had suffered property damage in 2011, apparently greasing the hands of Social Council members and their allies.[164] It also managed to put 500 of Bani Walid's men on the payroll of the police.[165] But these were paltry acts of charity. They were vastly insufficient to undermine the Social Council's standing, as the members of the Local Council planned to do, much less to reconcile the town with the revolutionary order. An attempt by notables not represented in the Social Council to establish an alternative Shura Council for Bani Walid with a more conciliatory stance towards Tripoli also fell flat. The Shura Council never gained any local traction.[166] Although some in the town continued to blame the Social Council's stubbornness for the catastrophe of October 2012, the overall impact of the town's renewed humiliation was to cement the Social Council's position in the community.

By moderating its approach and integrating a number of younger men as members
᛫᛫ers, the Social Council broadened its support in the town.[167] Earlier in 2012,

the Council had sought to join forces with other marginalized groups by holding two conferences of tribal politicians; after the town's second capture, it refrained from organizing such meetings to avoid provoking the renewed ire of revolutionary forces.[168] The influence of the Cairo-based former regime officials on the Council waned; they had encouraged the Council in its uncompromising stance, but had not suffered the consequences of this approach, nor had they been able to help defend Bani Walid.[169] Following Barghuthi's release, the Council embarked on a reconciliation effort with Zawiya that eventually led to an agreement in June 2014 – the first cautious step to normalize relations with a former revolutionary stronghold.[170] The Council succeeded in overcoming resistance from local opponents of reconciliation who had forcefully prevented a delegation from Zawiya from entering Bani Walid.[171]

While Bani Walid was increasingly united in its rejection of the revolutionary order, it remained marked by deep divisions as a result of the painful experiences of the 1990s and 2011. The political divides of the past reverberated within families. In April 2014, I spent an evening with an extended family from the Rababsa subtribe. Two members present that evening had demonstrated against the regime in 2011, were imprisoned until the fall of Tripoli, and had supported the revolutionaries in their first capture of Bani Walid. Among the other attendees were several staunch regime supporters. The two sides heatedly threw reproaches at each other for around an hour, and upon leaving, my host told me that this happened all the time. These men continuously dealt with past divides, thereby strengthening social cohesion at the level of the extended family. But when two of my interlocutors who did not know each other well happened to run into each other, the distrust between them was often palpable. Indeed, my hosts would commonly try to keep me from seeing people they distrusted or disliked, in most cases for reasons related to their role in past struggles. This occurred in other research locations too, but was far more common in Bani Walid.

After the army units dispatched by Tripoli withdrew in spring 2013, Bani Walid was wholly demilitarized. There were no forces claiming to represent the state, nor were there local armed groups, though most households possessed weapons. When I visited in April 2014 and expressed surprise at the remarkable stability in the town despite the absence of security forces, I was consistently told that family and tribal solidarities ensured a modicum of security. In this telling, conflict resolution by tribal elders prevented disputes from escalating, the threat of retaliation by the prospective victim's family dissuaded potential criminals from acting, and a settlement pattern whereby most neighbourhoods were inhabited by relatives of the same clan provided additional security. There was undoubtedly a lot of truth in this analysis, although it frequently came with allegations that residual security problems were due to internally displaced people who had found refuge in Bani Walid since 2011. This was less convincing, because the principle of mutual deterrence on a tribal basis actually placed refugees from other towns at a disadvantage, and turned them into easy prey.

Over time, Bani Walid's fragile security came under pressure. In 2013 and early 2014, the town saw several politically motivated assassinations or attempts.[172] Road banditry became more common in the town's environs, and disproportionately targeted motorists who were not from Bani Walid. Young men in the town began ferrying irregular migrants, initially working for networks run by Zintanis and others, then gradually forming their own gangs. The growth of drug abuse and prostitution suggested that social control was eroding.[173] Security deteriorated further with the massive influx of refugees into the town from July 2014 onwards; in September 2014, over a thousand families fled to Bani Walid from Warshafana alone, most of whom would stay there until early 2015.[174] Among the refugees were young men who had fought in Warshafana, including members of criminal gangs, some of whom teamed up with local youth to engage in banditry in Bani Walid's environs.

More broadly, insecurity was the outcome of a prolonged absence of security forces, combined with the lack of alternative opportunities, particularly for young men in the town. Developments in nearby Sirte also increased the sense of vulnerability, in particular the rise of Ansar al-Sharia and, from early 2015 onwards, the city's gradual takeover by a local affiliate of the Islamic State.[175] Sirte had a large Warfalla population with close ties to Bani Walid, implying that the Islamic State could establish itself in Bani Walid, too. In 2016, thousands of families fled to Bani Walid from Sirte, where Misratan forces were fighting IS.

In response to the eroding security, the Social Council in October 2014 established a security battalion drawn from volunteers, taking care to include members from all subtribes of the Warfalla. Though the battalion benefited from small funds mobilized by the Bayda-based justice minister Mabruk Greira, formerly the head of Bani Walid's Local Council, it was a purely local initiative and not affiliated with either of the country's two governments.[176] The unit's day-to-day work involved manning checkpoints and reacting to reports of crimes.

The security battalion's beginnings were difficult, since suspects at times mobilized family members against what they saw as undue interference by an armed group of questionable legitimacy. To minimize the risk of backlash, the battalion worked with Social Council members who engaged with families to persuade them to hand over suspects before the battalion entered into action.[177] This was also a way of shielding members of the battalion from possible prosecution in the future, should they injure or kill someone while on duty. Murder was typically dealt with through customary law ('urf), the perpetrator handed over to a third party from another town for safeguarding, and dispute resolution generally involving his family's exile from Bani Walid.[178] To deal with other crimes, the battalion later began cooperating with the prosecutor in neighbouring Tarhuna.

The battalion was deeply socially embedded. It had several prominent figures, but no leader. I did not have to seek its members out; people I met by chance at the homes of my hosts turned out to be volunteers in the unit. One of them, a man in his forties, told me:

> I am an engineer. On duty nights, I go out in my military fatigue with my Kalashnikov. There are young guys and old men with us. It's not that we are particularly happy about this, but there are no other solutions to insecurity right now. We'd love to have the army and the police secure the town, but there is no state.[179]

The battalion progressively gained recognition in Bani Walid, even among sceptics of the Social Council.[180] But its authority remained contested due to acts by armed locals and transgressions of its own members. After a suspected IS operative died under torture in the battalion's prison, in March 2016, his relatives assassinated a prominent figure in the battalion whom they held responsible.[181] On another occasion, the battalion suspended its work in response to allegations by a damaged party, only to be reactivated following pressure from the community.[182] Armed locals repeatedly freed their relatives from the prison.

The battalion remained a temporary stopgap measure devised by the collectivity, with a minimal remit. For example, it did not clamp down on migrant smuggling networks in the town, which by 2016 had become powerful and hugely profitable. The number of dead migrant bodies found in the town's environs at times numbered in the dozens per week, but the Social Council and its battalion stopped short of confronting the smugglers, except to demand that they circumvent the town to reduce the pressure on its morgue.[183]

Nevertheless, the battalion and the Social Council ensured a modicum of stability in an environment marked by pervasive conflict, rampant criminality and growing extremist activity. The battalion embodied a notable change from the unruly gangs that had emerged in early 2012, within what was then a shattered community. It remained the only organized armed group in Bani Walid until mid-2017. Throughout this time, the Social Council preserved a neutral position in Libya's conflicts, and prevented the warring parties from using the town as a base. This struggle for neutrality is discussed in the next chapter.

Bani Walid regained a degree of cohesion after suffering deep divides through the conflicts of 2011 and 2012. Its social fabric remained dense despite all the rifts. By focusing more clearly on communal interests after the catastrophe of October 2012, the Social Council gradually managed to establish a largely unchallenged position of collective leadership. For all its deficiencies, the collective solution to insecurity provided some stability, and closed the road to the establishment of armed groups affiliated to the conflicting parties.

Tobruk: The backwater

The civil war of 2011 left Tobruk's social order largely untouched. It had neither provoked significant rifts in the city, nor promoted stronger local cohesion. It had not produced a new elite, nor brought the downfall of the local establishment. There was no revolutionary leadership in Tobruk. The city's political players adopted the revolutionary discourse dominant nationwide after the war, but few could claim to have played a meaningful role in the revolution. Only a few dozen men from Tobruk had fought at the front, and they were too small a minority to establish themselves as a dominant force in the city once the war was over. The head of the Local Council, Faraj Yasin al-Mabri, drew his influence as much from well-established patronage networks and traditional legitimacy as from his temporary imprisonment under Qadhafi and his early support for the revolution. The former commander of Tobruk military region, Gen. Suleiman Mahmoud, was reluctant to play politics after the war, and his influence declined. Tribal notables who had been key figures in local politics under Qadhafi, such as al-Tayyeb al-Sharif, tried to make people forget their previous role by changing their tune, seizing on issues such as the unavenged murder of Gen. Abdelfattah Younes or the region's nascent autonomy movement.

Unlike many other Libyan cities, Tobruk did not witness a mushrooming of militias after the war. This was likely the result of a combination of factors. First, because the revolution provoked no salient divides in the city, residents felt no acute threat that would have caused them to form or join armed groups. Because no such divides emerged, tribal identities in Tobruk were not politicized, at least not in a way that set the city's three main tribes – the Obeidat, Mniffa and Qutaan – against each other. Tobruk's isolated geographical setting meant that there were no significant external threats, even if locals eyed the jihadist groups in neighbouring Darna with increasing suspicion. Already under Qadhafi, arbitration in property disputes and the dispensation of justice for capital offences had commonly occurred outside the framework of the state in Tobruk and its surrounding region, through the use of customary law and mediation – although this system had come under increasing pressure in the years preceding the revolution.[184] Much as in Bani Walid, this system of mutual deterrence and conflict resolution was the principal safeguard against the erosion of security after state authority collapsed. It also reproduced a patriarchal order that likely deterred prospective militia leaders from setting themselves up.

Second, the city was ill-positioned to partake in the post-revolutionary struggles over the militia economy. Tobruk's arsenals had mostly been destroyed by loyalist officers before they fled; Tobruk's revolutionaries were few, and most of them fought with groups from other cities, hence they did not possess great amounts of weaponry; finally, their peripheral location left them with little leverage over the struggles unfolding in Tripoli. As local politicians watched these struggles from afar, the urge to take action against their marginalization grew.

Before Haftar harnessed such local resentment for his operation, it manifested itself in a form that reflected these specific local circumstances. When forces loyal to Ibrahim al-Jadhran closed down the oil export terminals in the 'oil crescent' in mid-2013, they found an ally in a group from Tobruk that – like Jadhran himself – demanded autonomy for eastern Libya, and shut down Tobruk's al-Hariqa terminal to increase the pressure on the Zeidan government. In contrast to the closures in the oil crescent, however, the action in Tobruk was not led by a young militia leader, but by a senior tribal politician of the Obeidat, Mansur al-Salihin al-Mabri. Moreover, the actors in Tobruk were not a clearly identifiable armed group; it sufficed that Salihin threatened to send armed men to attack any tanker entering the port.[185] Salihin had public opinion in Tobruk against him, and a prominent opponent at the head of the Local Council, his cousin Faraj Yasin al-Mabri. The two had long been bitter rivals, and Salihin publicly embarrassed his cousin when the latter held a press conference with Zeidan in October 2013 to announce that the port would be reopened, only to return to Tobruk and find Salihin immune to his pleas and offers.[186] Salihin took advantage of the fact that his cousin and others in Tobruk were reluctant to confront him for fear of provoking internal discord – particularly as little could be gained by backing the government.[187] He eventually lifted the blockade after Zeidan's successor Thinni struck a deal with Jadhran, in April 2014.

Meanwhile, Tobruk remained on the margins of post-revolutionary distributive struggles. In autumn 2013, the chief of staff chose the city as the location of one out of three newly created brigades that were to be recruited from all across Libya, receive training abroad and form the core of a new national army. The recruitment committee established for that purpose in Tobruk predictably subverted the plan; the 1,000 recruits were overwhelmingly from Tobruk and its environs.[188] This was a lone opportunity for local military players to appropriate a small share of the resources that were fought over by militia leaders in Tripoli.

The resources Tobruk's political players were able to mobilize from Tripoli paled in comparison to the interests at stake in the city's transborder economy. Contrary to developments along the western and southern borders, in Tobruk the revolution did not overturn the balance of power between rival networks operating in this economy. These networks had not been involved on opposing sides of the civil war, nor had they accumulated large stocks of arms. The war produced no losers in the smuggling business – only winners, since the collapse of central authority further reduced the constraints placed on smuggling.

Since the 1970s, Tobruk had become a hub for consumer goods imported tax-free into Libya, then smuggled into Egypt; more recently, Moroccan hashish had also become an important merchandise.[189] The 2011 revolution at first saw weapons being smuggled into Libya, and then much greater outflows of weapons as the regime fell. After the war, a thriving trade in used cars imported tax-free via Tobruk's port developed, and growing quantities of expired, often hazardous, Egyptian foodstuffs were illicitly imported into Libya, exploiting weak or complicit customs controls.[190] Finally, flows of irregular migrants expanded rapidly after the war, including both Egyptian labour migrants circumventing the constantly changing visa regimes, and migrants from Egypt and beyond seeking to travel on to Europe. Most of these smuggling activities were controlled by, and socially embedded in, clan-based networks associated with the Awlad Ali tribe, which spanned the border.[191]

For a while, two units recruited from former revolutionary fighters tried to impose their control over the border, thereby threatening the vested interests associated with this economy. In the war's final days, Mustafa Abdeljalil charged a revolutionary commander and former political prisoner from Tobruk with assembling a unit named 'Shield of Tobruk' to secure the border crossing with Egypt. In early 2012, the new deputy defence minister in charge of the border guard, a former LIFG member and longtime prisoner called al-Siddiq al-Mabruk, who was an Obeidi from the Darna area, put another revolutionary commander from Tobruk in charge of forming a border guard unit, Battalion 71. The Shield of Tobruk was made up mostly of civilians, many of whom had been at the front with the unit's commander, whereas Battalion 71 included young men who had fought with the unit's head, an officer named Muftah Omar Hamza, as well as regular soldiers from the Omar al-Mukhtar Brigade.[192]

Both units repeatedly clashed with smugglers, seizing illicit goods and arresting irregular migrants.[193] Having suffered numerous injuries in its ranks, the Shield withdrew from the crossing for the first time in mid-2012. In early 2013, it returned to the crossing in a concerted effort with Battalion 71, which patrolled the border. Both units were again drawn into repeated clashes with smugglers, and both commanders were themselves injured in such altercations. Tired of its Sysiphean struggle with vested interests, the Shield dissolved itself in August 2013.[194] Battalion 71 continued its patrols, but when the Egyptian air force bombed one of them, in December 2014, it emerged that some members of the unit were using their vehicles to transport drugs.[195] Hamza and the commander of the Omar al-Mukhtar Brigade suspended the patrols and pledged to tighten oversight, but were removed from their posts by Haftar's chief of staff, Abderrazeq al-Nadhuri. Both officers opposed Haftar's operation, contrary to some rank and file in their units, who had proclaimed their support.[196]

The smuggling networks that had caused the downfall of the two units were deeply socially embedded, and generally structured on kinship ties.[197] These networks had long infiltrated security institutions on both sides of the border, and continued to do so after 2011. The revolutionary fighters were too small a minority to prevail against the interests associated with these networks. Some of these fighters had been part of such networks even before the war, or were drawn into them afterwards.

Haftar's operation, which from its beginnings used Tobruk as one of its main bases, did not confront such networks. It was concerned with the conflict in Benghazi, 400 kilometres to the west of Tobruk. Haftar was able to mobilize substantial local support in Tobruk. Given the weakness of revolutionary leadership in Tobruk, few local leaders had an interest in opposing Haftar, and those who did lacked the capacity. The operation's promise to restore the position of the old army, whose members had become the target of an accelerating assassination campaign in Benghazi, resonated with many officers in Cyrenaica, including in Tobruk.

Haftar also began courting local tribal elders early on. His campaign appeared designed to reinstate an order in which senior notables and officers retained their social and political pre-eminence over the younger men whose armed groups had taken control of Benghazi and Darna. Proponents of eastern autonomy saw in Haftar – a declared nationalist, and member of the Firjan tribe of central Libya – a useful instrument to attack the government in Tripoli and its eastern allies, and gambled that they could sideline him once he had served his purpose.

But for all the sources of support for Haftar's operation, it did not emerge from socially embedded forces. Although it initially resembled a loosely linked coalition of armed groups, Haftar progressively centralized the operation's command structure, and sidelined challengers within the coalition. His ability to do so stemmed in large degree from the support he received from Egypt and the UAE. Foreign support and centralized command provided Haftar with wide-ranging autonomy from local actors. The next chapter analyses Haftar's rise in detail.

Elsewhere: The reign of militias

The preceding four case studies cannot claim to be representative of Libya's post-revolutionary conflict landscape. The socially embedded forces of Misrata and the Nafusa Mountains were key players in Libya's political scene from 2011 onwards. Bani Walid and Tobruk were not the only towns where social mechanisms for conflict resolution offered temporary stopgap measures after the collapse of central authority. Indeed, many areas of Libya witnessed an astounding degree of stability in the years after 2011, and the conflicts that raged from 2014 onwards largely bypassed them. But in key arenas for conflicts, including Tripoli and Benghazi, armed groups dominated whose political or economic interests set them much more clearly apart from their social surroundings. Most of them emerged under conditions that differed markedly from those described in these four cases.

Some of these armed groups emerged out of tight-knit networks of revolutionary fighters, while others only formed after the war. Some had been embedded in the social fabric but progressively isolated themselves, such as by defining themselves more explicitly through Islamist ideology, or by acquiring notoriety for criminal activity. Others set themselves up as extremist or criminal groups from the start, or were formed by political players. Like more deeply rooted networks, the vast majority of these armed groups financed themselves at least in part with state salaries and inflated operating budgets, since most were nominally part of state security institutions such as the army, the Supreme Security Committee, the Libya Shield Force, the border guards or the PFGs.[198] State salaries for such groups became only gradually scarcer after the split through government institutions in mid-2014.

What the social and political conditions in which such groups formed had in common was that they were not marked by the strong degree of communal cohesion induced by collective struggle, such as in Misrata and the Nafusa Mountains during the revolution, and in Bani Walid in the post-revolutionary period. Beyond this commonality, the contexts that gave rise to such groups can be analytically separated into three types.

The first type of setting were large cities, which not only had a social fabric that was not as dense as that of smaller communities, but also an experience of the civil war that differed from that of revolutionary strongholds and loyalist towns. Misrata was the only large city where the revolutionary struggle had forged local cohesion and a strong communal identity. In Benghazi, the threat of regime forces returning to take the city vanished one month into the uprising, and suspicion among the armed groups in the city grew as the war continued. With the exception of Ajdabiya, other eastern cities were far removed from the front line.

In the west and south, all cities except Misrata were firmly under regime control from early March onwards. This meant that these cities' revolutionaries organized underground, or went to liberated areas to join the armed struggle. In neither case could they form the socially embedded fighting groups that emerged in revolutionary strongholds. When they eventually established themselves in their hometowns, they immediately moved to seize control of strategic locations or lucrative assets, at times clashing with other local armed groups that had emerged after the regime's collapse. In Tripoli, this pattern was aggravated by the rivalry over the control of government institutions, which led political players to invest in firepower in the city, such as in the form of the Qa'qa' and Sawaeq Brigades, or that of the armed groups affiliated with the Libyan Revolutionaries Operations Room (LROR).[199] The volatile situation in such cities offered a fertile environment for the development of armed groups marked by various strands of Salafi or jihadi ideology. These groups often put themselves forward as purveyors of order, and claimed to clamp down on the criminal activity of their rivals.

The second setting was that of communities that had been acquiescent or supportive of the regime during the war, and were vanquished and decapitated of their elites at its end. Such communities typically saw a small, revolutionary minority establish itself by force, backed by outside actors with whom they had fought during the war. The leading local figures associated with the regime often fled abroad, and the impotence of the remaining community leaders in the face of defeat, victimization and marginalization undermined their standing. In such settings, armed groups led by young or middle-aged men faced no significant counterweights.

Bani Walid might well have provided a textbook example for such a setting, had locals not compelled revolutionary forces to leave on two occasions. The town otherwise appeared predestined to follow a trajectory akin to that of Sirte, where local revolutionaries with a strong jihadist component imposed themselves with support from Misratan allies, later forming a local offshoot of Ansar al-Sharia, which eventually evolved into an affiliate of the Islamic State that took complete control of the city.[200] Other examples included the Warshafana area southwest of Tripoli, where elements of the myriad armed groups from Zintan and Tripoli established themselves in properties belonging to former senior regime figures, and gradually linked up with local criminals to engage in banditry, looting and extortion, impervious to the efforts of local elders at re-establishing order.[201] As Libya's conflicts raged on, former regime officials added to the volatile mix in such communities by setting up their own armed groups, some of which were themselves little more than criminal gangs.

The third were peripheral regions that had been under regime control for most of the war, and where regime collapse triggered a sudden mushrooming of new armed groups that scrambled for control of arsenals and economic assets, including oilfields, refineries and transborder traffic. In some areas, the regime had favoured networks associated with particular tribes in the management of the illicit transborder economy. The regime's demise prompted at times sudden and violent reversals of such orders.

These struggles, which erupted in late 2011 and early 2012, frequently escalated into inter-communal conflicts as conflicting parties retaliated indiscriminately against members of the community to which their adversaries belonged. But although the inter-communal tensions provoked by such conflicts were real and affected entire tribes or ethnic groups, there could be no mistaking that the armed groups at the core of these struggles were not champions of their communities' interests. Most frequently, they were narrow-based enterprises concerned primarily with predation. Examples of such struggles included the conflicts in Kufra and Sabha, as well as those between armed groups from Zuwara and Rigdalain, all of which were primarily over control of the illicit economy.[202] Many of the armed groups that established themselves in oilfields across the country's south and the export terminals in the oil crescent rapidly devolved into protection rackets. They obtained official sanction by being nominally integrated into the Petroleum Facilities Guard. The leaders of such groups gradually strengthened their influence and centralized control, thanks to the profits from these rackets. Some of them – most prominently Ibrahim al-Jadhran in the oil crescent – imposed themselves as indispensable interlocutors for the Tripoli government and external actors.[203]

Few of the groups that emerged in these three types of settings could pass as rebels, with the exception of Ansar al-Sharia, the Islamic State and armed proponents of regional autonomy. Nor did they fit into the militia category in its narrow definition as irregular counterinsurgent forces.[204] In a less restrictive sense, 'militia' does, however, appear to be the most appropriate collective term for them, much as it has been applied to a variety of armed groups in other cases where the collapse of central authority erased distinctions between government proxies and insurgents, and where non-state armed groups often claimed to represent the state, such as in Lebanon and Somalia.[205] In any case, these armed groups could serve as units of analysis. Compared to socially embedded forces, they could be more clearly distinguished from their communities, from which they were separated by virtue of defining themselves ideologically, operating as profit-making schemes for certain individuals, or following the directions of political actors based outside their communities.

Conclusion

An analysis of Libya's conflicts as an interaction between armed groups would miss central aspects of the processes unfolding since 2011. Key forces in Libya's conflict landscape could not be adequately understood as discrete organizations. Instead, they resembled networks that were deeply rooted in local communities, in some cases to the point of being indistinguishable from them. Whether and how they became active in Libya's conflicts depended not exclusively, or even primarily, on self-maximizing calculations by warlords, militia leaders or politicians. Rather, their actions responded to complex local processes of consultation, coordination and collective decision-making that often stubbornly resisted the schemes of individual political players. Social embeddedness imposed significant constraints on actors in Libya's conflicts, just as it ensured much of their resilience and fighting power.

The social embeddedness of forces in Libya's conflicts was not an expression of their communities' innate characteristics. The pre-war social fabric of Misrata had much in common with that of a city such as Zawiya, which became a base for predatory militias that escaped social control. A much smaller town inhabited by a single tribe, Zintan differed considerably from Misrata, and more closely resembled Bani Walid, which only narrowly escaped a downward trajectory of internal conflict and rule by an armed minority. And yet, the forces that emerged in Misrata and Zintan were both deeply embedded in their communities. The tight-knit networks and communal identity that underpinned these forces had been shaped by several months of common struggle against regime forces. The dominance of socially disembedded armed groups in localities that had not experienced such common struggle supports the present argument about the origins of social embeddedness.

Forces that were deeply embedded in communities changed with their communities. In Misrata, these forces lost their erstwhile unity as political divisions deepened in the city, and regained it only in the face of an external threat to the entire community. In Zintan, socially embedded forces were eclipsed by the rise of militia conglomerates that disintegrated only when the community faced an existential threat. Bani Walid only gradually restored the cohesion and the collective leadership necessary for the emergence of socially embedded security structures. It did so largely in response to the community's victimization and forced isolation. In Tobruk, no strong leadership emerged in 2011 or thereafter, and the city was little transformed by the conflict, in part due to its peripheral location. The weakness of local leadership and of socially embedded forces in Tobruk would provide a favourable setting for the establishment of Haftar's power structure.

The process of fragmentation (2015–19)

When defending their lack of success in brokering a meaningful solution to Libya's conflicts, Western officials often pointed to the extraordinary fragmentation of Libya's political landscape. Libya, they said, just was like that, and always had been. UN Special Representative Martin Kobler attributed this fragmentation to '42 years of autocracy and nepotism' under Qadhafi.[1] UK foreign secretary Philip Hammond told the House of Commons:

> We should be clear about Libya's historical context: it is a country that has traditionally had a high degree of devolution in its governance structure, which is often held together by a strong man at the centre. …
>
> If only it were so simple as there being two sides; there are about 120 sides as far as I can make out.[2]

For close observers of developments in Libya, of course, the countless divisions emerging in the wake of the 2014–15 civil war were not a reflection of unchanging societal characteristics. In fact, they represented a rather novel form of fragmentation – one shaped in no small measure by the UN-led negotiations themselves.[3]

This chapter offers a theoretical understanding of Libya's fragmentation as the product of conflicting pressures originating from strong local social ties and changing strategic conditions. Twice – in 2011 and again in 2014 – communities and their leaders closed ranks against a common enemy, only for local unity to dissolve into internal rivalry as civil war gave way to political bargaining. Each time strategic conditions changed, local actors in the conflict repositioned themselves, entering into new alliances and enmities, and thereby inflicting ever new rifts onto the local social fabric. Where communities remained cohesive, local actors were constrained in their external alliances and their action against internal rivals. Haftar's establishment of a centralized power structure in eastern Libya benefited from the dearth of cohesive local forces and the weakness of leadership in peripheral areas of Cyrenaica. Empirically, this chapter focuses on the unravelling of the two opposing camps of 2014 in western Libya, and the consolidation of Haftar's rule over the east.

Is fragmentation a game?

Whether as an explicit framework or by shaping underlying assumptions, rational choice theory has acquired hegemonic influence in the recent literature on civil wars.

The vast majority of contributions to this literature see actors in civil wars as defined by their relative power, and driven by varying combinations of threats, opportunities and uncertainty. Formal models based on such assumptions have the advantage of parsimony, but necessarily discount fundamental aspects of social reality, such as social structure, history and its collective memory, ideology, legitimacy, as well as the social construction of threats.[4] In their crudest form, these models reduce the causes of civil war and its persistence to a cost-benefit analysis of rebellion or bargaining failures caused by imperfect information and commitment problems.[5] Such models are ahistorical, asocial and apolitical; they collapse under any careful empirical analysis of particular cases.[6] Even more sophisticated and more empirically grounded rational choice models are necessarily reductionist in their exclusive focus on rational calculations, and their dismissal of the social in shaping them.[7]

The bulk of the literature on fragmentation in civil wars draws on rational choice theory. The general assumption is that the leaders of armed groups are perfectly flexible in their pursuit of wealth and power, as well as their response to threats. Warlords or rebel leaders defect due to pressure or incentives by governments or other rebel groups.[8] Even where this literature registers the role of social ties, it is unable to integrate them into its models.[9]

The most compelling game-theoretic model of alliance formation and fragmentation has been developed both as a theory of tribal war and as an approach to contemporary civil war.[10] In a reformulation of the Hobbesian security dilemma, groups competing in a struggle without arbiter seek to maximize their military power by entering into alliances against adversaries. Factions within groups may disagree with decisions of war and peace due to the associated costs or benefits, prompting them to split and ally with former adversaries. Groups seek to strike alliances that allow them to win, but at the same time want to ensure that they enjoy maximal weight and benefits within the alliance.[11] Pervasive distrust between groups means they prefer to defect from a winning coalition to join their former adversaries if they fear being marginalized or even annihilated by the strongest group in the coalition. 'The result is a process of constant defection, alliance reconfiguration, and group fractionalization.'[12]

A variant of that model emphasizes that rebel groups are organizations that seek to ensure their members' survival against a perceived threat; if the organization is losing, it can no longer credibly guarantee survival; if it is winning, the unifying threat dissipates, exacerbating collective action problems. As a result, 'only battlefield stalemate ... can preserve organizational cohesion'.[13]

The problem with such theories – leaving aside the more fundamental issues with conceptions of perfectly flexible, self-maximizing actors – is their assumption that, despite unceasing alliance formation and fragmentation, *nothing else changes*. This recalls segmentary lineage theory, as Evans-Pritchard applied it to Libyan politics in the mid-twentieth century, thereby grafting an equilibrium model onto a society that, in reality, was undergoing momentous changes.[14] What we observe in Libya and other collapsed states is not simply that groups fragment into their more cohesive components. Civil wars tend to become increasingly complex as they drag on.[15] This is not least because two assumptions of rational choice models do not hold: first – albeit to varying degrees – leaders of armed groups are not free to follow their individual whims, but are bound by social obligations and loyalties. Second, the rifts provoked by fractionalization profoundly transform the societies in which armed groups are embedded. As the conflict rages on, layers upon layers of divides are superimposed onto each other. Cohesion and trust are not constants; conflict deeply affects such properties of social ties and transforms social groups – pre-war groups may cease to exist, new groups may come into being. In sum, game-theoretic models cannot grasp fragmentation as a process.

However, this does not mean that we should dispense with rational choice theory altogether when analysing fragmentation. While choice-theoretic models are excessively reductionist, they nonetheless capture critical aspects of behaviour among actors in civil wars. These actors may not be unconstrained in their pursuit of wealth and power, or may not dedicate themselves exclusively to these aims. They may overcome certain instances of uncertainty by drawing on ties of trust or their ideological convictions. But the criticality of security threats and the pervasiveness of uncertainty mean that these factors nevertheless fundamentally shape their actions – as the analysis of the revolution's first weeks has shown.

Previous approaches that combined the insights of rational choice theory with a sociological understanding of agency have focused on the analysis of medium-to-long-term historical processes.[16] So have social network theorists, who argue that the complex web of social ties in which individuals are embedded often drives them to act at cross-purposes: in a context marked by relative institutional continuity, social structure is produced by the sedimentation of micro-level interactions over decades.[17] Civil wars, however, tend to involve processes of wide-ranging institutional destruction and creation through violence, and inflict abrupt changes on social structures. The rules of the game often change rapidly in civil wars and collapsed states, impelling individuals to strike up new relations, and cut off old ones. To understand the role of social ties for actors in conflict, as well as the pressures on individual action captured by rational choice theory, we need to understand how the two interact.

Let us assume that actors in civil wars respond to the constraints and incentives of a given strategic situation – the 'rules of the game' of rational choice theorists, or what I prefer to call the strategic conditions. Their action is also enabled and constrained by the social networks they are embedded in, including the conceptions of interests and identities these networks are infused with. Nevertheless, the immediacy and criticality of threats and opportunities, as well as the rapid changes in the capabilities of actors – in particular, their changing relative power – all encourage ruthless, determined action that runs counter to, and reconfigures the constraints emanating from, social ties. The violence wielded by these actors transforms social ties, creating new rifts and loyalties.

If we combine this insight with the idea that constantly changing strategic conditions force actors to frequently redefine alliances and enmities, two hypotheses follow: first, social ties and strategic conditions frequently exert contradictory pressures on actors. Second, strategic action inflicts ever new rifts on the social fabric, which are superimposed onto each other as one set of strategic conditions supersedes another. Taken together, these two propositions provide a theory for the process of fragmentation in Libya.

Before moving on, a rough definition of strategic conditions is in order. By the strategic conditions in a civil war or collapsed state, I mean the configuration of three parameters: threat, opportunity and uncertainty. In responding to the pressures and incentives of these conditions, the defining property of actors is their relative power vis-à-vis other actors. Threats, opportunities and uncertainty are a function of the interplay of all actors on the scene: the government (if it exists), foreign governments, other external actors and other local parties to the conflict. They include such diverse aspects as the threat of force or other penalizing measures, the opportunity of access to resources from criminal activity, foreign sponsors or the central government, and the presence or absence of factors that reduce uncertainty, such as effective central authority, a foreign power acting as arbiter, or local institutions that provide a degree of order and trust.

Changes in strategic conditions (2011–19)

During the period under investigation, strategic conditions in Libya underwent rapid change. Five distinct phases can be distinguished, each placing radically different constraints on actors: three phases of civil war, in 2011, 2014–15 and 2019, separated by two periods of relative détente in which violent conflict escalated only intermittently, or was confined to specific local theatres. Such a succession of distinct strategic circumstances is nothing unusual in situations where central authority has collapsed, or is extremely weak, and where the interests and involvement of foreign governments undergo dramatic shifts; Lebanon, Somalia and Afghanistan can all serve as examples.[18] I argue that the aggregate impact of the conflicting pressures emanating from these different conditions is crucial, but has not yet been systematically studied in the literature on civil wars.

Between February and October 2011, actors were forced to unequivocally take sides in the civil war between revolutionary forces and the regime. In revolutionary strongholds and liberated areas, this required closing local ranks against suspected regime collaborators and neighbouring communities that were considered as loyalist. In areas under regime control, it could mean discouraging, or informing on, clandestine activity by 'the rats', as official discourse called the revolutionaries; supporting the regime's propaganda machine by taking part in meetings, rallies and media campaigns; or joining the war effort. The imperative of choosing sides conflicted with the great uncertainty over the prospects for victory. Several regime officials later claimed to have secretly cooperated with the revolutionaries, or sabotaged the counterinsurgency efforts. The opportunities for political advancement required radically different strategies from actors on both sides of the divide: in regime-controlled areas, survival and power depended primarily on the support one could mobilize from the centre in Tripoli. In revolutionary strongholds, it required mobilizing local support, and gaining local recognition. There was little to be obtained from the NTC, though networking to access assistance from foreign governments became more important as the war continued.

Between October 2011 and May 2014, these clear divides blurred. The collapse of central authority locked in a newly fragmented landscape: opportunities to access state resources were no longer counterbalanced by a central leadership able to enforce compliance, leading to a free-for-all that forestalled the re-establishment of central authority. In revolutionary strongholds, the external threat that had induced local cohesion vanished with the fall of the regime, and local unity gave way to competition. Across the country, the combination of vast new opportunities to accumulate wealth and power with the generalization of diffuse security threats fuelled a proliferation of armed groups. New patronage networks formed that competed over access to state resources, within an unstable context marked by two successive governments and frequent changes in ministerial positions. Although the institutional rules of the game remained vaguely defined and were routinely violated, the consensus of dominant political forces on the founding myth of the 17th February revolution and the legitimacy of the GNC limited the uncertainty over the political outlook. Those who had sided with the regime in 2011 remained excluded from political participation, and political actors were careful not to associate themselves with them publicly.

From May 2014 to the spring of 2015, a clear-cut divide split the national political landscape anew. A major escalation of violence yet again left little room for ambivalent positions. Entire communities were equated as being associated with one side or another; massive displacement occurred as citizens perceived to be associated with the adversary fled cities and regions under the control of one camp, such as Tripoli, Benghazi and the Warshafana area. Open dissent with the political stance of the forces controlling an area was often dangerous. The line between friends and enemies now ran elsewhere; the former allies of 2011 found themselves in opposing camps, one of which reached out to former regime elements to improve its chances of winning the war, while the other allied with jihadists whom it billed as 'revolutionaries'. Few communities managed to stay out of the conflict. On both sides, the prospects were highly uncertain; each camp represented a coalition of diverse players, all gambling that they would prevail over their allies once they had won a decisive advantage over the enemy camp. The patronage networks built up over the preceding years collapsed as state institutions split, and foreign support – political, financial, military – as well as the shadow economy supplanted state budgets as a key source of actors' capabilities. Initially, the proponents on each side insisted that the institutions they supported represented the legitimate order. But as the conflict dragged on without a victory for either side, it became clear that the tug-of-war had obliterated the very basis for legitimate institutions.

During the spring of 2015, this state of polarization gave way to a more fragmented landscape. Local leaders in the west, suffering the consequences of a war that seemed impossible to win, negotiated a series of local ceasefires. The UN-led mediation effort lured political actors across the spectrum with the possibility of joining a unity government. Former allies began accusing each other of being traitors or war profiteers, depending on the choice they made in this situation. These divides also ran through formerly united communities. The degree of fragmentation was such that the UN had difficulties identifying the relevant interlocutors, and resorted to a growing array of dialogue tracks to incorporate different stakeholders. Whether the negotiations would lead to an agreement was as uncertain as the gains to be made from joining a unity government, should it be formed. The final stage of the negotiations and the early months of the Libyan Political Agreement (LPA) therefore saw much fence-sitting and side-switching. Many actors maintained an ambivalent position even after the Presidency Council (PC) established itself in Tripoli in March 2016. Given the PC's military impotence, its politically diverse composition, and its poor access to Central Bank funding, limited benefits were to be had from outright support or opposition to the PC.

In few regions did the divide between opponents and supporters of the PC translate into existential threats to representatives of either side. Even in Tripoli, the struggle between the two camps remained confined to a few larger confrontations that were each limited to a specific location and subsided after three or four days of fighting. The exception was Cyrenaica, where strategic conditions had become increasingly uncoupled from the rest of the country. There, Haftar saw PC supporters as a challenge to his pre-eminence and persecuted them with increasing relentlessness, driving them to Tripoli, abroad or into silence.

Instead of a new macro-divide between supporters and opponents of the unity government, the political landscape became even more fragmented. The enmities of the two civil wars lost their power, but so did the rhetoric of reconciliation and national unity. Supporters of the unity government grew disillusioned with its ineffectiveness, and its reluctance to confront its challengers. Instead of acting as a counterweight to Haftar, the unity government increasingly allowed Haftar's structures to finance themselves through a web of ties linking them to the Tripoli institutions. There no longer appeared to be any limits to opportunistic alliances – former Haftar supporters in the east now sided with Haftar's enemies; senior regime figures met with former jihadist leaders to examine the possibilities of collective political action. But although everything now appeared possible, in reality nothing was: such alliances had no way of altering the balance of power. The Presidency Council and its government existed because Western governments and the UN considered them to be the sole legitimate authority. Haftar was too weak to seize power by force; for the other armed groups, toppling the government militarily held no prospect of assuming power, nor could political forces that were outside the LPA institutions renegotiate executive authority. There was no way out of the impasse.

In April 2019, Haftar's surprise offensive on Tripoli suddenly caused the political landscape to split in two yet again. In western Libya, the offensive sparked widespread rejection and resistance. Tripoli officials who had been conciliatory towards Haftar, or even suspected of colluding with him, now banded together with the hardline revolutionaries who had long rejected the unity government, to form a united front against Haftar. The divide was now more clearly between east and west, with some exceptions: Zintan was split between fierce opponents and supporters of Haftar, while the Kaniyat militia had drawn the city of Tarhuna into the war on Haftar's side. In opposing Haftar, Misrata rediscovered a unity of purpose its business elite and armed groups had long been missing.

The following case studies examine how the impulses emanating from changing strategic conditions conflicted with the constraints imposed by social ties, and to what extent these contradictions promoted political fragmentation.

Trajectories of fragmentation

Misrata: Social cohesion, political fragmentation

The preceding two chapters have provided accounts of developments in Misrata during 2011–14, of which only the broad outlines shall be recalled here. The revolutionary war spawned cohesive, socially embedded forces underwritten by a strong collective identity, and led by a newly powerful elite. The new Misratan identity was built on a clear definition of the enemy: the former regime and its supporters, including entire communities such as Tawargha and Bani Walid, as well as certain residents of Misrata deemed to have been collaborators.

As the revolutionary coalition disintegrated following Qadhafi's demise, hard-liners came to dominate Misrata. They demanded the wholesale exclusion of former officials from politics and entered into conflict with other former revolutionaries, including Zintani armed groups in Tripoli. They also sidelined Misratan figures who opposed their uncompromising stance.

During this period, from late 2011 to mid-2014, the unity Misrata had displayed during the war crumbled not only over the disagreements between revolutionary hard-liners and moderates, but also over rivalries over access to state offices and resources. One example was the emergence of two separate Misratan units of the Libya Shield Force: the Central Shield and the Third Force. Another was the distributive struggle over the allocation of compensation payments for damages incurred during the 2011 war, which eventually forced the Local Council to suspend the payments in early 2013.[19] There was growing disillusionment in the city over Misratan figures in Tripoli, who were increasingly seen as defending parochial – rather than communal – interests. This went, for example, for the chairman of the Libyan Investment Authority (LIA) Mohsen Derregia, Deputy Defence Minister al-Tuhami Buzian, and GNC member Abderrahman al-Sweihli.[20]

Such rivalries were swept under the rug during the 2014 airport war. Most opponents of the war were reluctant or afraid to speak out. The operation was engineered by a few leading figures who drove the majority of Misratan battalions into joining the war.[21] But when I visited Misrata in October 2014, only long-standing, trusted acquaintances admitted to having opposed the war; many businessmen and politicians who would later emerge as the city's moderates defended the operation.[22]

The justification for the war relied on the spectre of counter-revolutionary forces, much in line with the dominant political discourse in the city since 2011. Nevertheless, uniting the city behind the war required redefining the enemies of the revolution and hardening the divide. Although the declared primary targets of the July 2014 operation were Haftar and his allies in Tripoli, the Qa'qa' and Sawaeq Brigades, the belligerent discourse of the time often expanded this hostility to Zintan and the eastern tribes who were thought to be supporting Haftar – or simply 'the Bedouins'. Supporters of that camp were deemed traitors, and dialogue with its representatives was ruled out while the war in Tripoli continued. The war demonstrated the power of a handful of Misratan leaders to unite the city behind them, and draw it into a fateful conflict in pursuit of their political goals.

This strategy, however, came at a heavy cost for Misrata's political leaders as strategic conditions changed. The attempts of the operation's masterminds at turning their military victory in Tripoli into political advantage rapidly revealed the limits of their influence, and left Misrata more divided than ever before. As soon as the objective of dislodging the Zintanis from Tripoli was achieved and the UN began mediating, Misratan unity dissolved. In early October, the central political figure behind the operation, Fathi Bashagha, began positioning himself in favour of negotiations. He thereby parted ways with several of his close allies from before and during the operation, including fellow HoR boycotter Mohamed Ibrahim al-Dharrat and religious figure Ibrahim ben Ghashir. When I met Dharrat in October 2014, he warned that he did not feel represented by the figures with whom UN envoy Leon was speaking.[23] Later, such subtleties would give way to open hostility towards Bashagha.

Many of the city's businessmen supported Bashagha's stance early on. Their representatives claimed to me that they could easily rein in 'hotheads' such as Salah Badi, 'extremists' such as Dharrat, and 'opportunists' like Sweihli, and would have no difficulties in negotiating a political deal.[24] Many commanders of armed groups joined this position, distancing themselves from the 'Islamists' with whom they had fought in Tripoli. They rejected the calls of hardliners for laying siege to Zintan itself. These commanders sought direct influence in negotiations, complaining that foreign envoys did not engage with them.[25] Other commanders and politicians, including Sweihli, supported the self-appointed government of Omar al-Hassi, either as a bargaining tactic or out of a mistaken belief that they could turn territorial control over Tripoli into international recognition for Hassi.

The difficulty of deciding who was competent to represent Misrata was one among several dilemmas that emerged from the city's united position during the war, as one set of strategic conditions succeeded another. Mobilization had principally relied on social pressure to prevail upon fighters to join the war in solidarity and defence of the city's revolutionary values. While a small clique had engineered the operation, its military command structure was diffuse. Many people could claim to have made a significant contribution, and now felt entitled to having their say in shaping the new realities created by the war. The cult of martyrdom, well established in the city since 2011 and revived to honour the fallen in the airport war, allowed hardliners to accuse the emerging conciliatory leadership of betraying the 'blood of the martyrs'. Tellingly, Bashagha repeatedly invoked his commitment to Misratan collective interests and his respect for the martyrs' sacrifices when he first publicly expounded his choice to negotiate.[26]

The differentiation of political positions following victory in Tripoli also provoked growing dillusionment, as fighters realized that they had been exploited for political ends. As one commander put it: 'after the airport war, we lost our convictions. We no longer understood what we were fighting for.'[27] This had two consequences: on the one hand, many commanders became increasingly wary of the justifications politicians were advancing when seeking to mobilize support from among armed groups. On the other, money – which had not featured in the mobilization for the airport war – took on increasing importance in motivating people to fight. By all accounts, major sums of money were paid out to persuade some Misratan battalions to move to the new front at the Wutiya air base, in late November 2014, and towards the oil export terminals in December.[28] The forces engaged on these fronts represented a minor proportion of Misratan fighters, demonstrating the limits of using cash for mobilization. The oil ports offensive provoked significant disagreements among leading political and military players in the city, with many contesting its utility.[29] It also caused some cracks in battalions. Only some battalions – or parts of battalions – of the Mahjub Brigade participated, while others refused.[30]

The growing role of financial incentives came at a time when established patronage networks had fallen into disarray. Salary payments to fighters registered with the Central Shield, for example, had run out in August 2014, and after state institutions split in two, it became much more difficult to prolong such contracts or place fighters on new payrolls.[31] The Hassi government in Tripoli, facing increasing reluctance on the part of the Central Bank to approve its disbursement requests, was working mainly with funds left over from the Zeidan government's budget.[32] Nevertheless, these funds still supplied hundreds of millions of dinars, to be spread among commanders and fighters. In January 2015, supported by Hassi, Misrata's Third Force began peeling Chadian rebels away from Misrata's adversaries, including the Zintanis in al-Wutiya, the Tubu in Ubari and Jadhran in the oil crescent. The Third Force eventually gathered around 1,200 of these foreign fighters.[33] When some Misratan battalions threatened to withdraw from the Wutiya front, in February 2015, the Hassi government began paying fighters there LD 1,000 per week, and Abderrahman al-Sweihli made a visit to the front, trying to take credit for the move.[34] Two months later, the Tripoli government – now led by Khalifa al-Ghwell, a Misratan businessman and former local council member – cut off the salaries of the Halbus and Mahjub Brigades after they entered into a ceasefire with their former enemies in the Warshafana area. When battalion leaders and notables went to see Ghwell in November 2015, he offered not only to resume but also to increase salary payments if the two brigades reneged on the cease-fire agreements, according to two people who attended the meeting.[35]

Given the limits to available state funding, access to foreign backing became more important. According to numerous concordant accounts, the mobilization for the operation against the oil export terminals involved the disbursement of dozens of millions of dollars transferred from Qatar via several Misratan conduits.[36] The division of these funds caused a major dispute. Some commanders tried to force Sweihli, one of the conduits, to hand over the money to the military council to oversee its distribution.[37] To be sure, the foreign assistance available to the fractious alliance in western Libya paled in comparison to the blatant Egyptian and Emirati support to Haftar's forces. Investigations by the UN Panel of Experts found ample proof for the latter, but little evidence to support allegations that Qatar and Turkey backed the Dawn alliance – although Qatar probably paid for Sudanese arms shipments to Dawn forces.[38]

At least as important as material and financial backing was foreign political support, or its simulation. To mobilize Misratan forces for the airport war, Bashagha claimed that he had 'got the green light for the operation' from the United States and the United Kingdom.[39] Sweihli made similar claims in a meeting with battalion commanders, who accused him of lying, pointing to airstrikes by unidentified warplanes on Misratan positions in Tripoli.[40] As unity gave way to rivalry between Misratan politicians, courting foreign governments became even more critical. The Misratan businessman Abdelhamid Dabeiba hired a Canadian lobbyist to promote the standing of the Tripoli authorities in Washington and Moscow – incidentally the same Iranian-born, self-declared former employee of Israeli intelligence who had already been contracted by Ibrahim al-Jadhran in 2013, and would provide services for Haftar in 2016.[41]

The most comical expressions of such efforts were the tireless attempts of the Tripoli government and the rump GNC to portray random foreign visitors as government officials portending international recognition for the Tripoli authorities. I experienced this first-hand when, shortly after I met with Omar al-Hassi at the request of one of his advisers in February 2015, rumours spread that an official German envoy had met Hassi and announced the opening of formal relations with his government. Around the same time, a number of political figures in Misrata began advocating an offensive against the Islamic State in Sirte, arguing that this would enable local forces to obtain Western support; some even reached out to foreign governments for that purpose. But they faced opposition from others promoting a reinforcement of the Warshafana and Wutiya fronts. Equally important, commanders were wary of these politicians' motives in seeking to draw them into another war.[42] Only one unit deployed on Sirte's outskirts, and the offensive against IS would have to wait another year.[43]

As the negotiating process went through twists and turns, the ripple effects of such rivalries spread through the Misratan social fabric. In late January 2015, Bashagha, Suleiman al-Faqih and the Local Council threw their full support behind the UN-led negotiations in Geneva. In response, Salah Badi castigated them for presenting themselves as doves and portraying the 'brave revolutionaries' as warmongers, 'pretending to have forgotten that it was the blood of the martyrs which brought you to Geneva', and 'seeking to exchange these blessed victories against backroom deals for your personal benefit', at the cost of splitting ranks and undermining morale.[44] When the Local Council in February formed a committee to open ceasefire negotiations in the oil crescent, it initially faced resistance from some of the operation's most prominent commanders, due not least to the money involved.[45] In late March, Misratan forces retreated from the oil crescent following a ceasefire, to the ire of proponents of continuing war.

When leaders in the Halbus and Mahjub Brigades entered into a ceasefire in the Warshafana area, in April 2015, hardliners such as Sweihli attacked them as traitors, and persuaded several commanders to oppose the move, causing tensions within both brigades.[46] Sweihli and Badi then engineered the integration of dozens of fighters from both brigades into the 'Presidential Security' unit guarding the GNC, to cement the split in political allegiances.

Between April and early July 2015, Misratan commanders and notables held a series of meetings with Zintani representatives, drafting agreements on security arrangements for Tripoli that would have seen Zintani forces return to the capital. This provoked tensions with those Misratan groups who backed the Ghwell government along with Tripolitanian armed groups, several of them Islamist-leaning. In June, Bashagha and his allies mobilized Misratan fighters to move against the 'Islamists' in Tripoli and take control of the capital together with the Zintanis.[47] This would have raised the risk of a confrontation between Misratan forces on opposite sides of the divide. The move was aborted at the last minute, when several key battalion commanders spoke out against it.[48] Meanwhile, the truces reached in meetings with Zintan were repeatedly violated by Misratan or Zawiyan forces opposed to the negotiations, and no draft agreement was ever finalized, let alone implemented – a fact which the Zintanis correctly attributed to internal divisions in Misrata.[49]

Commanders from the Halbus, Mahjub and other Misratan brigades also made repeated visits to Tunis during the summer and autumn of 2015 to meet with UNSMIL officials and Western diplomats, claiming that they could secure the entry of a unity government into Tripoli, potentially together with forces from Zintan. But back home, other leaders in the same units contested the authority of these emissaries to speak on their behalf.[50] In the run-up to the signing ceremony in the Moroccan beach resort of Skhirat, in December 2015, Presidency Council member Ahmed Maitig caused further splits in the Mahjub Brigade and other Misratan forces by buying off battalion commanders to establish a force to protect the Council in Tripoli.[51]

Such divides eventually prompted Mahjub battalion commanders to seek the mediation of local notables, who forged an understanding that commanders were free to choose their political affiliation, but remained bound by ties of social solidarity in the neighbourhood.[52] This was not much more than a recognition of the status quo: the primacy of social ties over fleeting political affiliations. In early January 2016, Serraj and several other members of the Tunis-based Presidency Council made their first visit to Libyan territory to offer their condolences to victims of a terrorist attack in Zliten, a town neighbouring Misrata. Upon their arrival at Misrata airport, the Presidency Council members were escorted to Zliten by a force including Mahjub and Halbus fighters. When they tried to return to Misrata, a battalion commander in the Mahjub Brigade named Abdellatif al-Krik and dozens of other opponents of the Presidency Council blocked the road at Misrata's western entrance. After a dramatic standoff, Krik was briefly arrested, then excluded from the Brigade the next day.[53]

Misratan hardliners continued to mobilize against the Presidency Council after its move to Tripoli. The very night of the Council's arrival in Tripoli, on 30 March 2016, a major confrontation with Tripolitan armed groups was only narrowly avoided. Salah Badi was dissuaded at the last minute from launching an attack on the forces protecting the Council. Social ties linking Misratan proponents and opponents of the Presidency Council were key to averting escalation. Supporters of the Presidency Council mobilized close allies of Badi to intercede with him, arguing that the political divides were not worth pushing Tripoli – and potentially Misrata – into war. Those who prevailed upon Badi to desist included the head of Misrata's Military Council Ibrahim ben Rajab, who had lost two sons in the airstrikes on Misratan positions in Tripoli in August 2014, and the religious figure Ibrahim ben Ghashir, who had long been a leading revolutionary hardliner.[54]

Though the camp supporting the Presidency Council had become the dominant one in Misrata, it had to tread cautiously vis-à-vis the Council's opponents. The political divide ran between erstwhile brothers-in-arms, business partners, neighbours and close relatives. The dense network of social ties, loyalties and obligations that had ensured the city's unity during the airport war now prevented a clampdown on the adversaries of the dominant group. The leading figures in both camps remained fairly constant, with the notable exception of Sweihli, who proved his opportunism by suddenly throwing his support behind the agreement to have himself elected president of the newly formed State Council, a reinvented GNC.[55] But some prominent proponents on both sides, and many influential figures who preferred to stay in the background, maintained relationships across this divide that made their position appear ambivalent. Meanwhile, many battalion commanders and second-tier political figures refrained from taking sides, having grown wary of being drawn into political struggles between parochial interests, and lost confidence in the leading proponents of both camps.

*

Dense social networks were also a principal reason for ambivalent Misratan attitudes towards armed groups in Benghazi that included extremist elements, and had support networks in Misrata. From mid-2014 onwards, Misrata had become the principal hub for the coordination of logistical support, weapons shipments, and movements of fighters to the Benghazi Revolutionaries Shura Council (BRSC), and the evacuation of its injured fighters. This partly reflected a tactical alliance between Libya Dawn leaders and the BRSC in their fight against a common enemy: Haftar. But there were also deeper ties at work. Some protagonists in Benghazi portrayed the conflict as pitting Cyrenaican tribes, most prominently the Awaqir, against families of Misratan origin who had migrated to Benghazi decades, if not centuries ago, and constituted much of the city's educated and commercial elite.[56] Many BRSC leaders and their supporters came from such families. As neighbourhood militias and Awaqir armed groups started seizing territory from the BRSC in October 2014, they began burning the homes of such families, and several of their leaders threatened that they would expel all 'Misratans' from Benghazi.[57] Thousands of such families fled to western Libya; in early 2017, Misrata alone hosted around 20,000 displaced from Benghazi.[58] The young men of these families supplied recruits for the BRSC. Many were motivated first and foremost by the desire for revenge and restitution of their homes, rather than by the jihadist ideology some BRSC leaders promoted.

Although it was widely known that the BRSC included members of Ansar al-Sharia and fought together with Islamic State elements against Haftar's forces, many in Misrata long downplayed the role of the extremists, or even denied their presence. From March 2015 onwards, Misratans found themselves in a confrontation with the rapidly growing IS presence in neighbouring Sirte, but continued to host networks that supported Ansar al-Sharia and IS in Benghazi.[59] In May 2015, a security service in Misrata arrested a BRSC operative who was in charge of evacuating the wounded from Benghazi, on charges of having facilitated the evacuation of injured IS fighters from Sirte.[60] Hardliners including Ibrahim ben Ghashir unsuccessfully exerted pressure to secure his release.[61] But no measures were taken to end the logistical support for the BRSC, much of which left from the port of Misrata's iron and steel plant, in plain sight of Misrata's political leaders. Such support negatively affected the entire community: in eastern Libya, it alimented a hateful discourse about the 'death boats' from Misrata, and contributed to the demonization of the city and its inhabitants as a whole.

The extensive social ties between BRSC supporters and Misratans meant that any attempt to close down the support networks risked triggering a backlash. The displaced

Benghazi families supporting the war in Misrata included powerful figures with extensive family relations and business ties in Misrata. Among them, for example, was the Karshini family, who owned Misrata's most expensive hotel. As late as April 2016, shortly before the Misratan offensive against IS in Sirte began, a member of the Local Council told me:

> We cannot stop the support for the *thuwwar* and *Daesh* in Benghazi. There are thousands of refugees from Benghazi here. Many of them are rich and influential. If we tried to cut off the logistics for Benghazi, we might run into very bad internal problems.[62]

These attitudes shifted after Misrata entered into full-scale war with IS in Sirte in May 2016. As they seized documents and captured fighters, advancing Misratan forces found clear evidence of BRSC cooperation with IS in Sirte. After several BRSC fighters were arrested in Misrata on their way to evacuation, the group's support networks in the city significantly scaled down their operations.[63] Some former BRSC members and other enemies of Haftar's forces formed a new group, the Benghazi Defence Brigades (BDB). The BDB partly accommodated Misratan concerns by distancing itself from IS and flying the independence flag, rather than the black jihadi banner. Several of the BDB's leaders were based in Misrata, from where they plotted their offensive towards Benghazi, supported by Misratan hardliners such as Abdellatif al-Krik and Salem al-Zufri's Marsa Battalion.[64] Their presence in the city was controversial, given the BDB's association with extremists and their offensives towards the oil crescent and Ajdabiya, which threatened to draw Misrata into a direct confrontation with Haftar. But for the same reasons that had applied to the BRSC's support networks earlier, as well as the Qatari funds at the BDB's disposal, no action was taken against the BDB and its allies in Misrata.[65]

Given all these divides, the city's unity in the war against IS in Sirte was astounding. Politicians associated with the Presidency Council, most notably Bashagha, had been trying for months to mobilize forces for an offensive against IS. Encouraged by these figures, Colonel Salem Jha returned from his posting as defence attaché in the UAE that had cost him so much support in the city. In early 2016, he sought to assemble officers from across Libya to launch an operation against IS in Sirte with the backing of the Presidency Council, anticipating that this would create a nucleus of forces around which a new, united army would form, and expose Haftar's 'Libyan National Army' as a partisan operation aimed at seizing power. But the official backing from the internally divided Presidency Council never materialized.[66]

A confluence of developments in April and May 2016 raised the stakes for Misratan politicians in the expected offensive against IS. Haftar's propagandists announced an imminent battle to free Sirte from IS, threatening to strip Misratan politicians of their opportunity to gain foreign support through counterterrorism.[67] In early May, Haftar began deploying forces towards the oil crescent, many of them officers and civilians from Sirte itself, who had joined Haftar's forces on the promise that they would help liberate their city.[68] At the same time, the BDB moved into the Jufra area south of Sirte, clashing with Haftar's forces.[69] These developments prompted Misratan politicians to mobilize their own forces. Because any Misratan offensive towards Sirte would now be in direct competition with Haftar's, it could no longer be the unifying fight against IS Jha had envisaged. Indeed, Jha refused to join the command structure the Presidency Council established on 6 May.[70] Misratan mobilization raised the risk of a direct confrontation with Haftar's forces – an alluring prospect for the BDB and its Misratan allies. In sum, the offensive was launched in a highly politicized context, and Misrata's internal divisions could have been expected to bog it down.

In mid-May, Misratan fighters mobilized in the face of a creeping IS advance towards the city and several attacks on Misratan-held checkpoints. Rival political players in the city tried to take the reins of the operation and capitalize on it politically – but failed. A day after the Presidency Council had formed its operations room, the Ghwell government formed its own body of Misratan officers and battalion commanders for an operation against IS in Sirte.[71] While the Presidency Council's body initially had little to offer, Ghwell's people supplied ammunition to the forces.[72] Thanks to its access to support from Western Special Forces and, from August onwards, US airstrikes, the body reporting to the Presidency Council gradually won out over Ghwell's group. Its name for the Sirte operation, *al-Bunyan al-Marsus* ('solid structure'), was universally adopted by Misratan forces in Sirte irrespective of their political tendencies. Bashagha played a key role in the operation – officially, he was the liaison between the operations room and the Presidency Council – and regularly visited the forces in Sirte.

However, the offensive gained its momentum from the widespread perception that it aimed at protecting Misrata against an acute threat from IS, and that the objective of defeating IS transcended all political divides. Battalions and commanders who had positioned themselves on opposite sides of these divides joined the operation, and often fought side by side.[73] Moreover, even battalion commanders who had supported the Presidency Council complained bitterly about the lack of support they received. Misratan forces ate into the ammunition they had stored since 2011, and networks of businessmen bought ammunition on the black market. As in 2011, women formed associations to prepare food for the fighters.[74] When Sweihli and the operation's commander, Brigadier Bashir al-Qadhi, went to meet battalion commanders outside Sirte in late May, they were both physically assaulted in an altercation over the lack of logistical support and ammunition for the operation.[75] In the evening discussions among fighters, talk about a move to Tripoli to 'throw the Presidency Council back into the sea' after the defeat of IS was common.[76] While the operation allowed figures such as Bashagha to strengthen their ties with Western states, they failed to cement their local leadership over battalion commanders and the rank and file, who were increasingly disillusioned with politicians of all stripes.[77]

*

Misrata united in the fight against IS as a struggle for self-preservation; its unity no longer extended to political positions. While the Sirte war dragged on, all certainties about Misratan identity vanished. Fighters grew wary of war, and many insisted that the Sirte offensive would be the last one. It dawned on Misratans that the aggressive posture of their leaders in the past had provoked widespread enmity towards Misrata. Haftar's expansion, and hostility in communities that had been humiliated by Misratan armed groups, fuelled perceptions of a looming threat for the city. But hardliners failed to benefit from these perceptions. In May 2017, the Third Force was implicated in a mass killing of forces loyal to Haftar in southern Libya.[78] In the ensuing Misratan deliberations over how to react, proponents of a stronger presence in the south lost out, compelling the Third Force to vacate not only Sabha, but also the Jufra area, which Haftar took over. The sphere of Misratan influence shrank rapidly.

Meanwhile, exiled moderates who had previously been attacked as 'traitors', such as Salem Jha and Fawzi Abdelali, were back in Misrata leading the outreach to former adversaries across the country. Various groups of Misratan politicians and notables competed over reconciliation initiatives with former regime officials and neighbouring communities such as Bani Walid or the Qadhadhfa. Dissident voices arguing that Misrata and Haftar shared the same enemy in IS were no longer afraid to be silenced, and began to resonate with a minority.[79] Others continued to invoke the heroism of the revolutionary war, and rejected any talk of compromise with Haftar. There was no longer any basis for a united Misratan position.

Disillusionment with the unity government in Tripoli compounded Misrata's loss of direction. Not only had the Presidency Council failed to provide meaningful support for the Sirte operation, but more broadly, Misratan backing for the establishment of the unity government had not translated into strong influence within that government. The reason was that the influence of Misratan armed groups in Tripoli had declined. A handful of militias from Tripoli gradually divided up much of the capital between themselves, dislodging their rivals in a series of clashes between mid-2016 and May 2017, and acquiring unprecedented influence in state institutions. Misratan armed groups opposed to the unity government repeatedly confronted the Tripolitan militias, but eventually withdrew because their destabilizing role in Tripoli enjoyed little support in Misrata. A few Misratan-led militias that supported the Presidency Council remained in Tripoli – including Brigade 301, whose leaders hailed from the Halbus Brigade, but whose recruits were mostly not from Misrata – but were confined to the southwestern outskirts, and the benefits they gained by virtue of controlling part of the capital were narrowly distributed within a fraction of Misrata's political spectrum.

As the Tripoli militias brazenly pillaged state institutions and assets, Misratan politicians and battalion leaders repeatedly attempted to mobilize forces for a return to Tripoli, in late 2017 and early 2018. But several times, internal divisions – in addition to pleas from UNSMIL chief Ghassan Salamé – prevented such an operation.[80] The power struggles in Tripoli even had ripple effects in Misrata: in March 2018, a Salafi-leaning Misratan armed group aligned with the Tripoli-based, Salafi-dominated Special Deterrence Force (SDF) captured the commander of a powerful Misratan brigade, Hisham Musaimir, who had offered refuge to fighters from Tajura that had attacked the SDF's base at Mitiga airport. The group seized part of Musaimir's arsenal and held him in prison for several weeks, before releasing him again – an exceptional incident in tight-knit Misrata.[81] The city, as a leading battalion commander told me that month, was no longer split in two or three, but in fifteen, or fifty.[82]

When, in August 2018, Tarhuna's Kaniyat eventually launched the offensive against Tripoli militias some Misratan figures had so long been mobilizing for, only a handful of marginal Misratan factions joined – among them Musaimir's group, as well as fighters loyal to revolutionary hardliner Salah Badi. In Tripoli, those Misratan factions fought the Misratan-led Brigade 301, which rapidly collapsed – though Misratan interlocutors consistently played down the significance of a confrontation between Misratans. Brigade 301, they argued, was Misratan only in its leadership, and in contrast to real Misratan forces was not a cohesive unit – as its defeat showed.[83]

As the conflict continued, larger Misratan forces deployed to Tripoli's outskirts with unclear intentions, but internal divisions within those forces forestalled their entry into the conflict.[84] Power brokers such as Fathi Bashagha then succeeded in converting their opposition to the offensive into political influence. In January 2019, only a few months after Bashagha had become interior minister as part of the arrangements that ended the Tripoli war, the same Misratan commanders and politicians began yet again mobilizing for another operation, complaining that the Tripoli militias' stranglehold over state institutions was unbroken.[85] But as in the previous year, they failed to mobilize substantial support from Misratan armed groups. As a representative of those armed groups said: 'some businessmen have assembled a force of a few dozen vehicles to go to Tripoli, to get access to budgets. But they can't wage war. Misrata will no longer let itself be instrumentalized for political aims.'[86]

Misrata had closed ranks twice against an external enemy, only for Misratans to discover that politicians exploited such divides for their individual benefit, and against the collective interest. This eroded the credibility and standing of political leaders, who also found it difficult to maintain stable patronage networks amid the tumultuous changes Libya was experiencing. With each twist and turn, political players faced greater constraints in adapting their alliances and enmities to evolving strategic conditions. When hard-liners sought to expand the war to Zintan after its defeat in Tripoli, they faced resistance from battalion leaders who had fought against Qadhafi together with the Zintanis. When Bashagha tried to mobilize for an offensive against armed groups supporting the Ghwell government, in June 2015, he encountered reluctant commanders. When politicians attempted to capitalize on the 2016 war in Sirte, they found Misratan fighters wary of being instrumentalized.

The repeated shifts in the positions of political players had ramifications for social relationships. Misratan interlocutors sometimes told me that they had fallen out with a close companion of 2011, or that they had reconciled – but even after making up, the relationship would not regain its previous quality. Some prominent Misratans had been exiled, returning to Misrata only with caution and under protection; others had been attacked as traitors. The animosities thus created were not easily transcended. In June 2015, Mohamed Ibrahim al-Dharrat publicly made a thinly veiled reference to Bashagha – his former close ally – and his effort to marshal a military operation in Tripoli:

He entered the war and pushed it to the limit, splitting Misrata in two. It didn't work, so he changed his flag and bet on peace and dialogue, splitting Misrata in four. Now he turns to another war; God help us into how many parts Misrata will split.[87]

Bashagha had been tight with al-Dharrat during 2013 and 2014, up until the victory in Tripoli. During the Tripoli war, he had allied closely with the battalion leaders Salem al-Zufri and Salah Badi, both of whom felt betrayed by Bashagha when he emerged as Misrata's foremost proponent of a political deal. During the negotiations, he was inseparable from Suleiman al-Faqih and the mayor, Mohamed al-Shtiwi. During the war in Sirte, and as he reached out to political adversaries in the east, he began working closely with Salem Jha and Fawzi Abdelali, both of whom had fiercely opposed the Tripoli war Bashagha had masterminded, and who had been castigated as traitors by Bashagha's allies. But as a key Misratan figure – and close associate of Bashagha at the time – told me in September 2016:

> Believe me, Fathi will eventually lose out from his manoeuvering. He has invested everything in playing this city off against others. He has managed to keep on top throughout the various changes of direction. But when this story is over, he will be finished.[88]

Overall, however, the social fabric remained cohesive in spite of these splits; indeed, this cohesion was a principal constraint on actors in the conflicts. Once the city's united position dissolved in autumn 2014, no political camp could monopolize the right to speak for Misrata, or subdue its political rivals. For months during 2015 and 2016, opponents of the UN-led negotiations would hold rallies after Friday prayers, while supporters demonstrated on Mondays and Thursdays. The two camps did not clash with each other.

In 2018 and 2019, I repeatedly spent long evenings with a group of battalion leaders from eastern Misrata; they were prosperous businessmen from the same area, close friends who regularly met on weekend nights, or on social occasions such as circumcisions, weddings and condolence receptions. That core group often received Misratan figures of conflicting political alignments; sometimes, a guest would be taken aback when unexpectedly encountering a person whose politics he had rejected. Once, a staunch supporter of the unity government ran into the commander of the Benghazi Defence Brigades; then again, an army officer known for his attachment to principles was surprised to find the infamously rich businessman and former Qadhafi companion Ali Dabeiba. Sometimes, heated arguments would develop; sometimes, the guests would later share their unease privately with me. Clearly, however, social networks helped bridge the political rifts that afflicted Misrata.

At times, social ties across political divides prevented political players from resorting to force, as when social pressure dissuaded Badi from attacking the forces protecting the Presidency Council on the day of its arrival in Tripoli. At others, such ties ensured that rival political actors could not prevent each other from pursuing their objectives: certain battalion leaders joined the BDB's eastward offensives despite the fact that they clearly undermined the fragile political settlement Misratan leaders supported. The cases where leading figures could threaten or use force against their local opponents were rare exceptions that confirmed the rule: Abdellatif al-Krik was released shortly after having been arrested for his brazen behaviour at Misrata's western entrance. The killing of Misrata's mayor, Mohamed al-Shtiwi, in December 2017, was an isolated act of violence, and its background remained unclear.[89] But the capture of Hisham Musaimir in March 2018 raised the question whether such incidents were becoming more common as political divisions tore at the city's social fabric.

Despite all the rifts, there was no escape from consultation and collective decision-making, even if it was ad hoc, and never wholly inclusive. The tumultuous political struggles of Misrata's elite forestalled the establishment of agreed-upon mechanisms for decision-making. During the UN-led negotiations, the Local Council was pigeonholed by its support for the talks, while Sweihli assembled the opponents of that camp in a 'Council of Wise Men and Notables of Misrata'.[90] Contrary to a widespread perception, Misrata therefore never became a city-state.[91] But when individual actors tried to override the collectivity, they failed – such as Prime Minister Serraj and his Misratan deputy Ahmed Maitig, who in early 2018 committed to a UN-backed agreement on the return of displaced Tawarghans to their abandoned town, despite resistance to the plan in Misrata. When Tawarghans arrived on 1 February, they were turned back by Misratan fighters, dealing an embarrassing blow to Maitig.[92] Unrelated to the Presidency Council, a new Misratan negotiation effort then consulted more widely in the city, and successfully brokered a deal in June 2018 that led to the return of Tawarghans to their town. 'Whoever tells you that he represents all of Misrata is lying,' a leading battalion commander said. 'Nobody can impose his will on Misrata. You need at least a dozen people to represent the various groups in Misrata, and even then, they will have to consult with those they represent.'[93]

Due to social cohesion, the disintegration of Misrata's unity after 2014 led neither to one camp forcefully imposing its leadership on the city, nor to violent confrontations between rival political forces. It also imposed constraints on the ability of politicians to adapt their alliances to shifting conditions. The more the opportunism of leading figures became apparent, the more their standing declined. Misrata's political leaders were unable to deliver the city's socially embedded forces for the national alliances they entered. Amid rapidly changing strategic conditions, social cohesion produced political fragmentation.

*

In February 2019, as Haftar expanded in southern Libya, I returned to Misrata and encountered a marked change in threat perceptions. Though politically divided, my Misratan interlocutors shared an anxiety over Haftar's next steps. Seemingly oblivious to the threat, some businessmen and commanders continued plotting a move to Tripoli, to enlarge their share of the spoils from predation. But when I asked a senior Misratan army officer, he told me: 'Misrata's forces can no longer be used for political ends. They will not mobilize unless someone attacks Misrata. Nothing else will make them move.'[94]

That acute threat to Misrata materialized with Haftar's offensive on Tripoli, in April 2019. Fighters who had not mobilized since the 2016 Sirte war joined their groups and moved to Tripoli or Sirte. Hardliners like Salah Badi fought together with Misratan brigades they had formerly considered 'traitors', and with Tripoli militias whom they had confronted less than a year earlier, under the nominal authority of the unity government, against Haftar's forces. This war, Misratan interlocutors of all stripes told me, had been forced upon them. They had not chosen it. And yet, underneath the veneer of unity, the rifts that had emerged over the preceding years were all too apparent. There was no doubt they would soon return to the fore, compounded by new divides wrought by Libya's third civil war.

Western/Nafusa Mountains: Zintan, from corporatism to fragmentation

As the previous chapter showed, revolutionary strongholds in the mountains followed trajectories parallel to that of Misrata until the eruption of the 2014–15 civil war. They united during the revolution, providing the terrain for the formation of socially embedded forces. Subsequently, local rivalries emerged as their representatives entered the struggles over state institutions. In Zintan, the rise of militia leaders transformed the revolutionary social order more profoundly than in Misrata and the Amazigh towns. Nevertheless, Zintan long presented a remarkably unified face, at least to outsiders. Serious divisions only became apparent after the town had closed ranks for a second time, in 2014–15.

The post-revolutionary rivalries redefined community identities and enmities. Amazigh towns had been united with Zintan and Rujban in their fight against the regime. Following the regime's collapse, leaders in Amazigh towns voiced demands for cultural and language rights – to which many Zintanis reacted with alarm – and rejected the participation of former regime elements in politics. The latter issue was decisive in structuring the political landscape in 2012–14, and pushed the representatives of Amazigh towns into an alliance with those of other revolutionary strongholds – most notably Misrata – as well as Islamist movements.

Zintanis found themselves in the opposite camp. In part, this was due to the rivalry of Misratan with Zintani-led armed groups over control of Tripoli. In part, it emerged from the close relationship between the Zintani Mlegta brothers, who led the Qa'qa' Brigade, and Mahmoud Jibril, who was the most prominent target of the drive to exclude former regime officials from political life. While Zintanis continued to stress their decisive role in the revolutionary war and their aversion to those who had sided with the regime in 2011, they also discovered a new adversary in 'the Islamists'.

This was a departure that directly affected personal relationships: during the 2011 war, several Islamist figures fought in Zintan who would later gain prominence in the Coordination for Political Isolation and the Libyan Revolutionaries Operations Room – among them Mohamed al-Kilani from Zawiya and Omar al-Mukhtar al-Madhhuni from Sabratha. These figures had developed close relations with their Zintani brothers-in-arms, which now deteriorated. The Zintani head of the Libya Shield's Western Division fell out with his former comrade from Zawiya, who had been with him in the Shield leadership: 'After Mohamed al-Kilani was elected to the GNC, I no longer recognized him. I increasingly disagreed with the guys from Zawiya, Sabratha, and Zuwara. Eventually, I resigned.'[95]

As in Misrata, competition over the spoils of power also began eroding internal cohesion in Zintan after 2011. Nevertheless, during 2012 and 2013, my Zintani interlocutors – notables, academics, battalion commanders – generally defended the prominent Zintanis engaged in the struggles in Tripoli. When they stressed that the Qa'qa' and Sawaeq were not Zintani groups but units recruited from all across Libya, this was not to distance themselves, but to highlight the supposed professionalism of these units. During this period, Zintani acquaintances made claims to political influence that far outsized the town's demographic weight – claims that had been born out of Zintan's role in the 2011 war. For a long time, many in Zintan saw the Mlegta brothers and the Sawaeq's Emad Trabelsi as defending Zintani interests.[96]

As tensions escalated in the first half of 2014, notables and former revolutionary commanders surrounding Usama al-Juwaili began voicing their opposition to the role of the Qa'qa' and Sawaeq in Tripoli. Some of them retained ties to figures who were now on the other side of the divide. As one commander recalled:

> Before the 2014 war, Omar al-Mukhtar [al-Madhhuni] asked me to come to Sabratha. There, he told me that his *azlam* [former regime officials] prisoners had informed him that Mlegta was conspiring with former regime loyalists. We convened a meeting with Juwaili and Zintan's Social Committee, and exerted pressure on Mlegta's people. But then they attacked the GNC, something we opposed completely. I went to see Mlegta and Trabelsi on the day of the attack, trying to calm things down, get them to retreat. They were the ones who were causing all the problems in Tripoli, acting as if they owned the city.[97]

Such internal Zintani dissent was only expressed behind closed doors. It remained a minority view in the town, and ultimately had little impact on the posture of the Qa'qa', Sawaeq and associated Zintani-led groups in Tripoli prior to the airport war. These groups could be certain that majority opinion in Zintan viewed them as a guarantee of their community's influence, and shared their definition of the enemy, 'the Islamists'.

The airport war forced Zintanis to close ranks. It was seen in Zintan not as an attack on the Qa'qa' and Sawaeq but on the town as a whole. The Qa'qa' and Sawaeq disintegrated in the war, and their leaders lost much of their influence as Zintanis grew resentful of the figures who had drawn them into the conflict without being able to defend them. Following this debacle, Haftar's local allies – among them the Mlegta brothers and Trabelsi, as well as several army officers – lacked the sway needed to bring the town's forces under their control. The assistance Haftar was able or willing to offer was paltry compared to the resources available to the military council, which had stockpiled weapons in 2011. Equally important, the town's self-image as a revolutionary bulwark continued to underpin local cohesion, and defined how the forces led by Juwaili's Military Council viewed themselves. Juwaili and his commanders stubbornly refused to submit to Haftar's authority, suspecting him of seeking to re-establish a dictatorship under the guise of fighting terrorism, and frowning upon his promotion of officers who had fought on Qadhafi's side in 2011.

Nevertheless, Juwaili's revolutionaries and Haftar's local allies were bound together by strong local social ties and the necessity of mustering all available resources for the community's defence. This uneasy cohabitation placed constraints on both camps in the town. Juwaili and his commanders had to tread carefully in reaching out to former brothers-in-arms who were now their enemies, lest they expose themselves to accusations of treachery from within their own community. The first contacts with figures on the other side of the divide were therefore conducted in utmost secrecy.[98]

Haftar's allies, on the other hand, were constrained in their alliances with former regime loyalists who had fought against Zintan in 2011, and who made no secret of their counter-revolutionary views. A key component among the forces supporting Haftar in western Libya was the 'Army of Tribes', an armed group drawn from tribal constituencies that were stigmatized as regime loyalists. The Military Council's revolutionaries were deeply suspicious of such elements. In December 2014, Haftar's commander for the western region Idris Madi – a Zintani officer who had himself remained loyal to Qadhafi in 2011 – found it necessary to publicly deny the existence of the 'Army of Tribes' and denounce as 'fantasists' those pretending that his forces were fighting to bring back the former regime.[99] In October 2015, Madi openly admonished his ally Omar Tantush from Warshafana – a former loyalist officer who had been in Zintani custody since 2011, and was released to lead forces from Warshafana against Libya Dawn – after the latter delivered a fiery speech in front of former regime nostalgists.[100] As a result of such tensions, forces from Warshafana that had allied with the Zintanis since the airport war increasingly emancipated themselves from Zintani control after winning their home region back in a May 2015 offensive.

The debilitating impact of these divisions was such that in March 2015, tribal elders formed a Supreme Council of the Tribes of Zintan with the aim of mediating between the competing camps in the town, and promoting outreach to neighbouring communities to alleviate the pressure on Zintan. Elders from that body joined and supported the Military Council's talks with its adversaries. They even attempted – unsuccessfully – to set up a joint operations room for the military council and Madi's forces.[101]

Zintan's internal divisions complicated both the military advance of its forces in the coastal plain in early 2015, and the parallel efforts to negotiate local ceasefires. For their adversaries, Zintan's divisions and internal balance of power were difficult to read at the time, because communication across the political divide had largely stopped since mid-2014. According to a commander from Misrata's Halbus Brigade who negotiated with the Zintanis:

> As the talks continued, it became clear to us that there were two camps: one led by Usama al-Juwaili, which was the stronger one militarily, and another one represented by Khaled al-Amiani, who was associated with Idris Madi. While we came to understand this, we ourselves became divided in Misrata.[102]

In line with Haftar's uncompromising stance, Madi, Trabelsi and their allies were opposed to the détente with the former components of Libya Dawn. They were too weak to wage war without the support of Zintan Military Council. But they could try to torpedo ceasefire negotiations by posing their own conditions, or mobilizing the sizeable group of forcibly displaced families in Zintan against the talks. Moreover,

Zintan's adversaries risked exploiting these internal rivalries. As a negotiator for the military council recalled:

> After we met with the Misratans to stop the fighting in Warshafana [in May 2015], they also contacted Idris Madi and asked him to stop shelling Gharyan. They told us that Idris had agreed to stop the bombardment, even though it was us [the Military Council] doing the shelling. Idris didn't know about our meetings with the Misratans. When we asked him about his talks with them, he denied having committed to anything, and agreed to let us take the lead, saying he would support our decisions. So the Misratans started trying to play different groups in Zintan against each other. We've become used to that.[103]

Zintani negotiators, in turn, were irritated by the divisions among their adversaries, which posed obstacles in negotiations over agreements. Dawn leaders initially demanded that Zintanis negotiate with them as a bloc. But a May meeting in Sabratha between Zintani emissaries and leaders from all main Dawn factions proved fruitless – predictably so, given that several groups within Dawn were in favour of continuing war.[104] The Zintanis were already in direct talks with leaders from the Misratan Halbus and Mahjub Brigades, though other armed groups from Misrata and Zawiya repeatedly violated the ceasefires negotiated with these two brigades. Commanders from Gharyan and Sabratha who had fought in Zintan in 2011 then agreed to open separate talks with the Zintanis, hastening the disintegration of the Dawn alliance.[105] Even so, growing local divisions and the opacity surrounding them encumbered the negotiations. According to another negotiator for Zintan Military Council:

> Because they were divided, Gharyan had difficulties committing to the agreement, despite the fact that it was so favourable to them. The deal almost collapsed at the last minute. And that's precisely what happened with Zawiya. Omar al-Mukhtar [al-Madhhuni, from Sabratha] had mediated an agreement between us and Zawiya. He had told us, these are the people you need to speak to in Zawiya. But shortly before we were to sign the deal, they stepped back from it. I asked Omar what had happened. He said that a third party from Zawiya had intervened. So we wondered, first you tell us that these are the key people in Zawiya, and then they can't commit?[106]

As a patchwork of local ceasefire agreements contained the war in Tripolitania, the political divisions in Zintan that had been shelved over the need to defend the community came back to the fore. But the fact that competing local factions were bound together in a tight-knit community still made it difficult for Zintani political players to move. In early July 2015, Juwaili's Military Council intended to exploit the fragmentation of Libya Dawn and tentative agreements with its Misratan interlocutors to return to Tripoli by force, against the resistance of a variety of other Misratan and Tripolitanian armed groups. However, the military council sought to prevent its local rivals – Haftar's Zintani allies – from moving into Tripoli alongside its own forces. The issue provoked serious tensions in Zintan. On 7 July, the Supreme Council of the

Tribes of Zintan called a meeting of local elders as well as political and military figures which resulted in ruling out any forcible return to Tripoli. Prominent Zintani religious figures subsequently backed this decision with legal opinions against renewed war in the capital.[107] Thereafter, the military council shifted towards (ultimately unsuccessful) negotiations with Tripolitanian armed groups, while its Zintani rivals continued to clamour for a return in arms to the capital, but lacked the necessary firepower.

Because of the social constraints on Zintani political actors, their political positions remained ambivalent even as local divisions became increasingly apparent. Against resistance from Haftar's local allies, Zintani negotiators aligned with Juwaili backed the Skhirat agreement. But the terms they were able to negotiate in Skhirat were insufficiently attractive to sway the many sceptics of such engagement in Zintan. Under pressure from their critics, Zintani supporters of the unity government turned into its detractors, and the Zintani Presidency Council member Omar al-Aswad withdrew from the body within a month of the agreement being signed.[108] The military council and other Zintani representatives insisted on security arrangements in Tripoli that could allow Zintani families to return to the capital – which, in the absence of neutral and professional units, would have required deploying Zintani forces to Tripoli. When the Presidency Council moved to Tripoli in late March 2016 without taking any steps to address such concerns, it alienated its supporters in Zintan.[109] Nor did the Presidency Council have much to offer to its potential Zintani allies. In other words, the costs of unequivocally choosing sides between the unity government and Haftar, and defending this choice against their local rivals, exceeded the benefits for the military council.

Such constraints on the political ambitions of Zintani actors were evident in several other incidents. In May 2016, the military council obtained assurances from Madi that his men at Zintan's airport would facilitate a visit of the Italian general and senior UNSMIL security adviser Paolo Serra to Zintan. But when Serra arrived, he was prevented from leaving the airport and forced to fly back by al-Ejmi al-Atiri, an officer then aligned with Haftar. Meanwhile, Madi was nowhere to be found.[110]

Later that month, Madi, Atiri and Trabelsi signalled their continued alignment with Haftar when they welcomed his chief of staff on a visit to Zintan.[111] But in July, Atiri diverged with Haftar when he claimed that he had released Qadhafi's son Saif al-Islam, who had been in his custody since 2011 and was the subject of an arrest warrant issued by the International Criminal Court.[112] By that point, Atiri was openly portraying his prisoner as Libya's future saviour. Atiri's unabashed promotion of Saif al-Islam and the prospect that he could, indeed, release him put him on a collision course with Juwaili's revolutionaries. Military council forces surrounded the base of Atiri's battalion following the announcement, trying to force him to surrender Saif al-Islam, but tribal elders intervened to mediate, and the issue died down again. As a commander close to Juwaili said in September 2016:

> Al-Ejmi is now Saif al-Islam's prisoner, not the other way round. He's crazy, he really believes Saif can bring Libyans together and lead the country. He's out of control, he submits neither to the Military Council nor to Madi. But because of tribal relations, we can't just throw him out.[113]

In March 2017, Atiri once again declared that Saif was free, and would lead Libya in the future. This time, Juwaili's men forced their way into Atiri's house and seized Saif, then surrendered him to a committee of Zintani tribal elders – who, unable to shoulder that responsibility, returned him to Atiri a few weeks later. Juwaili met with Atiri for an awkward reconciliation attempt, though the two men continued to loathe each other.[114] Both, however, were constrained in their options for dealing with Saif by the social ties in which they were enmeshed. Ajmi could not actually free Saif, nor allow him to become openly politically active. Juwaili and his military council could neither violently attack Atiri, nor imprison Saif or surrender him to the ICC. Haftar's command faced no such constraints, and declared Atiri's battalion dissolved in June 2017, when he again sang Saif's praises.[115]

As the rifts of the 2014–15 war faded and the lines of conflict in western Libya blurred, Zintani actors became more flexible. In March 2017, the military council overcame its ambivalence towards the UN-backed unity government by agreeing that Zintanis would establish a unit as part of that government's new Presidential Guard.[116] In June 2017, Prime Minister Serraj appointed Juwaili as commander of the western military region, posing a direct challenge to Madi, who performed the same function in Haftar's command structure.[117] In November, Juwaili moved Zintani forces into the Warshafana area and dislodged Haftar loyalists from several bases there, thereby significantly weakening Haftar's position in western Libya. Trabelsi's forces cooperated with Juwaili in that move, and Trabelsi effectively defected from Haftar in March 2018, when his second-in-command was appointed deputy interior minister in Tripoli.[118] Trabelsi's force eventually became fully integrated into the unity government's structures in July 2018. Throughout that time, Madi's and Atiri's associates increasingly openly (and absurdly) attacked Juwaili as an *ikhwani* – a covert Muslim Brother – and castigated the Military Council's accommodation with the UN-backed Presidency Council as treason.[119]

Among Libyan interlocutors of varying local backgrounds, Zintanis had long been the ones who presented the most united picture of their community to me, and who most frequently spoke of Zintani virtues and corporate Zintani interests. They were also among the most reluctant to discuss internal disagreements with an outsider such as myself. But eventually, the façade of unity crumbled. A prominent notable minimized the severity of the divisions when he told me in March 2017: 'it's true, Zintan does not have one position. We are diverse, and that is a good thing. But we're good at managing our disagreements.'[120]

Having closed ranks in 2011 and 2014, Zintan no longer had the capacity to adopt a unified political position after the imperative of unity receded during 2015. Zintan's self-image as a revolutionary bulwark had been shattered by the tactical alliances of some Zintani actors with Haftar, as well as with former regime loyalists the Zintanis had fought against in 2011. There was nothing to replace this common identity. As of 2017, Zintanis no longer had a common enemy: the *azlam*, Haftar, and the former component elements of Libya Dawn all counted as allies among the various political interest groups within the town.

The most eloquent expression of these divisions was the loss of consensus over who should represent Zintan. Haftar's local allies opposed the military council. Zintan's two members in the Tobruk-based House of Representatives had been elected prior to the 2014 war, and had delivered little since. The Supreme Council of the Tribes of Zintan, founded as local divisions widened in March 2015, competed with the parallel Social Committee, and repeatedly found it necessary to insist that the Supreme Council was 'the only legitimate body competent to speak in the name of all sons of Zintan'.[121] Such claims did not go unchallenged, particularly after the Supreme Council threw its support behind the UN-led negotiations in the fall of 2015. Thereafter, the Supreme Council's local standing declined. In January 2017, elders formed the Council of Notables of Zintan (*majlis a'yan al-Zintan*), which similarly claimed to be the only legitimate representation of Zintani interests.[122] But the positions of that Council favoured Haftar, and it rapidly lost support. By mid-2017, several of Zintan's tribes had declared their withdrawal from the body.[123] The competition between various would-be brokers over who could represent Zintan only deepened the divides.

And yet, their embeddedness in a tight-knit community continued to constrain rival Zintani forces in their actions. During the first half of 2018, Juwaili negotiated for months with Misratan commanders and Tarhuna's Kani brothers over a joint operation against the big Tripoli militias. The fact that none of the three parties trusted one another other kept delaying the offensive.[124] When the Kaniyat finally moved on Tripoli in August, Juwaili consulted closely with his commanders, but hesitated – not least because with Salah Badi, a nemesis of Zintanis had also joined the offensive. Siding with Misratan hard-liners in the operation would have exposed Juwaili and his associates to intense criticism in Zintan. Eventually, the Juwaili faction took advantage of the situation by helping Trabelsi's forces redeploy to the western Tripoli districts from which they had been forcibly dislodged in 2014 – but in coordination with the Presidency Council and the Tripoli militias, rather than in alliance with the Kaniyat.[125]

The constraints under which Juwaili and his commanders operated became even more salient during the escalation into the third civil war. As Haftar expanded in southern Libya and began sending weaponry to allies in the west, Juwaili intensified his outreach to leaders of armed groups in western Libya, to block further inroads by Haftar. Particularly problematic for Juwaili in that respect was the fact that forces from Zintan and Rujban loyal to Haftar – most of them Salafi-leaning – controlled the Wutiya air base in the coastal plain, to which Haftar was delivering arms supplies throughout March 2019. Juwaili's forces threatened to take over the air base by force unless the deliveries stopped, prompting Zintani tribal elders to step in and mediate. The elders reached an agreement that stipulated that al-Wutiya should remain under Zintani control, but should not be exploited by any party, and that neither of the two factions in Zintan should participate in any conflict.[126] But only a week after the agreement was reached, another flight touched down at al-Wutiya to deliver supplies to Haftar's forces. One of Juwaili's commanders told me that the imperative of keeping the social peace in Zintan kept forestalling a more forceful approach to the Wutiya group, 'but if they don't stop violating the agreement, we'll resort to other means'.[127] It never happened.

As the war escalated, the rift dividing Zintan widened. The core of Juwaili's forces mobilized under the banner of defending the revolution against an attempt to establish a military dictatorship. A number of smaller Zintani armed groups – some of them

Salafi-leaning – joined Haftar's forces, whose rallying cry was the fight against 'criminal militias' and heretics. Many Zintani fighters refused to fight, seeing how the war divided their community. On several occasions, Juwaili's men were targeted by combat aircraft that had taken off from al-Wutiya. And still, the Juwaili faction remained reticent to attack the base. Juwaili's forces generally avoided deploying to front lines where they would face the Zintani fighters who had joined Haftar's offensive.[128] Still, they now fought together with their former enemies from Misrata, Zawiya, the Amazigh towns and Tripoli against a coalition of armed groups that included fellow Zintanis. The rift long simmering beneath the surface had finally emerged into the open, splitting Zintan in two.

*

Zintan's fragmentation was the product of shifting alliances and rifts with outside actors that had successively added one fault line after another onto the social fabric. This contrasts with the trajectory of Zintan's Amazigh neighbours, which had avoided such repeated shifts in political alignments. Their involvement in the rivalries that led up to the eruption of the civil war was largely limited to the role of the National Mobile Force (NMF), which included units from Amazigh towns in the mountains, Zuwara, as well as several other coastal cities. The bulk of Amazigh forces refrained from entering the struggles in Tripoli. The Amazigh boycotted the February 2014 elections to the constituent assembly, as well as the June HoR elections; they had no stake in the tug-of-war over the legitimacy of the HoR's Tobruk sessions. Their only elected HoR member, Salem Gnan from Nalut, later mediated between boycotting and Tobruk-based parliamentarians. Several Amazigh GNC members remained active in the rump GNC, but they no longer commanded significant support within their communities. Most Amazigh leaders had stopped seeing GNC president Abusahmain as a representative of their interests long before the tensions escalated into civil war.

The 2014 war initially threatened to draw in the Amazigh towns in the mountains, where sympathies clearly tended towards the Dawn camp. Although these towns nominally adopted a neutral position, several hundred of their men, most of them associated with the NMF, fought against the Zintanis in Tripoli, Kikla and the Wutiya air base. Until late 2014, there was a real possibility that the bulk of the forces from Amazigh towns could enter the fray, thereby following the lead of Zuwara, the coastal Amazigh city whose forces were deployed at al-Wutiya. Such a move would have provoked serious internal divisions; in each town, prominent figures were busily working to keep their communities out of the conflict.[129] It would also have cut personal relationships of trust and comradeship established between revolutionary leaders in Zintan and Amazigh towns in 2011, and more broadly upended peaceful inter-communal coexistence between them. But the choice of neutrality won out, forestalling the formation of rival camps within Amazigh communities.

Personal connections between Zintan and Amazigh towns dating back to 2011 suffered amid the war, but some key channels remained intact. For example, the Naluti commander of the Wazin border crossing with Tunisia explained to me in March 2015 that he had continued to allow the evacuation of wounded fighters from Zintan despite pressure from Dawn leaders to stop all cross-border movements of Zintanis: 'I have friends among the *thuwwar* of Zintan and Rujban going back to 2011. If they want to pass through the crossing, I can't refuse. They all deal with me personally.'[130]

In the end, it was not communal unity but the NMF itself that disintegrated over the political squabbles it had become entangled in. After the Dawn victory in Tripoli, NMF leaders nominated several ministers and deputy ministers for the Hassi government, who then channelled funds to NMF commanders from their towns. Abusahmain also backed an NMF commander from Zuwara. These commanders established their own units, which became independent of the NMF leadership under Said Gujil.[131] Meanwhile, Amazigh officers who had opposed Libya Dawn peeled off dozens of NMF fighters and other Dawn veterans and integrated them into army or police units.[132] The disparate NMF factions were battered in the struggles between armed groups in Tripoli during 2016 and early 2017.[133] Only the core of the NMF under Gujil remained, staying put in its base at Tripoli's western gates.

Because the Amazigh towns avoided taking sides in the political tug-of-war and the military conflict, it was natural for them to support the UN-led negotiations over the formation of a unity government – despite the fact that they were weakly represented in the talks and the government. Their reaction to the agreement was positive. At the same time, Amazigh leaders remained staunchly opposed to Haftar due to his Arabist discourse, his reliance on the Zintanis, and his obvious ambitions to re-establish authoritarian rule. Amazigh towns therefore saw no realignments that were susceptible to causing internal divisions.

People in the Amazigh towns continued to look back on their role in the revolution as a source of communal pride. But as the 2014 war called into question old certainties over friends and enemies, these towns' leaders and elders softened their stance towards former regime loyalists. At a September 2016 National Reconciliation Forum in Nalut, the hosts even agreed to take down the monarchy-era flag and cancel the performance of the monarchy-era national anthem to assuage representatives of communities that had experienced the revolution as a defeat.[134] Contrary to what happened in Misrata and Zintan, however, such outreach to former loyalists did not aim at striking tactical alliances, but at overcoming divisions. As a result, such efforts did not provoke new rifts within Amazigh communities.

As Haftar's forces became stronger and began exploring ways of expanding in western Libya, tentative contacts between his emissaries and Amazigh commanders underlined the Amazigh communities' immunity from the temptations of political struggles. During 2018, Haftar's representatives sought several meetings with commanders and officers from Jadu and Nalut, offering them money and vehicles if they joined his forces. The response was consistent: Haftar should first alter the name of his 'Libyan Arab Armed Forces', and submit to civilian authority.[135] Meanwhile, Amazigh communities and their forces watched with unease as Salafi-dominated armed groups loyal to Haftar established themselves in the Si'aan communities of Tiji and Badr, and kept growing in Zintan and Rujban. Struggles over the control and repartition of the fuel smuggling economy between the Zawiya refinery and the Tunisian border also fuelled tensions between armed groups from Zintan and the Amazigh towns.[136] But the approach that prevailed in Amazigh communities throughout the years that followed the 2014–15 civil war was to avoid armed confrontations with their neighbours.

If Zintan's outsized role in post-revolutionary power struggles resulted in serious divisions within an exceptionally tight-knit community, then, the Amazigh towns preserved their internal cohesion by withdrawing from these struggles. As a result, when Haftar's offensive on Tripoli provoked renewed civil war, the Amazigh communities were at little risk of being divided over how to respond. Community leaders came out in open condemnation of the offensive early on.[137] Fighters joined the National Mobile Force in Tripoli or formed battalions on the basis of individual towns, such as Kabaw and Jadu, that fought in close coordination with Juwaili's Zintani forces on the front line between Tripoli and Gharyan. A significant proportion of forces remained in the Amazigh towns and their surroundings to guard against threats from adjacent areas that were under the control of forces loyal to Haftar.[138] The defence of their towns, their identity, and the fight against an obvious attempt to reinstall authoritarian rule united Amazigh communities.

Bani Walid: From cohesion through self-isolation to fragmentation

Bani Walid restored a degree of cohesion by preserving neutrality in the second civil war. It did so from a very different starting point than the Amazigh towns. Whereas the latter were tight-knit and militarily powerful communities proud of their role in the revolution, Bani Walid at the eve of the second civil war was a vanquished, demilitarized and deeply divided town.

The Social Council, as will be recalled, began as a weakly legitimized body whose members were mostly second-tier notables. It also suffered from divisions between hard-line Qadhafists who were linked to exiled former regime officials, and more conciliatory figures concerned primarily with addressing immediate local grievances, such as Bani Walid's prisoners in revolutionary strongholds, and the town's political and economic marginalization.

In October 2012, Bani Walid had made the bitter experience that, without the necessary firepower to defend the town, its defiance of revolutionary armed groups only led to renewed defeat and humiliation. Some in Bani Walid blamed the Social Council's intransigent stance for this catastrophe, and the Social Council changed track in its aftermath. It began cautious reconciliation efforts with Zawiya – whose armed groups had participated in the October 2012 operation and had captured several prisoners – and henceforth refrained from provocative moves such as hosting meetings of counter-revolutionary tribal notables. This new approach, combined with the October 2012 operation's unintended consequence of uniting Bani Walid in opposition to the revolutionary order, allowed the Social Council to gain broader acceptance in the town, and gradually cement its position. The Council easily warded off a challenge from a rival body of tribal notables who presented themselves as an enlightened alternative to obstinate nostalgists of a bygone era. The Local Council also tried to erode the Social Council's monopoly on collective decision-making, and failed –

not least because the resources it was able to mobilize from Tripoli were limited, slow in being disbursed and subject to the turmoil in state institutions from mid-2014 onwards.

But while the Social Council's position in the town had become uncontested by 2014, the Council continued to be torn by the rifts afflicting the community: the legacy of suffering and distrust left by the repression of the 1993 coup plot; the killings of 28 May 2011; the violent confrontation between Bani Walid's revolutionary minority and its adversaries; the struggle between hardliners longing for revenge and the return of the former regime; and pragmatists seeking to normalize Bani Walid's relations with the new authorities in Tripoli. These rifts lingered underneath the surface of a fragile consensus reached after the October 2012 operation, according to which Bani Walid was not party to the struggles raging between former components of the revolutionary alliance in Tripoli, and had fundamental grievances with the revolutionary order that first needed to be addressed before Bani Walid could participate in routine politics. (Of course, this was not the view of the hard-line revolutionaries who had supported the renewed capture of Bani Walid in 2012, and were forced to leave the town once the Social Council regained control.) An illustration of this position came in April and May 2014, when the Misratan would-be prime minister Ahmed Maitig sought to win over six or seven political figures from Bani Walid as his deputies in a proposed cabinet – some of them close to the Social Council, others closer to the revolutionaries – but all declined.[139]

With the escalation into civil war from May 2014 onward, this fragile consensus was sorely tested. Both camps began courting Bani Walid. At the same time, political players in the town were gauging whether the crisis offered an opportunity for Bani Walid and other losers of the 2011 revolution to re-emerge as a military force. In late May 2014, the Social Council sent representatives to a gathering of tribal politicians from constituencies considered as former regime loyalists in al-Aziziya, the main city in the Warshafana area. From the Social Council's perspective, the gathering and its aim of forming a 'Supreme Council of Libyan Cities and Tribes' stood in continuity with the meetings it had itself organized in 2012. But the hosts of the meeting wanted it to come out in favour of Haftar's operation in Benghazi, which had started just ten days earlier and was already dividing the country. Bani Walid's representatives successfully thwarted the planned expression of support for Haftar. They were suspicious of Haftar, who had joined the revolution and participated in the 2011 capture of Bani Walid. They did, however, sign up to the Supreme Council, and vowed to engage with Haftar to 'make absolutely sure we understand his intentions before we agree to support him', as one of Bani Walid's representatives at the meeting said.[140]

When war erupted in Tripoli in July, Zintani leaders, Haftar and their political allies all sought to gain Bani Walid's backing against the Misratan-led Dawn alliance. The ambassador to the UAE Aref al-Nayed, himself a Warfalli with weak ties to Bani Walid, reached out to local dignitaries, seeking to persuade them to enter the conflict.[141] Zintan released dozens of former regime loyalists from prisons in Zintan, on condition that they join their fight against Libya Dawn.[142] Politicians associated with the Supreme Council helped form the 'Warshafana battalion' and the 'Army of Tribes' to accommodate these fighters.[143] A few dozen men from Bani Walid joined the

'Army of Tribes' and fought in the Warshafana area. It remains unclear whether this occurred at the instigation of individual Social Council members in defiance of the Council's official policy of neutrality, or whether the Social Council covertly backed the effort to hedge its bets. At the time, a member of Bani Walid's Social Council who oversaw the mobilization into the 'Army of Tribes' explained the rationale as follows:

> The airport war did not concern us. It was a power struggle between two camps of February [i.e. the 2011 revolution], both of them serving foreign interests. But the war in Warshafana concerns our brothers and allies. That's why we mobilized, under the authority of the Supreme Council. Five martyrs in the Warshafana war came from Bani Walid. We are still weak, but the attack on Warshafana has strengthened us. It has shown the need for us to exist: everyone knows that they could be next after Warshafana.[144]

But the Social Council never officially expressed support for the 'Army of Tribes', let alone admit to the participation of men from Bani Walid at the behest of Council members. In fact, in January 2015, shortly before the Supreme Council of Cities and Tribes was due to hold a big meeting in Tobruk and would clearly position itself in support of Haftar, the Social Council withdrew from the body.[145] Now, Social Council members – including the very same person who had previously detailed Bani Walid's contribution to the war in Warshafana to me – denied that the 'Army of Tribes' had ever existed.[146]

By that point, the Social Council had settled its position towards the civil war: the parties to the conflict were two sides of the same coin, as both were led by the revolutionaries of 2011; Bani Walid represented a third force of tribes who rejected the revolutionary order altogether. Bani Walid had withdrawn from the Supreme Council because the latter had picked sides in the civil war, and because its leadership was under the thumb of Qadhafi's Cairo-based cousin Ahmed Qadhafeddam, who had betrayed Qadhafi in the revolution's first weeks, and was now allied with Haftar.[147]

This, in any case, was the explanation several Council members volunteered. It had broad support in Bani Walid. The town's neutrality in the second civil war also served to rewrite the history of Bani Walid's role in the 2011 war, which was now said to have been neutral. The Warfalla, the discourse went, had divined that the international conspiracy of 2011 would lead to internecine conflict between foreign-backed factions, and had therefore refrained from joining the revolution. In January 2015, I often heard in Bani Walid that 'everyone in Libya is now saying: the Warfalla were right from the beginning. Everyone now respects Bani Walid for having a principled position from the start, and sticking to it.'[148]

This explanation, however, did not reflect the full story of why and how Bani Walid disentangled itself from the civil war. In addition to ethical principles and personal enmities, more eminently political factors also played a role. Bani Walid had learned the hard way in 2012 that picking fights without a defensive capacity was suicidal. To enter the civil war, Bani Walid would need to have the necessary weaponry to guarantee its protection against attacks from outside.[149] But prospective allies were reluctant to supply Bani Walid with arms. Some alleged that Haftar had repeatedly promised to send weapons, but failed to deliver, perhaps because he was unsure of his local allies' loyalty.[150] Aref al-Nayed had organized two weapons shipments from the UAE via an airstrip in southern Libya, but the Tubu commanders he relied on had kept most of the weapons themselves, instead of delivering them to Bani Walid.[151] In this sense, Bani Walid's neutrality was a sign of weakness.

Second, Bani Walid's politicians watched closely as elements in Haftar's alliance reacted with unease to reports of former regime loyalists joining Haftar.[152] Many in Cyrenaica and Zintan still insisted on the February revolution as the foundation of political legitimacy. A month before my interlocutors in Bani Walid denied that the 'Army of Tribes' existed, Haftar's man in Zintan Idris Madi had already done the same – to distance himself from his counter-revolutionary allies.[153] For Bani Walid, such reservations towards regime loyalists raised the risk that Haftar would dump them once they had served their purpose.

Both of these factors are consistent with the assumptions of game-theoretic approaches that emphasize considerations of relative power and commitment problems. However, a third factor was probably crucial. Taking sides would have provoked open rifts in Bani Walid, including through the Social Council, upending the fragile consensus that allowed the community to overcome its deep divides, as well as threatening the Social Council's position in the town, and possibly also its existence. Were the members and supporters of the Social Council ready to run such a risk amid the profound uncertainty over who would prevail in the civil war, and how reliable their prospective allies in the war would be?

On the one hand, then, Bani Walid's neutrality was a sign of military weakness and a reflection of underlying internal divisions that threatened to come to the fore if political actors in Bani Walid were to align themselves unequivocally with the rival camps. On the other hand, it was a sign of social cohesion that came along with Bani Walid's self-isolation. The underlying divisions could have prompted politicians from Bani Walid to explicitly affiliate themselves with one side or another. While majority opinion was suspicious of Haftar or even hostile towards him, a handful of locals could plausibly have established a small armed group aligned with Haftar that would then have drawn Bani Walid gradually into Haftar's orbit, provoking divisions within the town. The fact that the Social Council managed to forestall such moves was a sign of strength.

Of course, the Social Council was not able to prevent individual members, let alone other political actors in Bani Walid from engaging with the conflicting parties. To hedge their bets, some politicians from Bani Walid maintained discreet contacts with forces from outside the town. But the Social Council was able to ensure that such engagement remained low profile, generally behind closed doors, and that any involvement of the Social Council could be plausibly denied, or dismissed as 'individuals who only represent themselves'. In sum, the Social Council's principal achievement was to preserve its neutral position during the second civil war and its aftermath.

The price to pay for this achievement was political paralysis. Any meaningful political move risked fuelling tensions within the Council and the town, threatening the fragile consensus that underpinned neutrality. This explains why Bani Walid withdrew from the Supreme Council; why, in January 2015, it rejected an invitation to the negotiations in Geneva, which would later move to Skhirat; and why, one year later, the Social Council staunchly denied that its former president Mohamed al-Barghuthi had met with the newly formed Presidency Council to discuss government formation.[154] After the Presidency Council moved to Tripoli, the Social Council initially avoided any public contact with the body. The Local Council was more flexible – it did not pretend to represent Bani Walid politically – and began meeting with Presidency Council members early on.[155]

A rare exception to the Social Council's reluctance to engage publicly with external political actors were several meetings, in May 2016, that brought together the Council's president and former president with Aref al-Nayed. Nayed had supplied substantial funds to help Bani Walid deal with the influx of displaced families from neighbouring Sirte.[156] He subsequently enrolled Barghuthi in the activities of his organization, claiming to Western diplomats that he enjoyed excellent relations with Bani Walid and was coordinating the Social Council's reconciliation efforts with similar initiatives elsewhere.[157]

In actual fact, Barghuthi was fiercely attacked by his adversaries within the Social Council and the town at large for associating himself with Nayed, who had been an early and important backer of the 2011 revolution, and barely concealed his ambitions to hold top offices.[158] And while Nayed's supporters in the Council claimed that he had apologized to them for his revolutionary stance in 2011, Nayed never did so publicly.[159] Many in Bani Walid continued to harbour deep resentment against Nayed, and subsequent contacts remained discreet or confined to Barghuthi who, as several of my interlocutors clamoured, 'represented only himself' in his dealings with Nayed.[160]

Constrained by its internal divisions, Bani Walid was unable to exploit its neutral position to act as a mediator between the conflicting parties, despite the Social Council's best intentions. From early 2015 onwards, the Social Council pursued various initiatives to form yet another Council representing the 'real' elders of all cities and tribes, or to hold a big meeting of such figures in an effort at national reconciliation.[161] Nothing ever came of these projects. Bringing them to fruition would have required courageous moves, such as reaching out to Misrata and other former revolutionary strongholds, without whom there could be no meaningful effort to bring the conflicting parties together. These cities were only too eager to reciprocate: from early 2016 onwards, the Misratans gradually released the majority of prisoners from Bani Walid and other former regime strongholds, attempting to demonstrate their goodwill.[162] Bani Walid's Local Council quietly engaged with the Misratans on the prisoner releases. The Social Council, however, consistently rebuffed Misratan advances, or confined them to deniable exchanges between individuals.[163] Genuine engagement with Misrata would have provoked an outcry among those who had lost relatives or suffered property damage due to the actions of Misratan armed groups.

Bani Walid's self-inflicted isolation came under pressure as the divides of the second civil war gave way to a fragmented landscape in western Libya, and former revolutionaries no longer hesitated to reach out to former regime loyalists. The Presidency Council had no qualms about placing former regime officials in senior positions, which softened the rejectionist stance prevailing in Bani Walid. Misratan politicians supported the delivery of new police vehicles to Bani Walid. The Zintani education minister appointed a hardline member of Bani Walid's Social Council, Abdelhamid al-Shanduli, as dean of the town's university. In November 2017, the boycotting Presidency Council member and close Haftar ally Ali al-Qatrani led a delegation of eastern representatives to visit Bani Walid – but as Shanduli insisted, it was a purely social visit of condolence after two Social Council members had been assassinated near Mizda a month earlier.[164] A number of military officers in Bani Walid began joining Haftar's Libyan Arab Armed Forces. This relationship was largely administrative – the salaries were higher – and did not translate into the establishment of actual units on the ground, rather than on paper.[165] Nevertheless, the affiliation of local officers with Haftar's forces began undermining Bani Walid's isolationist stance. So did the continuing involvement of former Social Council presidents Mohamed al-Barghuthi and Saleh Mayouf with Aref al-Nayed.

The municipal elections in September 2018 – which had been delayed since 2014, partly due to resistance from the Social Council – dealt another severe blow to isolationism. Once he had taken office, the new mayor immediately met with Prime Minister Serraj, and made a point of establishing a good working relationship with the Tripoli authorities, to mobilize budgets for Bani Walid. In April 2018, I had spent an evening with a group of men at a sheep farm in the desert outside Bani Walid; none of them had been to Tripoli – a two-hour car ride – since 2011. But clearly, these diehard Qadhafi nostalgists, who placed their hopes for salvation in the return of his son Saif al-Islam to the centre of politics, were a vanishing type.

At the same time, the Social Council proved powerless to prevent a renewed proliferation of armed groups in Bani Walid. One of the prisoners released from Misrata in March 2017, Adel Sultan, had led an armed group in Bani Walid before and during the town's defence in 2012. Upon his release, he reconstituted it and gave it an official-sounding name. Within the security battalion – which was under the Social Council's authority and had until then been the only armed entity in Bani Walid – a separate subunit emerged that carried the name of a leader in the battalion, Mohamed Salama, who had been assassinated in 2016. At Bani Walid's northern entrance, a local military police unit that administratively reported to the government in Tripoli began manning a checkpoint. During late 2017 and early 2018, repeated attempts by the Social Council to bring these various groups under a common structure failed. In the town's dense social fabric, no body could centralize authority over groups that were deeply embedded in family and neighbourhood networks.[166]

The fundamental driver behind the proliferation of these groups was the increasing competition over new sources of income. Among these sources were funds and vehicles provided by the rival governments in Tripoli and al-Bayda. But more important than those was the rise of Bani Walid as a hub in the business of smuggling and extortion of migrants, from late 2015 onward. Several gangs specializing in the business emerged, the largest one being led by Musa Diab, a onetime member of the 28 May Battalion.[167] As the business grew, it provoked increasing competition among rival gangs, which at times turned violent.[168] The security battalion became complicit with migrant smugglers; its reputation plummeted, and it repeatedly clashed with Adel Sultan's group. Financial incentives were also key in driving Sultan and several members of his group to join the Kaniyat in their attack on Tripoli in August 2018, along with some

Misratan armed groups who were considered archenemies by most people in Bani Walid.[169] The pursuit of economic gain, then, joined the association with rival political camps in eroding Bani Walid's self-isolation and cohesion.

For several years after 2011, Bani Walid withstood the temptation to shift its alignments with the changing strategic conditions. This was not only a function of its weakness and internal division. It was also due to the fact that rival local networks valued social cohesion and the existence of a unified representative body for the town more highly than uncertain gains from fleeting political alignments. Because of the Social Council's immobility, the pattern of fault lines adding onto fault lines that had eroded local unity in Misrata and Zintan did not emerge in Bani Walid.

But eventually, the centrifugal forces of Libya's conflicts eroded the unifying impact of isolationism. In September 2016, one of my interlocutors, a man in his thirties who worked with the Social Council, acknowledged that men from Bani Walid were joining Haftar's forces in the east, but stressed that majority opinion in the town rejected Haftar for his past record, and was determined to maintain neutrality.[170] What would happen, I asked, if Haftar took over neighbouring Sirte? In that case, he admitted, anything was possible in Bani Walid.

Three years later, the scenario materialized, in the form of Tarhuna's Kaniyat joining Haftar's forces in their offensive against Tripoli. Immediately before the offensive, Haftar had sent a substantial shipment of weapons to Tarhuna via Bani Walid's airport, where a military unit was stationed that had joined Haftar's forces. Tarhuna, and not Bani Walid, bore the brunt of the pressure from Tripoli and Misratan armed groups when news of the shipment spread. Once the war erupted, however, Haftar's many opponents in Bani Walid – including those newly aligned with the Tripoli government, but also former regime purists – imposed limits on his local allies. Their use of the airport was limited to occasional medical evacuation flights. A few dozen men announced their support for Haftar and joined the operation, but Haftar's opponents forestalled attempts to issue statements in the name of Bani Walid.[171] The Social Council, however, was too divided to even announce its neutrality in the conflict. Social cohesion clearly continued to constrain Haftar's local allies in their actions. But the myth of Bani Walid's unity, and its moral superiority as a third force separate from Libya's warring factions, had been shattered.

Tobruk: The rise of Haftar

How, given the pervasive local rifts and tenacious localism evident in the preceding case studies, can we explain that Khalifa Haftar gradually established uncontested control over the quasi-entirety of eastern Libya between mid-2014 and late 2016? Haftar's supporters in Cyrenaica commonly venture that he gained the support of 'the tribes' in the east – a line that much foreign commentary has adopted.[172] Tribal leaders in Cyrenaica, the narrative goes, tired of the post-revolutionary chaos, and mobilized to stop the assassinations haunting Benghazi in 2013 and early 2014, which were decimating their tribesmen. In Haftar, they saw a saviour who could rebuild the army, and drive out armed groups and extremists. Haftar was all the more attractive because he belonged to a tribe from central Libya, the Firjan, and therefore did not threaten to disturb the tribal balance in Cyrenaica as he would have, had he been a member of an eastern tribe. Such accounts of Haftar's rise are often rounded off with assertions that 'the tribes' in the east could easily dispose of Haftar, should they so wish.

The present analysis runs exactly counter to this narrative. Haftar was initially able to mobilize support from a variety of disgruntled eastern factions, none of which could be seen as representing the position of a tribe. Several of these groups refused to submit to Haftar's authority; they intended to use him to advance their own interests, then turn on him when the opportunity offered itself. That Haftar gradually centralized control over the loose alliance he led, and established his primacy across the east, was not due to the support of supposedly powerful tribes – quite to the contrary. Revolutionary and post-revolutionary mobilization had largely bypassed the peripheral areas of eastern Libya. In this eastern periphery, for which Tobruk can stand as an archetype, local leadership was weak, and communities had developed neither the internal cohesion nor the clearly defined external enemies that violent conflict had created in many areas of western and southern Libya. This setting offered fertile terrain for Haftar's structures of patronage and repression. These structures did make use of tribal notables, but in a way that relegated them to the position of mere clients. Most of all, Haftar owed his rise to his access to steady foreign support of a magnitude unavailable to any other actor in Libya.

What explanatory value does a case study of developments in Tobruk have in charting Haftar's ascension? Admittedly, Tobruk was exceptionally isolated, both geographically and politically, from the struggles unleashed by the revolution, until the House of Representatives (HoR) moved to the city in August 2014. But other towns in the east, such as al-Qubba or al-Marj, had equally seen little political and military mobilization during the revolution, had also been largely spared the violent local conflicts that developed in other parts of the country, and were similarly marginalized in the post-revolutionary power struggles.

These types of places were not the scene of the conflict that made Haftar a figure of national importance: that conflict raged in Benghazi, where deep political divides had developed since 2011, and powerful armed groups had formed. But without this eastern periphery, Haftar's rise would have been unthinkable. Control over Tobruk's port and airport was essential for Haftar to receive weapons shipments from abroad, and launch his fighter jets to bomb enemy positions in Benghazi. The HoR's move to Tobruk allowed Haftar to exert direct influence over the legislature. The environs of al-Marj provided a sufficiently secure location to host both Haftar's headquarters and an air base used by his Emirati supporters.[173] Such provincial Cyrenaican towns also furnished an important supply of recruits for units that were under Haftar's immediate control – as opposed to the armed groups from Benghazi and its environs, which were loyal first and foremost to their leaders, whose relationship with Haftar was often fraught with tensions. Finally, mobilizing support from across the east allowed Haftar to tap into rising regionalist sentiment in Cyrenaica and portray himself as benefiting from the backing of 'the tribes in the east', whereas a campaign focused on Benghazi alone would have turned him into just another local warlord.

Tobruk, as discussed in the previous two chapters, did not suffer serious divides during the revolution, nor witness the formation of new tight-knit groups or strong identities through violent conflict. As in other peripheral regions of southern and eastern Libya, Tobruk's politicians were more flexible and opportunistic in their political alignment than was the case in settings where new collective identities placed tight constraints – such as in Misrata, the Nafusa Mountains or Bani Walid. The three independent GNC members from Tobruk adopted no unequivocal positions in the post-revolutionary struggles, and, instead, floated between competing blocs in the legislature – until February 2014, when two resigned under pressure from local proponents of the campaign to dissolve the GNC. Tribal politicians such as al-Tayyeb al-Sharif moved from being pillars of Qadhafi's rule to proponents of eastern autonomy.[174] Others, such as Faraj Yadam Buatiwa, dabbled in revolutionary rhetoric and denounced the federalists as former members of Qadhafi's Popular Social Leadership (PSL) seeking to make a comeback. (Ironically, Buatiwa had himself been a PSL member, and clamoured for the suppression of protests at the Tobruk PSL's final meeting on 18 February 2011).[175] Al-Siddiq al-Mabruk al-Ghithi, a former member of the Libyan Islamic Fighting Group from neighbouring Darna with political connections and a clientele in Tobruk, moved from the jihadist spectrum to the autonomy movement.[176]

Contrary to the southern periphery, however, the east did not witness violent conflicts along tribal lines between 2011 and 2014. No armed groups emerged that claimed to protect their communities from hostile neighbours. The eastern periphery was not affected by the processes that split the landscape in western and southern Libya into rival local forces.

To be sure, tribal identity did matter in Tobruk, and local politicians used it as a resource. But these tribal politicians did not amount to a tribal leadership. They were notoriously divided by political rivalries and, in some cases, long-standing personal enmities. For example, six or seven figures competed over influence within the Obeidat section dominant in Tobruk, the Ait Mariam. Several of them loathed each other. Faraj Yasin and Mansur al-Salihin, though first cousins, had long been on bad terms with each other. Faraj Yasin bitterly opposed al-Tayyeb al-Sharif, with whom he had a long-standing dispute over land ownership. A fourth *Marimi* notable, Ahmed Harun, also hated al-Sharif, and during an encounter in April 2015, he exploded in anger when he found out that I had met with al-Sharif. Yet three others – Faraj Hashem Bulkhatabiya, Faraj Yadam Buatiwa and Faraj Buhassan al-Marimi – engaged in changing alliances with the four aforementioned figures, as well as with outside actors.[177]

Such personal rivalries conditioned political positions and ensured that there could never be a position of 'the tribe' – the Ait Mariam, let alone the Obeidat as a whole – on any given issue. The fact that al-Tayyeb al-Sharif and Mansur Salihin lobbied for eastern autonomy, for example, practically guaranteed that Faraj Yasin would oppose federalism – which he did. In promoting regional autonomy, Al-Sharif and Salihin claimed to speak for their tribes, while their opponents organized meetings of notables purporting to show that these same tribes opposed regional autonomy.[178] In the 2012 GNC elections, Obeidat tribal politicians failed to agree on a common candidate, and as a result, the Obeidat – numerically the largest tribe in Tobruk – failed to elect a single representative in the city. In the May 2014 Local Council elections, nine candidates from the Ait Mariam once again split the Obeidat vote. In the June HoR elections, the

Qutaan – one of the other two large tribes in Tobruk, the third one being the Mniffa – were too divided to elect one of their own.[179] Nor were the jealousies between Tobruk's tribal politicians a new phenomenon: already under Qadhafi, the same actors had been at loggerheads over access to state resources and the levers of the administration, and had contested each other's right to represent their tribe.[180]

Privately, several of my interlocutors in Tobruk were dismissive of these notables. They ridiculed their petty disputes among each other, listed their corrupt dealings during the Qadhafi era, and most of all scorned their opportunism and venality. 'They're hypocrites,' a young professional told me in April 2015. 'They pledged allegiance to Qadhafi. Then they pledged allegiance to [Mustafa] Abdeljalil. Now they pledge allegiance to Haftar.'[181] It was an open secret in Tobruk that Haftar had given cars to al-Tayyeb al-Sharif to gain or cement his support. The declarations of tribal support for Haftar in Tobruk, then, had to be seen against the background of this weak and internally divided leadership.

Following his February 2014 television coup, Haftar toured the east to mobilize support among disgruntled constituencies. He found considerable endorsement. Resentment ran high over the post-revolutionary chaos and the east's marginalization in the struggles in Tripoli. Such resentment played into the hands of an eastern autonomy movement that resorted to increasingly brazen actions. Officers of the old army and security services felt outpowered by revolutionary armed groups in Benghazi and Darna, and were furious at government inaction in the face of the accelerating assassination sprees targeting them in both cities. In the environs of Benghazi, remnants of the army coalesced with civilians from the same communities to form militias that clashed with Islamist-leaning and jihadi groups. In late 2013, GNC president Abusahmain and the government added insult to injury by retiring hundreds of army officers – among them Haftar, as well as several of his future associates.[182]

The component elements of Haftar's alliance in its initial form, in the spring and summer of 2014, reflected this variety of alienated eastern groups. Officers at eastern air bases were among the first to answer Haftar's call, not only because Haftar made a particular effort at courting them, but also because members of the air force had been disproportionately represented among the victims of assassinations. In early March, shortly after Haftar had reached out to them, officers at the air base in Tobruk publicly denounced the killings targeting military officers, asked the government to take action, and demanded that the authorities respond to their statement.[183] Officers at the al-Bayda, Benghazi and Sirte air bases, where Haftar had also drummed up support, followed suit shortly afterwards.

The chief of staff did respond – by dismissing the head of the air force, and referring him to the military prosecutor, along with four other officers who were involved with Haftar.[184] Among the four was Hamed al-Hassi, commander of the self-styled Cyrenaica Defence Force, a group that had repeatedly appeared as the armed wing of autonomy activists. The previous year, Hassi had himself escaped an assassination attempt in which one of his close associates was killed.[185] Hassi was at Haftar's side throughout his tour of the east. Another close associate was Saqr al-Jarushi, who had been commander of Tobruk's air base up until the revolution and was appointed chief of staff of the air force in early 2012, but was dismissed and retired by a ruling of the

Integrity Commission a year later.[186] Al-Jarushi became Haftar's air force chief, and reactivated his old connections to Tobruk air base in that capacity. Haftar's declared intention of restoring the Libyan army therefore particularly resonated with officers who had very personal reasons to rebel against Tripoli.

Even before the start of military operations in mid-May, Haftar coupled his message to army officers with the repertoire of eastern tribal politics. At his meetings in the east, he invoked the historical record of the tribes whose support he professed to be seeking.[187] Tribal politicians at these meetings arrogated the right to speak in the name of their entire tribes, and Haftar claimed to have obtained declarations of loyalty from the region's largest tribes.[188]

In reality, when he launched his operation against other armed groups in Benghazi, Haftar's support in the east resided in two specific constituencies, in addition to that of disgruntled military officers: first, proponents of regional autonomy, who saw in Haftar's rebellion against the army leadership an opportunity to weaken the central government further and advance their agenda; second, leaders of armed groups from the environs of Benghazi, most of them dominated by members of the Awaqir tribe, whose stated motivations ranged from avenging killings they attributed to armed groups from Benghazi, to expelling the 'Misratan' families they saw as leading these armed groups, and seizing their properties.[189]

Both of these constituencies, and many eastern army officers, came to share a common discourse that extolled the valour and nobility of the tribes of *Barqa*, or Cyrenaica. Their discourse and interests diverged from Haftar's, whose professed goal was to restore a central authority backed up by a strong army. Many saw Haftar not as a leader they would support, but as a temporary ally whom they could use to advance their goals, then discard when opportune. But in the operation's first months, their backing was critical for allowing Haftar to mobilize support across the east. A particularly important backer was Hassan Tatanaki, a Benghazi businessman whose TV station *Libya Awalan* was widely watched in the east, who strongly promoted both Haftar and the autonomy movement.

In Tobruk, the launch of Haftar's operation met with expressions of support early on. Almost immediately, soldiers and civilians came out in small demonstrations of support for Haftar, and the commander of Tobruk military region openly endorsed his operation.[190] Three days after the fighting erupted in Benghazi, officers at Tobruk's air base as well as its border guards unit announced that they had joined Haftar.[191] The next day, al-Tayyeb al-Sharif and several other notables declared their backing for Haftar's operation in the name of the Obeidat.[192] Over the following week, Al-Sharif, Buatiwa and other Haftar allies then mobilized demonstrations and meetings in support of Operation Dignity.[193]

This groundswell of support, remarkable though it was, concealed a more ambiguous mix of attitudes towards Haftar. The commanders of Tobruk's Omar al-Mukhtar Brigade and the border guards unit refused to back Haftar, but they felt sufficient pressure from his supporters not to openly oppose him.[194] Gen. Suleiman Mahmoud, the former commander of Tobruk military region and a Haftar opponent since the latter attempted to designate himself chief of staff in 2011, issued an ambivalent statement in which he voiced his support for the 'people's choice' and for building a strong army under civilian control, but failed to mention Haftar and Operation Dignity.[195] Several of the Tobruk Obeidat's leading notables, including Faraj Yasin and Mansur Salihin, refrained from joining al-Tayyeb al-Sharif's declaration of Obeidat support for Haftar, whether out of aversion towards al-Sharif or opposition to Haftar.

Still, Haftar enjoyed sufficient support in Tobruk to prevent any open resistance from forming. The use of Tobruk air base for bombing sorties on Benghazi provoked no local protests. Haftar's declared goals of fighting extremists and restoring the army resonated in Tobruk, and his open defiance of the Tripoli authorities was shrugged off – after all, the government had done little to reach out to faraway Tobruk, and counted few supporters there.

In other peripheral areas of eastern Libya, the reaction was similar to that in Tobruk. In Benghazi, Darna and Ajdabiya, however, armed groups whose self-image ranged from revolutionaries to jihadis fiercely opposed Haftar, who had declared war on them. Outside these cities, only al-Bayda counted a sizeable group of former revolutionaries, at their core the Ali Hassan Jaber Battalion, who openly rejected Haftar's renegade army command. In Tobruk, as in most of the east, opposition to Haftar would henceforth manifest itself in meetings behind closed doors, and in attempts at fomenting mutiny within his loose alliance.

Haftar's operation, then, did not prompt Tobruk to close ranks against a common enemy. Rather, a small number of influential allies managed to draw Tobruk into Haftar's orbit. A wider range of political actors feigned approval for the operation, ready to part ways with Haftar later on, or stay with him, as would suit their political interests. A small group of staunch opponents remained in Tobruk, but decided to lie low for the moment. As a result, behind the façade of unshakeable tribal loyalty, Haftar's authority in Tobruk remained fragile until at least early 2016. Ambivalence was the name of the game.

With the arrival of the House of Representatives (HoR) to Tobruk in August 2014, the city that had always been at Libya's margins entered the spotlight. The HoR's appointment of his close associate Abderrazeq al-Nadhuri as chief of staff left little doubt over the legislature's support for Haftar's operation – even though Haftar's command structure still remained outside official state institutions. But the HoR's presence in Tobruk and the choice of its president – Agila Saleh from al-Qubba, a member of the Obeidat's Ghaith section with extensive social relations in Tobruk – also opened up new opportunities for playing politics by maintaining an ambivalent position towards Haftar. Proponents of eastern autonomy who intended to dump Haftar at the earliest opportunity could now profess to recognize the legitimacy of the HoR and its 'army', without even a nod to Haftar. In November 2014, for example, three of Tobruk's tribal politicians appeared with Ibrahim al-Jadhran to affirm their loyalty to the HoR and its Bayda-based government, while at the same time threatening eastern secession, thereby positioning themselves in clear conflict with Haftar.[196]

The costs Tobruk incurred by supporting the Haftar-led alliance were all relative. In November 2014, a terrorist attack killed three people in Tobruk, and in December, a car bomb exploded in front of the hotel that housed the HoR, but caused only minor injuries.[197] Thereafter, the attacks stopped. Haftar and his allies refrained from provoking an open confrontation with the armed groups in neighbouring Darna, though they began controlling movements to and from the city, and occasionally carried out airstrikes on targets there. (Haftar eventually launched an offensive to capture Darna in May 2018.). The conflict in Benghazi was far away. In fact, Tobruk benefited from the diversion of trade from Benghazi and Darna after Haftar's air force repeatedly bombed vessels that approached these ports.[198]

At a meeting of tribal politicians I attended in Tobruk in April 2015, one of the participants deplored the lukewarm commitment of eastern tribes to Haftar's war in Benghazi. There were around 700,000 men of fighting age in *Barqa*, he said, but only 800 to 1,000 of them were fighting in Benghazi. This was hyperbole, but it touched a sore spot. To be sure, hundreds of men from Tobruk joined Operation Dignity; they did so as volunteers, initially without receiving salaries, and volunteer organizations mobilized food for these fighters. They fought with Brigade 309, a unit Haftar set up in Tobruk during the autumn of 2014 that was staffed with young men from Tobruk and al-Qubba, most of them civilians. By April 2015, thirty-seven of its members had been killed in fighting in Benghazi, but only four of them were military personnel.[199] Not a single military officer from Tobruk went to fight in Benghazi.[200] In Tobruk, young men from modest backgrounds bore the costs of Haftar's war, among them Egyptian citizens from the Awlad Ali tribe. This stood in stark contrast to the socially embedded armed groups in Misrata and the Nafusa Mountains.

Brigade 309 did not build on pre-existing local networks. The armed groups that joined Operation Dignity in al-Bayda, al-Marj and the environs of Benghazi all had a core membership and established leaders. They often pursued goals that only partly corresponded to Haftar's. In Tobruk, however, there was no existing group Haftar could mobilize, and no local leader to build a militia from among his clientele. Instead, Haftar charged a member of the Firjan tribe from Tobruk with setting up Brigade 309. After that commander was killed in battle in February 2015, Haftar appointed another fellow tribesman, from Sirte, in his place.[201]

*

On my first visit to Tobruk, in April 2014 – only one month before Haftar launched his operation – the local politicians and activists I met knew no common enemy. The discourse was not confrontational, and I heard no slogans about fighting terrorism or rebuilding the army. A year later, these slogans had become articles of faith, and most tribal politicians I talked to had adopted a vicious rhetoric that stigmatized eastern Libyans with roots in Misrata and other parts of western Libya as the cause of Cyrenaica's problems.[202] But this did not mean that Tobruk had closed ranks. In fact, this discourse appeared designed to distract from the actual politics these figures were busying themselves with: the struggle over leadership in Tobruk and eastern Libya, including within the Bayda-based government of Abdallah al-Thinni that in 2015 retained its status as the internationally recognized authority. Haftar, during the first year of Operation Dignity, was one among several players competing for influence in eastern Libya. Only from early 2016 onward did he begin centralizing control by forcefully sidelining challengers from within his coalition.

In early 2015, several commanders in Benghazi, backed by Thinni and his defence minister Massoud Arhuma, began openly contesting Haftar's authority, alleging that he was withholding ammunition from them to assert control. On videos circulating on social media, leading figures in the Benghazi operation attacked Haftar as 'sitting in al-Marj preparing to seize power, while we die on the battlefield'.[203] Haftar tried to dismiss the most prominent of these commanders, Faraj al-Barassi, but proved powerless to do so.[204] Meanwhile, Haftar successfully lobbied the HoR to appoint him general commander of the Armed Forces, a position superior to that of chief of staff, though nominally subordinate to HoR president Agila Saleh. With this move, Haftar finally gained an official position, and established his formal supremacy over both the Thinni government and his unruly commanders.

Still, many of Tobruk's political players were uncertain on which horse to bet. In April 2015, one of Tobruk's leading actors downplayed eastern support for Haftar, assuring me of his certain downfall at the hands of Benghazi commanders, as well as Ibrahim al-Jadhran, who was by then in open conflict with Haftar.[205] Other than Jadhran, Barassi also continued to reach out to military figures in Tobruk and al-Bayda to plot Haftar's overthrow.[206] Another Tobruk tribal politician, Faraj Hashem Bulkhatabiya, associated himself with the Benghazi businessman Hassan Tatanaki in a scheme to bring down the Thinni government.[207]

It was such local rivalry, as well as the absence of cohesive local forces, that allowed Haftar to gradually establish control over Tobruk, and other peripheral eastern cities like it. While local factions were occupied with their intrigues, Haftar steadily reinforced his position. His most important resource was external backing from Egypt and the UAE in the form of weapons, equipment, and, almost certainly, cash. No other Libyan actor benefited from support even remotely comparable in magnitude and constancy to that available to Haftar.[208]

To strengthen his hand vis-à-vis the unreliable commanders and militias in his alliance, Haftar recruited fighters from Darfur and Chad.[209] More importantly, he empowered two other forces in the east. First, he enrolled ultraconservative Salafis – dogmatic followers of the Saudi scholar Rabi' al-Madkhali – in his military operation, and supported their takeover of mosques and police stations.[210] These groups not only shared Haftar's hostility to the Muslim Brotherhood, but also promoted absolute obedience to authority – which meant Haftar – and offered a counterweight to the clan-based *Barqa* supremacists.

Second, Haftar encouraged former members of Qadhafi's security services and loyalist army officers to return from exile and work for him. Unlike established local commanders, these returnees had not built their own stocks of weapons and vehicles over the past years, and many of them came from cities or regions they could only hope to return to by military conquest. For both reasons, they were much more dependent on Haftar than the groups he had initially mobilized for his campaign. Senior regime figures also returned to eastern Libya and, even if they played no formal role in Haftar's structure, showed their gratitude by publicly endorsing Haftar. The most prominent such figure in Tobruk was al-Tayyeb al-Safi, a long-standing regime official from the Mniffa tribe who had been Qadhafi's right-hand man in the attempts to suppress the rebellion in eastern Libya in February 2011.[211]

With these resources at his disposal, Haftar entered protracted struggles with his eastern opponents. In Darna, a coalition of local armed groups called the Darna Mujahidin Shura Council (DMSC), which included jihadist, Islamist and non-Islamist elements, began waging war on the local affiliate of the Islamic State in June 2015. Haftar exploited the conflict by deploying armed groups recruited from areas bordering Darna, thereby moving closer to the city and obstructing the DMSC's struggle against IS. In September 2015, army officers and former revolutionaries from al-Bayda's Ali Hassan Jaber Brigade issued a statement in opposition to Haftar, and moved with their erstwhile brothers-in-arms from Tobruk to join the DMSC in fighting IS in Darna.[212] This was not only a direct challenge to Haftar's authority in a key eastern city, but also a threat to undermine the narrative that Haftar was indispensable for leading the fight against terrorists in the east.

Haftar responded by attacking the Ali Hassan Jaber Brigade in al-Bayda, forcing it to surrender its base.[213] As fighters from Darna, al-Bayda and Tobruk advanced against IS, Haftar's men gradually tightened the noose around Darna, harassing or arresting anti-IS combatants on their way to or from the front line, and cutting off supplies to their forces.[214] By the time the Darna-based alliance vanquished IS in April 2016, Haftar's hold over Tobruk and al-Bayda had become such that these former revolutionaries could no longer return as a group to their home cities. Many left for western Libya – including Muftah Omar Hamza, the officer from Tobruk who had led the joint forces in Darna since November 2015.

In the meantime, political rivalries among eastern actors had crystallized into a contest between those aligned with Haftar, and those supporting a future UN-backed unity government. Since October 2015, Thinni's education minister Fathi al-Majbari was a prime eastern candidate for Presidency Council membership. Majbari and his principal backer, Ibrahim al-Jadhran, worked to win over figures from across eastern Libya. But Haftar's allies in the HoR prevented all attempts to hold a vote on the draft. In late November, the Tobruk tribal politician Faraj Yadam Buatiwa, a staunch Haftar supporter, ran into an HoR session shouting threats against parliamentarians who intended to vote on the draft, and HoR president Agila Saleh – in obvious collusion with Buatiwa – adjourned the session.[215] Saleh also prevented all future attempts to formally vote on the agreement after it was signed.

Haftar's associates and supporters of the Skhirat agreement in the east made competing claims to tribal support. In Tobruk, tribal politicians were predictably split. While al-Tayyeb al-Sharif and Faraj Yasin backed Haftar, several figures who had previously allied with Jadhran now supported the unity government, and voiced their support for the agreement in the name of the Obeidat.[216] Tobruk's Local Council and its associated Council of Elders, in which supporters of the agreement prevailed, called on the HoR to vote on the deal.[217] But Agila Saleh assembled loyal tribal figures from across the east who announced that they would support the agreement only if Haftar remained head of the army.[218]

Across the country, it was increasingly common for rival groups of tribal notables from one and the same tribe to come out and pretend to speak for their communities. The political process had collapsed and elected bodies had entered a deep crisis of legitimacy; hence, self-declared tribal leaders had ample opportunity to pose as the true representatives of the people, and promote tribal leadership as a more authentic and successful model than representation through democratic elections. Ironically, Agila Saleh himself appeared as often as a tribal notable, and orchestrated political displays of tribal elders, as he chaired HoR sessions.

Foreign governments and the UN also encouraged the practice by hosting tribal representatives whose support base was often questionable. The most blatant such move was a meeting of Libyan tribal figures organized by the Egyptian government in May 2015 to voice support for Haftar, in line with Egypt's position.[219] One of the Benghazi-based militia leaders seeking to emancipate themselves from Haftar promptly derided the attendees as '1,000-Dinar-sheikhs, Tatanaki's sheikhs.'[220] But as the struggle between Haftar and his opponents in eastern Libya intensified, staged expressions of tribal support were taken to their extreme and ultimately turned into a parody of themselves, thereby revealing their hollowness.

A televised audience Haftar gave to eastern tribal elders in late January 2016 at his headquarters in al-Marj showed the way. It took place shortly after the Presidency Council proposed a government line-up whose nominee for defence minister was Colonel al-Mahdi al-Barghathi, a Benghazi commander from the Awaqir tribe who had long been at loggerheads with Haftar. It was clear that Presidency Council member Fathi al-Majbari as well as Barghathi and Jadhran intended to pull the Haftar-led alliance apart by integrating various eastern networks into the unity government. Haftar's appearance before tribal leaders sought to convey that Cyrenaica was united in its rejection of the Skhirat agreement and its government. Its choreography of successive exaltations of Haftar leading up to a long speech by the leader was more than reminiscent of Qadhafi's meetings with tribal figures.[221]

The contest shifted into high gear with Barghathi's move to Tripoli in May 2016, to take up his post. It was now clear that Barghathi directly challenged Haftar's authority. On his way to Tripoli, Barghathi appeared with Jadhran, Suleiman Mahmoud and several leaders of Awaqir armed groups from Benghazi, thereby revealing the outlines of an eastern alliance opposed to Haftar. With Jadhran, this alliance appeared to command control over eastern oilfields and export terminals; with the Awaqir figures, substantial firepower in Benghazi; and taken together, influential supporters in several of Cyrenaica's largest tribes.

Once Barghathi returned to Benghazi a week later, a tug-of-war over eastern allegiances began – and much of it was staged in the form of a contest over tribal loyalties. Awaqir militia leaders supporting Barghathi publicly accused Haftar of being behind several of the assassinations and bombings that had fuelled the anger Haftar then exploited for his operation. One such militia leader, Faraj Qa'im, had captured a Haftar operative who supposedly confessed to his involvement in such plots.[222] Social media was abuzz with videos of Qa'im expounding Haftar's alleged conspiracies before Awaqir tribal elders.[223] For a while, many Awaqir figures were reluctant to take sides in a conflict whose outcome was unclear, and pretended to mediate between Haftar and Barghathi.[224] But Haftar forced the tribe's notables to take sides by organizing several carefully choreographed pledges of loyalty.[225]

A similar struggle played out in parallel among the Magharba between Jadhran and the tribe's most prominent notable, Saleh Latiwish, who had assured Qadhafi of his loyalty as late as 14 February 2011 before throwing his support behind the revolution, then joined the movement for regional autonomy in 2012 but opposed Jadhran when he tried to take the reins of that movement. Latiwish emerged as a key Haftar ally in late 2015, when he facilitated the movement of forces loyal to Haftar into Ajdabiya.[226] Throughout the first half of 2016, Latiwish mobilized against Jadhran at tribal meetings that, he claimed, 'testified to Magharba tribal unity and showed that anyone who tries to divide the Magharba has no place here'.[227]

Jadhran, for his part, declared he was willing to abide by the word of Magharba elders: 'the real sheikhs, not these prepaid sheikhs who one day declare their loyalty to Mu'ammar [al-Qadhafi], the next day to the Muslim Brothers, and then to the vanquished prisoner-of-war [Haftar]'.[228] He also mobilized Magharba elders to stage shows of support for him rivalling those of Latiwish.[229] But in September, Haftar's forces took over Jadhran's oil export terminals with hardly a bullet fired. Some commentators explained this surprising development as reflecting 'tribal support' for Haftar: 'tribal leaders managed to convince many of Jadhran's men to lay down their weapons'.[230] More plausibly, given the divided loyalties of Magharba tribal politicians, major sums of money changed hands, with tribal elders as key conduits, to smooth the advance of Haftar's forces.[231]

In Tobruk, the stakes for supporters and opponents of Haftar were lower, since the city had no representatives in the unity government. Nevertheless, in August 2016, Haftar's local adversaries, led by Colonel Muftah Omar Hamza, persuaded a dozen prominent Obeidat notables from Tobruk and a-Qubba to meet with Misratan representatives in Tunis and issue a statement in favour of reconciliation.[232] In al-Qubba, the Obeidat heartland, a group of people immediately denounced 'dubious meetings of traitors with terrorists', while in Tobruk, Faraj Yasin and Faraj Yadam Buatiwa appeared with figures from other regions to reject the Skhirat agreement and voice their support for 'the army' in the name of Libya's tribes.[233]

Haftar's takeover of the oil crescent foiled the ploys to erode his position in the east by drawing eastern figures into the unity government. With Jadhran gone, Barghathi's position in Benghazi became untenable. The tug-of-war over political allegiances in eastern tribes receded, but Haftar's instrumentalization of tribal elders took on ever more extravagant forms. Haftar appointed a 'social affairs coordinator' to liaise with tribal figures, Belaid al-Shikhi, who had formerly specialized in odes to Qadhafi, and whose rhetorical style was closer to that of an agitator in a totalitarian regime than to a tribal dignitary.[234] Declarations of loyalty and support by tribal politicians were no longer spontaneous local actions; rather, they were now slickly produced by Haftar's media office – among them a statement of Obeidat sheikhs read by Faraj Yasin.[235] From early 2017 onwards, stage-managed gatherings of tribal figures with Haftar degenerated into increasingly absurd sequences of adulation.[236]

Eastern tribal politicians, then, sank from being figureheads of rival political interests to acting as mere pawns in propaganda performances staged by Haftar. The changes that underlay this transformation were real, and deeply affected the ability of political actors in the east to organize and express their interests independently of Haftar's power structure. To enforce compliance, Haftar had since late 2015 overseen a string of abductions among long-standing adversaries and former allies in the east. The first prominent such case was that of former deputy defence minister and erstwhile LIFG member al-Siddiq al-Mabruk, scion of a notable family from the Obeidat's Ghaith section, who was abducted in the town of Susa in December 2015. Over the next three months, over a dozen individuals were abducted in Tobruk, al-Bayda as well as al-Marj, and held incommunicado.[237] Among them were activists in the autonomy movement, vocal supporters of the unity government, as well as people who had shown support for the forces from Tobruk and al-Bayda who were fighting IS in Darna. A few of them, such as a son of the Tobruk notable Faraj Hashem Bulkhatabiya, were released after influential local figures pleaded with Haftar. In Bulkhatabiya's case, local notables successfully pressured local Haftar allies to close down the secret prison in which Bulkhatabiya had been held.[238] But in most cases, such pressure remained fruitless. Several Obeidat notables from Tobruk and the Darna area mobilized to obtain al-Siddiq al-Mabruk's liberation – among them many of the same figures who were also voicing support for the Skhirat agreement. They temporarily closed down the Tobruk-Darna road in protest, and intervened with HoR president Agila Saleh as well as Haftar himself – all to no avail.[239]

At first, the disappearances met with vocal protest by relatives, once they had established the location of the abductees and the fact that Haftar's operatives were responsible. But such dissent quickly died down as fear won out. One of my interlocutors from Tobruk, who was only marginally involved in politics but known to oppose Haftar, told me in May 2016 that he had reason to fear being abducted or arrested.[240] Many prominent figures from the east, among them army officers opposed to Haftar and leaders in the autonomy movement, left their hometowns during 2016 to seek refuge in Tripoli or abroad. In Tobruk, they included Suleiman Mahmoud and Muftah Omar Hamza.[241] Some tribal politicians who had previously supported Barghathi tried to redeem themselves by declaring their loyalty to Haftar – among them the Awaqir sheikh Brik al-Lawati. He was assassinated in a car bomb attack, likely as retribution for his previous disloyalty.[242] The autonomy movement that had been such a critical source of support for Haftar in the first year of his campaign now was no longer able to organize and mobilize openly.

Meanwhile, Haftar continued to consolidate control in the east. During the second half of 2016, he appointed military governors to replace elected local councils in eight municipalities, including in Benghazi, where he installed former senior regime official Abderrahman al-Abbar.[243] Throughout 2017, Haftar's forces spread terror across the east with a series of mass executions in Benghazi. Video recordings of the killings circulated on social media.[244]

Haftar's opponents tried to seize on the growing eastern disillusionment with such acts by once again challenging Haftar's authority. They attempted to mobilize support on a tribal basis, but ultimately failed. In August 2017, Suleiman Mahmoud returned to Tobruk, where a large group of relatives welcomed him at the airport to protect him. Shortly afterwards, Barghathi's ally Faraj Qa'im – whom Serraj had just named deputy interior minister – used the same tactic to return to Benghazi.[245] In October, Colonel Muftah Omar Hamza did the same when returning to Tobruk for the first time in over a year. The following month, a crowd protected Tobruk's mayor upon his return from Tripoli; his dealings with the Presidency Council had earned him an arrest warrant from the Bayda-based government.[246]

But Qa'im narrowly escaped an assassination attempt in November; he reacted by openly calling for Haftar's dismissal, and was then captured by Haftar's forces.[247] Repeated demonstrations and roadblocks by his relatives to demand his release in the name of the Awaqir were in vain. Hamza, who had protected himself in Tobruk by keeping his relatives close, returned to Tripoli after a few weeks. Suleiman Mahmoud stayed, but stopped publishing his virulent criticism of Haftar and Agila Saleh. The mayor made it clear that his dealings with Tripoli were not an expression of political loyalty and solely aimed at mobilizing resources for the city.[248] Although their extended families afforded these figures some protection, the political acts of these individuals also created problems for family members – which eventually led them to desist.[249] In contrast to the constraints on political agency in Misrata, the Nafusa Mountains and Bani Walid, here the limitations did not emanate from the social networks of the community, but from Haftar's power structure.

Abuctions and assassinations in all impunity, along with the successful repression of the region's autonomy movement, put the lie to the narrative that Haftar's rule over eastern Libya was rooted in solid tribal support. The actions of Haftar's security apparatus violated tribal conceptions of honour, and exposed the impotence of established notables. Politically motivated kidnappings did occur in Tripoli, and they happened in western Libya between members of distinct communities that were in conflict with each other. But they were highly exceptional between members of the same community in cohesive local communities such as Misrata, Zintan or Bani Walid. Haftar's power structure had succeeded in disembedding itself from local social networks in the east. Its ability to do so stemmed from foreign backing, as well as from a local social setting in peripheral areas of eastern Libya that was characterized by weak, fractious leadership and the absence of socially embedded forces that could have withstood Haftar's creeping takeover.

Conclusion

The local forces that emerged in revolutionary strongholds during the 2011 war were both cohesive and deeply socially embedded. Their social embeddedness endowed them with much of their power, but it also posed important constraints on their political leaders as they sought to adapt to changing strategic conditions. While pursuing the capture of state resources and bargaining for government posts in 2012–13 and again in 2015–16, these leaders eroded the communal unity that was the source of their power. By redefining their communities' enemies in 2014 only to reach out to these same enemies several months later, they inflicted crisscrossing political rifts on the social fabric. Even so, social relations in such closely knit communities prevented these leaders from confronting their local rivals with utter ruthlessness, and from freely following their whims in the tumultuous struggles they were entangled in. In Bani Walid, which – unlike revolutionary strongholds – had suffered deep divides in 2011 and 2012 and lacked powerful leaders, the constraints of social embeddedness caused local actors to withdraw from these struggles for years, even as rival actors in Libya's conflicts solicited them as allies. In all of these settings, social cohesion and embeddedness prevented the penetration of supralocal political and military organizations.

These case studies reveal a counterintuitive finding: political fragmentation appears most durably in socially cohesive communities. Even where such communities had potent leaders who combined political and military influence, such as in Misrata or Zintan, these leaders' room for manoeuvre was noticeably constrained by the network of social ties that linked them to rivals in the same communities. In these cases, local political fragmentation was the chief impediment to the formation of more integrated national political forces or alliances.

Haftar built his power structure in a region where cohesive local forces were few and far between. To the extent that peripheral areas of eastern Libya had been affected by the divides of the 2011 revolution and by the controversy surrounding the autonomy movement, these rifts did not run deep. While Haftar's position was still fragile, he refrained from shifting his position in any way that would have called into question the definition of the enemy on which he had built his alliance, and he remained steadfast in his rejection of talks with political adversaries. Only after he consolidated power in the east, in mid-2017, did he begin to show flexibility – he could now afford to.

A key driver of fragmentation was the rapid succession of radically different strategic conditions. An important aspect of such instability was the turbulence in political players' access to resources: foreign support or the Qadhafi regime in 2011, both of which disappeared with the end of the war; state assets in 2012–14, to which access constantly changed amid a succession of short-lived governments, and then became more difficult after government institutions split in two; renewed backing from regional governments in 2014–16, and limited possibilities for capturing state resources through the three parallel, competing governments. Here, a newly unstable, multipolar regional order could be seen at work, fuelling fragmentation in Libya. This instability did much to encourage political actors to push the limits within the web of obligations and loyalties they were enmeshed in. The one actor who did not have to deal with such turbulence was Haftar, whose steady support from Egypt and the UAE furnished the material basis for his unyielding political stance.

Patterns of territorial control emerging in western Libya from early 2017 onward also support the present argument on the reasons for Haftar's rise in eastern Libya. In Tripoli, four large militias divided up the capital between themselves. In Tarhuna, a family-led militia established exclusive control over the town and the road to Tripoli. These processes occurred in cities that had not undergone the intense, community-based mobilization of revolutionary strongholds in 2011, and lacked socially embedded forces. In Misrata, the Nafusa Mountains and Bani Walid, the social cohesion forged through conflict prevented such consolidation.

Conclusion

This book has delved into the depths of politics in four Libyan localities, as they lived through the Libyan revolution and the struggles it unleashed. Taking an interest in the exploits of local political actors should not be misunderstood as a voyeuristic curiosity about family disputes. In the eight years following the eruption of protests in February 2011, local politics was central to developments at the national level. The revolutionary coalition fractured – and central authority disintegrated – due to the cohesion of local forces shaped by the revolutionary war. As local leaders built new alliances, this cohesion imposed constraints on them that clashed with their need to adapt to changing strategic conditions. The tensions between the constraints of local social ties and strategic political action not only thwarted all attempts at restoring central authority, but also caused ever-greater fragmentation locally.

At a more abstract level, the findings of this book can be summarized in five aspects of relevance to theoretical debates. First, approaches to the eruption of civil war should pay greater attention to micro-level escalatory processes through which the actors in such wars emerge. Second, comparative analyses of conflict dynamics would benefit from taking into consideration the sequential impact of changing strategic conditions, and their interplay with social changes wrought by conflict. Third, fragmentation can be conceptualized as a state of competition between enduring ties of social solidarity and more volatile relations of political alliance and patronage that are the result of strategic action. This concept can be usefully applied to – and refined in – other fragmented conflict landscapes. Fourth, accounting fully for the social embeddedness of actors in violent conflict may require abandoning organization-centric analytical frameworks, but more research is needed to theorize the origins of deep social embeddedness. Finally, variations in social embeddedness and community cohesion help explain why the warlord route to centralization, through a conventional mix of patronage and force, advances in some social settings, while facing stubborn obstacles in others.

How civil wars erupt: Onset versus escalation

In February and March 2011, the prevalent account of protagonists and external observers alike was that tribes and cities decided to enter into rebellion or stay loyal to Qadhafi. The underlying assumption was that such communities were socially cohesive enough to act collectively. By contrast, this book has shown that communities only became collective actors in the course of the conflict. Escalatory processes in the first weeks of the uprising – before the conflict lapsed into full-scale civil war – drew the divides that structured newly forming solidarities at the local level. More than pre-existing characteristics of communities, the conflict dynamics themselves determined whether these communities emerged from the war as more cohesive or divided. In other words, the actors in the conflict did not exist prior to it – they constituted themselves during the escalation, and were shaped by the civil war itself.

In contexts where social forces have greater latitude in organizing themselves than in Qadhafi's Libya, the formation of actors during escalatory processes may be less spectacular, and play out over longer periods. Nevertheless, the point has general applicability: calculating the correlation between structural properties and the outbreak of civil war, or identifying constellations that are particularly prone to bargaining failures, will not satisfactorily explain why civil wars break out. The problem with the vast literature on 'civil war onset' is summed up in the notion of 'onset' itself. That literature has largely ignored the processes of escalation that produce the actors, constellations and interests that make all-out war possible. Discovering and theorizing the mechanisms that underlie these processes, and the conditions under which they are aborted or reversed, should be central to the study of the eruption of civil war. *How* civil wars erupt is key to explaining *why* they erupt.

Processes in violent conflict: Social transformation and strategic conditions

Studies of contemporary violent conflict have often noted that civil wars generate interests in their own perpetuation, such as in the form of war economies.[1] However, efforts to theorize the endogenous relationship between social change and violent conflict have begun only recently.[2] This book has emphasized in particular the activation or formation of social boundaries and solidarities amid violent conflict as an important driver behind the transformation of socially embedded forces, and behind the constraints facing their leaders. Accounting for such transformations requires adopting a process-oriented perspective.

Taking processes seriously alters our understanding of the role of strategic conditions. Much of the literature on civil wars rightly accords central importance to what I call strategic conditions: the configuration of threat, opportunity and uncertainty. There is abundant comparative analysis of how the behaviour of actors in conflict differs under varying configurations of these conditions. Rarely, however, do comparative analyses of civil wars take into account the impact of *sequences* of divergent strategic conditions – in other words, of history. This is largely left to in-depth studies of individual country cases.[3] But as I have argued, it matters how distinct strategic conditions succeed each other and consecutively shape political forces.

Real-life violent conflict is a highly variable phenomenon. In any given war-affected country, patterns of violence and territorial control differ from one place to another. They also vary significantly over time.[4] Periods of relative calm alternate with phases of major escalation. Each phase leaves its trace on social ties, and over time – in the Libyan case, five distinct phases of conflict within the nine years under investigation here – these traces transform and produce social structure, much like the formation of sedimentary rock strata.

The contribution of this book is to combine the two levels of analysis – social transformation and strategic conditions – in a single, process-oriented theory. The model proposed here, of conflicting constraints emanating from social ties and rapidly changing strategic conditions, is certainly not the only way of thinking about how these two levels interact over time. Hopefully, however, it can trigger further attempts to theorize how the interplay of strategic conditions and social change influences behaviour in violent conflict.

Fragmentation and cohesion

A seemingly paradoxical finding of this book is that political fragmentation is most debilitating where rival local factions are bound together in cohesive communities. Where such cohesion is lacking, these factions are free to ally with outside actors – thereby strengthening the role of supralocal forces – and try to establish their pre-eminence by force. At some point, such areas are likely to see a concentration of military resources by a local monopolist, or a takeover by an external force. But where strong social ties preclude the ruthless suppression of local adversaries, and compel local leaders to tread carefully in their association with outside actors, competing factions will continue to coexist, narrowing each other's room for manoeuvre.

Fragmentation, then, is about the competition between two different types of social ties, each associated with a distinct framework for political action. The first are the ties of solidarity created by the collective struggle of a community against an external adversary – ties that are interlaced with quotidian relations of kinship, neighbourhood and long-standing friendship. Such relations are difficult to sever, and even more difficult to rebuild once they have been destroyed. The second are more strategically chosen relations of political alliance, patronage and employment – ties that go beyond everyday relationships, and establish local politicians as brokers between a particular locality and wider networks.

Fragmentation occurs in a situation where neither of these two political rationales can prevail over the other, nor settle into a stable relationship with each other. (A stable relationship being, for example, the sedimentation of a long-standing political alliance into deeply rooted ideological support within a community). This requires, first of all, that local ties of solidarity are strong enough to offer some resistance to the penetration of patronage-based relations and strategic alliances. Such cohesion, I have argued, is not an innate feature of communities, but an outcome of collective struggle against outside forces.

But communal cohesion as such is not enough to produce the kind of fragmentation Libya has exhibited since 2011. This book has shown that three conditions encourage the persistence of a situation in which the logics of strategic action and social embeddedness compete with each other, without one of them prevailing. One is the absence or weakness of central government, which otherwise functions as the pole around which alliances and patronage networks stabilize – hence the argument that the collapse of central authority in 2011 locked in fragmentation. A second is the existence of multiple competing poles, such as meddling foreign governments, that prevent patronage networks from stabilizing around a single centre. A third condition is the rapid alternation of strategic conditions, which disrupts the continuity of processes that favour one rationale over the other – the consolidation of patronage networks structured around a central government, or the reinforcement of local solidarities and communal cohesion. Where phases of collective struggle alternate with local competition over outside alliances and access to patronage, both types of relationships clash with each other. Local leaders shift back and forth between a role as coordinators harnessing local power against outside actors, and a role as brokers between local interest groups and outside actors.[5] Local elites have difficulties consolidating their position in such a context, and will face challenges from below when attempting to represent local constituencies.

The interplay between shifting political alliances and more resilient communal solidarities will be familiar to students of other highly fragmented conflicts. In northern Yemen, fickle state patronage and Huthi exploitation of local leadership disputes created a complex patchwork of local self-defence groups, mercenary armies and competing local big men, all within a society where tribal solidarities continue to hold sway.[6] In South Sudan, the Nuer White Army has oscillated between community defence and instrumentalization by the leaders of political faction, thereby contributing to the fragmentation of Nuer communities.[7] The present study has highlighted the processual character of fragmentation, and theorized it in a way that will make it applicable to such contexts.

What explains deep social embeddedness, and what are its implications?

I have argued that some military forces in contemporary violent conflicts are socially embedded to an extent that invalidates attempts to analyse them as armed groups, or to focus exclusively on the supposed interests of their leaders. The analysis has demonstrated the relevance of social embeddedness for understanding not only the nature of fragmentation in Libya, but also political agency amid violent conflict more generally. Deep social embeddedness suggests a degree of social control over fighters, and direct repercussions on local society from the actions of socially embedded forces. This does not necessarily mean that these fighters will be more amenable to compromise, or less likely to commit atrocities: attitudes towards the enemy may be widely shared by the community in which fighters are embedded. It does, however, have wide-ranging implications for how actors in a conflict conceive of their interests, and therefore the posture they adopt in bargaining processes, and the sway they exert over their constituencies while negotiating in their name.

The recent interest in social embeddedness in the literature has to date remained wedded to armed groups as the unit of analysis. Accounting fully for social embeddedness – and, where appropriate, shedding organization-centric frameworks for a broader analysis of social transformation – is likely to provide new perspectives to ongoing debates in the study of violent conflict. Among those where its contribution seems particularly relevant are the research on what determines varying patterns of violence; the study of divergent forms of governance and order amid violent conflict; the question why some armed groups consolidate into centralized organizations as they grow, while others fragment; as well as a set of more plainly policy-oriented issues concerning strategies for accommodating and demobilizing fighters and their leaders.[8]

Much remains to be explored. Numerous studies have shown that as groups are drawn into violent conflict, they almost inevitably develop new hierarchies and an organization specializing in warfare that is distinct from the social groups out of which it arose.[9] Why is it, then, that such organizations have remained so elusive, almost indistinguishable from their social surroundings, in many Libyan cities – as well as in other conflict contexts, as a glance at cases from South Sudan to Afghanistan suggests? Why have their leaders oscillated between collective decision-making and competition, but hardly ever established centralized, hierarchical structures? The argument made here about community cohesion as being less an antecedent condition of, than an outcome of, conflict dynamics could provide a new approach to this question. More fundamentally, a processual understanding of how collective struggle produces communal cohesion could offer a fresh perspective on the old sociological puzzle of why conflict causes fragmentation in some cases, and cohesion in others.

From fragmentation to consolidation

As extreme as the nature of fragmentation in Libya may be, as conventional are the pathways to centralization emerging from the case study on Haftar's rise. Unsurprisingly, the most important condition for establishing centralized authority over local forces is steady command over resources to build military capacity and buy off local politicians. Access to external support offers the best bet in a situation where access to state resources and the capture of local assets – such as oil infrastructure or smuggling routes – are inherently unstable, because they are subject to the vagaries of power struggles. Of course, this only works as long as one source of external support trumps all others. Where multiple external actors compete as patrons of local factions, the outcome is, at best, the consolidation of regional fiefdoms.

However, the case studies on fragmentation have also shown that this tried-and-tested strategy of centralizing power through a combination of patronage and force works better in some local contexts than in others. The eastern Libyan periphery, with its dearth of cohesive local political and military forces, offered a particularly favourable environment for the consolidation of Haftar's power structure. By contrast, Zintan, with its powerful, socially embedded forces, proved difficult terrain, despite the fact that Haftar allies could operate there from mid-2014 onwards. This finding is in line with evidence from other countries. In Afghanistan, for example, warlords – charismatic military leaders who are largely unconstrained by social loyalties – could only prosper in social environments where tribes had lost much of their political autonomy, and hence 'could not find roots in Pashtun territory'.[10]

Moreover, once a warlord begins exerting uneven territorial control, he will inevitably begin promoting the interests of loyal local elites over those of their adversaries. This, in turn, makes it more difficult for him to gain the support of political actors in areas not under his control. The costs of pursuing the warlord route to centralization – in the level of brute force needed, and the lives destroyed – then rise even more sharply once it enters the fiefdoms of cohesive local groups. There, a much more complex game begins in which patronage and force must be coupled with a shift towards ambiguity, a move from warring party to arbitrator.[11] Few political operators have the networks and track record necessary to credibly make such a transition and play that game. The social rifts and loyalties formed in violent conflict, I have argued, adapt more slowly to changing political conditions than pragmatic politicians would like them to.

Finally, the analysis tentatively suggests the sobering conclusion that today's processes of fragmentation may pave the way for consolidation tomorrow. Although the period under investigation has been too short to fully bear out this finding, the case studies on Misrata and the Nafusa Mountains indicate that the repeated alternation of fusion and fission, of closing ranks and pursuing more narrow interests, will make future returns to communal unity increasingly difficult. What we have witnessed was certainly not a sequence in a never-ending Khaldunian cycle. It may have been the beginning of the annihilation of the local solidarities that came so prominently to the fore in 2011.

The Libyan predicament

This book has shown that Libya's extreme fragmentation is not immutable, but has taken on very different forms amid a rapid succession of strategic conditions. Moreover, the local actors populating this fragmented landscape may be unwittingly contributing to their own demise, by exhausting local solidarities in the defence against changing external and internal enemies.

As Libya's predicament deepened, it became increasingly common for foreign pundits to prescribe stronger political and administrative decentralization as a response to what they saw as the intrinsic nature of Libya's political landscape. Some sought the remedy in the federal model of the 1950s, others even called for partition. Some began arguing that, maybe, the 'Western' model of the state did not suit Libyan society, and that the struggles underway could lead to the formation of more authentic local orders that would do away with central authority, borders and other imported artificials. Western diplomats often doubted the existence of Libyan national consciousness, as opposed to parochial loyalties.

Such verdicts, however, miss a crucial point. The collapse of central authority locked in fragmentation, and caused it to deepen. In other words, to overcome fragmentation, central authority has to be re-established. Equally important, Libya's entire economy remains inextricably tied to functioning central authority – unless the country were to undergo an extremely painful transition to a non-hydrocarbon economy, or an even more painful war of secession. Greater administrative devolution is certainly desirable, but without the re-establishment of central authority, local authorities will not be viable in the Libya we know.

Of course, re-establishing central authority first was the other increasingly popular prescription among Libyans and foreign observers alike – coupled with the diagnosis that only a strong man could hold such a fragmented country together. International momentum has increasingly gathered behind this strong man, and many have seen his continued expansion and eventual capture of power as inevitable. The analysis put forward in this book, and its caveats on the sway of opportunism in Libya's fragmented landscape, does not support this prognosis. Rather, it suggests that fragmentation might be overcome if patronage networks reaching from the centre down to the local level can consolidate around a central authority. Such networks would gradually erode cohesion in communities, and eat away at their socially embedded forces. This would require strategic conditions to remain sufficiently stable to avoid the repeated disruption of such processes of consolidation.

Finally, whereas Libya's fragmentation was not inevitable, the progressive internationalization of its conflicts was. The transnational repercussions of chaos in Libya have led an increasing array of foreign governments to get involved and begin striking direct arrangements with local actors. The range of sponsors potentially available to Libya's local forces now goes far beyond the regional governments that supported the warring parties of 2014. The priorities and strategies of these states vis-à-vis Libya change constantly, introducing an additional element of instability into the strategic context. Until foreign powers can agree that central authority in Libya should be rebuilt rather than conquered or circumvented, Libya's fragmentation will be there to stay.

Notes

Introduction

1 Cunningham (2016).
2 In a statistical analysis of 139 sub-Saharan African rebel groups, Woldemariam (2018, p. 21) finds that 'rebel fragmentation ... has been a consistent feature of civil wars over time'. But the timeframe for Woldemariam's sample ends in 2006, while academic interest in fragmentation increased noticeably from 2008 onward.
3 See, for example, Bakke et al. (2012); Pearlman and Cunningham (2012); Cunningham (2013); Metternich et al. (2013); and Jentzsch et al. (2015).
4 See Christia (2012); Cunningham (2013); Driscoll (2012); Seymour (2014); Seymour et al. (2016); Woldemariam (2018).
5 See Staniland (2012b, 2014).
6 The exceptions to this rule are Christia's (2012) and Woldemariam's (2018) models of alliance formation and fragmentation in multiparty civil wars, which do not assume the state as a central actor in conflict; and Staniland's (2012b, 2014) arguments about social structure and intrainsurgent violence.
7 See, for example, Staniland (2012b, 2014); Metternich et al. (2013); Walther, Christopoulos (2015); Zech, Gabbay (2016); Parkinson (2013).
8 See Granovetter (1985). In this regard, my notion of social embeddedness concurs with that of Parkinson (2013) and Stearns (2016).
9 On Afghanistan and Somalia, see Rubin (1995); Dorronsoro (2005); Simons (1995); and Besteman (1999).
10 Such arguments are consistent with a wide range of structuralist approaches, from the classical political development literature (Coleman, Almond 1960; Huntington 1968; Coleman 1977) and proponents of the rentier state concept (Luciani 1990; Karl 1997; Schwarz 2008) to a new generation of theorists who have resurrected the macro-historical designs of modernization theory, while drawing on neoclassical or new institutional economics (Fukuyama 2012, 2014; Acemoglu, Robinson 2012; North et al. 2009).
11 The former would apply to Migdal's (1988); the latter to rentier theorists such as Delacroix (1980).
12 Granovetter (1973), p. 1378.
13 See, for example, Gould (1991) and the contributions in Diani and McAdam (2003).
14 See Moore (1966); Scott (1976); Skocpol (1979); Petersen (2001).
15 See Hüsken (2009) and Dawod (2013).
16 Simmel (1908); Coser (1956); Murphy (1957); Stein (1976); Markides, Cohn (1982).
17 Taylor (1982); Petersen (2001).
18 For definitions of cohesion as network density see, for example, Tilly (1978), or Moody, White (2003: 109), who define a group's cohesion as 'equal to the minimum number of actors who, if removed from the group, would disconnect the group'. Other authors contest definitions of social cohesion exclusively based on network structure,

arguing that weak ties can be a source of cohesion, and that network density does not determine the conditions shaping the attitudes of group members (Friedkin 2004).

19 See Wood (2003); Kalyvas (2006); Walder (2009); Collins (2012); Della Porta (2014); Bosi et al. (2014).

20 Key contributions are Wood (2008); Schlichte (2009); and Baczko, Dorronsoro (2017).

21 Granovetter (1985), building on Polanyi (1944), made precisely this argument with regard to economists' models of economic action.

22 Granovetter (1985).

23 See Bakonyi, Stuvøy (2005); Boege et al. (2009); Debiel et al. (2009); Renders, Terlinden (2010); Mielke et al. (2011); Neubert (2011); Hüsken, Klute (2015); Arjona (2016).

24 By warlords, I mean charismatic and patrimonial leaders whose legitimacy is primarily military, and who exercise autonomous control over a military force maintaining a monopoly on the concentrated means of violence over a sizeable territory (Giustozzi 2009; Marten 2007; Ahram, King 2012). This definition runs counter to the common use of the notion as describing actors primarily driven by economic rationality and interested in predation (cf. Marchal 2007).

25 Della Porta (2013), p. 24.

26 Bennett, Elman (2006).

27 Grzymala-Busse (2011).

28 Tilly (2001); Falleti, Lynch (2009); McAdam, Tarrow (2011).

29 Elias (1939); Tilly (2001, 2003).

30 Lijphart (1971); Snyder (2001).

31 Wedeen (2010).

32 These are, first and foremost, Anderson (1986); Davis (1987); Ahmida (2009); Vandewalle (1998); Mattes (2001); Ouannès (2009); and Baldinetti (2010).

33 Massie (2013).

34 Malejacq, Mukhopadhyay (2016).

35 Peters (1967); Parkinson (2013).

36 Where I have used posts from individual social media pages, they generally come from people I was in direct contact with, allowing me to ascertain that the page really did belong to the person whose name it carried.

Chapter 1

1 This follows the definition of a revolutionary situation by Tilly (1993).

2 Hill (2011), Al-Fassi (2011), Bartu (2015).

3 Human Rights Watch (2011), Al-Tarifi (2013).

4 Smith (2011), Al-Ahmad (2014).

5 Gebauer (2011).

6 Mahmoud (2016a), Smith (2011).

7 UNHRC (2012).

8 Human Rights Watch (2011).

9 Lacher and Labnouj (2015).

10 UNHRC (2012).

11 Cole and Khan (2015a).

12 Mahmoud (2016b).

13 Roberts (2011).
14 National Transitional Council (2011).
15 Lacher (2011).
16 Bartu (2015).
17 Fitzgerald (2015).
18 Bartu (2015).
19 Cole and Khan (2015a).
20 Cole and Khan (2015b).
21 Lacher and Cole (2014).
22 Fitzgerald (2015).
23 Kirkpatrick and Fahim (2011).
24 Lacher and Labnouj (2015).
25 BBC (2011).
26 Bartu (2015), Kane (2015).
27 Collombier (2016), Wehrey (2016a).
28 Al-Tommy (2012).
29 Lowe and Murphy (2011).
30 Lacher and Cole (2014).
31 Holmes (2011).
32 Lacher and Cole (2014).
33 Lacher (2013).
34 Lacher and Cole (2014).
35 Interview 201.
36 Lacher and Cole (2014).
37 Shuaib and Al-Shalchi (2012).
38 Khan (2012).
39 Lacher (2013).
40 Interview 245.
41 Kane (2015).
42 Deshmukh (2012).
43 Kirkpatrick (2012).
44 The commission's full name was the High Commission for the Enforcement of the Principles of Integrity and Patriotism (*al-Hay'a al-Ulya li-Tatbiq Ma'ayir al-Nazaha wal-Wataniya*).
45 Carter Center (2012), Lacher (2013).
46 Lacher (2013).
47 Lacher (2013).
48 International Crisis Group (2013).
49 Lacher (2013).
50 *Al-'Azl al-Siyasi.*
51 *Kutlat al-Wafa' li-Dima' al-Shuhada'.*
52 Interview 82; Lacher (2013).
53 Interview 388; Sharqieh (2013).
54 Interviews 41, 82.
55 Shennib and Donati (2013), Lacher and Cole (2014).
56 Interviews 82 and 388; see also Mitri (2015), p. 130; and al-Shalwi (2015), p. 238ff.
57 See UNSC (2015), p. 116, Lacher and Cole (2014), p. 45.
58 Lacher and Cole (2014).
59 Reuters (2013).

60 National Forces Alliance (2013).
61 The Constitutional Declaration did not set a term limit for the GNC, but specified the maximum number of months by which successive steps on the roadmap towards the election of a fully constitutional government should have been completed. Taken together, these amounted to 18 months from the GNC's first meeting on 8 August 2012 (National Transitional Council 2011). The NFA and associated interests argued that this meant the GNC's mandate would expire on 7 February 2014. See also the sober assessment of the issue by the former head of the UN Support Mission to Libya (UNSMIL) Tarek Mitri (2015).
62 Interview 74.
63 Al-Gharyani 2013a, International Crisis Group (2015c).
64 Al-Watan al-Libiya (2013).
65 International Crisis Group (2015c).
66 Al-Khalidi (2013).
67 Human Rights Watch (2013b), Salah (2014), Wehrey (2014).
68 Human Rights Watch (2013a), Al-Obeidi (2014c).
69 Human Rights Watch (2013c).
70 Lacher and Cole (2014).
71 Lacher and Cole (2014).
72 Interviews 26, 84, 93, 229.
73 Lacher (2014).
74 Kirkpatrick (2014).
75 Shennib and Laessing (2014).
76 Mitri (2015).
77 International Crisis Group (2015a).
78 Mitri (2015).
79 BBC (2014a), Kouddous (2014).
80 Al-Wasat (2014a).
81 Elumami and Laessing (2014).
82 Mitri (2015).
83 Elumami and Al-Warfalli (2014a).
84 Carter Center (2014).
85 Interview 82; see also Al-Shuhubi (2014).
86 Interviews 76, 84, 174.
87 Interviews 95, 96, 100, 103, 106, 161.
88 Interviews 100, 174, 180.
89 BBC (2014b).
90 Fitzgerald (2014).
91 Interviews 93, 98, 104.
92 Elumami and Al-Warfalli (2014b).
93 House of Representatives (2014).
94 Interview 145.
95 Reuters (2014).
96 Interviews 95, 96, 100, 161, 201, 278. Bashagha himself denies having been involved in planning the operation (Interview 303).
97 Tanasuh (2014), al-Nabaa TV (2014), Al-Wasat (2014c).
98 Human Rights Solidarity (2014).
99 Interviews 97, 101, 102.
100 Interviews 101, 105, 116, 118.

101 Interviews 93, 104, 154.
102 Lacher and Cole (2014).
103 Middle East Eye (2014).
104 Interview 181, Alrseefa (2014b).
105 Tubiana and Gramizzi (2017).
106 Al-Bayyan (2014), Al-Arabiya (2014).
107 Kirkpatrick and Schmitt (2014).
108 Fitzgerald (2014).
109 Kirkpatrick and Schmitt (2014), Human Rights Watch (2015).
110 The UN Panel of Experts on Libya has documented Sudanese shipments to Libya Dawn (UNSC 2015, 2016). These were almost certainly paid for by a third party. On allegations of Qatari money flows to Libya Dawn, see the case study on Misrata in 'The Process of Fragmentation'.
111 Wehrey (2015).
112 International Crisis Group (2015c).
113 International Crisis Group (2015a).
114 Libya al-Mostakbal (2014).
115 International Crisis Group (2015a).
116 Kirkpatrick (2015a).
117 Interview 161.
118 Interview 180.
119 Lacher (2015).
120 Kirkpatrick (2015b).
121 Kirkpatrick et al. (2015).
122 Libya's Channel (2015a).
123 Personal communication, Western diplomat present in Skhirat, October 2015.
124 UNSMIL (2015a).
125 Interview 182.
126 UNSMIL (2015b).
127 Ramesh (2015), Kirkpatrick (2015c).
128 Personal communications with members of the negotiation committee and senior Western diplomats, November 2015.
129 Libya's Channel (2015b).
130 Moore (2015).
131 Personal communications with members of the negotiation committee and Western diplomats present in Skhirat, December 2015.
132 Al-Warfalli (2016a), Libyan Political Agreement (2015).
133 Interviews 176, 177, 178.
134 Ghaddar et al. (2016).
135 Reuters (2016).
136 Bensimon et al. (2016), Binnie (2016).
137 Al-Warfalli (2016b).
138 Al-Warfalli (2016c).
139 Libya al-Mostakbal (2016).
140 Ryan and Raghavan (2016).
141 Lacher and Al-Idrissi (2018).
142 Personal communications in November and December 2016 with former revolutionary commanders from Benghazi; a close associate of al-Mahdi al-Barghathi in the defence ministry; a senior Misratan commander involved in the transactions

with Chadian fighters; and Tubu politicians involved in the outreach to Chadian commanders; as well as Interviews 225, 226, 238, 244. See also Tubiana, Gramizzi (2017).

143 International Crisis Group (2016b, 2017).
144 Human Rights Watch (2017a).
145 Reuters (2017).
146 Lacher (2018).
147 Howden (2017), Elumami and Lewis (2017).
148 Interviews 270, 271, 285, 291, 295.
149 Al-Wasat (2017b).
150 Ben Said (2017).
151 Al-Motawaset (2017).
152 Walsh (2018), Lewis (2018).
153 Al-Warfalli and Ghaddar (2018).
154 International Crisis Group (2018a).
155 Lacher and Al-Idrissi (2018).
156 International Crisis Group (2018b), Badi (2019a), Interviews 322, 331, 335, 336, 344.
157 Interviews 322, 334, 366, 378, 384.
158 Interviews 323, 338, 348, 353, 356.
159 Badi (2019b), Profazio (2019), Interviews 361, 362, 363, 371, 374, 383.
160 Interviews 380, 381, 382, 385, 386, 389.
161 Interviews 385, 386, 387, 389.
162 Interviews 380, 381, 391.
163 Interviews 386 and 392, as well as correspondence with European diplomats in Tunis.
164 Interviews 393, 394, 395, 396, 397, 398, 401.
165 Lacher (2019).
166 Irish and Laessing (2019), Lasserre (2019).
167 Interview 402, Al-Atrush et al. (2019).
168 Malsin and Said (2019).
169 AFP (2019).
170 Roberts (2011).

Chapter 2

1 In the Egyptian case, however, conventional accounts have downplayed or even ignored the role of violence in allowing non-violent protests to grow (Ketchley 2017).
2 Reuters (2011).
3 Watkins (2011), Spiegel Online (2011), Channel 4 News (2011).
4 El Amrani (2011), Vandewalle (2011).
5 Lyall (2015).
6 Cramer (2002), Di John (2007), Nathan (2008), Florea (2018).
7 Walter (2009), Webster (2018).
8 Capoccia, Kelemen (2007).
9 Walder (2006, 2009), Schnell (2015).
10 Ermakoff (2015).
11 Granovetter (1978), Kuran (1991), Lohmann (1994).
12 Ermakoff (2015).

13 Trotha (1997).
14 Wood (2003), Kalyvas (2006), Della Porta (2014).
15 Johnston (2014).
16 Collins (2009), Bergholz (2016).
17 Pearlman (2016).
18 See Moore (1966), Scott (1976), Skocpol (1979), Barkey and van Rossem (1997).
19 Diani and McAdam (2003), Tarrow (2011).
20 Petersen (2001), Leenders and Heydemann (2012), Koehler et al. (2016). Cf. Baczko et al. (2013), who claim to counter the argument of Leenders and Heydemann (2012) about the role of dense social networks in facilitating popular mobilization in Syria, but make this very same point themselves.
21 Marchal (2013), cf. Bakonyi (2009).
22 Bergholz (2016).
23 Martin (2014).
24 Wood (2003), p. 227.
25 Baczko et al. (2013, 2016).
26 Johnston (2014).
27 Collins (2012).
28 Gould (1999), pp. 357, 376.
29 Schnell (2015).
30 Kalyvas (2006), p. 129.
31 Collins (2012).
32 Bergholz (2016).
33 Tilly (2003), Collins (2012).
34 Wood (2008), Klute (2011).
35 Wood (2008), Whitehouse et al. (2014), Marks (2019).
36 Anderson (1990), p. 288.
37 Anderson (1990), p. 301.
38 Hasan (1973), Anderson (1986).
39 Simon (1987), Ahmida (2009).
40 Anderson (1990), Vandewalle (2006).
41 Vandewalle (2006), p. 43.
42 Hasan (1973), Anderson (1990), Vandewalle (2006).
43 See Anderson (1990) and Ouannès (2009), pp. 128, 234ff. Al-Maqariaf (2008, pp. 820–39) provides details on prison and death sentences for prominent figures in the first year after the coup.
44 Fathaly and Palmer (1980).
45 Fitzgerald and Megerisi (2015).
46 Mattes (2008).
47 Khalaf et al. (2008).
48 Davis (1987).
49 Roumani (1983), p. 164.
50 Martinez (2007), Ouannès (2009).
51 Ouannès (2009), Mattes (2001).
52 Mattes (2004).
53 Interviews 27, 201, 208.
54 Mattes (2004, 2008).
55 For such arguments, see Amselle (1985) and Lentz (1995). González (2009, p. 15) even goes as far as claiming that 'few anthropologists today would consider using the

term "tribe" as an analytical category, or even as a concept for practical application'. For the defence, see Ben Hounet (2010), Bonte (2001), Glatzer (2002), Godelier (2004), and Tapper (2009).

56 See, for example, Bonte (2001), Bonte and Ben Hounet (2009), Ben Hounet (2010), Hüsken (2009), Tapper (2009), Dawod (2013).

57 Hüsken (2009), Hachemaoui (2012).

58 Benraad (2009), González (2009).

59 Godelier (2004), p. 290.

60 Evans-Pritchard (1949), Peters (1990).

61 Peters (1967).

62 See Ahmida (2009), Cauneille (1963) and Simon (1987), pp. 194–227.

63 See Lahmar (2006). The works Lahmar cites in support of his argument, including Despois (1935), Cauneille (1954), and Graziani (1934), contain little to substantiate – and much to contradict – his claims that tribes were imaginary as sociopolitical unities, and that tribal leaders exerted little authority over the groups they pretended to control. Graziani (1929, 1934) habitually speaks in terms of tribes when describing the population's relationships with the colonial power, and frequently emphasizes the influence of tribal leaders such as Abdelnabi Belkheir or Mohamed Fekini. Cauneille (1954, p. 42) notes with regard to the Magarha that 'while the links of the [tribal] confederation are weak and almost limited to the name and battle cry, the tribes, on the contrary, are united'. Elsewhere, Cauneille (1957, p. 76) speaks of the 'fierce *esprit de corps*' of the Zintan, their territorial dispute with the Riyayna, and their hostility towards the Mashashiya and Awlad Busaif. Despois (1935, pp. 160–2) discusses land use regimes and disputes between communities as a whole: Zintan, Riyayna and Yefren. While unsupported by the authors he refers to, Lahmar's argument closely mirrors that of Peters (1977), whose analysis of Cyrenaican tribes cannot be easily transposed onto Tripolitania.

64 Cauneille (1963), Cordell (1985), Ahmida (2009).

65 See, for example, Simon (1987, p. 214ff., 236ff.) for details on a politicized rift between two factions of the Warfalla during 1913–18. Cordell (1985, p. 338f.) records a split within the Awlad Suleiman in the early twentieth century, one tribal section fighting with the French in Chad against another.

66 Simon (1987).

67 Hasan (1973), Peters (1990).

68 Peters (1990), p. 119.

69 Obeidi (2001).

70 Davis (1987), p. 106.

71 Ibid, p. 95ff.

72 Ouannès (2009), p. 299ff.

73 Cauneille (1963).

74 Interview 245, Ouannès (2009, p. 313) and Shalqam (2012, p. 37f.) also relate this episode.

75 Mattes (2001), p. 60.

76 Mattes (2008, p. 68) dates the first announcement of the PSL to July 1994, and states that PSL branches were formed across Libya over the following two years. Obeidi (2008, p. 109f.) dates the establishment of the PSL to 1993.

77 Mattes (2001), Ouannès (2009), p. 199.

78 Interview 287.

79 Interviews 88, 90, 127, 137, 212. See also Saleh (2008).

80 Interview 151.

81 Interview 287.

82 Pliez (2006).

83 See the account of Mohamed Mahmoud Weddady, who served as Mauritania's ambassador to Libya during the 1970s and followed several of these operations closely (Weddady 2012).

84 Lacher (2014).

85 Interview 174.

86 Hüsken (2009), p. 189.

87 Hüsken (2011), p. 56.

88 Dorronsoro (2013).

89 Lyon (2011). Similarly, during the first weeks of the uprising, George Joffe (2011a) claimed that 'eastern Libya has long been hostile to the Jamahiriya … Colonel Gaddafi's government has deliberately neglected and persecuted people in Cyrenaica.' Joffe (2011b) also spoke of the 'tribal leaders from the Sa'adi tribes, traditionally hostile to the Gaddafi regime'. The Sa'adi are the 'free' Cyrenaican tribes who trace their origin back to a common ancestress, Sa'ada. They divide into two main groups of tribes (al-Harabi and al-Jabarna) whose larger constituents are the Obeidat, Barassa, Darsa, Hassa, A'ilat Fa'id, Abid, Urafa', Awaqir, Magharba, Majabra and Jawazi. See Peters (1990, p. 85) and Mina' (2013).

90 Abdul-Ahad (2011).

91 Murray (2015).

92 This claim is from Chorin (2012, p. 153), who wrongly assumes that '1000 of the Abu Selim victims were from Benghazi or nearby towns and villages'. In fact, according to the Geneva-based Libyan NGO Human Rights Solidarity (2016), which compiled a list of all 1,158 victims, the largest number (327) came from Tripoli, followed by Benghazi (282), Ajdabiya (126), Darna (100) and Misrata (80). Victims from the eastern region made up around half of the total number, meaning that the east was proportionally over-represented.

93 Al-Mogherbi (n.d.).

94 To name but the most prominent: Abdelfattah Younes al-Obeidi, who participated in Qadhafi's 1969 coup, commanded the Saeqa Special Forces for several years, subsequently became commander of the eastern military region, and was interior minister when the revolution erupted; Suleiman Mahmoud al-Obeidi, who was equally among Qadhafi's co-conspirators, held various senior military positions and in 2011 was commander of Tobruk military region; Abdelati al-Obeidi, who held numerous ministerial positions from 1969 to 2011; al-Tayyeb al-Safi, who was a prominent figure in the Revolutionary Committees during the 1980s and subsequently held positions as head of the internal security service for Benghazi, minister, head of al-Batnan province and director of major state-owned enterprises; al-Senussi al-Wuzri, who occupied senior positions in the internal security service; and Abderrahman al-Abbar, whose most important posts were head of the People's Court, general prosecutor, head of the Surveillance Authority (*jihaz al-riqaba wal-mutaba'a al-sha'abiya*), and justice minister.

95 Al-Mogherbi (n.d.).

96 Interview 130.

97 Interview 5.

98 Lacher (2014).

99 The name of the mountain range is disputed since Ottoman times. The Ottoman
    administration used the name al-Jabal al-Gharbi (the Western Mountain), as did
    Qadhafi. Amazigh communities as well as Western geographers and anthropologists
    of the nineteenth and twentieth centuries used the name Jabal Nafusa, from Infusen,
    the name by which the Amazigh population of the mountains historically referred
    to itself. Today, Amazigh communities claim the name of Jabal Nafusa, while Arab
    groups such as Zintan and Rujban insist on al-Jabal al-Gharbi. On Amazigh and
    Arabization in the mountains, see Despois (1935) and Lacher, Labnouj (2015).
100 Interview 11.
101 Interviews 9, 10.
102 Interviews 11, 232.
103 Interviews 5, 16, 240.
104 Interviews 6, 12, 18, 19.
105 Interview 5.
106 Interview 16.
107 The Qadhafi regime's recruitment of fighters in or from Mali, Niger, Chad and
    Sudan – including among Darfur rebel groups – during February and March 2011
    has been confirmed by multiple sources from these countries, as well as many recruits
    themselves. But some allegations may also have referred to dark-skinned Libyan
    soldiers. In other cases, African migrants appear to have been arrested by rebels on
    allegations of being mercenary fighters. It has not been established how extensively
    the regime used mercenaries in the first weeks of the uprising. See UNSC (2012),
    Deycard and Guichaoua (2011), Tull and Lacher (2012), Roberts (2011).
108 Roberts (2011).
109 Al-Rummah (2013).
110 Interviews 13, 16, 18, 19, 240.
111 Interviews 9, 236.
112 Interviews 1, 12, 15.
113 Interviews 4, 6.
114 Interviews 9, 14, 242.
115 Al-Azzabi (2011).
116 Cauneille (1957, 1963), Ahmida (2009).
117 Graziani (1929), Ahmida (2009), Baghni (2015).
118 Bin Dhilla (2013).
119 Interviews 6, 8, 11, 12, 16, 17, 18, 19, 240.
120 Interviews 3, 6, 8.
121 Interview 11.
122 Interviews 13, 240.
123 Interviews 16, 17, 18.
124 Interviews 10, 11.
125 Interviews 6, 17.
126 Cole, Khan (2015a), Lacher and Labnouj (2015).
127 Cole, Khan (2015b).
128 For example, Zintan lost 196 of its inhabitants (194 of them men) to the war, Nalut
    81 (all of them men). Each of the two towns had a population of around 30,000. See
    Historical Documentation Centre Zintan (2011) and Bin Dhilla (2013), pp. 376–8.
129 Al-Sweihli (2011).
130 McQuinn (2015, p. 236) claims that thirty to forty protesters were killed by security
    forces on the day of the funeral. In fact, not a single fatal casualty was recorded on

20 and 21 February, and only one casualty on 22 February. See Misrata Central Hospital (2011) and UNHRC (2012), p. 53.

131 Jha (2012a).

132 Al-Zawawi (2014), McQuinn (2015).

133 McQuinn (2015).

134 UNHRC (2012).

135 Interview 243.

136 Claims that Qadhafi was using rape as a weapon in the conflict were promoted by supporters of the revolutionary forces, and eagerly relayed by the foreign media. They became the subject of a controversy between the prosecutor of the International Criminal Court, Luis Moreno Ocampo and human rights organizations such as Human Rights Watch. The fact that Qadhafi's forces were responsible for numerous cases of rape in several revolutionary strongholds has been well established, though it remains unclear how extensive and systematic this was. See UNHRC (2012), p. 141ff.

137 Jha (2012b).

138 Interviews 237, 243, see also Jha (2012c), McQuinn (2015).

139 McQuinn (2015), cf. Whitehouse et al. (2014).

140 McQuinn (2015).

141 Jha (2012a).

142 From the mid-1970s until the mid-2000s, all governments included at least two of the following Misratan figures: Ali al-Triki, Muftah Ka'iba, Omar al-Muntasser, Fathi ben Shetwan, Mohamed Abdallah Bait al-Mal, al-Taher al-Juhaimi.

143 Interview 200.

144 This was notably the case of Muftah Ka'iba, Ali al-Triki and Suleiman al-Shuhumi. Ismail al-Karrami, head of the anti-narcotics agency at the time of the revolution and a senior Misratan figure in internal security, was captured by Misratan fighters after the fall of Tripoli, and imprisoned for six years in Misrata.

145 Interviews 81, 92, see also Jha (2012a).

146 The categories used in Misrata are firstly, the *Karaghla* (or Kouloughlis), descendants of Ottoman soldiers and administrators as well as Circassians (*Sharksi*, pl. *Sharaksa*), who mostly inhabited the city centre, and were structured into large families rather than tribes. Secondly, the *Awlad Sheikh*, a collective label for smaller tribes who had long sedentarized in the Misrata area, and for whom the tribe played a limited role; and third, the *Ahali*, more recently sedentarized semi-nomadic tribes, whose tribal identity remained strong. Interviews 45, 200; see also Mina' (2013), p. 289ff. On *Karaghla*, see Najem (2004).

147 Interview 200.

148 Interviews 92, 202, 206.

149 Interview 44.

150 Interviews 81, 92.

151 UNHRC (2012), p. 136.

152 Interview 202.

153 Interview 202.

154 Reuters (2011).

155 Al-Nayed (2011).

156 Interview 90.

157 Interview 52.

158 Interview 90.

159 Interview 55.

160 Sympathizers of the revolutionaries in Bani Walid also emphasized the geographic factor (Interview 111).
161 Interviews 52, 90, 138, 210.
162 Interviews 52, 56.
163 Interviews 90, 247, 248.
164 Interview 90.
165 Interviews 90, 138, 212.
166 Interview 138.
167 Cole (2015).
168 Interviews 212, 300.
169 Cole (2015).
170 Telegraph (2012), Reuters (2012).
171 The sections (*qism*, pl. *aqsam*) are an Ottoman-era structure established for taxation purposes. Each section comprises a number of tribes – fifty-two in total – each of which, in turn, is structured into several large families (*lahma*). Four sections (al-Jamamla, al-Sa'adat, al-Sbay'a, al-Faladna) cultivate an ideology of common origin; the al-Lotiyin section sees itself as including a number of smaller tribes of different origin. Interviews 55, 57, 168, see also Mina' (2013).
172 Interview 88.
173 Interview 57.
174 Interviews 56, 88, 249.
175 Interviews 56, 57, 138.
176 Interviews 56, 88, 90.
177 Interview 56.
178 Interview 130.
179 Interviews 138, 139.
180 Interview 87.
181 Interview 52.
182 Interviews 52, 56, 86.
183 Popular Social Leadership Tobruk (2011a).
184 Interviews 59, 61, 207.
185 Interview 67.
186 Interview 207, Mahmoud (2016a).
187 Mahmoud (2011, 2016b).
188 Interviews 59, 207.
189 Interview 59.
190 Interviews 59, 63, 67.
191 Interviews 27, 67.
192 Interview 91.
193 Interview 27.
194 Hüsken (2011).
195 Including myself, in an earlier analysis; see Lacher (2011), Kane (2015), Eljarh (2017a).
196 Kane (2015).
197 Mahmoud (2016a).
198 Interview 147.
199 Evans-Pritchard (1949), Simon (1987).
200 Peters (1990), p. 49.

201 On the history and collective memory of population movements from western Libya to Benghazi and Darna, see Najem (2004), p. 186ff.
202 Baldinetti (2010).

Chapter 3

1 BBC (2016).
2 Markey and Laessing (2014).
3 The seminal texts are Moore (1966), Wolf (1969), Scott (1976), Skocpol (1979), and Horowitz (1985).
4 Key proponents of this overall and diverse trend were Kaldor (1999), Collier and Hoeffler (2000), and Reno (1998). For critiques, see Cramer (2002), Kalyvas (2001), Marchal and Messiant (2002), Bakonyi and Stuvøy (2005).
5 Key contributions are Weinstein (2007) and Staniland (2014). For an overview, see Parkinson and Zaks (2018).
6 Wood (2015).
7 Roy (1995), p. 70.
8 Roy (1995), p. 64.
9 Young (2016), Stringham, Forney (2017), Terry, McQuinn (2018).
10 Guichaoua (2012).
11 Grégoire (2013), p. 13.
12 Debos (2008).
13 Bakonyi and Stuvøy (2005), Tubiana (2011).
14 Vlassenroot et al. (2016), Stearns (2016), Verweijen (2019).
15 Daly (2014).
16 Gellner (1990), p. 109, cf. Trotha (2011).
17 Granovetter (1985), p. 487.
18 Schlichte (2009), Staniland (2012b, 2014).
19 Parkinson (2013).
20 The exception is Stearns (2016), who conceptualizes social embeddedness as ongoing and changing relationships between armed groups and their constituencies, each influencing and transforming the other.
21 The overwhelming focus of the literature on 'rebel groups' and 'insurgencies' has very recently been broadened with a number of studies analysing militias – that is state-sponsored armed groups – as a distinct category. However, such studies do not shed the lens of state-insurgent conflict. See Jentzsch et al. (2015) and the other articles in the same issue of *Journal of Conflict Resolution*.
22 Schlichte (2009), Staniland (2014).
23 Bearman (1991), Wood (2009).
24 Goodwin (1997), Wood (2009), Schlichte (2009), p. 159ff.
25 Schlichte (2009), p. 172ff.
26 Guichaoua (2013).
27 Cohen (2013).
28 Della Porta (2013).
29 This typology bears a partial resemblance to Brian McQuinn's (2016), who categorizes the internal organization of armed groups according to their command profile and financing architecture. The typology presented by Terry, McQuinn (2018)

comes close to the one proposed here, since it takes into account the isolation of a group from its social surroundings.

30 Gellner (1990), Peters (1967), Helbling (1999).
31 Wood (2009), Mampilly (2011), Staniland (2014).
32 Malthaner (2015).
33 Della Porta (2013).
34 Fitzgerald (2016).
35 International Crisis Group (2015b). Such loose alliances correspond to Schlichte's (2009) 'ad-hoc associations' and Staniland's (2014) 'fragmented organizations'.
36 Mandraud (2013).
37 Clapham (1998).
38 Taylor (1982), Petersen (2001).
39 Malthaner (2015), p. 433.
40 Kalyvas (2006), Parkinson (2013). On strong and weak social ties, see Granovetter (1973).
41 Guichaoua (2010), Meagher (2012), Young (2016).
42 Rashad et al. (2005).
43 Reuters (2009).
44 Peters (1990).
45 Interviews 317, 363.
46 Kalyvas (2006), p. 356.
47 McQuinn (2015).
48 Interview 237.
49 Interviews 250, 251; author's observations during visit to Misrata in November 2011, including to the prison holding civilian detainees.
50 Examples include the leading army officer commanding Misrata's forces in 2011, Salem Jha (a descendant of historic Misratan rebel leader Ramadhan al-Sweihli); NATO liaison Fathi Bashagha and head of military council Suleiman al-Faqih, both of them former air force pilots-turned-businessmen; former public prosecutor and revolutionary of the first hour Fawzi Abdelali; Abderrahman al-Sweihli; Suleiman al-Furtiya and religious sheikh Ibrahim ben Ghashir, both of them NTC members; as well as businessman Mohamed al-Raedh.
51 The former applied to the head of the anti-drugs agency Ismail al-Karrami; the latter to the longtime ministers Muftah Ka'iba, Suleiman al-Shuhumi and Ali al-Triki.
52 Two Tripoli-based former regime officials from Misrata were the former Navy chief of staff Hamdi al-Sweihli (Abderrahman's brother) and former government spokesperson Mohamed Omar Bayou. Qadhafi confidant Ali Dabeiba initially stayed abroad, but cultivated local support by spreading largesse and operating through his nephew and associate Abdelhamid.
53 Interview 200; personal communication, Misratan journalist, November 2015.
54 They included interior minister Fawzi Abdelali; housing and infrastructure minister Ibrahim al-Squtri; chairman of the Libyan Investment Authority (LIA) Mohsen Derregia; the chairman of the Economic and Social Development Fund (ESDF) Mahmud Badi; the general manager of the Libyan Investment and Development Holding Company (LIDCO) Abdelhamid Dabeiba; and the chairman of the steering committee for the holding company of the state-owned air carriers Abubaker al-Furtiya.
55 UNSC (2015), p. 118.
56 Interviews 43, 44.

57 Author's observations, Benghazi, June 2012.
58 Interview 204.
59 Interview 201.
60 Interviews 39, 201, 220.
61 Interviews 201, 220. See also UNSC (2015), p. 116.
62 Interview 161.
63 Interview 209.
64 Interviews 43, 164.
65 Interview 305.
66 Interviews 103, 203, 209.
67 Interview 44.
68 Key figures in the Shura Council in 2012–14 were its chairman Suleiman al-Faqih, who headed the military council in 2011; Fathi Bashagha, NATO liaison in 2011; Mohamed Ibrahim al-Dharrat, in charge of media and communications in 2011; and the head of the first Local Council, Khalifa al-Zawawi (Interview 43).
69 Al-Amin (2013b).
70 The leading figures mobilizing for the war were Abderrahman al-Sweihli and former revolutionary commander Salah Badi, both of them GNC members; Suleiman al-Faqih and Khalifa al-Zawawi; military council member Imhemmed Abdelkafi; as well as former NTC member and religious sheikh Ibrahim ben Ghashir (Interviews 43, 82, 201).
71 Interviews 57, 135, 201.
72 International Crisis Group (2013).
73 Interviews 108, 126.
74 Interview 131.
75 Interview 253.
76 Interview 82.
77 Al-Amin (2013a).
78 Al-Amin (2013b).
79 Interview 81.
80 Interviews 40, 43, 45, 107, 253.
81 See, for example, Economist (2013) or Heneghan (2013). Media outlets affiliated with Mahmoud Jibril's NFA included the al-Asema channel owned by businessman Jum'a al-Usta and the Libya al-Dawliya channel owned by the Mlegta brothers, as well as dozens of Facebook pages. Libya Awalan TV, owned by the Benghazi businessman Hassan Tatanaki, backed the federalist movement and later Haftar, and also stirred up sentiment against Misrata and 'the Islamists'.
82 The president of the Brotherhood's Justice and Construction Party (JCP), Mohamed Sawan, was from Misrata. The chairman of the city's iron and steel plant, Mohamed Abdelmalek al-Faqih, initially joined the JCP but later left it again, and was not a member of the Brotherhood. The prominent revolutionary hardliner Mohamed Ibrahim al-Dharrat had in 2012 been associated with Abdelhakim Belhaj's al-Watan party, though he later fell out with Belhaj. A member of the military council, Imhemmed Abdelkafi, was considered close to the Brotherhood by his colleagues. Mohamed Thabet Abdelmalek held various senior positions in the Brotherhood, but while hailing from Misrata did not play a leading role in the city. The list of prominent Misratan Islamist figures ends there. The Qatar-based scholar Ali Sallabi was widely perceived as Misratan because his family had Misratan roots, even though it had moved to Benghazi from Misrata many generations ago.

83 Human Rights Watch (2013c).
84 Misrata Local Council (2013).
85 Interviews 39, 43, 94.
86 Interviews 43, 84, 105.
87 Interview 161.
88 Interview 81.
89 Interviews 100, 103, 161, 278.
90 Interviews 174, 180.
91 Interview 100.
92 Interviews 97, 104.
93 Interviews 95, 96, 100, 107.
94 Interview 161.
95 Interview 206.
96 Interview 195, Faruq (2016).
97 Kirkpatrick and Schmitt (2014).
98 Interview 105.
99 Interview 103.
100 Interview 98, 99, 105.
101 Interviews 161, 164, 228.
102 Interview 237.
103 Interview 239.
104 Interviews 46, 96, 252, 254 and informal interactions with members of both families
     in Misrata in November 2011; April 2013; April, June and October 2014; June and
     September 2016; and March 2017.
105 Interview 196.
106 Interview 197.
107 Cole and Khan (2015b).
108 Interview 230.
109 Interview 26.
110 Interviews 26, 34, 68, 166.
111 Interview 35.
112 Interview 17, 233.
113 In one example among many, an executive at a state-owned infrastructure
     development company told me in April 2013 that the company's management had
     in vain sought to negotiate the return of its heavy machinery, which was displayed
     for sale in Zintan (Interview 256). Tales of carjackings along the Zintani-controlled
     airport road in Tripoli were common in 2013 and 2014. For attacks on state
     institutions, see the incidents listed in Lacher and Cole (2014), p. 61; p. 76, fn. 34;
     p. 80, fn. 90.
114 Interviews 174, 181.
115 Interviews 174, 230.
116 Shennib and Laessing (2014).
117 Interview 174.
118 Interviews 17, 240.
119 Interviews 3, 12, 17.
120 Lacher and Cole (2014).
121 Interview 26.
122 Interview 17.
123 Interview 112.

124 Interview 14.

125 Interview 16, Libya News Agency (2013).

126 Interviews 230, 235.

127 Interview 230.

128 Interviews 181, 233.

129 The statement was issued by Zintan's mayor, the military council and the social committee, as well as the Qa'qa' and Sawaeq Brigades (Zintan 2014). For typical media coverage depicting the conflict as one between Islamists and nationalists, see AFP (2014), Penketh and Stephen (2014).

130 On the 'Army of Tribes', see the Bani Walid case study in 'The Process of Fragmentation'.

131 Alrseefa (2014b).

132 Three days after Zintan's withdrawal from the airport, Madi arrived in Cairo along with Othman al-Mlegta and Col. al-Ejmi al-Atiri, a former revolutionary commander who held Qadhafi's son Saif al-Islam captive, and later turned into a champion of a political role for Saif al-Islam. The three commanders sought to enrol former regime loyalists including Col. al-Mabruk Sahban in their war effort (Interview 245).

133 Interviews 102, 112.

134 Interview 105.

135 Interview 174.

136 Interview 171.

137 Al-Aneizi (2014).

138 UNSMIL, OHCHR (2014).

139 The community of Kikla had been Arabized by the early twentieth century, but cherished the memory of its Amazigh heritage, and was seen by its Amazigh neighbours as one of them (Interviews 241, 242, Despois 1935).

140 Interview 229.

141 Interview 242.

142 Interviews 229, 240.

143 Interviews 112, 120.

144 Interviews 241, 259.

145 On the first day of the airport offensive, Zintani commander Abdallah Naker incensed Misratan public opinion with a TV interview in which he called the attackers 'remnants of Janissaries', a derogatory way of referring to the Ottoman ancestry of a part of the Misratan population (Naker 2014). During the 2011 war, the regime had encouraged the portrayal of Misratan rebels as 'Jews', playing on the rumour that the city's Jewish community had never left. 'Janissaries', 'Turks' and 'Jews' subsequently became a common designation for Libya Dawn forces in social media accounts linked to the Qa'qa' and Sawaeq Brigades, as well as the 'Army of Tribes'. For example, following their withdrawal from Tripoli in late August 2014, the Qa'qa', Sawaeq, and Madani Brigades issued a statement in which they described the battle as one between 'the noble Arab tribes' and 'the remnants of the Janissaries and Turks' (Ben Hamel 2014).

146 Interviews 110, 147, 151, 153. Cf. Pelham (2015).

147 Interviews 161, 180.

148 Interviews 170, 174.

149 Interviews 161, 180.

150 This paragraph draws on interviews 159, 161, 171, 174, 175, 180, 181. Copies of the agreements are on record with the author.

151 Interview 161.
152 Interview 120.
153 Interview 174.
154 Interview 175.
155 Interviews 230, 233.
156 Interviews 161, 180.
157 Interview 180.
158 Interview 161.
159 Interview 178.
160 Interviews 55, 56.
161 Interviews 56, 57, 138.
162 Interview 58.
163 Interview 55.
164 Interviews 52, 55, 57.
165 Interview 52.
166 Interviews 129, 130.
167 Interviews 55, 133.
168 Interview 54.
169 Interviews 133, 134.
170 Libya Herald (2013), Mzioudet and Abdul-Wahab (2014).
171 Al-Ruaf (2014e).
172 In September 2013, the head of Bani Walid's Local Council narrowly escaped an assassination attempt in the town's environs (Al-Gharyani 2013b). In February 2014, unknown assailants assassinated an influential elder who in 2011 had helped promote support for the regime (Alrseefa 2014a).
173 Interviews 57, 132.
174 Al-Wasat (2014d).
175 Lacher (2015).
176 Interviews 126, 133.
177 Interviews 126, 128.
178 Interview 210.
179 Interview 219.
180 Interviews 213, 214.
181 Interviews 210, 218.
182 Afrigatenews (2017).
183 Interviews 210, 211.
184 Hüsken (2009).
185 Interviews 59, 62, 63, 64. See also Lacher (2016).
186 Yasin (2013).
187 Interviews 59, 64.
188 Interviews 63, 67, 148, 244.
189 Pliez (2009), Hüsken (2017).
190 Interview 66.
191 Hüsken (2017).
192 Interviews 27, 244.
193 See, for example, Murasil Tobruk (2011, 2012a, b), Al-Ruaf (2013), Al-Shuhubi (2013), Libya al-Mostakbal (2013).
194 Ain Libya (2013).
195 Interview 148, Solidarity News Agency (2014).

196 Libya 24 (2014).
197 Hüsken (2017).
198 McQuinn (2012), Lacher and Cole (2014).
199 Lacher and Al-Idrissi (2018).
200 Collombier (2017).
201 Interviews 192, 193.
202 Cole (2012), Lacher (2014).
203 International Crisis Group (2015c).
204 Jentzsch et al. (2015).
205 Picard (2000), Zahar and Kingston (2004), Menkhaus (2007), Grajales and Le Cour Grandmaison (2019). For the problems associated with definitions of militias, see Tapscott (2019).

Chapter 4

1 'As any political mediator knows, concluding an agreement is difficult but implementing one is infinitely harder. In a country as fragmented as Libya, coming out of 42 years of autocracy and nepotism, the challenges are particularly immense' (Kobler 2016).
2 Hammond (2016). Likewise, the Italian foreign minister Paolo Gentiloni, speaking at the Italian Senate a few weeks earlier, defended Italy's support for the formation of a unity government by saying, 'how could such a plan be anything other than fragile given the fact that the region had been subject to a permanent and dramatic disorder? How could such a path not be stony in Libya? Those who know this country, even only superficially, are well aware of its complex and fragmented conditions, which are certainly not only connected to the two institutions – the HoR of Tobruk and the GNC of Tripoli – on which the mediation process and the United Nations Agreement depend' (Gentiloni 2016).
3 International Crisis Group (2016a), Collombier (2016).
4 For analyses showing how the role of these factors clashes with the assumptions of rational choice theory, see Wood (2003), Bakonyi and Stuvøy (2005), Malthaner (2015), and Shesterinina (2016).
5 Collier and Hoeffler (2000), Walter (2009).
6 Cramer (2002), Baczko and Dorronsoro (2017). For broader critiques of rational choice theory in political science, see Green and Shapiro (1994) and Cox (2004).
7 Malthaner (2015), Shesterinina (2016).
8 Staniland (2012a), Christia (2012), Driscoll (2012), Findley and Rudloff (2012), Seymour (2014), Seymour et al. (2016), Woldemariam (2018).
9 Lee Seymour (2014), for example, builds an argument on the opportunistic behaviour of warlords before eventually concluding that 'commanders' social ties can act as a break on opportunism' (p. 131) – but taking these ties into account would require an entirely different explanatory framework. Fotini Christia (2012) distinguishes between warring groups and their subgroups – though she defines neither – arguing that the latter are marked by high levels of trust that allow their members to overcome commitment problems. But the assumption of consistently cohesive subgroups is not only unrealistic; it also leaves the real puzzle of fragmentation unexplained by what is essentially a tautology: warring

groups fracture into subgroups because the former are fractious, whereas the latter are cohesive.

10 Helbling (1999, 2009), Christia (2012).
11 Both draw on Barth (1959) and Riker (1962) for this argument.
12 Christia (2012), p. 32.
13 Woldemariam (2018), p. 7.
14 Peters (1990).
15 Marchal (2007), p. 1091.
16 This includes the New Institutionalism, which pointed to institutions as shaping actors' preferences and constraints (North 1990; Ostrom 1990), as well as the literature on institutional choice in state formation, which relies on macrosociological theory to define the parameters of individual action, as they are posed by institutions, social structures, and modes of production (Levi 1988; Boone 2003).
17 Bearman (1993), Padgett and Ansell (1993).
18 Menkhaus (2007), Giustozzi and Orsini (2009), Haugbølle (2011).
19 Interviews 253, 255.
20 Interviews 37, 94, 257.
21 The leading figures behind the launch of the operation and mobilization in its favour during its first week, according to concordant statements by well-informed local observers and participants, were the Misrata Shura Council members Fathi Bashagha, Suleiman al-Faqih, and Mohamed Ibrahim al-Dharrat (all of whom had just been elected to the HoR); the religious figure Ibrahim ben Ghashir; as well as the battalion leaders Salah Badi and Salem al-Zufri (I 95, 96, 100, 103, 161, 201).
22 Interviews 101, 104, 108.
23 Interview 102.
24 Interviews 93, 94, 97, 104.
25 Interview 105.
26 Bashagha (2014).
27 Interview 161.
28 Interviews 161, 164, 199, 200, 201, 228.
29 Interviews 159, 201, 228.
30 Interviews 160, 164.
31 Interview 103.
32 International Crisis Group (2015c).
33 Interviews 203, 277, cf. Tubiana and Gramizzi (2017).
34 Interviews 158, 161, see also Rajhi (2015).
35 Interviews 159, 161.
36 Most local observers and protagonists alleged that the Qatar-based Libyan Islamic scholar Ali Sallabi was the primary conduit for these funds, with several Misratan politicians and battalion leaders functioning as secondary conduits (Interviews 125, 158, 161, 199, 200, 228).
37 Interviews 125, 158, 228.
38 UNSC (2015, 2016).
39 Bashagha asserted that he had warned the UK and US ambassadors of an imminent offensive against Zintani positions in Tripoli and had encountered no opposition, interpreting this as signalling their approval (Interviews 158, 195, 303).
40 Interviews 105, 158.

41 Dabeiba headed the Libyan Investment and Development Company (LIDCO), which was the contracting party on the registration documents filed in November 2014 (US DoJ 2014). Dabeiba's uncle, Ali, denied he had been involved in hiring the lobbyist (Interview 236). For the lobbying contracts with Jadhran and Haftar, see US DoJ (2013, 2016). On the lobbyist, Ari Ben-Menashe, see Hutchinson (2014).

42 Personal communications, Misratan activists and commanders, February-March 2015.

43 Kirkpatrick (2015b).

44 Badi (2015).

45 Interviews 159, 160, 164. See also a letter and statement by the operation's most prominent battalion commander, Salah al-Jabbu, in which he expressed his reservations towards the negotiation efforts (Al-Jabbu 2015a, b).

46 Interviews 237, 238.

47 Interviews 161, 163.

48 Interview 209.

49 Interviews 161, 180.

50 Personal communications, Misratan activists and commanders, June to October 2015.

51 Interviews 163, 164, 238.

52 Interview 238.

53 Interview 163, Al-Mahjub Brigade (2016). An accomplice of Krik's in the action, Abdelhafidh Qawasim, had been a commander in the Hatin Battalion, which had close links to Fathi Bashagha, and was excluded by that battalion at the same time as Krik (Hatin Battalion 2016).

54 Interviews 160, 195.

55 Leading Misratan supporters of the LPA and the Presidency Council were the boycotting HoR members Fathi Bashagha, Suleiman al-Faqih and Mohamed al-Raedh; the businessman Ahmed Maitig, who became a vice-president; the Local Council; JCP president Mohamed Sawan; as well as the majority of the battalion commanders in the Halbus, Mahjub and Hatin Brigades. Leading opponents were the boycotting HoR members Mohamed Ibrahim al-Dharrat and Hanan Shalluf; the businessman, former Local Council member and self-styled prime minister Khalifa al-Ghwell; the religious figure Ibrahim ben Ghashir; as well as battalion leaders Salah Badi, Salem al-Zufri and Abdellatif al-Krik. Sweihli fully threw his support behind the agreement only once he was securely installed as president of the State Council, in late January 2016.

56 Wehrey (2017).

57 Bulghib (2014).

58 Interviews 238, 243.

59 Kirkpatrick et al. (2015).

60 The man, Hamdi al-Abbasi was a native of Benghazi who had fought in Misrata in 2011. He was arrested and held by Misrata's *Amn al-Mu'allumat* (security intelligence) (Interviews 163, 205).

61 Ben Ghashir (2015).

62 Interview 159.

63 Interviews 205, 206.

64 Interviews 183, 198, 207.

65 Several people directly involved in, or close to, the transactions and preparations for the BDB's December 2016 offensive in the oil crescent confirmed to me that

Defence Minister al-Mahdi al-Barghathi and Tubu commander Hassan Musa had travelled to Doha, Qatar, in November to mobilize support for the offensive. Shortly afterwards, they appeared in al-Jufra together with BDB leader Ismail al-Sallabi and large amounts of cash, which they used among other things to buy off Chadian and Sudanese fighters whom Haftar had deployed in the region. Misratan fighters who joined the BDB's December 2016 and March 2017 offensives also received substantial cash payments. According to several people close to BDB commanders, Sallabi had already benefited from Qatari funding to set up the BDB in the spring of 2016. Sallabi himself denies this. Personal communications in November and December 2016 with former revolutionaries from Benghazi; a close associate of al-Mahdi al-Barghathi in the defence ministry; a senior Misratan commander involved in the transactions with Chadian fighters; and Tubu politicians involved in the outreach to Chadian commanders; as well as Interviews 225, 226, 238, 244, 261, 271, 277. See also International Crisis Group (2016b), Tubiana and Gramizzi (2017).

66 Interviews 166, 201, 208.
67 Ben Hamel (2016a).
68 Al-Bayyan (2016).
69 Al-Wasat (2016).
70 Al-Sallahi (2016).
71 Afrigatenews (2016a).
72 Personal communications, Misratan activists and battalion commanders, May 2016.
73 Interviews 197, 204.
74 Interviews 196, 197, 208.
75 Interviews 199, 204, Libya 24 (2016).
76 Interviews 196, 197.
77 Interviews 204.
78 Human Rights Watch (2017a).
79 Interviews 157, 159, 162, 196, 197, 204, 206, 237.
80 Lacher and Al-Idrissi (2018).
81 Interviews 274, 276, 290, 302.
82 Interview 276.
83 Interviews 323, 325.
84 Interviews 319, 322, 323.
85 Interviews 355, 356.
86 Interview 359.
87 Al-Dharrat (2015).
88 Identification with interview number withheld.
89 BBC (2017).
90 Al-Nas (2015).
91 Among many others labelling post-2011 Misrata a city-state, see Caryl (2013), Hüsken and Klute (2015), Toaldo (2016).
92 Interviews 276, 277, 280, 290.
93 Interview 276.
94 Interview 353.
95 Interview 233.
96 Interview 26, 76, 258.
97 Interview 230.
98 Interviews 180, 181.
99 Western Region Operations Room (2014).

100 Afrigatenews (2015).
101 Supreme Council of the Tribes of Zintan (2016).
102 Interview 161.
103 Interview 180.
104 Interview 180.
105 Interviews 161, 180.
106 Interview 181.
107 Interviews 184, 231. See also the account of the Supreme Council of the Tribes of Zintan (2016) itself.
108 Cousins (2016).
109 Interviews 176, 179, 180.
110 Interview 184.
111 Sky News Arabia (2016).
112 France 24 (2016).
113 Interview 184.
114 Interviews 230, 235, 283, 309.
115 Al-Wasat (2017c).
116 Interviews 233, 235.
117 Al-Wasat (2017b).
118 Lacher and Al-Idrissi (2018).
119 Interview 236.
120 Interview 232.
121 Supreme Council of the Tribes of Zintan (2015).
122 Interviews 231, 232.
123 Tribes of Zintan (2017).
124 Interviews 276, 277, 282, 283, 304. 305, 307.
125 Interviews 331, 345.
126 Al-Zintan (2019), Interview 393.
127 Interview 393.
128 Bobin (2019), Interviews 399, 401.
129 Interviews 229, 241, 242.
130 Interview 259.
131 Interview 170.
132 Interviews 229, 242.
133 Interviews 190, 222.
134 Ben Hamel (2016b).
135 Interviews 344, 347, 348, 357, 378.
136 Interviews 232, 240, 241, 242, 331, 344, 347, 348.
137 The Libya Observer (2019), Amazigh Supreme Council Libya (2019).
138 Interviews 393, 399, 398, 401.
139 Interviews 83, 86, 89.
140 Interview 89.
141 Interviews 131, 210.
142 Al-Bayyan (2014).
143 The key organizer of the May gathering in al-Aziziya was Mabruk Buameid, a former regime official and major figure in conflicts in the Warshafana area (Interviews 89, 110, Faruq 2014). During the war in Tripoli, Buameid's relatives and associates repeatedly spoke in the name of the 'Army of Tribes' (Al-Aswad 2014; Al-Obeidi 2014d).

144 Interview 110.
145 Social Council of Warfalla Tribes (2015b).
146 Interviews 126, 136.
147 Interviews 126, 127, 128, 133, 136.
148 Interview 132.
149 Interviews 126, 136, 138.
150 Interviews 212, 213, 214.
151 Interviews 212, 213, 271.
152 Interview 133.
153 Western Region Operations Room (2014).
154 Interviews 210, 211, see also Social Council of Warfalla Tribes (2015a, 2016). Multiple sources confirmed that the meeting had taken place (Interviews 167, 168, 170, 187, 212, 213).
155 Interview 213.
156 Interview 210.
157 Libya Institute for Advanced Studies (2016), as well as personal communications with Western diplomats, May-September 2016.
158 Interviews 212, 214.
159 Interview 211.
160 Interviews 212, 213.
161 Interviews 126, 128, 210, 211.
162 Interviews 169, 165, 208. For some examples of such prisoner releases, see Digital Libya Agency (2016), Afrigatenews (2016c), Al-Obeidi (2016), Al-Haddad (2016).
163 Interviews 210, 211, 213.
164 Interview 296.
165 Interviews 300, 301.
166 Interviews 296, 297, 299, 300, 301.
167 Micallef (2019), Interview 376.
168 Fetouri (2018).
169 Interview 376.
170 Interview 210.
171 Interviews 394, 396, 397.
172 For example, Pusztai (2016, p. 7) claims that Haftar's 'position relies on the support of eastern tribal leaders'. Fikry Abdel Samei (2016, p. 178) asserts that 'Haftar also managed to ally with powerful tribes in the east, such as the Ubaydat, the Awaqir, and the Baraghitha' – an assertion that reveals the author's superficial subject knowledge, since the Baraghtha are a house of the Awaqir. Eljarh (2016, p. 12) states that 'in eastern Libya, tribes played a fundamental role in the formation and support of the Libyan National Army (LNA) led by Gen. Khalifa Haftar. The tribes supported the LNA in its attempts to establish a national army and fight extremist jihadist groups'. Fraihat (2016, p. 219) argues that tribes in Libya positioned themselves according to their 'geographical location, their own interests, and their understanding of the political process … many of Libya's tribes in the east supported Operation Dignity and General Haftar'.
173 UNSC (2017).
174 Interview 151. See also al-Sharif's speech at a meeting of the Cyrenaica Unionist Council headed by Ahmed Zubair al-Senoussi, the first attempt to declare regional autonomy in the east, in spring 2012 (Al-Sharif 2012).

175 See Buatiwa's speech at the 18 February meeting (Popular Social Leadership Tobruk 2011b) as well as at a demonstration protesting the March 2012 establishment of the Barqa Unionist Council (Buatiwa 2012).

176 Al-Siddiq al-Mabruk was not the only example for such a trajectory. Another LIFG veteran, Abdeljawad al-Badeen from Benghazi, became president of the Cyrenaica Council of Elders formed in April 2014 to broaden representation of the autonomy movement beyond Ibrahim al-Jadhran's Cyrenaica Political Bureau. Jadhran himself had spent time in prison under Qadhafi for ties to the LIFG.

177 Interviews 59, 62, 64, 147, 151, 153, 154.

178 Al-Asema TV (2013).

179 Interviews 63, 155, 156.

180 Interviews 59, 152, see Al-Zukra (2009) and Al-Satur (2011) for two contemporary accounts.

181 Interview 152.

182 See Lacher and Cole (2014) as well as Barakat (2013) and Alrseefa (2013).

183 Al-Ruaf (2014a).

184 Abdul-Wahab (2014).

185 Ellawati (2013).

186 Ministry of Defence (2013).

187 See, for example, his speech at a gathering in Qasr Libya, in March 2014 (Haftar 2014).

188 Al-Moheir (2014).

189 These armed groups included a militia led by Ezzeddine al-Wakwak, a close associate of Hamed al-Hassi in the Cyrenaica Defence Force who controlled Benghazi's Benina airport (Al-Obeidi 2014a). The *Awliya' al-Damm* (closest blood kins, that is those seeking revenge) militia was led by Ayad al-Fassi, who became infamous by openly threatening to expel Misratans from Cyrenaica and burn their houses (Al-Fassi 2015; Ben Hamel 2015). This group is alleged to have destroyed dozens of houses (Solidarity News Agency 2015). A militia led by Faraj Qa'im controlled the Barsis checkpoint and the prison in the town, and later called itself the Counter-Terrorism Unit. Another armed group was led by Salah Bulghib, whose brother and associate Khaled was equally on record threatening to expel all 'Misratans' from Benghazi (Bulghib 2014). Bulghib's group later assumed the label of Military Intelligence. Along with several others, these four armed groups were recruited primarily from civilian members of the Awaqir tribe, each group being dominated by residents of particular towns in the environs of Benghazi, and led by civilians. For an account of tribal and ethnic rhetoric on both sides of the conflict, see Wehrey (2017).

190 Al-Ruaf (2014b).

191 Al-Ruaf (2014c), Al-Obeidi (2014b).

192 Al-Obeidat (2014).

193 Al-Ruaf (2014d).

194 Interviews 91, 148.

195 Mahmoud (2014).

196 The three Tobruk representatives were Othman Bkhatra al-Qutaani and Faraj Buhassan al-Marimi, both of them former members of Tobruk's Popular Social Leadership; as well as Saad al-Tajun, a *Mniffi* notable, former political prisoner, and later a local regime official (Barqa Council of Elders 2014).

197 Reuters (2014).

198 Interview 150, Westcott (2015).

199 Interview 148.

200 Interview 244.

201 Libya 24 (2015a).

202 Interviews 147, 151, 153, 154.

203 Bulghib (2015a).

204 See Ain Libya (2015a), Al-Obeidi (2015), Libya al-Khabar (2015a).

205 Interview 154. In December 2014, Jadhran had hit back at derisive comments from
     Haftar's air force chief Saqr al-Jarushi by saying that he recognized only the chief of
     staff appointed by the HoR (Al-Jared 2014). In September 2015, after a failed attempt
     by Haftar's men to arrest Jadhran during his stay in Tobruk, Haftar's air force bombed
     a convoy of Jadhran's fighters. Jadhran responded by calling Haftar a 'vanquished
     colonel' (Ain Libya 2015b).

206 Interview 148.

207 At a meeting I attended in April 2015, Bulkhatabiya had invited a group of protesters
     from Benghazi and sought to gain other notables' support for staging demonstrations
     demanding Thinni's dismissal. Thinni had earlier alleged that Tatanaki was exerting
     pressure to obtain a top government post (Libya al-Khabar 2015b). In late May,
     after armed men shot at Thinni's convoy following his visit to the HoR, Thinni
     accused Bulkhatabiya of being behind the attack (Al-Wasat 2015). At the time,
     my interlocutors invariably described Bulkhatabiya as 'Tatanaki's man in Tobruk'
     (Interviews 149, 152).

208 See UNSC (2015, 2016, 2017).

209 Tubiana and Gramizzi (2017), UNSC (2017).

210 Operation Dignity obtained almost instantaneous backing from leading Saudi
     religious scholars (Al-Wasat 2014b). Two months into the war in Benghazi, the Salafi
     battalion leader Salem al-Mayyar from Benghazi joined the operation (Afrigatenews
     2014). His *Tawhid* (Monotheism) Battalion subsequently became one of the most
     powerful forces in Benghazi. On the rise of the Madakhila in Libya, see Wehrey
     (2016b).

211 Al-Safi (2016).

212 Ain Libya (2015c), Libya al-Khabar (2015c).

213 Interview 225, Libya 24 (2015b).

214 Personal communications, commander in anti-IS operation in Darna, and local
     observers in Tobruk, March and April 2016. Also see Al-Jared (2016c).

215 Libya 24 (2015c).

216 Libya 24 (2015d).

217 Libya 24 (2015e).

218 Libya's Channel (2015c).

219 Reuters (2015).

220 Bulghib (2015b).

221 Al-Rasmiya TV (2016).

222 Qa'im (2016a).

223 Qa'im (2016b).

224 See Barghathi's meeting with Awaqir elders in mid-May 2016, at which one Awaqir
     figure, Brik al-Lawati, tried to take a neutral position in Barghathi's conflict with
     Haftar (Al-Awaqir 2016). A month later, Lawati strongly backed Barghathi and Qa'im
     (Al-Lawati 2016). Around that time, Mohamed Buisir, a US-based businessman from
     the Awaqir tribe, also attempted to mediate (Afrigatenews 2016b).

225 Armed Forces General Command (2016a, b).

226 See Latiwish (2011, 2012, 2015).

227 Latiwish (2016).

228 Al-Jadhran (2016).

229 Al-Magharba (2016).

230 Eljarh (2017b), p. 4.

231 Interviews 183, 189, 225.

232 Ain Libya (2016), Solidarity News Agency (2016b).

233 Al-Obeidat (2016), Libya's Channel (2016).

234 See, for example, his March 2017 speech in front of members of the Fadhil Bu Omar Brigade, in which he denied that the brigade had fought protesters in February 2011 (Al-Shikhi 2017). Shikhi also became infamous for asserting in August 2016 that among the families of Benghazi Revolutionaries' Shura Council fighters surrounded by Haftar's forces in Benghazi's Qanfuda district, nobody over fourteen should get out alive. 'There is not a single honourable Libyan woman among them' (Al-Shikhi 2016).

235 Armed Forces General Command (2017a).

236 See Haftar's meeting with tribal politicians from across Libya on the occasion of Eid al-Fitr, on 27 June 2017 (Libya al-Hadath TV 2017) and a similar meeting several days earlier (Armed Forces General Command 2017b).

237 Al-Jared (2016a, b, c).

238 See Ali Al-Asbali's (2017) account of his abduction, detention and release, as well as Barqa TV (2016), a report on the incident featuring interviews with the victim, his father Faraj Hashem Bulkhatabiya, and the head of the Tobruk Council of Elders, Abdelqader Hamed.

239 In a meeting with the notables, Haftar admitted to holding al-Mabruk in custody, and said that he was not accused of any crimes. Personal communications, Ghithi notable involved in the efforts, April and May 2016. See also Solidarity News Agency (2016a).

240 Personal communication.

241 Interviews 189, 225, 244.

242 Al-Wasat (2017a).

243 Libya al-Khabar (2017).

244 Human Rights Watch (2017b, c).

245 Ben Said (2017).

246 Al-Nabaa TV (2017).

247 Al-Motawaset (2017).

248 Ben Ali (2017).

249 Interviews 267, 284, 289.

Conclusion

1 Keen (1998); cf. Stearns (2016) for an explanation of enduring violence in the Democratic Republic of Congo that grants a prominent role to the reshaping of society by conflict in ways that contribute to its perpetuation.

2 Wood (2008), Baczko and Dorronsoro (2017).

3 See, for example, Dorronsoro (2005) for an analysis of the conflict in Afghanistan that identifies distinct conflict dynamics with a succession of contrasting strategic conditions.

4 For two recent analyses that emphasize this point, see Debos (2016) and
   Staniland (2017).
5 Hillmann (2008).
6 Brandt (2013, 2014).
7 Breidlid, Arensen (2014); Young (2016); Terry, McQuinn (2018). Dorronsoro (2013)
   offers similar examples for southern Afghanistan. Stringham, Forney (2017: 179) argue
   that Nuer communities have largely 'resisted warlords' assaults on their cohesion'.
8 Terry, McQuinn (2018) analyse the implications of social embeddedness for
   identifying which actors can constrain armed groups in their use of violence.
9 Schlichte (2009), Schnell (2015).
10 Giustozzi and Noor Ullah (2006), p. 17. Cf. Rubin (1995) and Shahrani (2013) for
   analyses that support Giustozzi and Noor Ullah on this point.
11 Padgett and Ansell (1993).

Annex: List of interviews

No.	Interlocutor	Place	Date
1	Notable and former opposition activist from Yefren	Tripoli	January 2014
2	Political activist from Yefren/Tripoli	Tripoli	January 2014
3	Former leader in revolutionary war effort, Yefren	Yefren	January 2014
4	Notable from Yefren	Yefren	January 2014
5	Revolutionary and political activist, Yefren	Yefren	January 2014
6	Former leader in revolutionary war effort, Yefren	Yefren	January 2014
7	Notable and Amazigh activist from Yefren	Yefren	January 2014
8	Revolutionary fighter from Yefren	Yefren	January 2014
9	Notable and revolutionary leader from Zintan	Zintan	January 2014
10	Revolutionary activist from Zintan	Zintan	January 2014
11	Battalion leader from Zintan	Zintan	January 2014
12	Battalion leader from Jadu	Tripoli	January 2014
13	Battalion leader from Jadu	Jadu	January 2014
14	Notable, former member of Nalut local council	Nalut	February 2014
15	Revolutionary and Amazigh activist from Nalut	Nalut	February 2014
16	Revolutionary fighter, Amazigh activist	Nalut	February 2014
17	Battalion leader from Nalut	Nalut	February 2014
18	Army officer, former leader in revolutionary war effort, Nalut	Nalut	February 2014
19	Army officer, former member of Nalut military council	Nalut	February 2014
20	Army officer in defence ministry's training department, former revolutionary	Tripoli	February 2014
21	Senior government official from Benghazi	Tripoli	February 2014
22	Retired army officer, former revolutionary, interior ministry official	Tripoli	February 2014
23	Former leading figure in Benghazi battalion; official in Warriors' Affairs Commission	Tripoli	February 2014
24	Head of Ubari local council	Tripoli	February 2014
25	Tuareg notable from Ghat	Tripoli	February 2014
26	Zintani battalion leader in Tripoli	Tripoli	February 2014
27	Tobruk army officer	Tripoli	February 2014

No.	Interlocutor	Place	Date
28	Tubu activist	Tripoli	February 2014
29	Tubu politician	Tripoli	February 2014
30	Federalist politician from Benghazi, businessman	Tripoli	February 2014
31	Political activist from Yefren/Tripoli	Tripoli	April 2014
32	Businessman/politician from Misrata	Tripoli	April 2014
33	Tubu politician	Tripoli	April 2014
34	Tuareg army officer, loyalist in 2011	Tripoli	April 2014
35	Tubu activist	Tripoli	April 2014
36	Tuareg activist	Tripoli	April 2014
37	Fathi Bashagha: Misratan politician, battalion leader, businessman	Misrata	April 2014
38	Misratan politician, leader in revolutionary war effort, businessman	Misrata	April 2014
39	Misratan battalion leader, businessman	Misrata	April 2014
40	Misratan politician, academic	Misrata	April 2014
41	Misratan politician, official in Justice and Construction Party	Misrata	April 2014
42	Misratan revolutionary activist, former political prisoner	Misrata	April 2014
43	Misratan political activist, former revolutionary fighter	Misrata	April 2014
44	Misratan notable, religious figure, member of Shura Council	Misrata	April 2014
45	Misratan political activist, academic	Misrata	April 2014
46	Misratan student and civil society activist	Misrata	April 2014
47	Academic, human rights activist from Bani Walid	Tripoli	April 2014
48	Civil society activist from Bani Walid	Tripoli	April 2014
49	Academic, former member of Revolutionary Committees from Bani Walid	Tripoli	April 2014
50	Member of Bani Walid Social Council	Tripoli	April 2014
51	Member of Bani Walid notable family	Tripoli	April 2014
52	Member of Bani Walid Local Council	Bani Walid	April 2014
53	Member of Bani Walid Local Council	Bani Walid	April 2014
54	Member of Bani Walid Social Council, former member of Popular Social Leaderships	Bani Walid	April 2014
55	Member of Bani Walid Social Council	Bani Walid	April 2014
56	Academic, local government official from Bani Walid	Bani Walid	April 2014
57	Civil society activist from Bani Walid	Bani Walid	April 2014

No.	Interlocutor	Place	Date
58	Former fighter in defence of Bani Walid against revolutionary forces	Bani Walid	April 2014
59	Medical doctor, temporary ambassador from Tobruk	Tobruk	April 2014
60	Young local politician, Tobruk	Tobruk	April 2014
61	Young local politician, former revolutionary	Tobruk	April 2014
62	Obeidat notable, federalist politician	Tobruk	April 2014
63	Tobruk civil society activist, political figure	Tobruk	April 2014
64	Faraj Yasin al-Mabri: Obeidat notable, head of local council	Tobruk	April 2014
65	Tobruk academic	Tobruk	April 2014
66	Tobruk businessman	Tobruk	April 2014
67	Senior army officer, Tobruk	Tobruk	April 2014
68	Political activist from Tripoli/Yefren	Tripoli	June 2014
69	Tubu politician	Tripoli	June 2014
70	Tubu politician	Tripoli	June 2014
71	Tuareg notable from Ghat	Tripoli	June 2014
72	Army officer in defence ministry's training department, former revolutionary	Tripoli	June 2014
73	Chief executive at TV station	Tripoli	June 2014
74	Senior figure in National Forces Alliance	Tripoli	June 2014
75	Former member of Tripoli military council, Tripoli security figure	Tripoli	June 2014
76	Zintani politician, academic	Tripoli	June 2014
77	Former member of Benghazi battalion from Sabha	Tripoli	June 2014
78	Former leading figure in Benghazi battalion; official in Warriors' Affairs Commission	Tripoli	June 2014
79	Politician, civil society figure, former member of exiled opposition	Tripoli	June 2014
80	Misratan political activist, academic	Misrata	June 2014
81	Misratan politician, official in Justice and Construction Party	Misrata	June 2014
82	Mohamed Ali Abdallah al-Dharrat: Misratan GNC member, president of National Front Party	Tripoli	June 2014
83	Misratan student and civil society activist	Misrata	June 2014
84	Fathi Bashagha: Misratan politician, battalion leader, businessman	Misrata	June 2014
85	Misratan political activist, former revolutionary fighter	Misrata	June 2014
86	Bani Walid GNC member, notable	Tripoli	June 2014

No.	Interlocutor	Place	Date
87	Judge from Bani Walid	Tripoli	June 2014
88	Salem al-Ahmar: member of Bani Walid Social Council; former GNC member for Bani Walid	Tripoli	June 2014
89	Member of Bani Walid Social Council	Tripoli	June 2014
90	Former revolutionary from Bani Walid, former member of 28 May Battalion	Tripoli	June 2014
91	Army officer from Tobruk	Tripoli	June 2014
92	Former revolutionary activist, medic, Misrata	Misrata	June 2014
93	Fathi Bashagha: Misratan boycotting HoR member, former battalion leader, businessman	Misrata	October 2014
94	Misratan journalist	Misrata	October 2014
95	Misratan political activist, former revolutionary fighter	Misrata	October 2014
96	Misratan student and civil society activist	Misrata	October 2014
97	Member of businessmen's council in Misrata, former revolutionary leader	Misrata	October 2014
98	Misratan boycotting HoR member, former battalion leader	Misrata	October 2014
99	Misratan civil society activist	Misrata	October 2014
100	Misratan battalion leader (Mahjub Battalion), participant in July 2014 negotiations over Tripoli airport	Misrata	October 2014
101	Members of Misrata local council	Misrata	October 2014
102	Mohamed Ibrahim al-Dharrat: Misratan boycotting HoR member, former revolutionary leader	Misrata	October 2014
103	Ahmed Hadiya: Spokesman for Libya Dawn; former spokesman for Central Shield; member of Committee of 17	Misrata	October 2014
104	Mohamed Raedh: boycotting Misratan HoR member, businessman	Misrata	October 2014
105	Battalion leaders, members of Committee of 17	Misrata	October 2014
106	Misratan civil society activist	Misrata	October 2014
107	Misratan journalist	Misrata	October 2014
108	Misratan notable, religious figure, member of Shura Council	Misrata	October 2014
109	Bani Walid academic, former member of Revolutionary Committees	Tripoli	October 2014
110	Member of Bani Walid Social Council	Tripoli	October 2014
111	Judge from Bani Walid	Tripoli	October 2014
112	Political activist from Tripoli/Yefren	Tripoli	October 2014

No.	Interlocutor	Place	Date
113	Misratan politician	Istanbul	January 2015
114	Senior Muslim Brotherhood official from Misrata	Tripoli	January 2015
115	GNC member for Ajdabiya	Tripoli	January 2015
116	Former leading figure in Benghazi battalion	Tripoli	January 2015
117	Nizar Kawan: Head of Justice and Construction Party group in GNC	Tripoli	January 2015
118	Former member of Tripoli military council; Tripoli security figure; adviser to Omar al-Hassi	Tripoli	January 2015
119	Omar al-Hassi: prime minister of National Salvation Government	Tripoli	February 2015
120	Amazigh activist from Yefren	Tripoli	January 2015
121	Tuareg activist	Tripoli	January 2015
122	Several GNC members	Tripoli	January 2015
123	Former leader in Libyan Islamic Fighting Group; Tripoli security figure	Tripoli	January 2015
124	Benghazi politician, supporter of Benghazi Revolutionaries' Shura Council, adviser to Omar al-Hassi	Tripoli	February 2015
125	Misratan civil society activist	Tripoli	February 2015
126	Saleh Mayouf: Head of Bani Walid Social Council	Bani Walid	January 2015
127	Salem al-Ahmar: member of Bani Walid Social Council, former GNC member	Bani Walid	January 2015
128	Young political activist associated with Bani Walid Social Council	Bani Walid	January 2015
129	Bani Walid religious figure, member of Shura Council	Bani Walid	January 2015
130	Bani Walid notable, former GNC member, member of Shura Council	Bani Walid	January 2015
131	Former security official from Bani Walid	Bani Walid	January 2015
132	Bani Walid civil society activist	Bani Walid	January 2015
133	Young political activists working with Bani Walid Social Council	Bani Walid	January 2015
134	Bani Walid academic and local government official	Bani Walid	January 2015
135	Activist in Bani Walid Association of Families of Martyrs, Prisoners and Disappeared	Bani Walid	January 2015
136	Member of Bani Walid Social Council	Tripoli	January 2015
137	Former revolutionary from Bani Walid, former member of 28 May Battalion	Tripoli	January 2015
138	Judge from Bani Walid	Tripoli	January 2015

No.	Interlocutor	Place	Date
139	Former member of Popular Social Leadership, local amateur historian, Bani Walid	Tripoli	January 2015
140	HoR member for Benghazi	Tobruk	April 2015
141	HoR member for Shahat, federalist politician	Tobruk	April 2015
142	HoR member for Benghazi	Tobruk	April 2015
143	HoR member for Zliten	Tobruk	April 2015
144	HoR member for Tarhuna	Tobruk	April 2015
145	HoR member for Zawiya	Tobruk	April 2015
146	Qutaan notable from Msaid	Tobruk	April 2015
147	Faraj Yasin al-Mabri: Obeidat notable, member of local council	Tobruk	April 2015
148	Two army officers from Tobruk	Tobruk	April 2015
149	Young political analyst from Tobruk	Tobruk	April 2015
150	Businessman from Tobruk	Tobruk	April 2015
151	Al-Tayyeb al-Sharif: Obeidat notable	Tobruk	April 2015
152	Young Tobruk businessman	Tobruk	April 2015
153	Obeidat notable	Tobruk	April 2015
154	Obeidat notable, federalist politician	Tobruk	April 2015
155	Qutaan notable, former GNC member from Tobruk	Tobruk	April 2015
156	Member of constituent assembly for Tobruk	Tobruk	April 2015
157	Misratan politician, member of Libyan Elders Council for Reconciliation	Misrata	April 2016
158	Misratan academic/politician	Misrata	April 2016
159	Abubakr al-Hresh: Misratan religious figure, member of local council	Misrata	April 2016
160	Member of Misrata local council	Misrata	April 2016
161	Misratan battalion leader in Tripoli (Halbus Battalion); participant in ceasefire negotiations in 2015	Tripoli	April 2016
162	Misratan civil society activist	Misrata	April 2016
163	Misratan political activist	Misrata	April 2016
164	Misratan battalion leader (Mahjub Battalion)	Misrata	April 2016
165	Misratan notable	Misrata	April 2016
166	Senior Misratan army officer	Misrata	April 2016
167	Bani Walid academic, former member in Revolutionary Committees	Tripoli	April 2016
168	Judge from Bani Walid	Tripoli	April 2016
169	Former leader in Libyan Islamic Fighting Group; Tripoli security figure	Tripoli	April 2016
170	Political activist from Tripoli/Yefren	Tripoli	April 2016

No.	Interlocutor	Place	Date
171	Former revolutionary commander, community negotiator from Kikla	Tripoli	April 2016
172	Amazigh activist from Yefren	Yefren	April 2016
173	Notable from Yefren	Yefren	April 2016
174	Notable, community negotiator from Zintan	Zintan	April 2016
175	Notable, community negotiator from Zintan	Zintan	April 2016
176	Zintani political negotiator	Zintan	April 2016
177	Zintan HoR member	Zintan	April 2016
178	Abdallah Trabelsi: commander of the Special Operations Force, brother of Sawaeq commander Emad Trabelsi	Zintan	April 2016
179	Young Zintani political activist	Zintan	April 2016
180	Member of/negotiator for Zintan military council	Zintan	April 2016
181	Zintani battalion leader, negotiator for Zintan military council	Zintan	April 2016
182	Fadhil al-Amin: Independent member of UN-led Libyan Political Dialogue	Tunis	September 2016
183	Former battalion leaders from Benghazi	Tripoli	September 2016
184	Zintani battalion leader, negotiator for Zintan military council	Tripoli	September 2016
185	Former leader in Libyan Islamic Fighting Group; Tripoli security figure	Tripoli	September 2016
186	Senior official in Muslim Brotherhood	Tripoli	September 2016
187	Senior official in Muslim Brotherhood and Justice and Construction Party; adviser to member of Presidency Council	Tripoli	September 2016
188	Official in Tripoli security institution, former revolutionary fighter from Nalut	Tripoli	September 2016
189	Adviser in Ministry of Defence from Benghazi	Tripoli	September 2016
190	Former official in Tripoli security institutions, former revolutionary fighter from Jadu	Tripoli	September 2016
191	Senior official in Ministry of Defence from Benghazi	Tripoli	September 2016
192	President of Warshafana Shura Council	Tripoli	September 2016
193	Civil society activist, member of notable family from Warshafana	Tripoli	September 2016
194	Human rights activist from Sirte	Tripoli	September 2016
195	Misratan academic and civil society activist	Misrata	September 2016
196	Misratan fighter in Sirte war effort	Misrata	September 2016
197	Misratan fighter in Sirte war effort	Misrata	September 2016
198	Misratan political activist	Misrata	September 2016

No.	Interlocutor	Place	Date
199	Misratan academic, politician	Misrata	September 2016
200	Former senior regime official from Misrata	Tripoli	September 2016
201	Salem Jha: leading army officer in revolutionary war effort	Misrata	September 2016
202	Maadan notable from Misrata	Misrata	September 2016
203	Jamal al-Triki: commander of Third Force	Misrata	September 2016
204	Misratan academic, civil society activist	Misrata	September 2016
205	Misratan Islamist politician	Misrata	September 2016
206	Fawzi Abdelali: leading Misratan revolutionary figure, member of first local council, former interior minister, Libyan ambassador to Bahrain	Misrata	September 2016
207	Army officer from eastern Libya	Misrata	September 2016
208	Senior Misratan army officer, official in Sirte war effort	Misrata	September 2016
209	Misratan battalion leader (Mahjub Battalion)	Misrata	September 2016
210	Young political activist working with Bani Walid Social Council	Bani Walid	September 2016
211	Saleh Mayouf: Head of Bani Walid Social Council	Bani Walid	September 2016
212	Brother and associate of a 1993 coup plotter	Bani Walid	September 2016
213	Member of Bani Walid Local Council	Bani Walid	September 2016
214	Bani Walid civil society activist	Bani Walid	September 2016
215	Former fighter in Bani Walid's defence in 2012	Bani Walid	September 2016
216	Bani Walid religious figure	Bani Walid	September 2016
217	Qadhadhfa notable from Sirte	Bani Walid	September 2016
218	Bani Walid academic	Bani Walid	September 2016
219	Member in Bani Walid security brigade, former fighter in Bani Walid's defence in 2012	Bani Walid	September 2016
220	Youssef al-Mangoush: former Chief of Staff, army officer from Benghazi	Berlin	December 2016
221	Senior official in Muslim Brotherhood and Justice and Construction Party; adviser to member of Presidency Council	Tripoli	March 2017
222	Former official in Tripoli security institutions, former revolutionary fighter from Jadu	Tripoli	March 2017
223	Political activist from Tripoli/Yefren	Tripoli	March 2017
224	Former leader in Libyan Islamic Fighting Group, Tripoli security figure	Tripoli	March 2017
225	Army officer from al-Bayda	Tripoli	March 2017
226	Former leaders of Benghazi revolutionary battalions	Tripoli	March 2017

No.	Interlocutor	Place	Date
227	Senior official in Tripoli security institution, former leader in revolutionary battalion	Tripoli	March 2017
228	Senior Misratan politician	Tripoli	March 2017
229	Army officer from Jadu	Tripoli	March 2017
230	Zintani battalion leader, negotiator for Zintan military council	Tripoli	March 2017
231	Zintani politician	Zintan	March 2017
232	Zintani notable and community negotiator	Zintan	March 2017
233	Zintani army officer, member of military council	Zintan	March 2017
234	Young Zintani political activist	Zintan	March 2017
235	Member of/negotiator for Zintan military council	Zintan	March 2017
236	Zintani notable	Zintan	March 2017
237	Misratan battalion leader (Halbus Battalion) in Tripoli	Tripoli	March 2017
238	Misratan academic and civil society activist	Misrata	March 2017
239	Senior Misratan army officer, official in Sirte war effort	Tripoli	March 2017
240	Official in Tripoli security institution, former battalion leader from Jadu	Tripoli	March 2017
241	Members of Jadu local council, former revolutionary leaders	Jadu	March 2017
242	Senior army officer from Nalut	Tripoli	March 2017
243	Senior Misratan security figure, battalion leader, former intelligence official	Misrata	March 2017
244	Army officer from Tobruk	Tripoli	March 2017
245	Agil Hussein Agil: former minister under Qadhafi	By telephone	April 2017
246	Mustafa Saqizli: former leader in Benghazi revolutionary battalions, head of Warriors' Affairs Commission	Tripoli	April 2013
247	Member of Bani Walid local council	Tripoli	June 2012
248	Pro-revolutionary civil society activist from Bani Walid	Tripoli	November 2012
249	Judge from Bani Walid	Bani Walid	November 2012
250	Members of Misrata's Military Council	Misrata	November 2011
251	Head of Misrata local council	Misrata	November 2011
252	Misratan student and civil society activist	Misrata	November 2011
253	Misratan academic, politician	Misrata	April 2013
254	Misratan student and civil society activist	Misrata	April 2013
255	Misratan political activist	Misrata	April 2013
256	Manager in state-owned infrastructure company	Tripoli	April 2013
257	Group of Misratan political figures	Misrata	April 2013

No.	Interlocutor	Place	Date
258	Zintani academic and members of Zintan's Shura Council	Zintan	November 2012
259	Naluti commander of Dahiba-Wazin border crossing	Djerba	March 2015
260	Former leader in Benghazi revolutionary battalion	Istanbul	November 2017
261	Leader in Benghazi Defence Brigades	Istanbul	November 2017
262	Former leader in Libyan Islamic Fighting Group	Istanbul	November 2017
263	Ali Dabeiba: businessman from Misrata	Istanbul	November 2017
264	Former official in interior ministry in Tripoli	Istanbul	November 2017
265	Former leader in Libyan Islamic Fighting Group	Istanbul	November 2017
266	Commander in Misratan revolutionary battalion	Istanbul	November 2017
267	Awad al-Barassi: former deputy prime minister	Istanbul	November 2017
268	Mustafa Saqizli: former leader in Benghazi revolutionary battalions	Istanbul	November 2017
269	Senior official in Justice and Construction Party	Tripoli	March 2018
270	Tubu politician from Murzuq	Tripoli	March 2018
271	Tubu battalion leader	Tripoli	March 2018
272	Misratan politician	Misrata	March 2018
273	Commander in Misratan forces in Sirte	Misrata	March 2018
274	Misratan businessman	Misrata	March 2018
275	Misratan military officer	Misrata	March 2018
276	Misratan battalion leader	Misrata	March 2018
277	Leaders in Third Force and other Misratan battalions	Misrata	March 2018
278	Leaders in al-Marsa and other Misratan battalions	Misrata	March 2018
279	Battalion leaders from Sabratha	Misrata	March 2018
280	Member of Misrata local council	Misrata	March 2018
281	Young professional from Zawiya	Tripoli	March 2018
282	Misratan battalion commander	Tripoli	March 2018
283	Zintani battalion commander	Tripoli	March 2018
284	Former leader in Benghazi revolutionary battalions	Tripoli	March 2018
285	Former member of exiled opposition from Sabha	Tripoli	March 2018
286	Senior military officers	Tripoli	March 2018
287	Military officer from Bani Walid, member of 1993 coup plotters	Tripoli	March 2018
288	Civil society activists, mediators	Tripoli	March 2018
289	Military officer from Tobruk	Tripoli	March 2018
290	Misratan academic	Tripoli	April 2018

No.	Interlocutor	Place	Date
291	Former member of exiled opposition from Sabha	Tripoli	April 2018
292	Senior military officer	Tripoli	April 2018
293	Prominent businessman from Tripoli	Tripoli	April 2018
294	Misratan battalion commander	Tripoli	April 2018
295	Awlad Suleiman notable from Sabha	Tripoli	April 2018
296	Member of Bani Walid Social Council	Bani Walid	April 2018
297	Activist working for Bani Walid Social Council	Bani Walid	April 2018
298	Activist working for Bani Walid Social Council	Bani Walid	April 2018
299	Journalist from Bani Walid	Bani Walid	April 2018
300	Military officer from Bani Walid, member of 1993 coup plotters	Bani Walid	April 2018
301	Volunteer in Bani Walid security brigade	Bani Walid	April 2018
302	Misratan businessman	Misrata	April 2018
303	Fathi Bashagha: Misratan politician	Misrata	April 2018
304	Group of Misratan battalion leaders	Misrata	April 2018
305	Misratan battalion commander	Misrata	April 2018
306	Al-Siddiq Al-Kabir: governor of Central Bank	Tripoli	April 2018
307	Zintani battalion leader	Tripoli	April 2018
308	Military officer from Jadu	Tripoli	April 2018
309	Military officer from Zintan	Tunis	April 2018
310	Former member of Presidency Council	Tunis	April 2018
311	European diplomat	Tunis	July 2018
312	Mahmoud Jibril: founder of National Forces Alliance	Tunis	August 2018
313	Leader of Tubu armed group	Tunis	August 2018
314	Former leader in Libyan Islamic Fighting Group	Berlin	October 2018
315	Senior international official working on Libya	Berlin	October 2018
316	Tubu politician, former Nigerien rebel leader	Niamey	October 2018
317	Awlad Suleiman businessman, former member of exiled opposition	Agadez	October 2018
318	Zwayya businessman, Nigerien parliamentarian	Niamey	October 2018
319	Misratan businessman	Misrata	November 2018
320	Commander of Benghazi Defence Brigades	Misrata	November 2018
321	Leaders in Benghazi Defence Brigades	Al-Sdada	November 2018
322	Senior army officer	Misrata	November 2018
323	Group of Misratan battalion leaders	Misrata	November 2018
324	Ahmed Maitig: deputy president of Presidency Council	Misrata	November 2018
325	Misratan academic	Misrata	November 2018
326	Commander in Sirte security force	Misrata	November 2018

No.	Interlocutor	Place	Date
327	Member of displaced Benghazi family	Misrata	November 2018
328	Civil society activist	Tripoli	November 2018
329	Former member of exiled opposition from Sabha	Tripoli	November 2018
330	Tubu activist	Tripoli	November 2018
331	Zintani battalion leader	Tripoli	November 2018
332	Senior Muslim Brotherhood official	Tripoli	November 2018
333	Politician from notable Awlad Suleiman family	Tripoli	November 2018
334	Senior official in economic institution	Tripoli	November 2018
335	Security official, former commander in Tripoli Revolutionaries Battalion	Tripoli	November 2018
336	Commander in National Mobile Force	Tripoli	November 2018
337	Members of Zawiya municipal council	Zawiya	November 2018
338	Zawiya parliamentarian, former leader of armed group	Zawiya	November 2018
339	Leaders in Zawiya armed groups	Zawiya	November 2018
340	Leader in armed groups from Sabratha	Zawiya	November 2018
341	Young professional from Zawiya	Zawiya	November 2018
342	Sabratha politician	Tripoli	November 2018
343	Political adviser to leader in Tripoli armed group	Tripoli	November 2018
344	Politician, battalion leader from Nalut, former commander in Tripoli Revolutionaries Battalion	Tripoli	November 2018
345	Zintani academic	Zintan	November 2018
346	Nalut elders	Nalut	November 2018
347	Commander in Nalut armed groups	Nalut	November 2018
348	Nalut military officer	Nalut	November 2018
349	Member of Nalut municipal council	Nalut	November 2018
350	European diplomat	Tunis	November 2018
351	Ambassador of European state	Tunis	November 2018
352	Diplomat of Middle Eastern state	Tunis	November 2018
353	Misratan military officer	Tunis	January 2019
354	Misratan academic	Misrata	February 2019
355	Misratan businessman	Misrata	February 2019
356	Group of Misratan battalion leaders	Misrata	February 2019
357	Military officers from Zintan and Rujban	Misrata	February 2019
358	Misratan military officer	Misrata	February 2019
359	Liaison between military command and armed groups in Misrata	Misrata	February 2019
360	Local mediator between Tripoli armed groups	Tripoli	February 2019

No.	Interlocutor	Place	Date
361	Tuareg activist	Tripoli	February 2019
362	Tubu politician	Tripoli	February 2019
363	Former member of exiled opposition from Sabha	Tripoli	February 2019
364	Zintani battalion leader	Tripoli	February 2019
365	Civil society activist	Tripoli	February 2019
366	Senior official at economic institution	Tripoli	February 2019
367	Young professional from Tarhuna	Tripoli	February 2019
368	Political adviser to leader in Tripoli armed group	Tripoli	February 2019
369	Senior technocrat under former regime	Tripoli	February 2019
370	Former leader of Benghazi armed group	Tripoli	February 2019
371	Tubu notable	Tripoli	February 2019
372	Ahmed Maitig: deputy president of Presidency Council	Tripoli	February 2019
373	Security official, former commander in Tripoli Revolutionaries Battalion	Tripoli	February 2019
374	Young professional from Ubari	Tripoli	February 2019
375	Tripoli businessman, former commander of armed group	Tripoli	February 2019
376	Judge from Bani Walid	Tripoli	February 2019
377	Misratan battalion commander	Misrata	February 2019
378	Military officer from Jadu	Tunis	February 2019
379	Aide to General Prosecutor	Tunis	February 2019
380	Ambassador of European state	Tunis	February 2019
381	European diplomat	Tunis	February 2019
382	European diplomat	Tunis	February 2019
383	Politician from Ubari	Tunis	February 2019
384	Senior economic official in Bayda-based government	By telephone	February 2019
385	US diplomats	Tunis	March 2019
386	European diplomats	Tunis	March 2019
387	Diplomat of Middle Eastern state	Tunis	March 2019
388	Official from Benghazi	Tunis	March 2019
389	French diplomats	Paris	March 2019
390	Former leading GNC member and former senior security official in Zeidan government	Berlin	March 2019
391	Senior US military official	Berlin	March 2019
392	German diplomats	Berlin	April 2019
393	Zintani commander	By telephone	April 2019
394	Misratan politician	By telephone	April 2019

No.	Interlocutor	Place	Date
395	Commander from Tajura	Berlin	April 2019
396	Misratan academic	By telephone	April 2019
397	Misratan academic, civil society activist	By telephone	May 2019
398	Civil society activist from Tripoli	By telephone	May 2019
399	Zintani commander	By telephone	May 2019
400	Misratan commander	By telephone	May 2019
401	Local mediator between Tripoli armed groups	By telephone	May 2019
402	Senior French diplomat	Berlin	May 2019
403	Senior Libyan politician, former intermediary between Serraj and Haftar	Berlin	May 2019

Bibliography

Abdul-Ahad, Ghaith (2011): Libya's Berbers Join the Revolution in Fight to Reclaim Ancient Identity. *The Guardian*, 28 March 2011. Available online at https://www.the guardian.com/world/2011/feb/28/libya-amazigh-identity-tribes-gaddafi, checked on 2 May 2017.

Abdul-Wahab, Ashraf (2014): Mismari dismissed as head of Air Force. *Libya Herald*, 21 March 2014. Available online at https://www.libyaherald.com/2014/03/21/mismari-dismissed-as-head-of-airforce/, checked on 5 September 2017.

Acemoglu, Daron and Robinson, James (2012): *Why Nations Fail: The Origins of Power, Prosperity and Poverty*. New York: Crown.

AFP (2014): Libya Islamist Militias 'Seize Tripoli Airport'. *The Telegraph*, 23 August 2014. Available online at http://www.telegraph.co.uk/news/worldnews/africaandindianoce an/libya/11053501/Libya-Islamist-militias-seize-Tripoli-airport.html, checked on 29 June 2017.

Afrigatenews (2014): الشيخ السلفي أشرف الميار ينضم الى كتيبة الصاعقة. *Afrigatenews*, 25 July 2014. Available online at http://www.afrigatenews.net/content/الشيخ-السلفي-أشرف-الميار-ينض م-الى-كتيبة-الصاعقة, checked on 12 September 2017.

Afrigatenews (2015): مادي يحمّل تنتوش مسؤولية اشتباكات العجيلات. *Afrigatenews*, 25 October 2015. Available online at http://www.afrigatenews.net/content/مادي-يحمّل-تنتوش-مسؤولي ة-اشتباكات-العجيلات, checked on 28 August 2017.

Afrigatenews (2016a): الغويل يشكل غرفة عمليات عسكرية لتحرير سرت. *Afrigatenews*, 8 May 2016. Available online at http://www.afrigatenews.net/content/الغويل-يشكل-غرفة-عمليات-عسكر ية-لتحرير-سرت, checked on 25 July 2017.

Afrigatenews (2016b): قبيلة العواقير تشكل لجنة لحل الاشكال بين البرغثي وحفتر. *Afrigatenews*, 15 June 2016. Available online at http://www.afrigatenews.net/content/قبيلة-العواقير-تشكل-لجن ة-لحل-الاشكال-بين-البرغثي-وحفتر, checked on 12 September 2017.

Afrigatenews (2016c): الافراج عن سجناء محتجزين بسجن الكلية الجوية بمصراتة | بوابة أفريقيا الإخبارية. *Afrigatenews*, 8 December 2016. Available online at http://www.afrigatenews.net/co ntent/الافراج-عن-سجناء-محتجزين-بسجن-الكلية-الجوية-بمصراتة, checked on 1 September 2017.

Afrigatenews (2017): سرية حماية بني وليد تعلن عودتها للعمل داخل المدينة. *Afrigatenews*, 28 January 2017. Available online at http://www.afrigatenews.net/content/سرية-حماية-بني-وليد-تعل ن-عودتها-للعمل-داخل-المدينة, checked on 25 July 2017.

Ahmida, Ali Abdullatif (2009): *The Making of Modern Libya. State Formation, Colonization, and Resistance*. 2nd ed. Albany: SUNY Press.

Ahram, Ariel and King, Charles (2012): The Warlord as Arbitrageur. *Theory and Society* 41 (2), pp. 169–86.

Ain Libya (2013): درع طبرق يحل تشكيلاته ويسلم أسلحته لقاعدة طبرق - عين ليبيا | آخر أخبار ليبيا. *eanlibya. com*, 15 March 2013. Available online at http://www.eanlibya.com/archives/19602, checked on 25 July 2017.

Ain Libya (2015a): إقالة "فرج البرعصي" يشعل الصراع داخل قبيلة البراعصة. *eanlibya.com*, 6 February 2015. Available online at http://www.eanlibya.com/archives/29765, checked on 12 September 2017.

Ain Libya (2015b): الجضران يتهم حفتر بمحاولة قصف رتل تابع له. *eanlibya.com*, 10 September 2015. Available online at http://www.eanlibya.com/archives/40038, checked on 12 September 2017.

Ain Libya (2015c): أبو غفَير : الأمن الداخلي ينتقم من بنغازي باسم الكرامة. *eanlibya.com*, 17 September 2015. Available online at http://www.eanlibya.com/archives/40264, checked on 12 September 2017.

Ain Libya (2016): إتفاق بين أعيان العبيدات ومصراته على وقف "إطلاق النار" في بنغازي ودرنه. *eanlibya.com*, 20 August 2016. Available online at http://www.eanlibya.com/archives/92215, checked on 12 September 2017.

Al-Ahmad, Shaher (2014): دماء البيضاء أشعلت الثورة الليبية. الجزيرة, 27 March 2014. Available online at http://www.aljazeera.net/news/reportsandinterviews/2014/2/26/دماء-الب يضاء-أشعلت-الثورة-الليبية, checked on 23 March 2017.

Al-Amin, Hassan (2013a): Televised interview. Libya li-Kull al-Ahrar, 5 March 2013. Available online at https://www.youtube.com/watch?v=VbCw6TucR9s, checked on 21 June 2017.

Al-Amin, Hassan (2013b): Discussion disseminated via social media, 12 March 2013. Palltalk conversation: Youtube. Available online at https://www.youtube.com/watch?v=ZHIBn4ortjY, checked on 21 June 2017.

Al-Aneizi, Ahmed (2014): انفجار سيارة مفخخة على الجسر الرابط بين مفترق تاغمة ومنطقة بئر الغنم. *Al-Wasat*, 10 October 2014. Available online at http://alwasat.ly/ar/news/libya/41057/, checked on 28 June 2017.

Al-Arabiya (2014): القبائل الليبية ترحب بإطلاق الزنتان للسجناء. العربية, 28 July 2014. Available online at http://www.alarabiya.net/ar/north-africa/libya/2014/07/28/القبائل-الليبية-ترحب-بإطلا ق-الزنتان-للسجناء.html, checked on 23 March 2017.

Al-Asbali, Ali (2017): سجن قرنادة. الداخل مفقود والخارج مولود. Available online at http://tripoli4 libya.blogspot.de/2017/02/blog-post_841.html, updated on 12 September 2017, checked on 12 September 2017.

Al-Asema TV (2013): Coverage of meeting of tribal representatives of al-Batnan province. Al-Asema TV, 10 December 2013. Available online at https://www.youtube.com/w atch?v=fxW5S7N5kOE, checked on 5 September 2017.

Al-Aswad, al-Habib (2014): رئيس مجلس القبائل الليبية لــ بوابة أفريقيا : سقوط ورشفانة يعني سيطرة التكفيريين على ليبيا. *Afrigatenews*, 21 September 2014. Available online at http://www.afri gatenews.net/content/رئيس-مجلس-القبائل-الليبية-لــ-«بوابة-أفريقيا-»-سقوط-ورشفانة-يعن ي-سيطرة-التكفيريين-على-ليبيا, checked on 29 June 2017.

Al-Atrush, Samer, Jacobs, Jennifer and Talev, Margaret (2019): Trump Backed Libyan Strongman's Attack on Tripoli, U.S. Officials Say. *Bloomberg*, 24 April 2019, checked on 14 May 2019.

Al-Awaqir (2016): Meeting of Awaqir elders from greater Benghazi, 14 May 2016. youtube. Available online at https://www.youtube.com/watch?v=zzozZf-ku74, checked on 12 September 2017.

Al-Azzabi, Massoud (2011): معارك نالوت نموذجاً. معارك ثوار 17 فبراير. Benghazi: دار و مكتبة الفضيل للنشر و التوزيع.

Al-Bayan (2014): القبائل الليبية تتجه إلى دعم لمعركة الكرامة. *Al-Bayan*, 27 July 2014. Available online at http://www.albayan.ae/one-world/arabs/2014-07-27-1.2172150.

Al-Bayan (2016): الجيش الليبي يبدأ معركة سرت الكبرى. *Al-Bayan*, 5 May 2016. Available online at http://www.albayan.ae/one-world/arabs/2016-05-05-1.2633071, checked on 25 July 2017.

Al-Dharrat, Mohamed Ibrahim (2015): Post on personal Facebook page, 2/6/2015. Available online at https://www.facebook.com/mohamed.da/posts/1020523806552 4035, checked on 21 August 2017.

Al-Fassi, Ayad (2015): Video statement disseminated via social media. youtube. Available online at https://www.youtube.com/watch?v=LRx_lMxH9QI, checked on 12 September 2017.

Al-Fassi, Sherifa (2011): حقائق وشهادات على أحداث ثورة فبراير بمدينة الشرارة الأولى بنغازي. *Al-Watan al-Libya*, 27 November 2011. Available online at http://www.alwatanlibya.com/more-18266-1-حقائق وشهادات على أحداث ثورة فبراير بمدينة الشرارة الأولى بنغازي, checked on 23 March 2017.

Al-Gharyani, Nirjis (2013a): سقوط قتيلين وأربعة جرحى في اشتباكات منطقة صلاح الدين. *Solidarity News Agency*, 25 June 2013. Available online at http://www.presssolidarity.net/news/ONENEWS/2271-أو جرحـ_ةعبرأو_يف_تاكابتش_ةقطنم_حلاص_طوقسنيدلا_نيليتـق/, checked on 23 March 2017.

Al-Gharyani, Nirjis (2013b): نجاة رئيس مجلس بني وليد المحلي من مُحاولة اغتيال و إصابة سائقه بجروح بليغة. *Solidarity News Agency*, 19 September 2013. Available online at http://www.presssolidarity.net/news/ONENEWS/23232-اغ_ةلواحُم_نم_يلحملا_ديلو_ينب_سلجم_سيئر_ةاجن بليغ_حورجب_هقئاس_ةباصإ_و_لايت.html.

Al-Haddad, al-Saghir (2016): إطلاق سراح 46 سجينًا من بني وليد كانوا بسجون مصراتة. *Al-Wasat*, 16 November 2016. Available online at http://alwasat.ly/ar/news/libya/124668/, checked on 1 September 2017.

Al-Jabbu, Salah (2015a): Letter to Misrata Local Council. Misrata, 11 February 2015.

Al-Jabbu, Salah (2015b): Statement on personal Facebook page, 26 February 2015. Misrata. Available online at https://www.facebook.com/permalink.php?story_fbid=938040589562150&id=100000686524039, checked on 21 August 2017.

Al-Jadhran, Ibrahim (2016): Video statement, disseminated via social media, 17 July 2016. youtube. Available online at https://www.youtube.com/watch?v=MrJBidd2Ed8, checked on 12 September 2017.

Al-Jared, Usama (2014): الجضران يستنكر تصريحات الجروشي. *Al-Wasat*, 28 December 2014. Available online at http://www.alwasat.ly/ar/news/libya/54084, checked on 12 September 2017.

Al-Jared, Usama (2016a): الناشط الخطابية يتهم جهات أمنية وعسكرية بخطفه وتعذيبه. *Al-Wasat*, 19 March 2016. Available online at http://www.alwasat.ly/ar/news/libya/99768, checked on 12 September 2017.

Al-Jared, Usama (2016b): اختطاف ناشط إعلامي في المرج. *Al-Wasat*, 28 March 2016. Available online at http://alwasat.ly/ar/news/libya/100803/, checked on 12 September 2017.

Al-Jared, Usama (2016c): خطف ثلاثة عسكريين قرب بلدة القبة. *Al-Wasat*, 13 March 2016. Available online at http://alwasat.ly/ar/news/libya/102561/, checked on 12 September 2017.

Al-Khalidi, Suleiman (1 September 2013): Analysis - Libya protests threaten stability as oil output dives. Reuters. Available online at http://in.reuters.com/article/libya-oil-stability-idINL6N0GV1YG20130901, checked on 22 March 2017.

Al-Lawati, Brik (2016): Speech at meeting of Supreme Council of Awaqir Tribe, Benghazi, 14 June 2016. youtube. Available online at https://www.youtube.com/watch?v=1rCJ_PwipnA, checked on 12 September 2017.

Al-Magharba (2016): Statement by Magharba elders, al-Zuwaitina, 15 August 2016. youtube. Available online at https://www.youtube.com/watch?v=xPUAlqS3Y40, checked on 12 September 2017.

Al-Mahjub Brigade (9 January 2016): بيان لواء كتائب شهداء زاوية المحجوب التابع للمجلس العسكري. Misrata. مصراتة.

Al-Maqariaf, Mohamed Youssef (2008): ليبيا من الشرعية الدستورية إلى الشرعية الثورية. دراسة توثيقية. Cairo: Dar al-Istiqlal. و تحليلية.

al-Mogherbi, Mohammed Zahi (n.d.): اتجاهات وتطورات تركيبة النخبة السياسية. Available online at http://www.zahi.iwarp.com/guvermental_elites_in_libya.htm, updated on 08.11.2003, checked on 2 May 2017.

Al-Moheir, Khaled (2014): الجزيرة. قبائل ليبية تبايع حفتر ومصراتة ترفضه, 11 March 2014. Available online at http://www.aljazeera.net/news/reportsandinterviews/2014/3/11/قبا ئل-ليبية-تبايع-حفتر-ومصراتة-ترفضه, checked on 5 September 2017.

Al-Motawaset (2017): أنباء عن القبض على اقعيم واقتياده إلى المرج. *Al-Motawaset*, 16 November 2017, http://almotawaset.com/2017/11/16/إل-أنباء-عن-القبض-على-اقعيم-واقتياده/.

al-Nabaa TV (2014): Interview with Deputy Defence Minister Khaled al-Sharif. al-Nabaa TV, 25 August 2014. Available online at https://www.youtube.com/watch?v=FJvZz7_X IwU.

al-Nabaa TV (2017): أعيان طبرق يستنكرون قرار توقيف عميد بلديتهم. *al-Nabaa TV*, 23 November 2017. Available online at https://alnabaa.tv/news/view/15948, checked on 4 July 2018.

Al-Nas (2015): مؤتمر أبو سهمين يعاقب مصراتة بتشكيل مجلس مطعم بشخصيات جدلية و بعض الأموات. *Al-Nas*, 12 May 2015.

Al-Nayed, Aref Ali (2011): Televised interview. Sky News, 22 February 2011.

Al-Obeidat (2014): Statement of Obeidat elders disseminated via social media, Tobruk, 20 May 2014. youtube. Available online at https://www.youtube.com/watch?v=rYWKLa3f 4zY, checked on 12 September 2017.

Al-Obeidat (2016): Declaration by members of the Obeidat, al-Qubba, 21 August 2016. youtube. Available online at https://www.youtube.com/watch?v=MXBo2qwnFio, checked on 12 September 2017.

Al-Obeidi, Salem (2014a): منسق الأمن بمطار بنينا: تسليم الموقوفين العرب لرئاسة الأركان. *Al-Wasat*, 23 February 2014. Available online at http://alwasat.ly/ar/news/libya/5655, checked on 12 September 2017.

Al-Obeidi, Salem (2014b): قاعدة طبرق تعلن الانضمام لقوات حفتر. *Al-Wasat*, 19 May 2014. Available online at http://alwasat.ly/ar/news/libya/18749/, checked on 12 September 2017.

Al-Obeidi, Salem (2014c): بوابة الوسط تنفرد بنشر إحصائيّة أحداث السبت الأسود. *Al-Wasat*, 11 June 2014. Available online at http://www.alwasat.ly/ar/news/libya/22207, checked on 12 September 2017.

Al-Obeidi, Salem (2014d): بو عميد: لجنة مشتركة لتأمين الطريق بعد هدم أسوار الـ27. *Al-Wasat*, 10 August 2014. Available online at http://alwasat.ly/ar/news/libya/30575/, checked on 29 June 2017.

Al-Obeidi, Salem (2015): البرعصي لـبوابة الوسط: نقص الذخيرة سبب تأخر تقدُّم الجيش. *Al-Wasat*, 19 February 2015. Available online at http://alwasat.ly/ar/news/libya/62068/, checked on 12 September 2017.

Al-Obeidi, Salem (2016): إطلاق 20 محتجزًا من سجن الكلية الجوية بمصراتة. *Al-Wasat*, 4 May 2016. Available online at http://alwasat.ly/ar/news/libya/104658/, checked on 1 September 2017.

Al-Rasmiya TV (2016): Coverage of meeting between Haftar and tribal leaders and mayors of Cyrenaica, Al-Marj, 24 January 2016. youtube. Available online at https:// www.youtube.com/watch?v=yDzWXrQoPmE, checked on 12 September 2017.

Alrseefa (2013): الرصيفة الأخبارية. أسماء بعض الضباط الذين تمت إحالتهم على التقاعد الاجباري, 30 October 2013. Available online at http://www.alrseefa.net/archives/5476, checked on 5 September 2017.

Alrseefa (2014a): الرصيفة الأخبارية. تفاصيل اغتيال الشيخ عبد الله نافع اسطيل بمدينة بني وليد, 24 February 2014. Available online at http://www.alrseefa.net/archives/9432, checked on 25 July 2017.

Alrseefa (2014b): كان أقل قسوة من فجر ليبيا والقذافي حفتر. مع نتحالف لم الجويلي أسامة. الأخبارية الرصيفة, 1 October 2014. Available online at http://www.alrseefa.net/archives/16935, checked on 27 June 2017.

Al-Ruaf, Abd al-Aziz (2013): وكالة - تونس في علاج رحلة بعد طبرق الحدود حرس 71 الكتيبة آمر عودة. *Solidarity News Agency*, 21 October 2013. Available online at http://www.presssolidarity.net/news/ONENEWS/30119-عودة_آمر_الكتيبة_71_حرس_الحدود_طبرق_بعد_رحلة_علاج_في_تونس/, checked on 25 July 2017.

Al-Ruaf, Abd al-Aziz (2014a): التطرف انتشار من يحذرون الجوية طبرق قاعدة منتسبو. *Al-Wasat*, 3 March 2014. Available online at http://www.alwasat.ly/ar/news/libya/6940/, checked on 5 September 2017.

Al-Ruaf, Abd al-Aziz (2014b): زملاؤنا اليوم حفتر مقاتلو طبرق: لمتظاهري الرفادي. *Al-Wasat*, 17 May 2014. Available online at http://alwasat.ly/ar/news/libya/18281/, checked on 12 September 2017.

Al-Ruaf, Abd al-Aziz (2014c): ليبيا كرامة لعملية ينضم بطبرق الحدود حرس. *Al-Wasat*, 19 May 2014. Available online at http://www.alwasat.ly/ar/news/libya/18815, checked on 12 September 2017.

Al-Ruaf, Abd al-Aziz (2014d): «الكرامة عملية» وتدعم الجيش تفوض طبرق». *Al-Wasat*, 23 May 2014. Available online at http://alwasat.ly/ar/news/libya/19403/, checked on 12 September 2017.

Al-Ruaf, Abd al-Aziz (2014e): يستقيل الاجتماعي والمجلس المصالحة يرفضون وليد بني من مسلحون. *Al-Wasat*, 20 June 2014. Available online at http://alwasat.ly/ar/news/libya/23624/, checked on 25 July 2017.

Al-Rummah, Ali Ahmad Ahmad (2013): فبراير ثورة على أوضاع. الجزاء الزنتان في الثورة أرشيف من Zintan. الثاني.

Al-Safi, Al-Tayyeb (2016): Speech in Belkhather near Tobruk, 16 April 2016. youtube. Available online at https://www.youtube.com/watch?v=GHk3Rzg6d10, checked on 12 September 2017.

Al-Sallahi, Mahmoud (2016): سرت تحرير المكلفة الأمنية الغرفة عضوية عن يعتذر جحا سالم. *Al-Wasat*, 11 May 2016. Available online at http://alwasat.ly/ar/news/libya/105411/, checked on 25 July 2017.

Al-Satur (2011): المطبق والصمت الكوارث بين طبرق. Available online at https://alsature.wordpress.com/2011/01/05/طبرق-بين-الكوارث-والصمت-المطبق/, checked on 12 September 2017.

al-Shalwi, Abd al-Fattah (2015): البرلمان قبة تحت أسرار. العام الوطني بالمؤتمر يوم سبعمنة Benghazi: الوطنية الكتب دار.

Al-Sharif, Al-Tayyeb (2012): Speech at Meeting of Cyrenaica Unionist Council. youtube. Available online at https://www.youtube.com/watch?v=pLkniy_WxUk, checked on 5 September 2017.

Al-Shikhi, Belaid (2016): Speech of at meeting of tribal elders in Benghazi, 28 August 2016. youtube. Available online at https://www.youtube.com/watch?v=_2MdQhsJ3vM, checked on 12 September 2017.

Al-Shikhi, Belaid (2017): Speech in front of members of the Fadhil Bu Omar Brigade, Benghazi, March 2017. youtube. Available online at https://www.youtube.com/watch?v=wlZvn_dAxGA, checked on 12 September 2017.

Al-Shuhubi, Jalal (2013): خلال شرعي غير مهاجر 100 من أكثر على القبض تلقي الحدود حرس 71 الكتيبة أسبوع. *Solidarity News Agency*, 28 August 2013. Available online at http://www.presssolidarity.net/news/ONENEWS/17986-الكتيبة_17_حرس_الحدود_تلقي_القبض_على_أكثر_من-100__مهاجر_غير_شرعي_خلال_أسبوع/, checked on 25 July 2017.

Al-Shuhubi, Jalal (2014): قزيط : قانون العزل السياسي سببَ التوتر التي تعيشه البلاد ويمكن طرحه والتعديل. فيه لأنه غير مقدس. *Solidarity News Agency*, 5 February 2014. Available online at http://www.presssolidarity.net/news/ONENEWS/48553-قزيط:_قانون_العزل_السياسي_سببَ-ال/توتر_التي_تعيشه_البلاد_ويمكن_طرحه_والتعديل_فيه_لأنه_غير_مقدس, checked on 23 March 2017.

Al-Sweihli, Abderrahman (2011): Televised interview. Al-Jazeera, 19 February 2011. Available online at http://www.dailymotion.com/video/xh3lsq, checked on 5 May 2017.

Al-Tarifi, Adel (2013): المستشار مصطفى عبد الجليل: لم أكن يومأ ضمن منظومة القذافي. وكنا مستعدين لقبول المصالحة. *Al-Sharq al-Awsat*, 21 October 2013. Available online at http://aawsat.com/home/article/6796, checked on 23 March 2017.

Al-Tommy, Mohammad (21 January 2012): Protesters Storm Libyan Government HQ in Benghazi. Reuters. Available online at http://www.reuters.com/article/us-libya-ntc-b enghazi-idUSTRE80K0OC20120122, checked on 22 March 2017.

Al-Warfalli, Ayman (25 January 2016): Libya's Recognized Parliament Rejects U.N.-Backed Unity Government. Reuters. Available online at http://www.reuters.com/article/us-libya-security-politics-idUSKCN0V31Q0, checked on 24 August 2017.

Al-Warfalli, Ayman (24 March 2016): Libya Military Makes Further Gains in Benghazi. Reuters. Available online at http://www.reuters.com/article/us-libya-security-bengha zi-idUSKCN0VW2N7, checked on 22 March 2017.

Al-Warfalli, Ayman (21 June 2016): Rival Libyan Forces Clash in Strategic Eastern Town. Reuters. Available online at http://www.reuters.com/article/us-libya-security-east-i dUSKCN0Z7285, checked on 3 May 2017.

Al-Warfalli, Ayman and Ghaddar, Ahmad (14 June 2018): Attack Shuts Major Libyan Oil Ports, Slashing Production. Reuters. Available online at https://www.reuters.com/articl e/us-libya-security-oil/attack-shuts-major-libyan-oil-ports-slashing-production-idUSKBN1JA23I, checked on 19 June 2018.

Al-Wasat (2014a): تحالف القوى الوطنية يعلن تأييده كرامة ليبيا. *Al-Wasat*, 21 May 2014. Available online at http://alwasat.ly/ar/news/libya/19031/, checked on 27 March 2017.

Al-Wasat (2014b): علماء سعوديون يدعون لدعم الجيش الليبي. *Al-Wasat*, 21 May 2014. Available online at http://alwasat.ly/ar/news/libya/19158/, checked on 12 September 2017.

Al-Wasat (2014c): صوان لـد ب أ: أكثر من ثلثي الشعب أيدوا فجر ليبيا. *Al-Wasat*, 25 August 2014. Available online at http://www.alwasat.ly/public/ar/news/libya/33165/, checked on 27 March 2017.

Al-Wasat (2014d): سليم: بني وليد استقبلت 3825 أسرة نازحة. *Al-Wasat*, 24 September 2014. Available online at http://alwasat.ly/ar/news/libya/38777/, checked on 25 July 2017.

Al-Wasat (2015): النبي يكشف تفاصيل جديدة حول حادث إطلاق الرصاص عليه في طبرق. *Al-Wasat*, 31 May 2015. Available online at http://alwasat.ly/ar/news/libya/76928/, checked on 12 September 2017.

Al-Wasat (2016): زياد بلعم: قواتنا محاصرة في الجفرة. *Al-Wasat*, 9 May 2016. Available online at http://alwasat.ly/ar/news/libya/105130/, checked on 25 July 2017.

Al-Wasat (2017a): مقتل أحد شيوخ قبيلة العواقير ابريك اللواطي في تفجير سيارة مفخخة بسلوق. *Al-Wasat*, 19 May 2017. Available online at http://alwasat.ly/ar/news/libya/142310/, checked on 12 September 2017.

Al-Wasat (2017b): الرئاسي يعين أسامة جويلي آمرًا للمنطقة العسكرية الغربية. *Al-Wasat*, 4 June 2017. Available online at http://alwasat.ly/ar/news/libya/143803/, checked on 28 August 2017.

Al-Wasat (2017c): العتيري يعلق على قرار حل كتيبة أبوبكر الصديق. *Al-Wasat*, 12 June 2017. Available online at http://alwasat.ly/ar/news/libya/144604/, checked on 28 August 2017.

Al-Watan al-Libya (2013): وزارة الداخلية تكشف تفاصيل اقتحامها والهجوم عليها. *Al-Watan al-Libya*, 4 July 2013. Available online at http://www.alwatan-libya.net/more.php?newsid=28419 &catid=1, checked on 27 March 2017.

Al-Zawawi, Khalifa (2014): Televised interview. al-Nabaa TV, 12 February 2014. Available online at https://www.youtube.com/watch?v=DV124tjZYVs.

Al-Zintan (20 March 2019): *Protocol of Agreement by Zintani Elders on al-Wutiya Air Base.* Zintan.

Al-Zukra, Saleh (2009): موت الضمير وضياع المدينة ومافيا طيب الشريف. Available online at http://www.libya-watanona.com/letters/v2009a/v31dec9c.htm, updated on 25 September 2015, checked on 12September 2017.

Amazigh Supreme Council Libya (7 April 2019): Statement of Amazigh Supreme Council Libya. Available online at https://www.facebook.com/AmazighSC/photos/a.165504 5648116074/2414539322166699/?type=3&theater.

Amselle, Jean-Loup (1985): Éthnies et Espaces: Pour une Anthropologie Topologique. In Jean-Loup Amselle and Elikia M'Bokolo (Eds.): *Au Coeur de l'Éthnie. Éthnies, Tribalisme et État en Afrique.* Paris: La Découverte, pp. 11–48.

Anderson, Lisa (1986): *The State and Social Transformation in Tunisia and Libya,* 1930–1980. Princeton: Princeton University Press.

Anderson, Lisa (1990): Tribe and State: Libyan Anomalies. In Philip S. Khoury and Joseph Kostiner (Eds.): *Tribes and State Formation in the Middle East.* Berkeley: University of California Press, pp. 288–302.

Arjona, Ana (2016): *Rebelocracy.* Cambridge: Cambridge University Press.

Armed Forces General Command (2016a): Declaration of Support by Supreme Council of Awaqir Tribe, 6 June 2016. youtube. Available online at https://www.youtube.com/w atch?v=a6R3pwnGkSg, checked on 12 September 2017.

Armed Forces General Command (2016b): Meeting of Khalifa Haftar with elders of greater Benghazi, 22 June 2016. youtube. Available online at https://www.youtube. com/watch?v=Ib9287hKRxY, checked on 12 September 2017.

Armed Forces General Command (2017a): Statement of support for Haftar by Obeidat elders, 2 April 2017. youtube. Available online at https://www.youtube.com/watch? v=k8nGf_q8dNI, checked on 12 September 2017.

Armed Forces General Command (2017b): Coverage of Haftar's meeting with representatives of Libya's tribes, 22 June 2017. youtube. Available online at https://ww w.youtube.com/watch?v=MRV-BE5t820, checked on 12 September 2017.

Baczko, Adam; Dorronsoro, Gilles (2017): Pour une Approche Sociologique des Guerres Civiles. *Revue Française de Science Politique* 67 (2), pp. 309–27.

Baczko, Adam; Dorronsoro, Gilles; Quesnay, Arthur (2013): Mobilisations par Délibération et Crise Polarisante. Les Protestations Pacifiques en Syrie (2011). *Revue Française de Science Politique* 63 (5), pp. 815–39.

Baczko, Adam; Dorronsoro, Gilles; Quesnay, Arthur (2016): Le Capital Social Révolutionnaire. L'Exemple de la Syrie entre 2011 et 2014. *Actes de la recherche en sciences sociales* 211 (1), pp. 24–35.

Badi, Emad (2019a): Mergers and Assassinations as Tripoli Remains under Militia Control. Middle East Institute. Available online at https://www.mei.edu/publications/ mergers-and-assassinations-tripoli-remains-under-militia-control, checked on 8 May 2019.

Badi, Emad (2019b): General Hifter's Southern Strategy and the Repercussions of the Fezzan Campaign. Middle East Institute. Available online at https://www.mei.edu/

publications/general-hifters-southern-strategy-and-repercussions-fezzan-campaign, checked on 13 May 2019.

Badi, Salah (2015): Statement distributed via Facebook, 10 February 2015. Available online at https://www.facebook.com/WeAreSalahBady/photos/a.772719872754622. 1073741825.508336262526319/1050604904966116/?type=3&theater, checked on 21 August 2017.

Baghni, 'Amru Sa'id (2015): حرب الجبل و الساحل. الفتنة و محاولات الاصلاح في القطاع الغربي من ليبيا مؤسسة تاوالت الثقافية :no location. 1921 - 1919.

Bakke, Kristin M., Cunningham, Kathleen Gallagher and Seymour, Lee J. M. (2012): A Plague of Initials. Fragmentation, Cohesion, and Infighting in Civil Wars. *Perspectives on Politics* 10 (2), pp. 265–83.

Bakonyi, Jutta (2009): Moral Economies of Mass Violence. Somalia 1988–1991. *Civil Wars* 11 (4), pp. 434–54.

Bakonyi, Jutta and Stuvøy, Kirsti (2005): Violence and Social Order Beyond the State. Somalia and Angola. *Review of African Political Economy* 32 (104–5), pp. 359–82.

Baldinetti, Anna (2010): *The Origins of the Libyan Nation: Colonial Legacy, Exile, and the Emergence of a New Nation-State*. London: Routledge.

Barakat, Mustafa (2013): قائد عسكري بالجيش للتقاعد بتوصيات قطرية 400 ليبيا تحيل بالمستندات. *Veto*, 20 October 2013. Available online at http://www.vetogate.com/646297, checked on 5 September 2017.

Barkey, Karen and van Rossem, Ronan (1997): Networks of Contention. Villages and Regional Structure in the Seventeenth-Century Ottoman Empire. *American Journal of Sociology* 102 (5), pp. 1345–82.

Barqa Council of Elders (2014): بيان مجلس الشيوخ والسياسي لأقليم برقة. youtube. Available online at https://www.youtube.com/watch?v=Okc59tRv5SM, checked on 12 September 2017.

Barqa TV (2016): Report on the abduction and detention of Othman Faraj Bulkhatabiya, 25 March 2016. Available online at https://www.youtube.com/watch?v=mUTditjN08A, checked on 12 September 2017.

Barth, Fredrik (1959): Segmentary Opposition and the Theory of Games: A Study of Pathan Organization. *The Journal of the Royal Anthropologica Institute of Great Britain and Ireland* l89 (1), p. 5.

Bartu, Peter (2015): The Corridor of Uncertainty. The National Transitional Council's Battle for Legitimacy and Recognition. In Peter Cole and Brian McQuinn (Eds.): *The Libyan Revolution and Its Aftermath*. London: Hurst, pp. 31–55.

Bashagha, Fathi (2014): كلمة السيد فتحي باشاغا الى ناخبيه وكل أهالي مصراته حول الحوار الوطني. youtube. Available online at https://www.youtube.com/watch?v=eqRe593Kp64, checked on 20 July 2017.

BBC (2011): Libya's Interim Leaders Reject UN Military Personnel. *BBC*, 31 August 2011. Available online at http://www.bbc.com/news/world-africa-14726292, checked on 22 March 2017.

BBC (2014a): Libya Clashes between Rival Militias in Benghazi. *BBC*, 16 May 2014. Available online at http://www.bbc.com/news/world-africa-27448224.

BBC (2014b): Libya Militias Seize Benghazi Special Forces Base. *BBC*, 30 July 2014. Available online at http://www.bbc.com/news/world-africa-28557772.

BBC (2016): Guide to Key Libyan Militias. *BBC*, 11 January 2016. Available online at http://www.bbc.com/news/world-middle-east-19744533, checked on 25 July 2017.

BBC (2017): 'Deep Grief' over Libyan Mayor's Killing. BBC, 18 December 2017. Available online at https://www.bbc.com/news/world-africa-42395678, checked on 3 July 2018.

Bearman, Peter (1991): Desertion As Localism. Army Unit Solidarity and Group Norms in the U.S. Civil War. *Social Forces* 70 (2), pp. 321–42.

Bearman, Peter (1993): *Relations into Rhetorics. Local Elite Social Structure in Norfolk, England* 1540–1640. New Brunswick: Rutgers University Press.

Ben Ali, Fares (2017): عميد بلدية طبرق: من يتعامل مع حكومة الوفاق ليس خائنًا. *Al-Wasat*, 16 November 2017. Available online at http://alwasat.ly/news/libya/149640, checked on 4 July 2018.

Ben Ghashir, Ibrahim (2015): Letter demanding recipients to form a committee to secure the release of Hamdi al-Abbasi and Mohamed al-Huti from the security intelligence agency to Mayouf, Mustafa Omar et al. Misrata, 9 July 2015.

Ben Hamel, Abd al-Baset (2014): الزنتان تقف مع القبائل الليبية الشريفة ضد عصابات الخوارج و الارهابيين. *Afrigatenews*, 25 August 2014. Available online at http://www.afrigatenews.net/co ntent/الزنتان-تقف-مع-القبائل-الليبية-الشريفة-ضد-عصابات-الخوارج-والارهابيين.

Ben Hamel, Abd al-Baset (2015): آمر كتيبة أولياء الدم من لم يمت فى الجبهات مات بالمستشفيات. *Afrigatenews*, 14 April 2015. Available online at http://www.afrigatenews.net/content آمر-كتيبة-أولياء-الدم-من-لم-يمت-فى-الجبهات-مات-بالمستشفيات//, checked on 12 September 2017.

Ben Hamel, Abd al-Baset (2016a): الجيش يستعد لعملية "القرضابية 2" لتحرير سرت. *Afrigatenews*, 27 April 2016. Available online at http://www.afrigatenews.net/content/الجيش-يستعد-لعملية-القرضابية-2-لتحرير-سرت, checked on 25 July 2017.

Ben Hamel, Abd al-Baset (2016b): أسباب انسحاب أعيان مصراتة من مؤتمر نالوت للمصالحة. *Afrigatenews*, 17 September 2016. Available online at http://www.afrigatenews.net/co ntent/أسباب-انسحاب-أعيان-مصراتة-من-مؤتمر-نالوت-للمصالحة, checked on 28 August 2017.

Ben Hounet, Yazid (2010): La Tribu comme Champ Social Semi-Autonome. *L'Homme* 194, pp. 57–74.

Ben Said, Asma (2017): الرئاسي يكلف النقيب فرج قعيم بمهام وكيل وزارة الداخلية. *Al-Wasat*, 31 August 2017. Available online at http://alwasat.ly/ar/news/libya/151517/, checked on 24 October 2017.

Bennett, Andrew and Elman, Colin (2006): Complex Causal Relations and Case Study Methods. The Example of Path Dependence. *Political Analysis* 14 (03), pp. 250–67.

Benraad, Myriam (2009): Une Lecture de la Sahwa ou les Milles et un Visages du Tribalisme Irakien. *Etudes Rurales* (184), pp. 95–106.

Bensimon, Cyril, Bobin, Frédéric and Zerrouky, Madjid (2016): Trois Membres de la DGSE Tués en Libye, le Gouvernement Libyen Proteste. *Le Monde*, 20 July 2016. Available online at http://www.lemonde.fr/international/article/2016/07/20/trois-mili taires-francais-tues-en-libye_4972142_3210.html, checked on 22 March 2017.

Bergholz, Max (2016): *Violence as a Generative Force. Identity, Nationalism, and Memory in a Balkan Community*. Ithaca: Cornell University Press.

Besteman, Catherine (1999): *Unraveling Somalia. Race, Violence, and the Legacy of Slavery*. Philadelphia: University of Pennsylvania Press.

Bin Dhilla, Muhammad (2013): نالوت الجهاد من الأجداد إلى الأحفاد. Benghazi: دار الكتب الوطنية.

Binnie, Jeremy (2016): UAE's Forward Operating Base in Libya Revealed. *IHS Jane's Defence Weekly*. Available online at http://www.janes.com/article/64980/uae-s-forw ard-operating-base-in-libya-revealed, checked on 22 March 2017.

Bobin, Frédéric (2019): En Libye, la Ville de Zinten Fracturée entre Pro et Anti-Haftar. *Le Monde*, 4 May 2019. Available online at https://www.lemonde.fr/afrique/article/2019/0 5/04/en-libye-la-ville-de-zinten-fracturee-entre-pro-et-anti-haftar_5458216_3212. html, checked on 15 May 2019.

Boege, Volker, Brown, Anne, Clements, Kevin and Nolan, Anna (2009): On Hybrid Political Orders and Emerging States. What is Failing – States in the Global South or Research and Politics in the West? In Martina Fischer and Beatrix Schmelzle (Eds.): *Building Peace in the Absence of States. Challenging the Discourse on State Failure.* Berlin: Berghof.

Bonte, Pierre (2001): Tribus et Pouvoirs dans le Monde Arabe et ses Périphéries. *La Pensée* 325 (1), pp. 43–63.

Bonte, Pierre and Ben Hounet, Yazid (2009): Introduction. *Etudes Rurales* (184), pp. 13–32.

Boone, Catherine (2003): *Political Topographies of the African State: Territorial Authority and Institutional Choice.* Cambridge: Cambridge University Press.

Bosi, Lorenzo, Demetriou, Chares and Malthaner, Stefan (2014): A Contentious Politics Approach to the Explanation of Radicalization. In Lorenzo Bosi, Chares Demetriou and Stefan Malthaner (Eds.): *Dynamics of Political Violence. A Process-Oriented Perspective on Radicalization and the Escalation of Political Conflict.* Farnham: Ashgate Publishing, pp. 1–23.

Brandt, Marieke (2013): Sufyān's 'Hybrid' War. Tribal Politics during the Ḥūthī Conflict. *Journal of Arabian Studies* 3 (1), pp. 120–38.

Brandt, Marieke (2014): The Irregulars of the Sa'ada War. 'Colonel Sheikhs' and 'Tribal Militias' in Yemen's Huthi Conflict (2004–2010). In Helen Lackner (Ed.): *Why Yemen Matters. A Society in Transition.* London: Saqi Books, pp. 105–22.

Breidlid, Ingrid Marie and Arensen, Michael J. (2014): 'Anyone Who Can Carry a Gun Can Go'. The Role of the White Army in the Current Conflict in South Sudan. Prio Paper. Peace Research Institute Oslo (PRIO). Oslo. Available online at https://www.prio.org/utility/DownloadFile.ashx?id=358&type=publicationfile, checked on 18 September 2017.

Buatiwa, Faraj Yadam (2012): Comments on video disseminated via social media, 7 March 2012. youtube. Available online at https://www.youtube.com/watch?v=NPBeMgjSJlg, checked on 5 September 2017.

Bulghib, Khaled (2014): Video message disseminated via social media, October 2014. youtube. Available online at https://www.youtube.com/watch?v=yrAxhaS3Xys, checked on 25 July 2017.

Bulghib, Khaled (2015a): Speech in front of Benghazi commanders, disseminated via social media, April 2015. youtube. Available online at https://www.youtube.com/watch?v=PKfvt1XONTY, checked on 12 September 2017.

Bulghib, Khaled (2015b): Video message disseminated via social media, 27 May 2015. youtube. Available online at https://www.youtube.com/watch?v=5ZU0_dkqfRU, checked on 12 September 2017.

Capoccia, Giovanniand Kelemen, R. Daniel (2007): The Study of Critical Junctures. Theory, Narrative, and Counterfactuals in Historical Institutionalism. *World Politics* 59 (3), pp. 341–69.

The Carter Center (2012): General National Congress Elections in Libya. Final Report. Atlanta. Available online at https://www.cartercenter.org/resources/pdfs/news/peace_publications/election_reports/libya-070712-final-rpt.pdf, checked on 22 March 2017.

The Carter Center (2014): The 2014 Constitutional Drafting Assembly Elections in Libya. Final Report. Atlanta. Available online at https://www.cartercenter.org/resources/pdfs/news/peace_publications/election_reports/libya-06112014-final-rpt.pdf, checked on 22 March 2017.

Caryl, Christian (2013): Islands in the Desert. The Problem, and the Promise, of Libya's New City-States. *Foreign Policy*, 14 August 2013. Available online at http://foreignp olicy.com/2013/08/14/islands-in-the-desert/, checked on 28 July 2017.

Cauneille, Auguste (1954): Le Nomadisme des Megarha. *Travaux de l'Institut des Recherches Sahariennes* (12), pp. 41–67.

Cauneille, Auguste (1957): Le Nomadisme des Zentân (Tripolitaine et Fezzân). *Travaux de l'Institut des Recherches Sahariennes* (16), pp. 73–99.

Cauneille, Auguste (1963): Le Semi-Nomadisme dans l'Ouest Libyen (Fezzan, Tripolitaine). In UNESCO (Ed.): *Nomades et Nomadisme au Sahara*. Paris: UNESCO, pp. 101–12.

Channel 4 News (2011): Libya Crisis: Gaddafi 'on Brink of Losing Power', 23 February 2011. Available online at https://www.channel4.com/news/libya-crisis-gaddafi-on-b rink-of-losing-power, checked on 18 April 2017.

Chorin, Ethan (2012): *Exit Gadddafi: The Hidden History of the Libyan Revolution*. London: Saqi Books.

Christia, Fotini (2012): *Alliance Formation in Civil Wars*. New York: Cambridge University Press.

Clapham, Christopher (1998): Introduction: Analysing African Insurgencies. In Christopher Clapham (Ed.): *African Guerillas*. Oxford: James Currey, pp. 1–18.

Cohen, Dara Kay (2013): Explaining Rape during Civil War. Cross-National Evidence (1980–2009). *American Political Science Review* 107 (3), pp. 461–77.

Cole, Peter (2012): Borderline Chaos? Stabilizing Libya's Periphery. Carnegie Endowment for International Peace. Washington, D.C. Available online at http://carnegieendow ment.org/files/stablizing_libya_periphery.pdf, checked on 20 July 2017.

Cole, Peter (2015): Bani Walid. Loyalism in a Time of Revolution. In Peter Cole and Brian McQuinn (Eds.): *The Libyan Revolution and Its Aftermath*. London: Hurst, pp. 285–302.

Cole, Peter and Khan, Umar (2015a): The Fall of Tripoli: Part 1. In Peter Cole, Brian McQuinn (Eds.): *The Libyan Revolution and Its Aftermath*. London: Hurst, pp. 55–79.

Cole, Peter and Khan, Umar (2015b): The Fall of Tripoli: Part 2. In Peter Cole, Brian McQuinn (Eds.): *The Libyan Revolution and Its Aftermath*. London: Hurst, pp. 81–104.

Coleman, James (1977): The Concept of Political Penetration. In Lionel Cliffe, James Coleman and Martin Doornbos (Eds.): *Government and Rural Development in East Africa: Essays on Political Penetration*. The Hague: Martinus Nijhoff, pp. 3–18.

Coleman, James and Almond, Gabriel (Eds.) (1960): *The Politics of the Developing Areas*. Princeton: Princeton University Press.

Collier, Paul and Hoeffler, Anke (2000): *Greed and Grievance in Civil War*: World Bank. Washington, DC (World Bank Research Paper, 2355).

Collins, Randall (2009): The Micro-Sociology of Violence. *The British journal of sociology* 60 (3), pp. 566–76.

Collins, Randall (2012): C-Escalation and D-Escalation: A Theory of the Time-Dynamics of Conflict. *American Sociological Review* 77 (1), pp. 1–20.

Collombier, Virginie (2016): Libya Urgently Needs New Mechanisms for Dialogue! FriEnt. Available online at https://www.frient.de/news/details/news/libya-urgently-needs -new-mechanisms-for-dialogue-1/, checked on 3 May 2017.

Collombier, Virginie (2017): Sirte's Tribes under the Islamic State. From Civil War to Global Jihadism. In Virginie Collombier and Olivier Roy (Eds.): *Tribes and Global Jihadism*. London: Hurst.

Cordell, Dennis D. (1985): The Awlad Sulayman of Libya and Chad. Power and Adaptation in the Sahara and Sahel. *Canadian Journal of African Studies* 19 (2), pp. 319–43.

Coser, Lewis (1956): *The Functions of Social Conflict*. New York: Free Press.

Cousins, Michel (2016): National Unity Government Built on Cronyism and Will Fail Says Presidency Council Member Aswad. *Libya Herald*, 23 January 2016. Available online at https://www.libyaherald.com/2016/01/23/national-unity-government-built-on-cronyism-and-will-fail-says-presidency-council-member-aswad/, checked on 28 August 2017.

Cox, Gary W. (2004): Lies, Damned Lies, and Rational Choice Analyses. In Ian Shapiro, Rogers M. Smith and Tarek E. Masoud (Eds.): *Problems and Methods in the Study of Politics*. Cambridge: Cambridge University Press, pp. 167–85.

Cramer, Chris (2002): Homo Economicus Goes to War. Methodological Individualism, Rational Choice and the Political Economy of War. *World Development* 30 (11), pp. 1845–64.

Cunningham, Kathleen Gallagher (2013): Actor Fragmentation and Civil War Bargaining. How Internal Divisions Generate Civil Conflict. *American Journal of Political Science* 57 (3), pp. 659–72.

Cunningham, Kathleen Gallagher (2016): Understanding Fragmentation in Conflict and its Impact on Prospects for Peace. Centre for Humanitarian Dialogue. Geneva (Oslo Forum Papers). Available online at https://www.hdcentre.org/wp-content/uploads/2017/02/Understanding-fragmentation-in-conflict.pdf, checked on 6 June 2017.

Daly, Sarah Zukerman (2014): The Dark Side of Power-Sharing. Middle Managers and Civil War Recurrence. *Comparative Politics* 46 (3), pp. 333–53.

Davis, John (1987): *Libyan Politics. Tribe and Revolution*. London: I. B. Tauris.

Dawod, Hosham (2013): Avant-Propos. In Hosham Dawod (Ed.): *La Constante 'Tribu'. Variations Arabo-Musulmanes*. Paris: Demopolis, pp. 7–13.

Debiel, Tobias, Glassner, Rainer, Schetter, Conrad and Terlinden, Ulf (2009): Local State-Building in Afghanistan and Somaliland. *Peace Review* 21 (1), pp. 38–44.

Debos, Marielle (2008): Fluid Loyalties in a Regional Crisis. Chadian 'Ex-Liberators' in the Central African Republic. *African Affairs* 107 (427), pp. 225–41.

Debos, Marielle (2016): *Living by the Gun in Chad: Combatants, Impunity and State Formation*. London: Zed Books.

Delacroix, Jacques (1980): The Distributive State in the World System. *Studies in Comparative International Development* 15 (3), pp. 3–21.

Della Porta, Donatella (2013): *Clandestine Political Violence*. Cambridge: Cambridge University Press.

Della Porta, Donatella (2014): On Violence and Repression. A Relational Approach (The Government and Opposition/Leonard Schapiro Memorial Lecture, 2013). *Government and Opposition* 49 (02), pp. 159–87.

Deshmukh, Jay (6 July 2012): Gunmen Close Five Libya Oil Terminals Ahead of Vote. AFP. Available online at https://www.modernghana.com/blogs/404864/gunmen-close-five-libya-oil-terminals-ahead-of-vote.html, checked on 22 March 2017.

Despois, Jean (1935): Le Djebel Nefousa (Tripolitaine): Étude Géographique. Paris: Larose.

Deycard, Frédéric and Guichaoua, Yvan (2011): Mali and Niger Tuareg Insurgencies and the War in Libya: 'Whether You Liked Him or Not, Gadaffi Used to Fix a Lot of Holes'. African Arguments. Available online at http://africanarguments.org/2011/09/08/whether-you-liked-him-or-not-gadaffi-used-to-fix-a-lot-of-holes-tuareg-insurgencies-in

-mali-and-niger-and-the-war-in-libya-by-frederic-deycard-and-yvan-guichaoua/, checked on 3 May 2017.

Di John, Jonathan (2007): Oil Abundance and Violent Political Conflict. A Critical Assessment. *The Journal of Development Studies* 43 (6), pp. 961–86.

Diani, Mario and McAdam, Doug (Eds.) (2003): *Social Movements and Networks: Relational Approaches to Collective Action*. Oxford: Oxford University Press.

Digital Libya Agency (22 April 2016): مصراتة الإفراج عن 21 سجيناً. Available online at http://www.eanlibya.com/archives/77089, checked on 1 September 2017.

Dorronsoro, Gilles (2005): *Revolution Unending. Afghanistan: 1979 to the Present*. New York: Columbia University Press.

Dorronsoro, Gilles (2013): Le Déclin de l'Institution Tribale en Afghanistan. In Hosham Dawod (Ed.): *La Constante 'Tribu'. Variations Arabo-Musulmanes*. Paris: Demopolis, pp. 93–117.

Driscoll, Jesse (2012): Commitment Problems or Bidding Wars? Rebel Fragmentation as Peace Building. *Journal of Conflict Resolution* 56 (1), pp. 118–49.

Economist, The (2013): Libya's Militias: Make or Break. *The Economist*, 23 October 2013. Available online at http://www.economist.com/news/middle-east-and-africa/21590581-showdown-militias-may-mark-turning-point-which-way-make-or-break.

El Amrani, Issandr(2011): Is There a Libya? *London Review of Books* 33 (9), pp. 19–20. Available online at https://www.lrb.co.uk/v33/n09/issandr-elamrani/is-there-a-libya, checked on 18 April 2017.

Elias, Norbert (1939): *Über den Prozess der Zivilisation. Soziogenetische und Psychogenetische Untersuchungen*. Basel: Haus zum Falken.

Eljarh, Mohamed (2016): Security Challenges and Issues in the Sahelo-Saharan Region. The Libya Perspective. Friedrich Ebert Stiftung. Bamako. Available online at http://www.fes-pscc.org/fileadmin/user_upload/documents/publications/Country_based_Study_Security-Dialogues_Libya_English.pdf, checked on 12 September 2017.

Eljarh, Mohamed (2017a): Libya: Between a Civil War and Western Intervention. In Abdulwahab Alkebsi, Nathan J. Brown and Charlotta Sparre (Eds.): *Reconstructing the Middle East: Political and Economic Policy*. London and New York: Routledge, pp. 100–12.

Eljarh, Mohamed (2017b): Struggling to Advance in Post-Spring Libya. Washington Institute for Near East Policy. Washington, D.C. Available online at http://www.washingtoninstitute.org/uploads/Documents/pubs/BeyondIslamists-Eljarh.pdf, checked on 12 September 2017.

Ellawati, Maha (2013): Hamid Al-Hassi Injured in Benghazi Attack – Two Companions Die. *Libya Herald*, 4 July 2013. Available online at https://www.libyaherald.com/2013/07/04/hamid-al-hassi-injured-in-benghazi-attack-two-companions-die/, checked on 5 September 2017.

Elumami, Ahmed and Al-Warfalli, Ayman (25 June 2014): Poor Turnout in Libyan Parliament Vote as Prominent Lawyer Killed. Reuters. Available online at http://www.reuters.com/article/us-libya-election-idUSKBN0F000720140626, checked on 22 March 2017.

Elumami, Ahmed and Al-Warfalli, Ayman (13 August 2014): UPDATE 2-Libya's Parliament Calls for UN Aid to Quell Militia Fighting. Reuters. Available online at http://af.reuters.com/article/libyaNews/idAFL6N0QJ3X520140813?sp=true, checked on 22 March 2017.

Elumami, Ahmed and Laessing, Ulf (19 May 2014): Gunmen Loyal to Ex-General Storm Libyan Parliament, Demand Suspension. Reuters. Available online at http://uk.reuters.

com/article/uk-libya-violence-idUKKBN0DY0IC20140519, checked on 22 March 2017.

Elumami, Ahmed and Lewis, Aidan (6 October 2017): Armed Force Claims Victory in Libyan Migrant Smuggling Hub. Reuters. Available online at https://www.reuters.com/article/us-libya-security-sabratha/armed-force-claims-victory-in-libyan-migrant-smuggling-hub-idUSKBN1CB15B, checked on 24 October 2017.

Ermakoff, Ivan (2015): The Structure of Contingency. *American Journal of Sociology* 121 (1), pp. 64–125.

Evans-Pritchard, Edward E. (1949): *The Sanusi of Cyrenaica*. Oxford: Clarendon Press.

Falleti, Tulia and Lynch, Julia (2009): Context and Causal Mechanisms in Political Analysis. *Comparative Political Studies* 42 (9), pp. 1143–66.

Faruq, Alaa (2014): السايح لـبوابة الوسط: جيش القبائل يقوده أتباع القذافي. *Al-Wasat*, 16 October 2014. Available online at http://alwasat.ly/ar/news/discussion/42094/, checked on 29 June 2017.

Faruq, Alaa (2016): محمد سوالم. من الحكومة والمصالحة إلى الشهادة. *Libya al-Mostakbal*, 22 May 2016. Available online at http://archive2.libya-al-mostakbal.org/news/clicked/96910, checked on 21 June 2017.

Fathaly, Omar I. and Palmer, Monte (1980): Opposition to Change in Rural Libya. *International Journal of Middle East Studies* 11 (2), pp. 247–61.

Fetouri, Mustafa (2018): How My Hometown Became Major Smuggling Route in Libya. *Al-Monitor*, 21 February 2018. Available online at https://www.al-monitor.com/pulse/originals/2018/02/libya-village-human-traffickers-smuggling-migrants.html, checked on 16 May 2019.

Fikry Abdel Samei, Marwa(2016): Keeping Democracy at Bay: Post-Revolutionary Dilemmas in Egypt and Libya. In Senén Florensa (Ed.): *The Arab Transitions in a Changing World*. Barcelona: Institut Europeu de la Mediterrània, pp. 167–83.

Findley, Michael and Rudloff, Peter (2012): Combatant Fragmentation and the Dynamics of Civil Wars. *British Journal of Political Science* 42 (4), pp. 879–901.

Fitzgerald, Mary (2014): Libya´s New Power Brokers? *Foreign Policy*, 27 August 2014. Available online at http://foreignpolicy.com/2014/08/27/libyas-new-power-brokers/, checked on 22 August 2017.

Fitzgerald, Mary (2015): Finding Their Place. Libya's Islamists during and after the 2011 Uprising. In Peter Cole and Brian McQuinn (Eds.): *The Libyan Revolution and Its Aftermath*. London: Hurst.

Fitzgerald, Mary (2016): Jihadism and its Relationship with Youth Culture and Ideology. The Case of Ansar al-Sharia in Libya. In Virginie Collombier, Agnès Favier and Luigi Narbone (Eds.): *Inside Wars: Local Dynamics of Conflicts in Syria and Libya*. Florence: European University Institute, pp. 44–8.

Fitzgerald, Mary; Megerisi, Tarek (2015): Libya: Whose Land Is It? Property Rights and Transition. Legatum Institute. London. Available online at https://lif.blob.core.windows.net/lif/docs/default-source/publications/libya---whose-land-is-it-2015-transitions-forum.pdf?sfvrsn=8.

Florea, Adrian (2018): Theories of Civil War Onset: Promises and Pitfalls. In William R. Thompson (Ed.): *The Oxford Encyclopedia of Empirical International Relations Theory*. New York: Oxford University Press.

Fraihat, Ibrahim (2016): *Unfinished Revolutions: Yemen, Libya, and Tunisia after the Arab Spring*. New Haven: Yale University Press.

France 24 (2016): حصري فرانس24: آمر الكتيبة المشرفة على سجن سيف الإسلام القذافي يؤكد الإفراج عنه. France 24, 8 July 2016. Available online at http://www.france24.com/ar/20160708-حصر

ي-القذافي-سيف-الإسلام-إفراج-آمر-كتيبة-زنتان-سجن-الـعجمي-العتيري, checked on 28 August 2017.

Friedkin, Noah (2004): Social Cohesion. *Annual Review of Sociology* 30 (1), pp. 409–25.

Fukuyama, Francis (2012): *The Origins of Political Order: From Prehuman Times to the French Revolution.* New York: Farrar Straus and Giroux.

Fukuyama, Francis (2014): *Political Order and Political Decay: From the Industrial Revolution to the Globalization of Democracy.* New York: Farrar Straus and Giroux.

Gebauer, Matthias (2011): The Battle for Al-Bayda. Fighting for Freedom against Tanks, Mercenaries and Bombs. *Spiegel Online,* 26 February 2011. Available online at http://www.spiegel.de/international/world/the-battle-for-al-bayda-fighting-for-freedom-aga inst-tanks-mercenaries-and-bombs-a-747909.html, checked on 22 March 2017.

Gellner, Ernest (1990): Tribalism and the State in the Middle East. In Philip S. Khoury and Joseph Kostiner (Eds.): *Tribes and State Formation in the Middle East.* Berkeley: University of California Press, pp. 109–26.

Gentiloni, Paolo (9.March 2016): Speech at the Italian Senate. Rome. Available online at http://www.esteri.it/mae/en/sala_stampa/archivionotizie/interviste/2016/03/genti loni-libia-non-ci-faremo-trascinare.html, checked on 12 September 2017.

Ghaddar, Ahmad, George, Libby and Lewis, Aidan (24 June 2016): Exclusive: Libya oil exports threatened as NOC warns against port deal. Reuters. Available online at http://www.reuters.com/article/us-libya-oil-exports-exclusive-idUSKCN1040DO, checked on 22 March 2017.

Giustozzi, Antonio (2009): *Empires of Mud: War and Warlords in Afghanistan.* London: Hurst.

Giustozzi, Antonio and Noor Ullah (2006): 'Tribes' and Warlords in Southern Afghanistan, 1980–2005. Crisis States Research Centre, London School of Economics. London (Crisis States Working Papers Series No. 2, 7). Available online at http://www.lse.ac.uk/internationalDevelopment/research/crisisStates/download/wp/wpSeries2/wp72.pdf, checked on 18 September 2017.

Giustozzi, Antonio and Orsini, Dominique (2009): Centre–Periphery Relations in Afghanistan. Badakhshan between Patrimonialism and Institution-Building. *Central Asian Survey* 28 (1), pp. 1–16.

Glatzer, Bernt (2002): The Pashtun Tribal System. In Deepak Kumar Behera and Georg Pfeffer (Eds.): Concept of Tribal Society. New Delhi: Concept Pub. Co, pp. 265–82.

Godelier, Maurice (2004): À Propos des Concepts de Tribu, Ethnie et État. Formes et Fonctions du Pouvoir Politique. In Hosham Dawod (Ed.): *Tribus et Pouvoirs en Terre d'Islam.* Paris: Armand Colin, pp. 287–304.

González, Roberto J. (2009): Going 'Tribal'. Notes on Pacification in the 21st Century. *Anthropology Today* 25 (2), pp. 15–19.

Goodwin, Jeff (1997): The Libidinal Constitution of a High-Risk Social Movement: Affectual Ties and Solidarity in the Huk Rebellion, 1946 to 1954. *American Sociological Review* 62 (1), pp. 53–69.

Gould, Roger V. (1991): Multiple Networks and Mobilization in the Paris Commune, 1871. *American Sociological Review* 56 (6), pp. 716–29.

Gould, Roger V. (1999): Collective Violence and Group Solidarity: Evidence from a Feuding Society. *American Sociological Review* 64 (3), pp. 356–80.

Grajales, Jacobo; Le Cour Grandmaison, Romain (2019): Introduction. In Jacobo Grajales, Romain Le Cour Grandmaison (Eds.): L'État Malgré Tout. Produire l'Autorité dans la Violence. Paris: Karthala, pp. 7–26.

Granovetter, Mark (1973): The Strength of Weak Ties. *American Journal of Sociology* 78 (6), pp. 1360–80.

Granovetter, Mark (1978): Threshold Models of Collective Behavior. *American Journal of Sociology* 83 (6), pp. 1420–43.

Granovetter, Mark (1985): Economic Action and Social Structure: The Problem of Embeddedness. *American Journal of Sociology* 91 (3), pp. 481–510.

Graziani, Rodolfo (1929): *Verso il Fezzan*. Tripoli: Cacopardo.

Graziani, Rodolfo (1934): *La Riconquista del Fezzan*. Milano: Mondadori.

Green, Donald P. and Shapiro, Ian (1994): *Pathologies of Rational Choice Theory: A Critique of Applications in Political Science*. New Haven: Yale University Press.

Grégoire, Emmanuel (2013): Islamistes et Rebelles Touaregs Maliens. Alliances, Rivalités et Ruptures. *EchoGéo*. Available online at https://echogeo.revues.org/13466.

Grzymala-Busse, Anna (2011): Time Will Tell? Temporality and the Analysis of Causal Mechanisms and Processes. *Comparative Political Studies* 44 (9), pp. 1267–97.

Guichaoua, Yvan (2010): How Do Ethnic Militias Perpetuate in Nigeria? A Micro-level Perspective on the Oodua People's Congress. *World Development* 38 (11), pp. 1657–66.

Guichaoua, Yvan (2012): Circumstantial Alliances and Loose Loyalties in Rebellion Making. The Case of Tuareg Insurgency in Northern Niger (2007–2009). In Yvan Guichaoua (Ed.): *Understanding Collective Political Violence*. Houndsmills: Palgrave Macmillan, pp. 246–66.

Guichaoua, Yvan (2013): Group Formation, Identities, and Violent Mobilization: Evidence from Nigeria and Niger. In Patricia Justino, Tilman Brück and Philip Verwimp (Eds.): *A Micro-Level Perspective on the Dynamics of Conflict, Violence, and Development*. Oxford: Oxford Univ. Press, pp. 68–91.

Hachemaoui, Mohammed (2012): Y a-t-il des Tribus dans l'Urne? Sociologie d'une Énigme Électorale (Algérie). *Cahiers d'études africaines* (205), pp. 103–63.

Haftar, Khalifa (2014): Speech in Qasr Libya, 8 March 2014. youtube. Available online at https://www.youtube.com/watch?v=2i2W8KyDs8M, checked on 12 September 2017.

Hammond, Philip (19 April 2016): Comments on Libya to the House of Commons. London. Available online at https://hansard.parliament.uk/commons/2016-04-19/d ebates/16041932000001/Libya, checked on 12 September 2017.

Hasan, Salaheddin Salem (1973): *The Genesis of the Political Leadership of Libya 1952– 1969: Historical Origins and Development of its Component Elements*. Washington, DC: The George Washington University, Diss., 1973.

Hatin Battalion (8 January 2016): الموضوع: قرار فصل. Misrata.

Haugbølle, Sune (2011): The Historiography and the Memory of the Lebanese Civil War. Online Encyclopedia of Mass Violence. Available online at http://www.sciencespo.fr/ mass-violence-war-massacre-resistance/en/document/historiography-and-memory -lebanese-civil-war, checked on 20 July 2017.

Helbling, Jürg (1999): The Dynamics of War and Alliance among the Yamomami. In Georg Elwert, Stephan Feuchtwang and Dieter Neubert (Eds.): *Dynamics of Violence: Processes of Escalation and De-escalation in Violent Group Conflicts*. Berlin: Duncker and Humblot (Sociologus, Beiheft, supplement I), pp. 103–15.

Helbling, Jürg (2009): Hobbes und seine Theorie des tribalen Krieges. *Schweizerische Zeitschrift für Soziologie* 35 (1), pp. 97–116.

Heneghan, Tom (23 August 2013): Libya Oil Port Blockade Reflects National Disarray. Reuters. Available online at http://www.reuters.com/article/libya-disarray-idUSL6N0G O26L20130823, checked on 21 June 2017.

Hill, Evan (2011): The Day the Katiba Fell. *Al Jazeera*, 1 March 2011. Available online at http://www.aljazeera.com/indepth/spotlight/libya/2011/03/20113175840189620.html, checked on 22 March 2017.

Hillmann, Henning (2008): Localism and the Limits of Political Brokerage. Evidence from Revolutionary Vermont. *American Journal of Sociology* 114 (2), pp. 287–331.

Historical Documentation Centre Zintan (2011): دليل معارك الزنتان ضد كتائب الطاغية. 16 من مركز التوثيق التاريخي بالزنتان: Tripoli. فبراير إلى إعلان التحرير.

Holmes, Oliver (9 September 2011): New Libyan PM Seeks Cash, Reassures Fighters. Reuters. Available online at http://af.reuters.com/article/libyaNews/idAFL6E7M9 5GY20111109?sp=true, checked on 22 March 2017.

Horowitz, Donald L. (1985): *Ethnic Groups in Conflict*. Berkeley, Los Angeles: University of California Press.

House of Representatives (23.08.2014): Declaration of the House of Representatives on the War Raging in Various Parts of Libya. Source: Tobruk.

Howden, Daniel (2017): The Central Mediterranean: European Priorities, Libyan Realities. News Deeply. Available online at http://issues.newsdeeply.com/central-mediterranean -european-priorities-libyan-realities, checked on 24 October 2017.

Human Rights Solidarity (2014): تحذير من جرائم تطهير عرقي و عقاب جماعي في بنغازي. Facebook. Available online at https://www.facebook.com/LHumanRightsSolidarity/posts/997358 003614363, checked on 27 March 2017.

Human Rights Solidarity (2016): ضحايا سجن أبو سليم. Geneva. Available online at https://ww w.facebook.com/LHumanRightsSolidarity/photos/a.1407112909305535.1073741833. 172338012783037/1407112929305533/?type=3&theater, checked on 2 May 2017.

Human Rights Watch (18 February 2011): Libya: Security Forces Kill 84 Over Three Days. End Attacks on Peaceful Protesters. Available online at https://www.hrw.org/news/ 2011/02/18/libya-security-forces-kill-84-over-three-days, checked on 22 March 2017.

Human Rights Watch (13 June 2013): Libya: No Impunity for 'Black Saturday' Benghazi Deaths. Investigate Killings, Clamp Down on Unlawful Militias. Available online at https://www.hrw.org/news/2013/06/13/libya-no-impunity-black-saturday-benghazi-de aths, checked on 22 March 2017.

Human Rights Watch (8 August 2013): Libya: Wave of Political Assassinations. Lack of Accountability Risks Escalating Violence. Available online at https://www.hrw.org/ news/2013/08/08/libya-wave-political-assassinations, checked on 22 March 2017.

Human Rights Watch (17 November 2013): Libya: Militias Kill Unarmed Protesters. 43 Dead, Many Wounded, as Security Forces Stand by. Available online at https://ww w.hrw.org/news/2013/11/17/libya-militias-kill-unarmed-protesters, checked on 22 March 2017.

Human Rights Watch (13 October 2015): UAE: Investigate Allegations of Torture of Foreign Nationals. Available online at https://www.hrw.org/news/2015/10/13/uae- investigate-allegations-torture-foreign-nationals, checked on 21 August 2017.

Human Rights Watch (2017a): Libya: Mass Executions Alleged at Military Base. Human Rights Watch. Available online at https://www.hrw.org/news/2017/05/21/libya-mas s-executions-alleged-military-base.

Human Rights Watch (2017b): Libya: Videos Capture Summary Executions. Available online at https://www.hrw.org/news/2017/08/16/libya-videos-capture-summary-execu tions, checked on 4 July 2018.

Human Rights Watch (2017c): Libya: Mass Extra-Judicial Execution. Available online at https://www.hrw.org/news/2017/11/29/libya-mass-extra-judicial-execution, checked on 4 July 2018.

Huntington, Samuel (1968): *Political Order in Changing Societies*. New Haven: Yale University Press.

Hüsken, Thomas (2009): The Neo-Tribal Competitive Order in the Borderland of Egypt and Libya. In Ulf Engel and Paul Nugent (Eds.): *Respacing Africa*. Leiden: Brill, pp. 169–206.

Hüsken, Thomas (2011): Politische Kultur und die Revolution in der Kyrenaika. In Fritz Edlinger (Ed.): *Libyen. Hintergründe, Analysen, Berichte*. Vienna: Promedia, pp. 47–69.

Hüsken, Thomas (2017): The Practice and Culture of Smuggling in the Borderland of Egypt and Libya. *International Affairs* 93 (4), pp. 897–915.

Hüsken, Thomas and Klute, Georg (2015): Political Orders in the Making. Emerging Forms of Political Organization from Libya to Northern Mali. *African Security* 8 (4), pp. 320–37.

Hutchinson, Brian (2014): Notorious Canadian Lobbyist Signs $2M Contract to Promote Libya Militants Aiming to Divide Country. *National Post*, 6 January 2014. Available online at http://nationalpost.com/news/notorious-canadian-lobbyist-hired-by-mili tants-seeking-breakaway-from-libya/wcm/ec518f8f-d924-463d-8854-9f538fd88bcf, checked on 25 July 2017.

International Crisis Group (2013): Trial by Error. Justice in Post-Qadhafi Libya. International Crisis Group. Brussels (Middle East/North Africa Report, 140), checked on 22 March 2017.

International Crisis Group (2015a): Libya: Getting Geneva Right. International Crisis Group. Brussels (Middle East/North Africa Report, 157). Available online at https://d2 071andvip0wj.cloudfront.net/157-libya-getting-geneva-right.pdf, checked on 22 March 2017.

International Crisis Group (2015b): Centrafrique: Les Racines de la Violence. International Crisis Group. Brussels (Africa Report, 230).

International Crisis Group (2015c): The Prize: Fighting for Libya's Energy Wealth. International Crisis Group. Brussels (Middle East/North Africa Report, 165). Available online at https://d2071andvip0wj.cloudfront.net/165-the-prize-fighting-for-libya-s-en ergy-wealth.pdf, checked on 22 March 2017.

International Crisis Group (2016a): The Libyan Political Agreement: Time for a Reset. International Crisis Group. Brussels (Middle East/North Africa Report, 170). Available online at https://www.crisisgroup.org/middle-east-north-africa/north-africa/libya/lib yan-political-agreement-time-reset, checked on 22 March 2017.

International Crisis Group (2016b): Oil Zone Fighting Threatens Libya with Economic Collapse. International Crisis Group. Available online at https://www.crisisgroup.org/ middle-east-north-africa/north-africa/libya/oil-zone-fighting-threatens-libya-econ omic-collapse, checked on 1 September 2017.

International Crisis Group (2017): New Libyan Militia's Oil Strike Risks Wider Conflagration. International Crisis Group. Available online at https://www.crisisgroup. org/middle-east-north-africa/north-africa/libya/new-libyan-militias-oil-strike-risks-w ider-conflagration.

International Crisis Group (2018a): After the Showdown in Libya's Oil Crescent. International Crisis Group. Brussels. Available online at https://d2071andvip0wj.cl oudfront.net/189-after-the-showdown-in-libyas-oil-crescent.pdf.

International Crisis Group (2018b): Libya's Economic Reforms Fall Short. Brussels. Available online at https://www.crisisgroup.org/middle-east-north-africa/north-africa/ libya/libyas-economic-reforms-fall-short, checked on 8 May 2019.

Irish, John and Laessing, Ulf (15 April 2019): Libya Offensive Stalls, but Haftar Digs in Given Foreign Sympathies. Reuters. Available online at https://www.reuters.com/articl e/us-libya-security-analysis/libya-offensive-stalls-but-haftar-digs-in-given-foreign-sympathies-idUSKCN1RR1R6, checked on 14 May 2019.

Jentzsch, Corinna, Kalyvas, Stathis N. and Schubiger, Livia Isabella (2015): Militias in Civil Wars. *Journal of Conflict Resolution* 59 (5), pp. 755–69.

Jha, Salem (2012a): الجزء الأول. سالم جحا. شاهد على الثورة الليبية. Al-Jazeera, 22 March 2012. Available online at http://www.aljazeera.net/programs/centurywitness/2012/3/22/ سالم-جحا-شاهد-على-الثورة-الليبية-ج1, checked on 5 May 2017.

Jha, Salem (2012b): الجزء الثاني. سالم جحا. شاهد على الثورة الليبية. Al-Jazeera, 30 March 2012. Available online at http://www.aljazeera.net/programs/centurywitness/2012/3/30/2سالم جحا-شاهد-على-الثورة-الليبية-ج, checked on 5 May 2017.

Jha, Salem (2012c): الجزء الثالث. سالم جحا. شاهد على الثورة الليبية. Al-Jazeera, 4 April 2012. Available online at http://www.aljazeera.net/programs/centurywitness/2012/4/4/3 سالم-جحا-شاهد-على-الثورة-الليبية-ج, checked on 5 May 2017.

Joffe, George (2011a): Libya: Past and Future? *Al Jazeera English*, 24 February 2011. Available online at http://www.aljazeera.com/indepth/opinion/2011/02/20112241293 4486492.html, checked on 2 May 2017.

Joffe, George (2011b): Libya's Hunt for a Gaddafi Alternative. *BBC*, 1 March 2011. Available online at http://www.bbc.com/news/world-africa-12612169, checked on 2 May 2017.

Johnston, Hank (2014): The Mechanisms of Emotion in Violent Protest. In Lorenzo Bosi, Chares Demetriou and Stefan Malthaner (Eds.): *Dynamics of Political Violence. A Process-Oriented Perspective on Radicalization and the Escalation of Political Conflict.* Farnham: Ashgate Publishing, pp. 27–47.

Kaldor, Mary (1999): *New and Old Wars: Organised Violence in a Global Era.* Cambridge: Polity.

Kalyvas, Stathis N. (2001): 'New' and 'Old' Civil Wars. A Valid Distinction? *World Politics* 54 (1), pp. 99–118.

Kalyvas, Stathis N. (2006): *The Logic of Violence in Civil War.* Cambridge: Cambridge University Press.

Kane, Sean (2015): Barqa Reborn? Eastern Regionalism and Libya's Political Transition. In Peter Cole and Brian McQuinn (Eds.): *The Libyan Revolution and Its Aftermath.* London: Hurst, pp. 205–27.

Karl, Terry Lynn (1997): *The Paradox of Plenty: Oil Booms and Petro-States.* Berkeley: University of California Press.

Keen, David (1998): *The Economic Functions of Violence in Civil Wars.* London: International Institute for Strategic Studies (Adelphi paper, 320).

Ketchley, Neil (2017): *Egypt in a Time of Revolution: Contentious Politics and the Arab Spring.* Cambridge: Cambridge University Press.

Khalaf, Roula, England, Andrew and Saleh, Heba (2008): Risky Foray: Why Gaddafi is Seeking to Shrink the Libyan State. *Financial Times*, 16 September 2008.

Khan, Umar (2012): Armed Protestors Try to Storm Prime Minister's Headquarters; 1 Killed. *Libya Herald*, 8 May 2012. Available online at https://www.libyaherald.com/20 12/05/08/armed-protestors-storm-governmental-headquarters/, checked on 22 March 2017.

Kirkpatrick, David D. (2012): Braving Areas of Violence, Voters Try to Reshape Libya. *New York Times*, 7 July 2012. Available online at http://www.nytimes.com/2012/07/08/

world/africa/libyans-vote-in-first-election-in-more-than-40-years.html, checked on 22 March 2012.

Kirkpatrick, David D. (2014): In Libya, a Coup. Or Perhaps Not. *New York Times*, 14 February 2014. Available online at https://www.nytimes.com/2014/02/15/world/middleeast/in-libya-a-coup-or-perhaps-not.html?_r=1, checked on 22 March 2017.

Kirkpatrick, David D. (2015a): Islamist Faction in Libya Now Strikes From the Sky. *New York Times*, 17 February 2015. Available online at https://www.nytimes.com/2015/02/18/world/middleeast/islamist-faction-in-libya-now-strikes-from-the-sky.html, checked on 22 March 2017.

Kirkpatrick, David D. (2015b): ISIS Finds New Frontier in Chaotic Libya. *New York Times*, 10 March 2015. Available online at https://www.nytimes.com/2015/03/11/world/africa/isis-seizes-opportunity-in-libyas-turmoil.html?_r=1, checked on 22 March 2017.

Kirkpatrick, David D. (2015c): Leaked Emirati Emails Could Threaten Peace Talks in Libya. *New York Times*, 12 October 2015. Available online at https://www.nytimes.com/2015/11/13/world/middleeast/leaked-emirati-emails-could-threaten-peace-talks-in-libya.html, checked on 22 March 2017.

Kirkpatrick, David D.and Fahim, Kareem (2011): Former Rebels' Rivalries Hold Up Governing in Libya. *New York Times*, 25 October 2011.

Kirkpatrick, David D., Hubbard, Ben and Schmitt, Eric (2015): ISIS' Grip on Libyan City Gives It a Fallback Option, 28 October 2015. Available online at https://www.nytimes.com/2015/11/29/world/middleeast/isis-grip-on-libyan-city-gives-it-a-fallback-option.html?smprod=nytcore-iphone&smid=nytcore-iphone-share&_r=1, checked on 22 March 2015.

Kirkpatrick, David D. and Schmitt, Eric (2014): Arab Nations Strike in Libya, Surprising U.S. *New York Times*, 25 August 2014. Available online at https://www.nytimes.com/2014/08/26/world/africa/egypt-and-united-arab-emirates-said-to-have-secretly-carried-out-libya-airstrikes.html, checked on 22 March 2015.

Klute, Georg (2011): From Friends to Enemies. Negotiating Nationalism, Tribal Identities, and Kinship in the Fratricidal War of the Malian Tuareg. L'Année du Maghreb (VII), pp. 163–75.

Kobler, Martin (2016): La Libye A Besoin d'Antibiotiques, Pas d'Aspirine. *Le Monde*, 16 December 2016. Available online at http://www.lemonde.fr/afrique/article/2016/12/16/martin-kobler-la-libye-a-besoin-d-antibiotiques-pas-d-aspirine_5050332_3212.html, checked on 12 September 2017.

Koehler, Kevin, Ohl, Dorothy and Albrecht, Holger (2016): From Disaffection to Desertion. How Networks Facilitate Military Insubordination in Civil Conflict. *Comparative Politics* 48 (4), pp. 439–57.

Kouddous, Sharif Abdel (2014): Libyan Prime Minister Refuses to Step Down; Confrontation with Ex-General Grows. *The Washington Post*, 21 May 2014. Available online at https://www.washingtonpost.com/world/middle_east/libyan-prime-minister-refuses-to-step-down-confrontation-with-ex-general-grows/2014/05/21/9350fd00-e125-11e3-9743-bb9b59cde7b9_story.html?utm_term=.0e071a62ece1, checked on 22 March 2017.

Kuran, Timur (1991): Now out of Never. The Element of Surprise in the East European Revolution of 1989. *World Politics* 44 (1), pp. 7–48.

Lacher, Wolfram (2011): Families, Tribes and Cities in the Libyan Revolution. *Middle East Policy* 18 (4), pp. 140–54.

Lacher, Wolfram (2013): Fault Lines of the Revolution. Political Actors, Camps and Conflicts in the New Libya. Stiftung Wissenschaft und Politik. Berlin (Research Paper).

Available online at https://www.swp-berlin.org/fileadmin/contents/products/resea
rch_papers/2013_RP04_lac.pdf, checked on 22 March 2017.

Lacher, Wolfram (2014): Libya's Fractious South and Regional Instability. Small Arms
Survey. Geneva (Security Assessment in North Africa Dispatch, 3). Available online at
http://www.smallarmssurvey.org/fileadmin/docs/R-SANA/SANA-Dispatch3-Libyas-
Fractuous-South.pdf, checked on 22 March 2017.

Lacher, Wolfram (2015): Libya: A Jihadist Growth Market. In: Jihadism in Africa. Local
Causes, Regional Expansion, International Alliances. Stiftung Wissenschaft und
Politik. Berlin (Research Paper), pp. 31–50.

Lacher, Wolfram (2016): Libya's Local Elites and the Politics of Alliance Building.
Mediterranean Politics 21 (1), pp. 64–85.

Lacher, Wolfram (2018): Libya: The Gamble That Failed. In Muriel Asseburg, Wolfram
Lacher and Mareike Transfeld (Eds.): *Mission Impossible? UN Mediation in Libya*, Syria
and Yemen. Berlin (Research Paper), pp. 15–27.

Lacher, Wolfram (2019): Think Libya's Warring Factions Are Only in it for the
Money? Think Again. *The Monkey Cage*, 10 April 2019. Available online at
https://www.washingtonpost.com/politics/2019/04/10/think-libyas-warring-
factions-are-only-it-money-think-again/?utm_term=.4a4f1caa72c2.

Lacher, Wolfram and Al-Idrissi, Alaa (2018): Capital of Militias. Tripoli's Armed Groups
Capture the State. Small Arms Survey. Geneva (Security Assessment in North Africa
Briefing Paper). Available online at http://www.smallarmssurvey.org/fileadmin/docs
/T-Briefing-Papers/SAS-SANA-BP-Tripoli-armed-groups.pdf.

Lacher, Wolfram and Cole, Peter (2014): Politics by Other Means. Conflicting Interests in
Libya´s Security Sector. Small Arms Survey. Geneva (Working Paper, 20). Available
online at http://www.smallarmssurvey.org/fileadmin/docs/F-Working-papers/SA
S-SANA-WP20-Libya-Security-Sector.pdf, checked on 29 March 2017.

Lacher, Wolfram and Labnouj, Ahmed (2015): Factionalism Resurgent: The War in the
Jabal Nafusa. In Peter Cole and Brian McQuinn (Eds.): *The Libyan Revolution and Its
Aftermath*. London: Hurst.

Lahmar, Mouldi (2006): Libyens et Italiens en Tripolitaine (1911–1928). Quels Territoires
d'Allégeance Politique? In Abdelhamid Hénia (Ed.): *Être Notable au Maghreb*. Tunis:
Institut de recherche sur le Maghreb contemporain, pp. 121–38.

Lasserre, Isabelle (2019): Jean-Yves Le Drian: 'La France est en Libye pour combattre le
terrorisme'. *Le Figaro*, 2 May 2019. Available online at http://www.lefigaro.fr/interna
tional/jean-yves-le-drian-la-france-est-en-libye-pour-combattre-le-terrorisme-20
190502, checked on 14 May 2019.

Latiwish, Saleh (2011): Speech at meeting of Qadhafi with Ajdabiya tribal notables, 14
February 2011. youtube. Available online at https://www.youtube.com/watch?v=fUc
bSNMPB90, checked on 12 September 2017.

Latiwish, Saleh (2012): Speech at Meeting of Barqa Unionist Council, April 2012. youtube.
Available online at https://www.youtube.com/watch?v=gtwZtKanqr4, checked on 12
September 2017.

Latiwish, Saleh (2015): Speech at the meeting of leaders and sheikhs of Ajdabiya, al-Jildiya,
8 December 2015. youtube. Available online at https://www.facebook.com/fiddasalah/
videos/1038975636166069/, checked on 12 September 2017.

Latiwish, Saleh (2016): Speech at meeting of Ajdabiya tribes, al-Jildiya, 21 August 2016.
youtube. Available online at https://www.youtube.com/watch?v=Kr7b8TZkmqA,
checked on 12 September 2017.

Leenders, Reinoud and Heydemann, Steven (2012): Popular Mobilization in Syria. Opportunity and Threat, and the Social Networks of the Early Risers. *Mediterranean Politics* 17 (2), pp. 139–59.

Lentz, Carola (1995): 'Tribalism' and Ethnicity in Africa. A Review of Four Decades of Anglophone Research. *Cahiers des Sciences Humaines* 31 (2), pp. 303–28, checked on 10 April 2017.

Levi, Margaret (1988): *Of Rule and Revenue*. Berkeley: University of California Press.

Lewis, Aidan (24 May 2018): Impact of Fighting on Civilians in Libya's Derna 'Devastating': U.N. Reuters. Available online at https://www.reuters.com/article/us-libya-security/impact-of-fighting-on-civilians-in-libyas-derna-devastating-u-n-idUSKCN1IP3HD.

Libya 24 (2014): كتيبة عمر المختار طبرق تنفي انضمامها لحركة الكرامة. *Libya 24*, 17 May 2014. Available online at http://www.akhbarlibya24.net/2014/05/17/كتيبة-عمر-المختار-طبرق-ت/انفي-انضمامها-ل, checked on 25 July 2017.

Libya 24 (2015a): الخرطوش: آمر الكتيبة 309 يتنازل عن منصبه. *Libya 24*, 26 February 2015. Available online at http://www.akhbarlibya24.net/2015/02/26/الخرطوش-آمر-الكتيبة-309-يتنازل-عن-منصبه/, checked on 12 September 2017.

Libya 24 (2015b): بعد رفض كتيبة "الجابر" تسيلم مافي عهدتها ... اشتباكات مع كتيبة حسين جويفي بالبيضاء. *Libya 24*, 28 September 2015. Available online at http://www.akhbarlibya24.net/2015/09/28/بعد-رفض-كتيبة-الجابر-تسيلم-مافي-عهدته, checked on 12 September 2017.

Libya 24 (2015c): مجلس النواب الليبي فوضى وضغوطات محلية ودولية وأخبار ليبيا 24 تكشف حقيقة اقتحام المجلس. *Libya 24*, 26 November 2015. Available online at http://www.akhbarlibya24.net/2015/11/مجلس-النواب-الليبي-فوضى-وضغوطات-محلية/, checked on 12 September 2017.

Libya 24 (2015d): أعيان و مشائخ برقة: حكومة الوفاق غير شرعية ... وقبيلة العبيدات في طبرق تؤيدها. *Libya 24*, 20 December 2015. Available online at http://www.akhbarlibya24.net/2015/12/20/أعيان-و-مشائخ-برقة-حكومة-الوفاق-غير-شرع, checked on 12 September 2017.

Libya 24 (2015e): طبرق تدعو مجلس النواب لاستئناف جلساته وترحب بالحكومة في حال اعتمادها. *Libya 24*, 20 December 2015. Available online at http://www.akhbarlibya24.net/2015/12/25/طبرق-تدعو-مجلس-النواب-لاستئناف-جلساته/, checked on 12 September 2017.

Libya 24 (2016): ضرب السويلحي أثناء زيارته غرفة عمليات البنيان المرصوص في منطقة أبوقرين. *Libya 24*, 28 May 2016. Available online at http://www.akhbarlibya24.net/2016/05/28/ضرب-السويلحي-أثناء-زيارته-غرفة-عمليات/, checked on 25 July 2017.

Libya al-Hadath TV (2017): Coverage of meeting between Khalifa Haftar and representatives of Libya's tribes, 27 June 2017. Available online at https://www.youtube.com/watch?v=JmXxrPz-jBI, checked on 12 September 2017.

Libya al-Khabar (2015a): البرغثي يقترح تعيين البرعصي قائداً لمعارك بنغازي. *Libya al-Khabar*, 26 February 2015. Available online at http://www.libyaalkhabar.com/news/2294/البرغثي-يق/اترح-ت-تعيين-البرعصي-قائداً-لم, checked on 12 September 2017.

Libya al-Khabar (2015b): الثني يكشف ضغوطات من طاطاناكي وجبريل. *Libya al-Khabar*, 1 April 2015. Available online at http://www.libyaalkhabar.com/news/2835/الثني-يكشف-ضغوط/ات-من-طاطاناكي-وجبريل, checked on 12 September 2017.

Libya al-Khabar (2015c): إطلاق عملية عسكرية ضد تنظيم الدولة بمنطقة الفتائح شرق درنة. *Libya al-Khabar*, 22 September 2015. Available online at http://www.libyaalkhabar.com/news/4768/إطلاق-عملية-عسكرية-ضد-تنظيم-الدولة-بمن, checked on 12 September 2017.

Libya al-Khabar (2017): الناطوري يكلف أحد رموز النظام السابق بمهام عميد بلدية بنغازي. *Libya al-Khabar*, 10 April 2017. Available online at http://www.libyaalkhabar.com/news/4635/الناطوري-يكلف-أحد-رموز-النظام-السابق-ب, checked on 12 September 2017.

Libya al-Mostakbal (2013): الجيش يوقف 102 مهاجر مصري غير شرعي. *Libya al-Mostakbal*, 27 December 2013. Available online at http://archive2.libya-al-mostakbal.org/news/clicked/42458, checked on 25 July 2017.

Libya al-Mostakbal (2014): باشاغا: حكومة الحاسي غير شرعية ويجب إعلان انتهاء فجر ليبيا. *Libya al-Mostakbal*, 8 December 2014. Available online at http://archive2.libya-al-mostakbal. org/news/clicked/59600, checked on 27 March 2017.

Libya al-Mostakbal (2016): بنغازي. قتل ضابطين وإيقاف آخرين من الكتيبة 204 دبابات. *Libya al-Mostakbal*, 11 June 2016. Available online at http://www.libya-al-mostakbal.org/1 بنغازي-قتل-ض ابطين-و إيقاف-آخ رين-من-اللكتيبة--204دبابات/9590/0.html, checked on 27 March 2017.

Libya Herald (2013): Bani Walid Elders Released from Prison. *Libya Herald*, 8 December 2013. Available online at https://www.libyaherald.com/2013/12/08/bani-walid-elders-released-from-prison/, checked on 25 July 2017.

Libya Institute for Advanced Studies (4 March 2016): Note on Recent Tribal Processes in Libya. Confidential Briefing.

AFP (6 May 2019): Libya Missile Strikes Point to Possible UAE Role: UN Report.

Libya News Agency (20 August 2013): ثوار نالوت يعترضون على فتح منفذ بري جديد بين ليبيا وتونس. Available online at http://archive2.libya-al-mostakbal.org/news/clicked/37809, checked on 25 July 2017.

Libyan Political Agreement (2015). Skhirat, 17 December 2015.

Libya's Channel (2015a): Insights on Leon's meeting with Libyan tribes in Cairo. *Libya's Channel*, 14 September 2015. Available online at http://en.libyaschannel.com/2015/09 /14/insights-on-leons-meeting-with-libyan-tribes-in-cairo/, checked on 22 March 2017.

Libya's Channel (2015b): Lawmakers Explore Alternative Dialogue amid Attempts to Reinvigorate UN-Led Peace Talks. *Libya´s Channel*, 4 December 2015. Available online at http://en.libyaschannel.com/2015/12/04/lawmakers-explore-alternative-dialogue-tr ack-amid-attempts-to-reinvigorate-un-led-peace-talks/, checked on 22 March 2017.

Libya's Channel (2015c): Coverage of meeting of eastern Libyan tribal elders, al-Bayda, 27 December 2015. Available online at https://www.youtube.com/watch?v=sl5-M9YQ 3lg, checked on 12 September 2017.

Libya's Channel (2016): اجتماع لعدد من أعيان ومشائخ القبائل في طبرق يعتبر المجلس الرئاسي بدون شرعية. *Libya´s Channel*, 23 August 2016. Available online at https://libyaschannel.com/2016 /08/23/اجتماع-القبائل-الليبية-يعتبـر-المجلس-ا/, checked on 12 September 2017.

Lijphart, Arend (1971): Comparative Politics and the Comparative Method. *American Political Science Review* 65 (3), pp. 682–93.

Lohmann, Susanne (1994): The Dynamics of Informational Cascades. The Monday Demonstrations in Leipzig, East Germany, 1989–91. *World Politics* 47 (1), pp. 42–101.

Lowe, Christian; Murphy, Francois (23 October 2011): Libyan Tribes Protest at New Government Line-Up. Reuters. Available online at http://www.reuters.com/article/us-l ibya-idUSTRE7AL0JM20111123, checked on 22 March 2017.

Luciani, Giacomo (1990): Allocation vs. Production States: A Theoretical Framework. In Giacomo Luciani (Ed.): *The Arab State*. London: Routledge, pp. 65–84.

Lyall, Jason (2015): Process Tracing, Causal Inference, and Civil War. In Andrew Bennett and Jeffrey Checkel (Eds.): *Process Tracing: From Metaphor to Analytic Tool*. Cambridge: Cambridge University Press, pp. 186–208.

Lyon, Alistair (21 February 2011): Analysis: Libya May Face Civil War as Gaddafi's Grip Loosens. Reuters. Available online at http://www.reuters.com/article/us-libya-chaos -idUSTRE71K48T20110221, checked on 2 May 2017.

Mahmoud, Suleiman (2011): Video of Suleiman Mahmoud declaring his defection, Tobruk, 20 February 2011: Youtube. Available online at https://www.youtube.com/ watch?v=-38s-Xby4nI, checked on 14 June 2017.

Mahmoud, Suleiman (2014): Televised statement. Al-Asema TV, 20 May 2014. Available online at https://www.youtube.com/watch?v=Rg3eya6wSQ4, checked on 12 September 2017.

Mahmoud, Suleiman (2016a): الجمعة 18 فبراير 2011. Post on personal Facebook page, 12 March 2016. Available online at https://www.facebook.com/permalink.php?story_fbid=198650523837180&id=100010767018976, checked on 3 May 2017.

Mahmoud, Suleiman (2016b): سطور من مفكرة عام 2011 ، كنت أكتبها لنفسى ، لتذكرنى ببعض الأحداث اليومية. الأحد 20 فبراير 2011. Post on personal Facebook page, 16 March 2016. Available online at https://www.facebook.com/permalink.php?story_fbid=201250863577146&id=100010767018976, checked on 3 May 2017.

Malejacq, Romain and Mukhopadhyay, Dipali (2016): The 'Tribal Politics' of Field Research. A Reflection on Power and Partiality in 21st-Century Warzones. *Perspectives on Politics* 14 (4), pp. 1011–28.

Malsin, Jared and Said, Summer (2019): Saudi Arabia Promised Support to Libyan Warlord in Push to Seize Tripoli. *The Wall Street Journal*, 12 April 2019. Available online at https://www.wsj.com/articles/saudi-arabia-promised-support-to-libyan-warlord-in-push-to-seize-tripoli-11555077600, checked on 14 May 2019.

Malthaner, Stefan (2015): Violence, Legitimacy, and Control. The Microdynamics of Support Relationships between Militant Groups and their Social Environment. *Civil Wars* 17 (4), pp. 425–45.

Mampilly, Zachariah Cherian (2011): *Rebel Rulers. Insurgent Governance and Civilian Life During War*. Ithaca: Cornell University Press.

Mandraud, Isabelle (2013): *Du Djihad aux Urnes. Le Parcours Singulier d'Abdelhakim Belhadj*. Paris: Stock.

Marchal, Roland (2007): Warlordism and Terrorism. How to Obscure an Already Confusing Crisis? The Case of Somalia. *International Affairs* 83 (6), pp. 1091–1106.

Marchal, Roland (2013): Des Somaliens, du Clan et de la Politique de la Guerre (1991–2009). In Hosham Dawod (Ed.): *La Constante 'Tribu'. Variations Arabo-Musulmanes*. Paris: Demopolis, pp. 171–213.

Marchal, Roland and Messiant, Christine (2002): De l'Avidité des Rebelles. L'Analyse Économique de la Guerre Civile selon Paul Collier. *Critique internationale* 16 (3), p. 58.

Markey, Patrick and Laessing, Ulf (30 March 2014): Armed Militias Hold Libya Hostage. Reuters. Available online at http://www.reuters.com/article/us-libya-militias-insight-idUSBREA2T05H20140330, checked on 25 July 2017.

Markides, Kyriacos and Cohn, Steven (1982): External Conflict/Internal Cohesion: A Reevaluation of an Old Theory. *American Sociological Review* 47 (1), pp. 88–98.

Marks, Zoe (2019): Gender, Social Networks, and Conflict Processes. *feminists@law* 9 (1), pp. 1–33. Available online at https://journals.kent.ac.uk/index.php/feministsatlaw/article/view/743/1455.

Marten, Kimberly (2007): Warlordism in Comparative Perspective. *International Security* 31 (3), pp. 41–73.

Martin, Jean-Clément (2014): *La Guerre de Vendée, 1793–1800*. Paris: Points.

Martinez, Luis (2007): *The Libyan Paradox*. London: Hurst.

Massie, Christopher (2013): Libya, a Country Under-Covered. *Columbia Journalism Review*, 27 August 2013. Available online at https://archives.cjr.org/behind_the_news/libya_coverage.php, checked on 5 July 2018.

Mattes, Hanspeter (2001): Bilanz der libyschen Revolution. Drei Dekaden politischer Herrschaft Mu'ammar al-Qaddafis. Hamburg (Wuquf-Kurzanalyse). Available online at http://www.wuquf.de/www/cms/upload/wuquf_2001_libyen.pdf.

Mattes, Hanspeter (2004): Challenges to Security Sector Governance in the Middle East: The Case of Libya. Geneva Centre for the Democratic Control of the Armed Forces (DCAF). Geneva (Conference Paper). Available online at http://www.dcaf.ch/PDF-File/ev_geneva_04071113_Mattes.pdf, checked on 21 April 2017.

Mattes, Hanspeter (2008): Formal and Informal Authority in Libya since 1969. In Dirk Vandewalle (Ed.): *Libya Since 1969. Qadhafi's Revolution Revisited.* New York: Palgrave Macmillan, pp. 55–81.

McAdam, Doug and Tarrow, Sidney (2011): Introduction: Dynamics of Contention Ten Years On. *Mobilization: An International Quarterly* 16 (1), pp. 1–10.

McQuinn, Brian (2012): After the Fall. Libya's Evolving Armed Groups. Geneva (Security Assessment in North Africa Working Paper, 12). Available online at http://www.smal larmssurvey.org/fileadmin/docs/F-Working-papers/SAS-WP12-After-the-Fall-Lib ya.pdf, checked on 20 July 2017.

McQuinn, Brian (2015): History's Warriors: The Emergence of Revolutionary Battalions in Misrata. In Peter Cole and Brian McQuinn (Eds.): *The Libyan Revolution and Its Aftermath.* London: Hurst.

McQuinn, Brian (2016): DDR and the Internal Organization of Non-State Armed Groups. *Stability: International Journal of Security and Development* 5 (1). Available online at http://www.stabilityjournal.org/articles/10.5334/sta.412/galley/384/download.

Meagher, Kate (2012): The Strength of Weak States? Non-State Security Forces and Hybrid Governance in Africa. *Development and Change* 43 (5), pp. 1073–1101.

Menkhaus, Ken (2007): Governance without Government in Somalia. Spoilers, State Building, and the Politics of Coping. *International Security* 31 (3), pp. 74–106.

Metternich, Nils W., Dorff, Cassy, Gallop, Max, Weschle, Simon and Ward, Michael D. (2013): Antigovernment Networks in Civil Conflicts. How Network Structures Affect Conflictual Behavior. *American Journal of Political Science* 135 (1), 892–911.

Micallef, Mark (2019): The Human Conveyor Belt Broken. Assessing the Collapse of the Human-Smuggling Industry in Libya and the Central Sahel. Global Initiative Against Transnational Organized Crime. Available online at https://globalinitiative.net/wp-content/uploads/2019/04/Global-Initiative-Human-Conveyor-Belt-Broken_March-2019.pdf.

Middle East Eye (2014): Libyan MP says Egyptian Planes Strike Benghazi as Haftar Mounts Attack. *Middle East Eye,* 15 October 2014. Available online at http://www.middleeasteye.net/news/airstrikes-hit-benghazi-haftar-aims-drive-ansar-al-sharia-city-531520445, checked on 22 March 2016.

Mielke, Katja, Schetter, Conrad and Wilde, Andreas (2011): Dimensions of Social Order. Empirical Fact, Analytical Framework and Boundary Concept. Center for Development Research, University of Bonn. Bonn (ZEF Working Paper Series, 78). Available online at http://www.zef.de/uploads/tx_zefportal/Publications/wp78.pdf.

Migdal, Joel (1988): *Strong Societies and Weak States: State-Society Relations and State Capabilities in the Third World.* Princeton: Princeton University Press.

Mina', Mohamed Abd al-Razaq (2013): الأنساب العربية في ليبيا. Revised edition. Benghazi: Dar Berenice.

Ministry of Defence (10 January 2013): وزير الدفاع يوقف العميد طيار صقر الجروشي. Tripoli. Available online at http://www.defense.gov.ly/modules/publisher/item.php?itemid=122, checked on 5 September 2017.

Misrata Central Hospital (2011): قائمة بالشهداء والجرحى في ثورة 17 فبراير. Libya al-Mostakbal. Available online at http://archive2.libya-al-mostakbal.org/news/clicked/7223, checked on 5 May 2017.

Misrata Local Council (2013): بيان المجلس المحلي مصراتة رقم 3 بشأن احداث غرغور. Misrata TV, 17 November 2013. Available online at https://www.youtube.com/watch?v=H3GVpzw7 JNI, checked on 21 June 2017.

Mitri, Tarek (2015): سنتان في ليبيا و من أجلها. مسالك وعرة. Beirut: Riad el-Rayyes Books.

Moody, James and White, Douglas (2003): Structural Cohesion and Embeddedness: A Hierarchical Concept of Social Groups. *American Sociological Review* 68 (2), pp. 103–27.

Moore, Barrington(1966): *Social Origins of Dictatorship and Democracy: Lord and Peasant in the Making of the Modern World*. Boston: Beacon Press.

Moore, Jack (2015): Rival Libya Parliament Leaders Hold First Meeting in Malta. In *Newsweek*, 16 December 2015. Available online at http://europe.newsweek.com/rival-libya-parliaments-leaders-hold-first-meeting-malta-405789?rm=eu, checked on 22 March 2017.

Murasil Tobruk (2011): كتيبة درع طبرق تقوم بأعدام كمية من الحبوب المخدرة. Available online at http://free-tobruk.blogspot.de/2011/09/14-9-2011.html, updated on 22 June 2017, checked on 25 July 2017.

Murasil Tobruk (2012a): مراسل طبرق كتيبة درع طبرق أعدام كمية من الكحول في معبر أمساعد الحدودي 2012 1 15. youtube. Available online at https://www.youtube.com/watch?v=iZzHVGA8 fxs, checked on 25 July 2017.

Murasil Tobruk (2012b): مراسل طبرق كتيبة درع طبرق ضبط كمية من النحاس مهربة في شاحنات لنقل الأسمنت 2011 1 11 معبر أمساعد الحدودي. youtube. Available online at https://www.youtube. com/watch?v=BMjj2KTV4j0, checked on 25 July 2017.

Murphy, Robert (1957): Intergroup Hostility and Social Cohesion. *American Anthropologist* 59 (6), pp. 1018–35.

Murray, Rebecca (2015): Libya's Tebu. Living in the Margins. In Peter Cole and Brian McQuinn (Eds.): *The Libyan Revolution and Its Aftermath*. London: Hurst, pp. 303–19.

Mzioudet, Houda and Abdul-Wahab, Ashraf (2014): Reconciliation Pact between Zawia and Bani Walid Hailed as Model for Libya. *Libya Herald*, 29 June 2014. Available online at https://www.libyaherald.com/2014/06/29/reconciliation-pact-between-zawia-and-bani-walid-hailed-as-model-for-libya/, checked on 25 July 2017.

Najem, Faraj (2004): Tribe, Islam and State in Libya. Analytical Study of the Roots of the Libyan Tribal Society and Interaction p to the Qaramanli Rule (1711–1835). PhD Dissertation. Westminster University, London. Available online at http://wes tminsterresearch.wmin.ac.uk/8559/1/Najem.pdf.

Naker, Abdallah (2014): Televised interview. Libya li-Kull al-Ahrar, 13 July 2014. Available online at https://www.youtube.com/watch?v=L6IoJ6Erlzc&feature=youtube_gdata_ player, checked on 29 June 2017.

Nathan, Laurie (2008): The Causes of Civil War. The False Logic of Collier and Hoeffler. *South African Review of Sociology* 39 (2), pp. 262–75.

National Forces Alliance (2013): Declaration of the National Forces Alliance to 933,000 Libyan Voters. National Forces Alliance. Tripoli. Available online at https://www.facebook.com/nfaingnc/, checked on 29 March 2017.

National Transitional Council (August 2011): *Constitutional Declaration of Libya*. Source: Benghazi.

Neubert, Dieter (2011): Competing Orders and the Limits of Local Forms of Socio-Political Organisation. In Georg Klute and Birgit Embaló (Eds.): *The Problem of Violence: Local Conflict Settlement in Contemporary Africa*. Köln: Rüdiger Köppe, pp. 49–68.

North, Douglass C. (1990): *Institutions, Institutional Change and Economic Performance.* Cambridge: Cambridge University Press.

North, Douglass C., Wallis, John Joseph and Weingast, Barry R. (2009): *Violence and Social Orders: A Conceptual Framework for Interpreting Recorded Human History.* Cambridge: Cambridge University Press.

Obeidi, Amal (2001): *Political Culture in Libya.* Richmond: Curzon.

Obeidi, Amal (2008): Political Elites in Libya since 1969. In Dirk Vandewalle (Ed.): *Libya Since 1969. Qadhafi's Revolution Revisited.* New York: Palgrave Macmillan, pp. 105–26.

Ostrom, Elinor (1990): *Governing the Commons: The Evolution of Institutions for Collective Action.* Cambridge: Cambridge University Press.

Ouannès, Moncef (2009): *Militaires, Élites et Modernisation dans la Libye Contemporaine.* Paris: L'Harmattan.

Padgett, John F. and Ansell, Christopher K. (1993): Robust Action and the Rise of the Medici, 1400–1434. *American Journal of Sociology* 98 (6), pp. 1259–1319.

Parkinson, Sarah E. and Zaks, Sherry (2018): Militant and Rebel Organization(s). *Development and Change* 50 (2), pp. 271–93.

Parkinson, Sarah Elizabeth (2013): Organizing Rebellion. Rethinking High-Risk Mobilization and Social Networks in War. *American Political Science Review* 107 (3), pp. 418–32.

Pearlman, Wendy (2016): Moral Identity and Protest Cascades in Syria. *British Journal of Political Science* 17, pp. 1–25.

Pearlman, Wendyand Cunningham, Kathleen Gallagher (2012): Nonstate Actors, Fragmentation, and Conflict Processes. *Journal of Conflict Resolution* 56 (1), pp. 3–15.

Pelham, Nicolas (2015): Libya Against Itself. *New York Review of Books*, 19 February 2015. Available online at http://www.nybooks.com/articles/2015/02/19/libya-against-itself/, checked on 20 July 2017.

Penketh, Anne and Stephen, Chris (2014): Libyan Capital under Islamist Control after Tripoli Airport Seized. *The Guardian*, 24 August 2014. Available online at https://www.theguardian.com/world/2014/aug/24/libya-capital-under-islamist-control-tripoli-airport-seized-operation-dawn, checked on 29 June 2017.

Peters, Emrys (1967): Some Structural Aspects of the Feud among the Camel-Herding Bedouin of Cyrenaica. *Africa* 37 (3), pp. 261–82.

Peters, Emrys (1977): Patronage in Cyrenaica. In Ernest Gellner and John Waterbury (Eds.): *Patrons and Clients in Mediterranean Societies.* London: Duckworth, pp. 275–90.

Peters, Emrys (1990): *The Bedouin of Cyrenaica: Studies in Personal and Corporate Power.* Cambridge: Cambridge University Press.

Petersen, Roger D. (2001): *Resistance and Rebellion: Lessons from Eastern Europe.* Cambridge: Cambridge University Press.

Picard, Elizabeth (2000): The Political Economy of Civil War in Lebanon. In Steven Heydemann (Ed.): War, Institutions, and Social *Change in the Middle* East. Berkeley: University of California Press, pp. 292–322.

Pliez, Olivier (2006): Nomades d'Hier, Nomades d'Aujourd'Hui. Les Migrants Africains Réactivent-Ils les Territoires Nomades au Sahara? *Annales de géographie* 115 (652), pp. 688–707.

Pliez, Olivier (2009): Salloum (Égypte), Une Bourgade Bédouine sur les Routes de la Mondialisation. *Espace géographique* 38 (1), p. 31.

Polanyi, Karl (1944): *The Great Transformation: The Political and Economic Origins of Our Time.* New York: Farrar & Rinehart.

Popular Social Leadership Tobruk (2011a): Declaration of the Popular Social Leadership Tobruk, 18 February 2011. youtube. Available online at https://www.youtube.com/watch?v=sre70CGkzjA, checked on 5 September 2017.

Popular Social Leadership Tobruk (2011b): Speech of Faraj Yadam Buatiwa at 18 February 2011 Meeting of Popular Social Leadership Tobruk. youtube. Available online at https://www.youtube.com/watch?v=ZpcmOrD165Q, checked on 5 September 2017.

Profazio, Umberto (2019): Push for Southern Libya Tests Ethnic Ties and Regional Alliances. IISS. Available online at https://www.iiss.org/blogs/analysis/2019/03/southern-libya, checked on 13 May 2019.

Pusztai, Wolfgang (2016): The End of a Country – The Break-Up of Libya? ISPI. Milano (ISPI Analysis, 305). Available online at http://www.ispionline.it/sites/default/files/pubblicazioni/analisi305_pusztai_27.09.2016.pdf, checked on 12 September 2017.

Qa'im, Faraj (2016a): Video statement disseminated via social media, 5 June 2016. youtube. Available online at https://www.youtube.com/watch?v=8ZPuWay2YTU, checked on 12 September 2017.

Qa'im, Faraj (2016b): Speech at meeting of Supreme Council of Awaqir Tribe, Benghazi, 14 June 2016. youtube. Available online at https://www.youtube.com/watch?v=N8V YWLrKoPk, checked on 12 September 2017.

Rajhi, Mohamed (2015): وفد من المؤتمر الوطني العام يتفقد أوضاع جبهة الوطية و بير الغنم. *Libyens.net*, 28 February 2015. Available online at http://libyens.net/أ-يتفقد-العام-الوطني-المؤتمر-من-وفد/ اوضا/, checked on 20 July 2017.

Ramesh, Randeep (2015): UN Libya Envoy Accepts £1,000-a-Day Job from Backer of One Side in Civil War. In *The Guardian*, 4 November 2015. Available online at https://www.theguardian.com/world/2015/nov/04/un-libya-envoy-accepts-1000-a-day-job-from-backer-of-one-side-in-civil-war, checked on 22 March 2017.

Rashad, Hoda, Osman, Magued and Roudi-Fahimi, Farzaneh (2005): Marriage in the Arab World. Population Reference Bureau. Washington, D.C. Available online at http://www.prb.org/pdf05/marriageinarabworld_eng.pdf, checked on 12 June 2017.

Renders, Marleen and Terlinden, Ulf (2010): Negotiating Statehood in a Hybrid Political Order. The Case of Somaliland. *Development and Change* 41 (4), pp. 723–46.

Reno, William (1998): *Warlord Politics and African States*. Boulder: Lynne Rienner.

Reuters (2 March 2009): Libya's Jobless Rate at 20.7 Percent: Report. Reuters. Available online at http://af.reuters.com/article/investingNews/idAFJOE52106820090302?sp=true, checked on 12 June 2017.

Reuters (20 February 2011): Libyan Tribe Threatens to Cut Oil Exports Soon. Reuters. Available online at http://af.reuters.com/article/commoditiesNews/idAFLDE71J0PP2 0110220, checked on 18 April 2017.

Reuters (25 January 2012): Libyan Government Concedes to Restive Town's Demands. Reuters. Available online at http://www.reuters.com/article/us-libya-talks-idUSTRE80 O1WN20120125, checked on 10 May 2017.

Reuters (4 July 2013): Libya's Largest Political Party Says Will Boycott Congress. Reuters. Available online at http://uk.reuters.com/article/uk-libya-congress-idUKBRE9630O K20130704, checked on 22 March 2017.

Reuters (25 August 2014): Libya's Ex-Parliament Reconvenes, Appoints Omar al-Hasi as PM. Reuters. Available online at http://in.reuters.com/article/libya-security-parliament s-idINKBN0GP18O20140825, checked on 22 March 2017.

Reuters (30 December 2014): Car Bomb Explodes Outside Libyan Parliament Building in Tobruk -Officials. Available online at http://af.reuters.com/article/topNews/idAFKBN 0K80ZA20141230, checked on 12 September 2017.

Reuters (25 May 2015): Libyan Tribes Meet in Cairo as Egypt Seeks Allies against Militants. Available online at http://www.reuters.com/article/us-egypt-libya-tribes/libyan-tribes-meet-in-cairo-as-egypt-seeks-allies-against-militants-idUSKBN0O A1CF20150525, checked on 12 September 2017.

Reuters (1 July 2016): Four Ministers Resign from Libya's U.N.-Backed Government: Statement. Reuters. Available online at http://www.reuters.com/article/us-libya-security-politics-idUSKCN0ZH535, checked on 22 March 2017.

Reuters (3 June 2017): East Libyan Forces Take Desert Air Base as They Push West. Available online at https://www.reuters.com/article/us-libya-security/east-libyan-forces-take-desert-air-base-as-they-push-west-idUSKBN18U0MA, checked on 23 October 2017.

Riker, William (1962): *The Theory of Political Coalitions*. New Haven: Yale University Press.

Roberts, Hugh (2011): Who Said Gaddafi Had to Go? *London Review of Books* 33 (22), pp. 8–18, checked on 22 March 2017.

Roumani, Jacques (1983): From Republic to Jamahiriya: Libya's Search for Political Community. *Middle East Journal* 37 (2), pp. 151–68.

Roy, Olivier (1995): *Afghanistan: From Holy War to Civil War*. Princeton: Darwin Press.

Rubin, Barnett R. (1995): *The Fragmentation of Afghanistan. State Formation and Collapse in the International System*. New Haven: Yale University Press.

Ryan, Missy and Raghavan, Sudarsan (2016): U.S. Special Operations Troops Aiding Libyan Forces in Major Battle against Islamic State. *The Washington Post*, 9 August 2016. Available online at https://www.washingtonpost.com/news/checkpoint/wp/2016/08/09/u-s-special-operations-forces-are-providing-direct-on-the-ground-support-f or-the-first-time-in-libya/?utm_term=.54d7c48412e9, checked on 22 March 2017.

Salah, Hanan (2014): Counting the Dead in Benghazi. *Foreign Policy*, 6 June 2014. Available online at http://foreignpolicy.com/2014/06/06/counting-the-dead-in-ben ghazi/, checked on 22 March 2017.

Saleh, Mohamed Ali (2008): للوطن عطاء (2) ... فى ذكرى استشهاد البطل حسين سوف الجدك. Libya al-Mostakbal. Available online at http://archive.libya-al-mostakbal.org/Shohada/huss ain_aljadak_130908.htm, updated on 31 January 2017, checked on 2 May 2017.

Schlichte, Klaus (2009): *In the Shadow of Violence: The Politics of Armed Groups*. Frankfurt am Main: Campus.

Schnell, Felix (2015): Von dörflicher Selbsthilfe zur paramilitärischen Miliz. Spontane Vergemeinschaftung durch Gewalt im Russischen Bürgerkrieg (1918). In Axel T. Paul and Benjamin Schwalb (Eds.): *Gewaltmassen. Über Eigendynamik und Selbstorganisation kollektiver Gewalt*. Hamburg: Hamburger Edition, pp. 312–36.

Schwarz, Rolf (2008): The Political Economy of State-Formation in the Arab Middle East. Rentier States, Economic Reform, and Democratization. *Review of International Political Economy* 15 (4), pp. 599–621.

Scott, James C. (1976): *The Moral Economy of the Peasant: Rebellion and Subsistence in Southeast Asia*. New Haven: Yale University Press.

Seymour, Lee (2014): Why Factions Switch Sides in Civil Wars. Rivalry, Patronage, and Realignment in Sudan. *International Security* 39 (2), pp. 92–131.

Seymour, Lee, Bakke, Kristin and Cunningham, Kathleen Gallagher (2016): E pluribus unum, ex uno plures. Competition, Violence, and Fragmentation in Ethnopolitical Movements. *Journal of Peace Research* 53 (1), pp. 3–18.

Shahrani, Nazif (2013): Centre-Periphery Relations in Afghanistan. In Conrad Schetter (Ed.): *Local Politics in Afghanistan: A Century of Intervention in the Social Order*. London: Hurst, pp. 23–37.

Shalqam, Abd al-Rahman (2012): أشخاص حول القذافي. Tripoli: دار الفرجاني.

Sharqieh, Ibrahim (2013): Reconstructing Libya: Stability through National Reconciliation. Brookings Doha Center (Brookings Doha Center Analysis Paper, 9). Available online at https://www.brookings.edu/wp-content/uploads/2016/06/Libya-National-Reconciliation-English.pdf, checked on 22 March 2017.

Shennib, Ghaith; Donati, Jessica (30 April 2013): Gunmen Stage Protest outside Libyan Justice Ministry. Reuters. Available online at http://www.reuters.com/article/us-libya-militia-idUSBRE93T0G220130430, checked on 22 March 2017.

Shennib, Ghaith; Laessing, Ulf (18 February 2014): Libyan Militias Threaten Parliament, Deploy Forces in Tripoli. Reuters. Available online at http://uk.reuters.com/article/uk-libya-politics-idUKBREA1H1KA20140218, checked on 26 June 2017.

Shesterinina, Anastasia (2016): Collective Threat Framing and Mobilization in Civil War. *American Political Science Review* 110 (03), pp. 411–27.

Shuaib, Ali and Al-Shalchi, Hadeel (9 April 2012): Libya Halts Cash for Ex-Fighters over Corruption. Reuters. Available online at http://www.reuters.com/article/us-libya-corruption-idUSBRE8380QZ20120409, checked on 22 March 2017.

Simmel, Georg (1908): *Soziologie. Untersuchungen über die Formen der Vergesellschaftung*. Leipzig: Duncker & Humblot.

Simon, Rachel (1987): *Libya between Ottomanism and Nationalism. The Ottoman Involvement in Libya during the War with Italy (1911–1919)*. Berlin: Klaus Schwarz Verlag.

Simons, Anna (1995): *Networks of Dissolution: Somalia Undone*. Boulder: Westview Press.

Skocpol, Theda (1979): *States and Social Revolutions: A Comparative Analysis of France, Russia, and China*. Cambridge: Cambridge University Press.

Sky News Arabia (2016): رئيس الأركان الليبي يتفقد القوات في المنطقة الغربية. *Sky News Arabia*, 24 May 2016. Available online at https://www.skynewsarabia.com/web/article/844031/رئيس-الأركان-الليبي-يتفقد-القوات-المنطقة-الغربية, checked on 28 August 2017.

Smith, Graeme (2011): A Rebellion Divided: Spectre of Revenge Killings Hangs over Eastern Libya. *The Globe and Mail*, 1 April 2011. Available online at http://www.theglobeandmail.com/news/world/a-rebellion-divided-spectre-of-revenge-killings-hangs-over-eastern-libya/article556267/?page=all, checked on 22 March 2017.

Snyder, Richard (2001): Scaling Down. The Subnational Comparative Method. *Studies in Comparative International Development* 36 (1), pp. 93–110.

Social Council of Warfalla Tribes (2015a): بيان المجلس الإجتماعي لقبائل ورفلة بخصوص دعوته لحوار. جنيف. 20 January 2015. youtube. Available online at https://www.youtube.com/watch?v=2RwmwhMX6EA, checked on 1 September 2017.

Social Council of Warfalla Tribes (2015b): بيان المجلس الاجتماعي لقبائل ورفلة يعلن الانسحاب من. مجلس القبائل والمدن الليبية. 20 January 2015. youtube. Available online at https://www.youtube.com/watch?v=F-dwqbRKhBI, checked on 1 September 2017.

Social Council of Warfalla Tribes (2016): Post on Social Council Facebook page, 3 January 2016. Available online at https://www.facebook.com/S.C.W.T.Libya/posts/922876444457956, checked on 1 September 2017.

Solidarity News Agency (2014): مصدر عسكري : مقتل أحد عناصر كتيبة عمر المختار في طبرق بعد. استهداف طائرة مصرية عن طريق الخطأ دورية تابعة للكتيبة. *Solidarity News Agency*, 17 December 2014. Available online at http://www.presssolidarity.net/news/ONENEWS/74985-مصدر

عسكري_: _مقتل_أحد_عناصر_كتيبة_عمر_المختار_في_طبرق_بعد_استهداف_طائرة_مصرية_ع
_ن_طريق_الخطأ_دورية_تابعة_للكتيبة/, checked on 25 July 2017.

Solidarity News Agency (2015): قوات تابعة للكرامة تهدم وتحرق 10 منازل في بنغازي. *eanlibya.com*,
8 April 2015. Available online at http://www.eanlibya.com/archives/33160, checked on
12 September 2017.

Solidarity News Agency (2016a): العبيدات يحملون قبيلة الفرجان مسؤولية اختطاف الصديق الغيثي ويهددون
بإغلاق المطارات والقواعد العسكرية إذا لم يطلق سراحه. *Solidarity News Agency*, 2 January 2016.
Available online at https://www.facebook.com/Press.Solidarity/photos/a.209817055
729092.57469.209796635731134/1075486259162163/?type=3&theater, checked on
12 September 2017.

Solidarity News Agency (2016b): وفد من مصراتة يصل إلي تونس للاجتماع بقبيلة العبيدات غدا.
Solidarity News Agency, 17 August 2016. Available online at https://www.facebook.
com/Press.Solidarity/photos/a.209817055729092.57469.209796635731134/123237
0633473724/?type=3&theater, checked on 12 September 2017.

Spiegel Online (2011): Uprising in Libya: 'Survival Hinges on Tribal Solidarity',
23 February 2011. Available online at http://www.spiegel.de/international/world/upr
ising-in-libya-survival-hinges-on-tribal-solidarity-a-747234.html, checked on
18 April 2017.

Staniland, Paul (2012a): Between a Rock and a Hard Place. Insurgent Fratricide, Ethnic
Defection, and the Rise of Pro-State Paramilitaries. *Journal of Conflict Resolution*
56 (1), pp. 16–40.

Staniland, Paul (2012b): Organizing Insurgency. Networks, Resources, and Rebellion in
South Asia. *International Security* 37 (1), pp. 142–77.

Staniland, Paul (2014): *Networks of Rebellion: Explaining Insurgent Cohesion and Collapse*.
Ithaca: Cornell University Press.

Staniland, Paul (2017): Armed Politics and the Study of Intrastate Conflict. *Journal of
Peace Research* 54 (4), pp. 459–67.

Stearns, Jason K. (2016): The Social Rebel--Society, Interests, and Conflict Duration. Why
Armed Violence Has Persisted in the Democratic Republic of the Congo. PhD
Dissertation. Yale University, New Haven.

Stein, Arthur (1976): Conflict and Cohesion. A Review of the Literature. *Journal of
Conflict Resolution* 20 (1), pp. 143–72.

Stringham, Noel and Forney, Jonathan (2017): It Takes a Village to Raise a Militia. Local
Politics, the Nuer White Army, and South Sudan's Civil Wars. *Journal of Modern
African Studies* 55 (02), pp. 177–99.

Supreme Council of the Tribes of Zintan (14 July 2015): بيان المجلس الأعلى لقبائل الزنتان بشأن
المستجدات الوطنية. Zintan.

Supreme Council of the Tribes of Zintan (2016): التقرير النهائي للمجلس الأعلى لقبائل الزنتان بعد إنهاء
دورته الأولى لمدة سنة من تأسيسه. Zintan.

Tanasuh (2014): لا تُسوّوا بين الفريقينِ في ميدان القتالِ. بسم الله الرحمن الرحيم, 21 August 2014.
Available online at http://www.tanasuh.com/online/leadingarticle.php?id=6043,
checked on 27 March 2017.

Tapper, Richard (2009): Tribe and State in Afghanistan: An Update. *Etudes Rurales* (184),
pp. 33–46.

Tapscott, Rebecca (2019): Conceptualizing Militias in Africa. In William R. Thompson
(Ed.): *Oxford Research Encyclopedia of Politics*. Online: Oxford University Press.

Tarrow, Sidney (2011): *Power in Movement: Social Movements and Contentious Politics*.
Revised and updated 3rd ed. Cambridge: Cambridge University Press.

Taylor, Michael (1982): *Community, Anarchy and Liberty*. Cambridge: Cambridge University Press.

Telegraph, The (2012): Libya: Gaddafi Loyalists 'Capture Bani Walid', 23 January 2012. Available online at http://www.telegraph.co.uk/news/worldnews/africaandindianoce an/libya/9033135/Libya-Gaddafi-loyalists-capture-Bani-Walid.html, checked on 10 May 2017.

Terry, Fiona and McQuinn, Brian (Eds.) (2018): *The Roots of Restraint in War*. Geneva: ICRC.

عمداء بلديات المنطقة الغربية والوسطى: العدوان على طرابلس حرب بين أنصار :(2019) The Libya Observer الدولة المدنية و أنصار عسكرة الدولة. *The Libya Observer*, 10 April 2019. Available online at https://ar.libyaobserver.ly/article/4236.

Tilly, Charles (1978): *From Mobilization to Revolution*. Reading, MA: Addison-Wesley.

Tilly, Charles (1993): *European Revolutions*, 1492–1992. Oxford: Blackwell.

Tilly, Charles (2001): Mechanisms in Political Processes. *Annual Review of Political Science* 4 (1), pp. 21–41.

Tilly, Charles (2003): *The Politics of Collective Violence*. Cambridge: Cambridge University Press.

Toaldo, Mattia (2016): Decentralising Authoritarianism? The International Intervention, the New 'Revolutionaries' and the Involution of Post-Qadhafi Libya. *Small Wars & Insurgencies* 27 (1), pp. 39–58.

Tribes of Zintan (10 June 2017): 2017 6 10 الموافق رمضان 15 بتاريخ الزنتان قبائل بيان. Zintan.

Trotha, Trutz von (1997): Zur Soziologie der Gewalt. In Trutz von Trotha (Ed.): *Soziologie der Gewalt*. Opladen, Wiesbaden, pp. 9–57.

Trotha, Trutz von (2011): The Problem of Violence. Some Theoretical Remarks about Regulative Orders of Violence, Political Heterarchy, and Dispute Regulation beyond the State. In Georg Klute and Birgit Embaló (Eds.): *The Problem of Violence: Local Conflict Settlement in Contemporary Africa*. Köln: Rüdiger Köppe, pp. 31–47.

Tubiana, Jérôme (2011): Renouncing the Rebels: Local and Regional Dimensions of Chad-Sudan Rapprochement. Small Arms Survey. Geneva (HSBA Working Paper, 25).

Tubiana, Jérôme and Gramizzi, Claudio (2017): Tubu Trouble. State and Statelessness in the Chad-Sudan-Libya Triangle. Small Arms Survey. Geneva (HSBA Working Paper, 43). Available online at http://www.smallarmssurveysudan.org/fileadmin/docs/work ing-papers/SAS-CAR-WP43-Chad-Sudan-Libya.pdf, checked on 20 July 2017.

Tull, Denis M. and Lacher, Wolfram (2012): Die Folgen des Libyen-Konflikts für Afrika. Gräben zwischen der AU und dem Westen, Destabilisierung der Sahelzone. Stiftung Wissenschaft und Politik. Berlin. Available online at https://www.swp-berlin.org/fil eadmin/contents/products/studien/2012_S08_lac_tll.pdf.

United Nations Human Rights Council (UNHRC) (2012): Report of the International Commission of Inquiry on Libya. Advance Unedited Version. United Nations. Geneva.

United Nations Security Council (UNSC) (2012): Report of the Assessment Mission on the Impact of the Libyan Crisis on the Sahel Region. 7 to 23 December 2011. New York (S/2012/42). Available online at http://www.un.org/ga/search/view:doc.asp?symbol=S/ 2012/42.

United Nations Security Council (UNSC) (2015): Final Report of the Panel of Experts Established Pursuant to Resolution 1973 (2011). New York (S/2015/128). Available online at https://documents-dds-ny.un.org/doc/UNDOC/GEN/N15/021/20/PDF/ N1502120.pdf?OpenElement, checked on 20 July 2017.

United Nations Security Council (UNSC) (2016): Final Report of the Panel of Experts on Libya Established Pursuant to Resolution 1973 (2011). New York (S/2016/209).

Available online at http://www.un.org/ga/search/view:doc.asp?symbol=S/2016/209, checked on 20 July 2017.

United Nations Security Council (UNSC) (2017): Final Report of the Panel of Experts on Libya Established Pursuant to Resolution 1973 (2011). New York (S/2017/466). Available online at https://documents-dds-ny.un.org/doc/UNDOC/GEN/N17/116/23/PDF/N1711623.pdf?OpenElement, checked on 12 September 2017.

United Nations Support Mission in Libya (UNSMIL) (2015a): Names of Government of National Accord Proposed. Available online at https://unsmil.unmissions.org/Default.aspx?ctl=Details&tabid=5662&mid=6187&ItemID=2099277, checked on 22 March 2017.

United Nations Support Mission in Libya (UNSMIL) (2015b): UNSMIL Calls on Libyan Political Stakeholders to Redouble Efforts to Reach Agreement to Form GNA. Available online at https://unsmil.unmissions.org/Default.aspx?ctl=Details&tabid=5662&mid=6187&ItemID=2099322, checked on 22 March 2017.

United Nations Support Mission in Libya (UNSMIL); Office of the United Nations High Commissioner on Human Rights (OHCHR) (2014): Update on Violations of International Human Rights and Humanitarian Law during the Ongoing Violence in Libya. Available online at http://www.ohchr.org/Documents/Countries/LY/UNSMIL_OHCHRJointly_report_Libya_23.12.14.pdf, checked on 28 June 2017.

US Department of Justice (11 December 2013): Exhibit AB to Registration Statement Pursuant to the Foreign Agents Registration Act of 1938, as amended. Dickens & Madson Canada Inc. Available online at https://www.fara.gov/docs/6200-Exhibit-AB-20131211-1.pdf, checked on 25 July 2017.

US Department of Justice (24 November 2014): Exhibit AB to Registration Statement Pursuant to the Foreign Agents Registration Act of 1938, as amended. Adams Jones Law Firm, P.A. Available online at https://www.fara.gov/docs/6202-Exhibit-AB-20141124-3.pdf, checked on 25 July 2017.

US Department of Justice (20 July 2016): Exhibit AB to Registration Statement Pursuant to the Foreign Agents Registration Act of 1938, as amended. Adams Jones Law Firm, P.A. Available online at https://www.fara.gov/docs/6202-Exhibit-AB-20160720-4.pdf, checked on 25 July 2017.

Vandewalle, Dirk (1998): *Libya since Independence: Oil and State-Building*. Ithaca: Cornell University Press.

Vandewalle, Dirk (2006): *A History of Modern Libya*. Cambridge: Cambridge University Press.

Vandewalle, Dirk (2011): Is this Libya's New Revolution? CNN, 21 February 2011. Available online at http://edition.cnn.com/2011/OPINION/02/21/vandewalle.libya.uprising/, checked on 18 April 2017.

Verweijen, Judith (2019): Inclusion amid Fragmentation. The Mai–Mai in the DRC. *Accord* (28). Available online at https://www.c-r.org/accord/inclusion-peace-processes/inclusion-amid-fragmentation-mai-mai-drc, checked on 14 May 2019.

Vlassenroot, Koen, Mudinga, Emery and Hoffmann, Kasper (2016): *Contesting Authority: Armed Rebellion and Military Fragmentation in Walikale and Kalehe*, North and South Kivu. Rift Valley Institute. London.

Walder, Andrew (2006): Ambiguity and Choice in Political Movements: The Origins of Beijing Red Guard Factionalism. *American Journal of Sociology* 112 (3), pp. 710–50.

Walder, Andrew (2009): *Fractured Rebellion: The Beijing Red Guard Movement*. Cambridge, MA and London: Harvard University Press.

Walsh, Declan (2018): A Libyan Strongman Returns Home and Asserts That He's Fit. *New York Times*, 28 April 2018. Available online at https://www.nytimes.com/2018/04/27/world/middleeast/libya-hifter-return-hospital.html.

Walter, Barbara (2009): Bargaining Failures and Civil War. *Annual Review of Political Science* 12 (1), pp. 243–61.

Walther, Olivier and Christopoulos, Dimitris (2015): Islamic Terrorism and the Malian Rebellion. *Terrorism and Political Violence* 27 (3), pp. 497–519.

Watkins, Tom (2011): Experts Expect More Chaos in Libya, Whatever Gadhafi's Fate. CNN, 22 February 2011. Available online at http://edition.cnn.com/2011/WORLD/africa/02/21/libya.transition.scenarios/, checked on 18 April 2017.

Webster, Kaitlyn (2018): Rethinking Civil War Onset and Escalation (Paper presented at the 2017 American Political Science Association Conference). Available online at https://kaitlynwebster.files.wordpress.com/2018/01/kwebsterrethinkingcivilwar.pdf.

Weddady, Mohamed Mahmoud (2012): الترابط مع ليبيا : الثامنة. أوراق عن أژواد. Available online at http://ewrag.blogspot.de/2012/09/blog-post.html, updated on 02.05.2017, checked on 2 May 2017.

Wedeen, Lisa (2010): Reflections on Ethnographic Work in Political Science. *Annual Review of Political Science* 13 (1), pp. 255–72.

Wehrey, Frederic (2014): The Battle for Benghazi. *The Atlantic*, 28 February 2014. Available online at https://www.theatlantic.com/international/archive/2014/02/the-battle-for-benghazi/284102/, checked on 22 March 2017.

Wehrey, Frederic (2015): The Battle for Libya's Oil. *The Atlantic*, 9 February 2015. Available online at https://www.theatlantic.com/international/archive/2015/02/the-battle-for-libyas-oil/385285/, checked on 22 March 2017.

Wehrey, Frederic (2016a): Why Libya's Transition to Democracy Failed. *The Washington Post*, 17 February 2016. Available online at https://www.washingtonpost.com/news/monkey-cage/wp/2016/02/17/why-libyas-transition-failed/?utm_term=.68f96572660b, checked on 22 March 2017.

Wehrey, Frederic (2016b): Quiet No More? Carnegie Endowment for International Peace. Available online at http://carnegie-mec.org/diwan/64846, checked on 12 September 2017.

Wehrey, Frederic (2017): 'Whoever Controls Benghazi Controls Libya'. *The Atlantic*, 1 July 2017. Available online at https://www.theatlantic.com/international/archive/2017/07/benghazi-libya/532056/, checked on 25 July 2017.

Weinstein, Jeremy M. (2007): *Inside Rebellion: The Politics of Insurgent Violence*. Cambridge: Cambridge University Press.

Westcott, Tom (2015): Box Services Axed as Shipping Insurers Say Libya Is Again a War-Risk Destination. *The Loadstar*, 9 February 2015. Available online at https://theloadstar.co.uk/libya-ports/, checked on 12 September 2017.

Western Region Operations Room (22 December 2014): بيان. Zintan.

Whitehouse, Harvey, McQuinn, Brian, Buhrmester, Michael and Swann, William B., Jr. (2014): Brothers in Arms: Libyan Revolutionaries Bond like Family. *Proceedings of the National Academy of Sciences of the United States of America* 111 (50), pp. 17783–5.

Woldemariam, Michael (2018): *Insurgent Fragmentation in the Horn of Africa: Rebellion and Its Discontents*. Cambridge: Cambridge University Press.

Wolf, Eric (1969): *Peasant Wars of the Twentieth Century*. New York: Harper & Row.

Wood, Elisabeth Jean (2003): *Insurgent Collective Action and Civil War in El Salvador*. Cambridge: Cambridge University Press.

Wood, Elisabeth Jean (2008): The Social Processes of Civil War. The Wartime Transformation of Social Networks. *Annual Review of Political Science* 11 (1), pp. 539–561.

Wood, Elisabeth Jean (2009): Armed Groups and Sexual Violence. When Is Wartime Rape Rare? *Politics & Society* 37 (1), pp. 131–61.

Wood, Elisabeth Jean (2015): Social Mobilization and Violence in Civil War and their Social Legacies. In Donatella Della Porta and Mario Diani (Eds.): *The Oxford Handbook of Social Movements*. Oxford: Oxford University Press, pp. 452–66.

Yasin, Faraj (2013): Press conference of Faraj Yasin with Ali Zeidan. Libya li-Kull al-Ahrar, 29 October 2013. Available online at https://www.youtube.com/watch?v=QY6-rpu2 4CQ, checked on 25 July 2017.

Young, John (2016): Popular Struggles and Elite Cooptation: The Nuer White Army in South Sudan's Civil War. Small Arms Survey. Geneva (HSBA Working Paper, 41).

Zahar, Marie-Joëlle and Kingston, Paul (2004): Rebuilding A House of Many Mansions. The Rise and Fall of Militia Cantons in Lebanon. In Paul Kingston and Ian Spears (Eds.): *States-Within-States: Incipient Political Entities in the Post-Cold war Era*. New York: Palgrave Macmillan, pp. 81–97.

Zech, Steven and Gabbay, Michael (2016): Social Network Analysis in the Study of Terrorism and Insurgency. From Organization to Politics. *International Studies Review* 18 (2), pp. 214–43.

Zintan, Local and Military Councils, Social Committee, Commanders of Qaʿqaʾ and Sawaeq (2 August 2014): بيان للرد على الشائعات التي تتهم بها مدينة الزنتان و قادتها بالدفاع عن العلمانية و الليبرالية. Zintan.

Index